Land in South Africa: Contested meanings and nation formation

EDITED BY

Khwezi Mabasa and Bulelwa Mabasa

MAPUNGUBWE
INSTITUTE FOR STRATEGIC REFLECTION (MISTRA)

First published by the Mapungubwe Institute for Strategic Reflection (MISTRA) in 2021

142 Western Service Road
Woodmead
Johannesburg

ISBN 978-1-928509-15-8

Production and design by Jacana Media, 2021
Text editor: Sally Hines
Copy editor: Glenda Younge
Proofreader: Lara Jacob
Designer: Sam van Straaten

Set in Stempel Garamond 10.5/15pt

Please cite this publication as follows:
MISTRA. 2021. *Land in South Africa: Contested meanings and nation formation.* Khwezi Mabasa and Bulelwa Mabasa (eds). Johannesburg: Mapungubwe Institute for Strategic Reflection

Contents

SECTION II: AGRARIAN REFORM AND SOCIAL JUSTICE

SECTION III: INTERNATIONAL EXPERIENCES: THE STATE, LAND AND POLITICAL AGENCY

Preface

The South African constitution emphasises land redistribution, restitution and tenure security as essential pillars in addressing the systematic land dispossession that was the essence of the colonial system. There is consensus across society that post-apartheid land reform programmes have, however, fallen short of the aspirations for broad-based land reform.

Given the minimal progress in this reform over more than two decades, there was bound to be intense contestation over how to address the country's land question. The reasons behind this pedestrian performance have variously been identified as lack of clear constitutional parameters on land redistribution, poor and vague formulations in legislation, and weak state capacity.

The recently published report of the Presidential Advisory Panel on Land Reform identifies some of these factors as being responsible for the failures in the implementation of these programmes. The report underlines what is perhaps the most fundamental question in debating land reform in South Africa: to what end?

Without deliberate focus on this issue, the debate can end up being dominated by narrow productivist agricultural approaches. Worse still, the genuine aspirations of the mass of the people can be appropriated by elites bent on securing assets for themselves, in a manner that perpetuates the inherited colonial relations with a change only to the colour of the land barons. This is irrespective of the precise form of redistribution – whether it is through the current tenure regimes or through state custodianship over land.

It is in this context that this volume on *Land in South Africa: Contested meanings and nation formation* departs from the standard discourses. It seeks to underline the interconnection between land reform, social cohesion and nation formation.

The authors do this by pointing to the limitations of reducing land to a commodity, explaining the tangible and intangible values that should underpin land reform perspectives. The varied and contested meanings of land are identified in relation to how they intersect with core elements of nation formation such as identity, citizenship, a sense of belonging, culture and heritage. These meanings, the authors argue, should be integrated into land reform policies and governance frameworks.

Documented sources and field research, largely in rural areas, are used to bring into sharper focus the voices of affected communities. Significant policy gaps in the area of land tenure emerge. These derive from the fact that most South Africans hold tenure rights that fall outside of the legal protections of the deeds registry systems and commercial markets. It is therefore necessary to develop a new land tenure system that recognises diverse landholdings – some of them originating in the precolonial era – including individual, family and homestead arrangements.

Consultation, informed consent and broad agreement on development projects are essential for resolving the many land disputes across the country. This requires commitment from government officials, traditional leaders and the private sector, especially large corporations. These decision-makers need to comply with legislative prescripts; but the prescripts themselves need refinement in order to ensure meaningful land-based citizenship based on democratic land policies.

The international case studies covered in the book underline issues ranging from the impact of colonial occupation and land seizures to postcolonial collaboration between political elites and private companies to secure commercial projects at the expense of local communities. Also critical in this regard are the gains that communities can make from persistent, organised campaigns to assert their rights and continually improve their utilisation of assets at their disposal.

The authors also draw attention to the experiences and expectations of labour tenants, and the profound impact that women-led subsistence agriculture has on households and communities in relation to poverty reduction and broader community imperatives. Further, there is much that needs to be done to strengthen and deepen the protection of, and access to, heritage resources that are important for the spirituality, religion and sense of belonging of communities.

The Mapungubwe Institute of Strategic Reflection (MISTRA) wishes to thank the authors and the teams across the publication chain, as well as those who contribute to the Institute's sustenance. We do hope that the insights and recommendations contained in this volume will help to broaden the discourse on land reform and nudge South Africa further towards the constitutional ideal of a country that truly belongs to all who live in it.

Joel Netshitenzhe
Executive Director

Acknowledgements

The Mapungubwe Institute for Strategic Reflection (MISTRA) would like to express its gratitude to the editors, Khwezi Mabasa and Bulelwa Mabasa, for editing this volume, and to the project team for their support: Wandile Ngcaweni, Keabetswe Mogosoane and Njabulo Zwane.

Thank you to the MISTRA staff who contributed to the successful outcome of this project: the project management directorate led by Xolelwa Kashe-Katiya, supported by Dzunisani Mathonsi and Towela Ng'ambi; Lorraine Pillay for fundraising and financial management activities, with support from Magati Nindi-Galenge; and Terry Shakinovsky for managing the publication process. Appreciation is also extended to Professor Susan Booysen for her intellectual guidance and Joel Netshitenzhe for his thorough reading of the manuscript.

We also wish to express our thanks to the authors who contributed to this volume: MISTRA is honoured to have worked with them. Our gratitude also goes to the peer-reviewers for their valuable insights.

MISTRA extends its appreciation to Jacana Media, who was responsible for the editing, proofreading, design, layout and production of this publication.

PROJECT FUNDERS

Intellectual endeavours of this magnitude are not possible without financial resources, and Standard Bank deserve our special thanks for their support of this project.

MISTRA FUNDERS

MISTRA would also like to acknowledge the donors not directly involved with this research project but who support the Institute and make its work possible. They include:

- Anglo American Platinum
- Anglo Coal
- Aspen Pharmacare
- Belelani Group
- Discovery Central Services
- Exxaro
- First Rand Foundation
- Goldman Sachs
- Harith General Partners
- Human Sciences Research Council (HSRC)
- Sishen Iron Ore
- National Institute for the Humanities and Social Sciences (NIHSS)
- Oppenheimer Memorial Trust (OMT)
- Pareto Ltd
- Phembani Group
- PEU
- Robinson Ramaite
- Safika
- Simeka
- The Department of Science and Innovation (DSI)
- Yellowwoods

Contributors

William Beinart is an Emeritus Professor at St Antony's College, University of Oxford. He did his undergraduate degree at the University of Cape Town and his master's and doctoral work in History at the University of London in the 1970s. Beinart was a Director of the African Studies Centre at Oxford and also served as President of the African Studies Association of the United Kingdom. His work focuses largely on the history of South Africa and environmental history.

Andrew Bennie has worked in grassroots organising, research and advocacy around the solidarity economy and food sovereignty, especially while he was at the Cooperative and Policy Alternative Centre (COPAC), and has remained active in the food and agrarian sector in South Africa. He is currently writing his PhD on the agrarian question and food politics in South Africa, and is a research and advocacy officer at the African Centre for Biodiversity in Johannesburg.

David B. Coplan is an Emeritus Professor and Chair of Social Anthropology at the University of the Witwatersrand, Johannesburg. His research interests include African ethnology, history and theory of anthropology, performing arts, urban anthropology, culture change, social organisation and border studies.

Peter Delius is an Emeritus Professor at the University of the Witwatersrand, Johannesburg. He has published numerous books, including *Forgotten World: The stone-walled settlements of the Mpumalanga escarpment* (Wits University Press, 2014); and with W. Beinart and M. Hay, *Rights to Land: A guide to tenure upgrading and restitution in South Africa* (Jacana Media, 2017). He has contributed to policy debates on land reform, poverty alleviation, public works programmes and heritage. In recent years, he has also undertaken research on especially intractable land restitution cases.

Bulelwa Mabasa is Director and Head of the Land Reform Restitution and Tenure practice area at Werksmans Attorneys, Johannesburg. Her career at Werksmans spans 18 years, mainly spent as an expert and leading lawyer in land reform and restitution, mining litigation, healthcare law, banking litigation and general commercial litigation. In 2018, Mabasa was appointed by President Cyril Ramaphosa as the only attorney on the Presidential Advisory Panel on Land Reform and Agriculture. Mabasa was also awarded 'Best Land Rights and Property Lawyer' in the Women in Law Awards in 2019. She holds a Bachelor of Arts (Psychology and Law) and a postgraduate LLB degree from the University of the Witwatersrand and Mining Law Honours from the Mandela Institute.

Khwezi Mabasa is a senior researcher in the Faculty of Political Economy at MISTRA. Mabasa has a Political Science background and obtained his master's (Political Science: Political Economy) from the University of Pretoria. He is currently working on a PhD in Development Sociology at the University of the Witwatersrand, focusing on a gendered analysis of South Africa's agrarian question. Prior to his MISTRA appointment, he served as the National Social Policy Coordinator at the Congress of South African Trade Unions, Programme Manager at Friedrich-Ebert-Stiftung and a Junior Lecturer in Political Science at the University of Pretoria. He is a Fellow in the Atlantic Fellows for Racial Equity Programme, hosted by the Nelson Mandela Foundation and Columbia University, New York.

David Matsinhe is the lusophone research specialist at Amnesty International, where his investigations focus on business and human rights, notably the adverse impact of mining and agribusiness on human rights and dignity in rural communities. He is an Adjunct Professor at the Institute of African Studies, Carlton University, where his research centres on nationalism, group relations, collective emotions and violence. Matsinhe holds a PhD in Political Sociology from the University of Alberta, where he was Canada Graduate Scholar of the Social Sciences and Humanities Research Council.

Kearabetswe Moopelo is a master's candidate in the field of Social and Cultural Anthropology with a focus on themes such as identity politics, tradition versus popular culture, popular media, the sacred versus the profane, and the social order of things. Recently, she has worked with pioneering anthropologist and ethnographer David Coplan on heritage sites as an assistant ethnographer/researcher for Werksmans Attorneys. She has worked in knowledge harvesting and knowledge management under WeKnow Consultants in conjunction with the Department of Rural Development and Land Reform.

Zenzo Moyo, a Zimbabwean based in South Africa, is a researcher at MISTRA. He holds an MA and a PhD in Development Studies, both obtained from the University of Johannesburg (UJ). Before joining MISTRA, he was a lecturer in the Department of Anthropology and Development Studies at UJ. His PhD research was on the relationship between human rights-oriented civil society and state structures in Zimbabwe, and how this relationship moderated democratisation processes in the country. His other research interests include civil society, southern African politics and opposition parties' socio-economic transformation, and the interlinkages between education and development.

Fani Ncapayi is a research associate of the Centre for African Studies at the University of Cape Town, as well as senior researcher for the Trust for Community Outreach and Education, which supports a national movement of landless and poor rural people called the

Inyanda National Land Movement. Ncapayi's research interests are on land and agrarian issues, as well as the democratisation of governance, particularly at the level of municipalities and traditional authorities. He is particularly interested in monitoring and understanding small producers' livelihood strategies.

Yacoob Abba Omar is Director: Operations at MISTRA. Previously, he was Head of Strategy and Communications at the Banking Association of South Africa. He also served as South Africa's Ambassador to Oman from 2003 to 2008, United Arab Emirates from 2008 to December 2012, and as Deputy Director-General of the Government Communication and Information System. His PhD from the University of the Witwatersrand was on 'Sovereignty and National Identity in South Africa'. He serves, inter alia, on the Steering Committee of the Indlulamithi Scenarios 2030 project, the board of Business Arts South Africa, and as Chair of the South African Banking Risk Information Centre and the South African National AIDS Council Board of Trustees.

Toendepi Shonhe is an Agrarian Political Economist/Research Fellow at the Thabo Mbeki School of Public and International Affairs. He holds a PhD in Development Studies and specialised in Land and Agrarian Studies at the University of KwaZulu-Natal. He also holds a master's in Public Policy Management from the University of the Witwatersrand. His main research interests are agrarian change and economic development, and he recently published *Reconfigured Agrarian Relations in Zimbabwe*. He is currently working on land and accumulation in Africa. Shohne leads longitudinal agricultural commercialisation, mechanisation and climate resilience research projects in Zimbabwe under the Future Agricultures Consortium (FAC), an Agricultural Policy Research in Africa programme covering nine African countries.

Quraysha Ismail Sooliman is a postdoctoral research fellow in the University of Pretoria's Faculty of Humanities/Mellon Foundation Public Intellectual Project. She completed her PhD in the Faculty of Law, Department of Jurisprudence, University of Pretoria. Her research considered the violence and theorisation of the Islamic State from a decolonial perspective. Her master's research considered South Africa's foreign policy on Israel in relation to Palestine.

Sithandiwe Yeni is a PhD candidate at the Institute for Poverty, Land and Agrarian Studies (PLAAS), University of the Western Cape. Her research is on land, livelihoods and belonging, and agrarian change in the context of dominant corporate control of South Africa's agri-food system. Yeni has over 13 years' experience in civil society organisations, working on land and agrarian transformation in South Africa. Before enrolling for a PhD, she was the national coordinator for Tshintsha Amakhaya, a network of 10 civil society organisations working on land, water and food justice in rural South Africa. In 2018, she was an inaugural Atlantic Fellow for Racial Equity, hosted by the Nelson Mandela Foundation and Columbia University, New York. Occasionally, Yeni writes opinion pieces.

Acronyms and abbreviations

AFRA	Association for Rural Advancement
ANC	African National Congress
ANCYL	African National Congress Youth League
BEE	Black Economic Empowerment
BBBEE	Broad-Based Black Economic Empowerment
BLF	Black First, Land First
CEO	chief executive officer
CIVILINFO	Civil Society News Agency (Angola)
CLARA	Communal Land Rights Act
Codesa	Convention for a Democratic South Africa
COPAC	Cooperative and Policy Alternative Centre
COSATU	Congress of South African Trade Unions
CPA	communal property association
CWP	Community Works Programme
DRDAR	Department of Rural Development and Agrarian Reform
DUAT	Direito de Uso e Aproveitamento da Terra (Mozambique)
EFF	Economic Freedom Fighters
EPWP	Expanded Public Works Programme
ESTA	Extension of Security of Tenure Act
EWC	expropriation without compensation
FTLRP	Fast-Track Land Reform Programme (Zimbabwe)
GEAR	Growth Employment and Redistribution
GTMDH	Angolan Working Group on Human Rights Monitoring
HRW	Human Rights Watch
IPILRA	Interim Protection of Informal Land Rights Act

JV	joint venture
KZN	KwaZulu-Natal
LCC	Land Claims Court
LNG	liquified natural gas
LRC	Legal Resource Centre
LSCF	large-scale commercial farmer
LTA	Labour Tenants Act
MDC	Movement for Democratic Change (Zimbabwe)
MISEREOR	German Catholic Bishops' Organization for Development Cooperation
MISTRA	Mapungubwe Institute for Strategic Reflection
MPRDA	Mineral and Petroleum Resources Development Act
MST	Movimento dos Trabalhadores Rurais Sem Terra (Rural Landless Workers' Movement, Brazil)
NDR	National Democratic Revolution
NEC	Native Economic Commission
NEMA	National Environmental Management Act
NGO	non-governmental organisation
NHRA	National Heritage Resources Act
NP	National Party
NSDF	National Spatial Development Framework
NUSAS	National Union of South African Students
OAM	Ordem dos Advogados de Moçambique (Mozambican Bar Association)
OPT	Occupied Palestinian Territories
PA	Palestinian Authority
PAC	Pan-Africanist Congress
PBQ	Brazil Quilombola Program
PLAAS	Poverty, Land and Agrarian Studies (University of the Western Cape)
PRAAG	Pro-Afrikaans Action Group
PT	Partido dos Trabalhadores (Workers' Party, Brazil)
PTO	Permission to Occupy
RDP	Reconstruction and Development Programme
RTV	Rede Terra Viva (Brazil)
SABC	South African Broadcasting Corporation

SAHRA	South African Heritage Resources Agency
SAIC	South Africa Indian Congress
SANAC	South African Native Affairs Commission
SASO	South African Students' Organisation
Stats SA	Statistics South Africa
SCA	Supreme Court of Appeal
SEKELEKANI	Centre for Studies in Communication and Development (Mozambique)
SMME	small, medium and micro enterprise
TBVC	Transkei, Bophuthatswana, Venda and Ciskei
THO	Traditional Healers Organisation
TIMB	Tobacco Industry and Marketing Board (Zimbabawe)
UDF	United Democratic Front
ULTRA	Upgrading of Land Tenure Rights Act
UNCTAD	United Nations Conference on Trade and Development
UNESCWA	United Nations Economic and Social Commission for West Asia
UNITA	National Union of Total Independence of Angola
WIPHOLD	Women Investment Portfolio Holding Limited
ZANU-PF	Zimbabwe African National Union-Patriotic Front

INTRODUCTION

Land, Agrarian Reform and Nation Formation

Khwezi Mabasa and Bulelwa Mabasa

One of the major post-apartheid policy failures is the perennial and unresolved land question (DRDLR, 2017; Presidential Advisory Panel on Land Reform and Agriculture, 2019). The pedestrian pace of transforming ownership patterns using several land reform programmes implemented since 1995 epitomises this poor implementation (Kepe and Hall, 2016). Bridget O'Laughlin et al. (2013) specifically cite the post-apartheid state's failure to achieve its land redistribution targets over the past 26 years. In 1994, the government set out to redistribute 30 per cent of the land within a time frame of five years. Only 1 per cent of land was redistributed by 1999, and there was minimal progress in the following years, with the figure reaching 7 per cent in 2011 (Jara, 2014; O'Laughlin et al., 2013). Recent reports indicate that redistribution programmes have 'transferred five per cent of commercial agricultural land' to beneficiaries (Kepe and Hall, 2016; Presidential Advisory Panel on Land Reform and Agriculture, 2019: 33). This policy failure exists in a volatile social context with landlessness, racial disparities and continued land dispossession, albeit in different forms (Mnwana et al., 2016; Yeni, 2018; Presidential Advisory Panel on Land Reform and Agriculture, 2019). In the following sections, we discuss the main arguments and themes presented in this volume. We begin with the book's core research questions and main contributions and then explain the conceptual framework and themes used to explore the land question in South Africa. The subsequent sections discuss the various authors' contributions within the framework of three themes.

This book draws attention to the limitations of reducing land to a commodity. It posits an alternative policy paradigm, which discusses contested meanings of land and their relation to nation formation. This view elevates inextricable connections between economic (livelihood), cultural, political and sociological factors that underpin land reform perspectives in South Africa. The emphasis on these connections and the varied meanings of land contributes to policy discussions in several ways. First, it highlights the limitations of reducing South Africa's land question to expropriation debates or productivist agricultural paradigms. Chapters in this volume illustrate that land reform in a post-apartheid context is intertwined with social cohesion, citizenship and nation-building. This approach is expressed in two central research questions: what form of land policy strategy is conducive for social cohesion and nation formation; and how can South African policy-makers design land reform policies that create a diverse but unified nation state?

The second contribution of this book relates to political agency and citizenship in land transformation processes. It emphasises the importance of deepening public participation and citizen oversight in land policy formulation and implementation. Previous accounts of land politics in post-apartheid South Africa focus on the following main policy actors: the ruling government led by the African National Congress (ANC), opposition political parties, large-scale commercial agricultural lobby groups, traditional leaders and research institutes. These analyses are confined mostly to the South African context and do not sufficiently examine political agency undertaken by citizens who fall outside the main policy actor groups.[1] The examination of

1 Some land academics and think tanks, such as PLAAS at the University of the Western Cape, have attempted to elevate voices of other civil society actors in their research.

land-driven citizenship and political agency in this book extends beyond South Africa; it also explores the politics of land reform in five countries located in different regions of the world. The country case studies provide lessons on the politics of land, with a specific focus on political activism, agrarian debates, citizenship and nation formation.

South African citizens' voices are elevated through several case studies based on extensive interview data and life histories. These accounts cut across rural, peri-urban and urban settings in order to appreciate how different geographic contexts influence land justice demands and the contested meanings of land. This volume illustrates how 'non-specialists' and marginalised 'policy stakeholders' interact with land-based social conflict and policy formulation processes (Du Plessis et al., 2014: 20). It brings to the fore citizen stakeholder perspectives from former labour tenants, citizens residing on communally owned land, urban dwellers, women subsistence farmers, peasant movements and land-reform civil society groups. The perspectives of urban citizens in other countries are included but this volume does not deal with the land struggle in South Africa's urban areas, though it does allude to some of the legislative debates around land tenure in urban townships and informal settlements.

All these perspectives of land enunciate inherent ties between land reform and social justice. The citizen stakeholder experiences cannot be understood without considering how they relate to state authorities and large corporations. Accountability and inclusiveness in land policy governance are cited as major challenges throughout the book. Relations between businesses, communities, government authorities and traditional authorities have an important bearing on land inequalities in South Africa.

The chapters present a case for strengthening political agency and active citizenship around land rights as solutions to address the unequal relations between the state, capital and marginalised citizens. This proposal emanates from the evidence presented in various chapters of this volume, which highlights contradictions, social justice demands and conflicts arising from land policy disputes. These factors deepen existing feelings of socio-economic exclusion that create barriers for social cohesion and nation formation. The authors advance arguments for developing land policy frameworks that appreciate the necessity of socio-economic redress, different societal values associated with land reforms, and sustainable economic livelihoods.

Third, the book addresses gaps between existing land policies and the lived experiences of citizens. The authors test if current legislated policy prescripts are adequate and whether they perpetuate the exclusion of most South Africans from not only access to land, but also the protection and recognition that may only be provided by formal legal or market instruments. This point comes out in different chapters of the book, especially those examining land tenure and restitution. Most South Africans' (31 million) land tenure systems fall outside the formal legislated system protecting land rights (Beinart et al., 2017; Presidential Advisory Panel on Land Reform and Agriculture, 2019). The various pieces of legislation introduced in the post-apartheid era have not protected these informal rights sufficiently. The authors in this book debate and advance new policy solutions to create a national tenure system that does not perpetuate apartheid land inequalities and social conflict. These arguments rest on removing colonial legislative biases, strengthening state capacity and avoiding purist market-driven approaches when developing and implementing land tenure policy.

The arguments in the various chapters elaborate on land restitution failures cited in other studies (Hall and Ntsebeza, 2007; Cousins and Walker, 2015). However, they emphasise land compensation policy considerations that transcend productivist agriculture and monetary redress measures. The intangible and non-material meanings associated with land are highlighted throughout this book in order to broaden the scope of developing and evaluating land restitution policy. Compensation frameworks in the land policy context must consider the underlying cultural, political and historical values attached to land in different communities.

CONCEPTUAL FRAMEWORK AND THEMES

We use a political 'nation formation' definition, which is aimed at creating 'a unified nation in a common territory with shared political institutions, a political history, common economic, legal and education systems, as well as equal rights for all its members' (MISTRA, 2014: 34). Developing national unity in a heterogeneous country like South Africa requires 'a society with diverse origins, histories, languages, cultures and religions to come together within the boundaries of a sovereign state' (DAC, 2012: 1). Socially cohesive nations are built by decreasing various forms of inequalities, especially in societies with historical dispossession and polarisation. These disparities include economic, cultural, gender and race inequalities across South Africa (MISTRA, 2014: 95). All the inequalities 'engender divisions, distrust and conflict' among citizens, as observed in the land debates during the 2019 parliamentary public hearings on amending section 25 of the Constitution of the Republic of South Africa (Act No. 108 of 1996) (MISTRA, 2014: 95).

This book is divided into three main themes. The first deals with land, citizenship and nation formation – it lays out the relationship between land policy reforms, citizenship agency and nation-building. The emphasis is placed on the gaps between intended land reform policy aims and the underlying legislated principles informing land tenure and restitution. This discussion takes place within the context of multi-stakeholder engagements on the future of land policy in South Africa. The second theme explores agrarian debates within the contemporary, finance-led, extractive, capitalist socio-economic context. These accounts illustrate that dispossession in the agrarian political economy persists, albeit in a different form. The experiences of peasant-based communities, former labour tenants and women subsistence farmers are discussed, with an emphasis on understanding how these groups exercise citizenship in advancing social justice causes related to land use in agrarian development. These chapters broaden the contemporary agrarian question in order to appreciate its intersection with social cohesion and the national question.

The existing literature on international case studies focuses primarily on Zimbabwe, citing agricultural production failures, patronage and economic stagnation (Goebel, 2005; Peters and Malan, 2009; Mkodzongi and Lawrence, 2019). The authors in Section III discuss case studies from South America, the Middle East and other countries in southern Africa. Their contributions examine how land shapes nation formation, identity, citizenship and political agency in these countries. This brings a new perspective that does not reduce international comparisons on land reforms to economic productivity, private sector investment and commercial property rights.

LAND, CITIZENSHIP AND NATION FORMATION

Contributions in Section I present several salient arguments highlighting the relationship between land, citizenship and nation formation. These accounts amplify the necessity of maintaining transparent and accountable stakeholder relations in land development negotiations. Social conflict and inequality persist when some of the stakeholders are excluded from decision-making, causing them to experience land tenure insecurity or dispossession. It is equally important to resist flawed stakeholder engagements that create divisions within communities. These trends are not appropriate for building a national land policy approach that strengthens social cohesion in the nation-formation process.

An additional argument advanced is the contradiction between different land policies and most citizens' relationships with land. The evidence presented here shows how South Africa's post-apartheid land policy framework fails to accommodate the tenure systems of the majority black African population. All authors emphasise this discord between policy intentions and real land–power relations on the ground. Society cannot pursue a socially inclusive nation-formation trajectory if land redress policies fail to recognise the lived realities across communities. Policy measures are proposed to resolve this contradiction in order to strengthen land tenure of the most marginalised citizens.

The importance of considering the diverse associations with land is highlighted when implementing tenure or restitution policies. Land is a contested concept with multiple, layered meanings permeating socio-economic, cultural and political aspects of human development. The authors show how different land policies introduced in the post-apartheid era have inadequately accommodated these meanings. South Africans' struggles for land have always been synonymous with political advocacy for the attainment of lost identity, heritage and belonging, and it continues to shape citizenship in urban and rural communities 27 years after the attainment of democracy. The evidence indicates that the goal of reclaiming identity, heritage and belonging has not been achieved, partly as a result of the unresolved land question.

The first chapter by Yacoob Abba Omar sets the background for debating land within the context of nation-building. It elevates links between land, citizenship and nation formation in South Africa. This contribution connects historical land debates with varied strands of nationalism that have shaped the modern South African state. Abba Omar focuses on the nationalisms articulated in the Afrikaner, Pan-Africanist and Black Consciousness traditions. He draws attention to how these contrasting nationalist strands inform beliefs on land policy. Nationalism is an important reference point in South Africa's historical and contemporary land debates. It reminds society that deep political engagement is required when attempting to resolve stakeholder differences around land (Hall and Ntsebeza, 2007: 13).

Yacoob Abba Omar's discussion lays the foundations for this engagement by tracing political, social and cultural beliefs shaping how the different nationalisms approach land policy. Debates on land justice cannot be pursued without rethinking nation-building and nation formation, especially in a South African society still dealing with apartheid legacies. The analysis in this chapter points to some essential considerations for taking this discussion forward. Abba Omar argues that strengthening social cohesion is essential for creating an inclusive nation-formation process. This necessitates ameliorating all forms of societal inequalities, especially in relation to land because it cuts across material and non-material forms of social exclusion. Land justice is at the heart of different nationalist strands that shape South Africa's nation-building efforts. It speaks directly to notions of belonging and ensuring land tenure security for different social groups without any discrimination or exclusion.

Abba Omar contends that South Africa's future land reform policies should be embedded in inclusive nationalism as articulated in the Constitution. He cautions society against adopting parochial nationalisms, which have emerged in recent policy discussions on amending the Constitution's property clause. This chapter recognises legitimate calls to review land reform policies that govern expropriation and compensation, but it encourages South Africans to undertake these policy reviews using the nation-building principles expressed in the National Development Plan, the Constitution and historical ANC documents on the national question.

In Chapter 2, Bulelwa Mabasa offers a legal perspective that engages with ongoing debates on South Africa's property and customary law policy frameworks. This includes discussing pre-democratic laws that survived the promulgation of the Constitution in 1996. She explains how these laws are at odds with the lived cultural and normative experiences of South Africa's black majority population, as they have failed to accommodate these citizens' interactions with land and property throughout different historical periods. The laws continue to exclude Africans, given the dichotomy between the formal property sector and real estate, and the manner in which land reform is treated as a concept that is positioned outside of markets and formality. Mabasa calls for an intentional decolonisation of formal property and customary laws to create a legal framework that is suitable for addressing historical land inequalities.

She argues that the weakness of land tenure is caused by the persistence of colonial influences in customary law jurisprudence and its application in the courts. Mabasa then proposes several policy measures for lawmakers to consider when amending land policies regulating customary tenure. The main point is the necessity of appreciating the nuances and precolonial features in customary laws for future lawmaking purposes. This approach will complement most black South Africans' interactions with land. An additional contribution of the chapter is broadening property law debates beyond the rural geographic area and agricultural sector focus. It amplifies the fact that property law and customary tenure policy issues exist in different social settings. Mabasa's contribution to property law debates nudges stakeholders to look at the underlying exclusionary practices within lawmaking and how property jurisprudence shapes policy implementation. The chapter's arguments support the book's main findings about the contradictions between established land laws and most South Africans' relationships with land.

Peter Delius and William Beinart expand on the intersection between property law and land tenure in Chapter 3. They argue that legislative policies regulating off-register land rights have failed to provide adequate tenure for two marginalised groups: black African rural citizens living in former bantustans and urban dwellers residing on informal land sites. The authors provide an account of the shortcomings in legislation aimed at strengthening tenure for marginalised citizens. Some prominent examples include the Interim Protection of Informal Land Rights Act (No. 31 of 1996), the Communal Land Rights Act (No. 11 of 2004) and the Upgrading of Land Tenure Rights Act (No. 112 of 1991, amended in 1996 and 1998).

The authors examine legal case history around land disputes between communities, private companies (mostly mining), traditional leaders and state authorities using these legislative frameworks. Delius and Beinart also assess the implementation of these laws since South Africa's transition to democracy, and the subsequent policy outcomes in urban and rural locations. Central to their argument is their challenge of traditional beliefs that reduce customary land laws to communalism. This core argument is substantiated by historical analysis proving that individual and family-based landholding is not foreign to Africans. The community and communalism principles, which run through South Africa's customary land tenure policies, are criticised on the basis of historical and legal inconsistencies. The authors use this critique as an explanation for ongoing disputes over land tenure and development projects across different provinces. They argue that the communal approach has benefited mainly chiefs, mining companies, government, and a few traditional leaders who receive direct economic gains from corporate-driven land development investments. This trend exacerbates existing tenure insecurities in the former rural bantustans, leading to social conflict and legal disputes. It exposes the disparities between tenure policies and historical land governance systems within black African communities in South Africa.

Delius and Beinart conclude their chapter with land tenure policy recommendations for lawmakers to take forward. The main one is accommodating different types of landholdings, with a primary emphasis on family, household and individual land rights. This proposal is different from established customary tenure policy frameworks organised around intermediaries, such as traditional leaders, community trusts or community property associations (CPAs). An additional takeaway from the chapter is the argument for transitioning to a unitary national system of land tenure in South Africa. The authors suggest practical measures related to politics, state governance and legal amendments, which could potentially facilitate this transition. They believe South Africa's current two-tiered land tenure system perpetuates apartheid and colonial segregated development strategies.

In Chapter 4, Fani Ncapayi illustrates the impacts of this two-tiered system on citizens in rural areas. He examines customary tenure policies and how these hand traditional authorities unchecked power. This ultimately leads to residents losing their land-based citizenship, which is intrinsically tied to heritage resources, identity and belonging.

This unchecked power afforded to traditional authorities also influences land development regulatory trends. Ncapayi uses case study evidence from Centane in the rural Eastern Cape to discuss the relationship between customary land tenure and land development processes. He finds that traditional authorities and private companies take decisions unliterally without consulting landholders sufficiently when initiating commercial activities in communally owned areas. This demonstrates how the absence of landholding protection measures and weak tenure directly impact rural communities. It creates conducive conditions for their exclusion in decision-making processes and prevents meaningful, transparent and fair engagement when deliberating on commercial land development proposals.

Ncapayi's primary argument is centred on the importance of active citizenship when defending land rights in a hostile authoritarian environment. He advocates for rural citizens to resist contemporary forms of dispossession by using their indigenous knowledge on customary tenure and historical links with the land. This land-based citizenship opposes reducing communal land ownership and development decision-making processes to traditional leaders' views. Ncapayi calls for a transparent and inclusive system of wide consultation and citizen oversight when private sector investors propose projects on communally owned land. This cannot happen if traditional leaders exercise unchecked legislated control over the land and continue to bypass rural citizens when negotiating with developers.

Ncapayi proposes redesigning customary land tenure policy so that rural citizens have full control over land tenure and use. This process must include, among other interventions, strengthening regulatory oversight in land development processes. His contribution illustrates that legislative changes ought to be complemented by political organising and education around land-based rights. These two factors are essential to address the precarious tenure in rural communities. Another significant finding in this chapter is community discontent and conflict over how private companies operate business ventures in communally owned areas. Disputes over land development agreements, decision-making and household financial benefits cause this social conflict. This discontent persists even when the corporate actors, state authorities and traditional leaders believe economic rewards are sufficient for addressing community concerns.

In Chapter 5, David Coplan and Kearabetswe Moopelo present deeper insights into the prevalence of discontent within communities, even when companies provide or offer economic benefits to households. It illuminates how contested land meanings broaden conventional development and compensation policies. Their chapter is based on an ongoing legal dispute over commercial land development in the Meletse mountain range in the Limpopo Province, which houses a sacred cave called Madimatle. This dispute between the mining company, its black economic empowerment (BEE) partner and civil society groups started six years ago when the licence to mine in the iron ore-rich area was awarded. The authors use material from their extensive ethnographic research in this community to highlight how the state and large private companies overlook deeper meanings and values attached to land. The advocacy groups opposing the mining activity have sustained their resistance, despite the promise of employment creation, local economic development and investment.

The authors argue that the community and broader civil society resistance stems from the religious, spiritual, ecological and cultural values associated with the land surrounding Meletse. Community members and other citizens, whose identities and cultural practices are tied to the Meletse mountains, cannot be compensated using market mechanisms such as BEE or local economic development. This contention challenges existing legislative frameworks governing land development and compensation. It calls for the inclusion of intangible dimensions, such as culture, heritage and spiritual value, in land restitution policies.

Coplan and Moopelo's account illustrates that land dispossession not only deprives citizens of economic livelihoods, but it also erodes the basis for cultural identity and a sense of belonging for community members, their descendants and other citizens who perceive the land as a non-monetary asset. This argument brings to the fore a wider and deeper notion of dispossession, which should be upheld by provisions in South Africa's Constitution that protect cultural, religious and heritage rights. This intangible dispossession – cited in several cases in the book – is largely overlooked when implementing land development and compensation policies in South Africa. Coplan and Moopelo propose that market-oriented land development policies be read with other constitutional clauses that protect the cultural, religious and heritage value of land.

AGRARIAN REFORM AND SOCIAL JUSTICE

Section II, which deals with agrarian reform and social justice, presents the following core arguments related to social cohesion and nation formation. First, agrarian reform in a social justice context is not limited to developing traditional commercial agriculture. Rather, it is related to comprehending the multiple agrarian livelihood sources developed around land use in low-income communities across different geographic locations. Governments should preserve and expand access to crucial natural resources such as land, which can sustain these community livelihoods. The dominant policy practices of pushing communities towards traditional agricultural markets or dispossessing their lands for extractive sector investments have not worked. Policy discourses on developing or modernising land overlook this important factor, thus decreasing the livelihood sources of the most marginalised citizens. This reproduces socio-economic inequality in society and undermines efforts aimed at building social cohesion.

Second, a land policy framework suited for strengthening social cohesion acknowledges and considers the multiple meanings of land ownership in society. This influences how property law, regulation and policy develop in societies, especially in states like South Africa that wish to build inclusive land policies. Chapters in this section show the disconnection between current land policies and citizens' conceptions of land use or ownership. The evidence illustrates that land ownership and use must not be reduced to commercial value. All the accounts point to myriad meanings and values associated with land across different communities. These varied conceptions of land include, but are not limited to, notions of belonging, heritage resources, social justice and gender rights.

Third, reclaiming citizenship and advancing causes for social justice come out strongly in all three chapters. This includes highlighting collective women-led agency and how it lays the foundation for rethinking agrarian development models. These models must consider gendered structural barriers. Another dimension of citizenship relates to the unresolved question of labour tenants and their descendants. This issue is a crucial part of agrarian debates, which explore class formation during different stages in the agrarian political economy's evolution. The discussion in this section develops a wider conception of the labour tenant, which challenges traditional Marxian class analyses. It emphasises how class categorisation intersects with other human identity markers that go beyond economic agency; this alludes to the agency undertaken by former labour tenants and its connection with different forms of redress. This discussion of class is taken further when considering the plight of contemporary rural peasants in Mozambique and Angola, whose agrarian livelihoods are under threat because of land dispossessions initiated by state authorities and private companies. In all these cases, there is an attempt – through different forms of political agency – to organise collectively around basic demands for inclusive citizenship, which deals with gender, class and spatial inequalities. Agrarian policies that promote social cohesion can only be developed by addressing the forms of inequality cited throughout this section.

Fourth, state capacity and orientation are essential for creating land policies that improve social cohesion. Governments need to strengthen implementation of regulatory prescripts guiding land use and development. Some stakeholders circumvent or disregard law in land development processes, which subsequently leads to land disputes that entrench social divisions or conflict. The autonomy and impartiality of state authorities at different levels is important for building the capacity to regulate effectively. It is easier to hold private-sector companies, traditional authorities and other stakeholders accountable in land development processes when state regulatory capacity is strong. Additionally, laws that facilitate state capture by elite interests in commercial land development decisions need to be reformulated. These pieces of legislation have failed to protect the livelihood and land tenure rights of poor communities. This emphasis on state capacity is not limited to land use and development issues. State failures also hinder the settlement of land claims, which remind people about historical dispossession daily. This is most vivid in a country like South Africa, with racialised landlessness, unemployment and unequal access to basic public goods. The settlement of these historical land claims is essential for social justice and social cohesion.

Land and agrarian policy debates are closely related, especially in countries like South Africa with a history of settler colonialism (Mafeje, 2003; Moyo et al., 2013). Agrarian developments in these social contexts were organised around systemic land dispossession and racialised segregated development. As Sam Moyo and Utsa Patnaik (2011: 64) explain: 'Africa of the labour reserves (which includes South Africa) had by the 1960s witnessed the first African wave of extensive land grabbing by European settlers.' This happened throughout the 20th century and eventually destroyed the traditional precolonial peasant livelihood structure (Bundy, 1988). The important connections between land and agrarian development are illustrated in this brief historical account. However, the two terms should not be conflated because agrarian policy issues go beyond land reform (Neocosmos, 1993; Moyo et al., 2013).

Sections II and III discuss land as one central component of the overall themes embedded in agrarian political economy debates.

Other important topics include class formation, gender relations, nation formation, political agency and the agro-food system's role in shaping capitalist development (Mafeje, 2003; Bernstein, 2006; Moyo et al., 2013). This wider conceptualisation of the agrarian question is developed throughout the book, and it signifies the importance of looking beyond the traditional productivist land and agrarian paradigms.

In Chapter 6, Khwezi Mabasa initiates the debate through an examination of South Africa's contemporary agrarian question, using a gendered lens. This contribution focuses on the experiences of black African women in Ermelo's peri-urban areas. He assesses how the women cope with, and respond to, a market-led agro-food system, which sustains food security at the national level but creates hunger in 50 per cent of households (Shisana et al., 2013). South Africa's food insecurity data amplify the general race, class and gender inequalities in society. Black women bear the brunt of this structural food distribution problem, with most studies pointing to higher food insecurity levels in women-headed households (Dodson et al., 2012; Shisana et al., 2013).

Mabasa argues that South Africa's agrarian political economy model, organised around dominant firms in all segments of the food value chain, produces gendered class inequality. It is foregrounded in a policy framework that favours a large commercially oriented industrial agro-food system, which marginalises small-scale subsistence farmers and other economic actors across the food value chain. This trend is gendered because most small-scale subsistence farmers in South Africa are black African women and white males dominate large-scale commercial farming. Additionally, this model sustains structural barriers limiting African women's access to land, crucial inputs and state support. Gender-based structural inequalities in the market-led agrarian model persist, highlighting the limitations of prioritising racial transformation within existing agrarian market structures. The author's findings show various ways in which this policy framework reproduces gendered hunger and the marginalisation of women-led, small-scale subsistence production. This gendered agrarian structural problem is juxtaposed with the women's agency, observed in subsistence home and communal garden farming.

Mabasa uses the work of feminist, political economy writers and interview data to highlight the women's agrarian citizenship. This approach departs from previous studies, which 'portray the poor as passive victims of "neo-liberal" transitions, negating their power and agency' (Kroll, 2016: 1). It shows how women's experiences amplify the necessity of decreasing gendered land-access disparities, reforming state food procurement practices and shifting government to supporting localised food systems. The women's agency highlights that agrarian livelihoods should not be restricted to food security and securing additional household incomes; their farming activities challenge gender stereotypes in agriculture, increase the women's economic independence and encourage collective agency. This contribution extends land policy development debates beyond the sphere of formal production. The women illustrate that social reproduction, organised around land and natural resources outside formal markets, is equally important.

Mabasa presents a gendered perspective on the book's overall demand for active citizenry and political agency in land development. He brings to the fore, the women's vision of an alternative agrarian structure, which can potentially decrease socio-economic inequality and support women-led organising around agrarian transformation in low-income communities. The findings shift the agrarian political economy redistribution debate from its preoccupation with transforming racial ownership patterns in large-scale commercial farming markets. A case is developed for supporting women-led subsistence farming in the informal economy, which presents innovative ideas on how to restructure South Africa's food system and address long-standing gendered inequalities.

Sithandiwe Yeni, in Chapter 7, takes the agrarian debate further by exploring former labour tenants' views on expropriation without compensation. She contextualises her chapter in historical and contemporary accounts of the struggles of labour tenants, through both literature debates and empirical evidence from her engagement with rural-based labour tenants' advocacy groups in KwaZulu-Natal. Her chapter posits several salient points for understanding the book's arguments on land restitution. The primary one is the post-apartheid state's failure to address, effectively, labour tenants' historical land claims. This has resulted in the land claimants using civil society advocacy and judicial recourse through the country's different courts over the past years, with minimal success. Another important point is the wave of post-apartheid dispossession in the form of illegal evictions of labour tenants or farm dwellers. This trend persists, despite the promulgation of the Labour Reform (Labour Tenants) Act (No. 3 of 1996) and the Extension of Security of Tenure Act (No. 62 of 1997). The labour tenants who remain on privately owned farms state that they reside in conditions and regulations similar to those in the apartheid era.

Yeni's main contribution relates to the deeper meanings associated with land ownership and compensation. She concludes, based on the interviewee's responses, that compensation should not be reduced to land transfers aimed at developing small-scale commercial or subsistence agriculture. Land compensation and ownership are inherently tied with citizens' notions of belonging, heritage resources, dignity and preserving land for future generations. These meanings cannot be separated from the basic human rights enshrined in South Africa's Constitution, especially in a social context of historical and contemporary forms of land dispossessions. The former labour tenants and their descendants perceive land restitution as an essential step towards achieving social justice and redress. Land claims and compensation processes are viewed as a mechanism for addressing historical injustices by restoring communities to their ancestral lands.

This perspective informs the former labour tenants' rejection of compensating private farmers for land parcels at the centre of ongoing claims. This chapter highlights the policy implementation gaps between the aims of post-apartheid land legislation and the beneficiaries' views on land use. The former labour tenants' demands for compensation cover the multiple and diverse meanings of land, discussed throughout this book. These interpretations of land cannot be confined to market value because they reveal deeper cultural, heritage and political relations with the land. This book emphasises the necessity of widening the land compensation policy frameworks so that they compel companies and the state to consider different values associated with land in communities.

In Chapter 8, David Matsinhe adds a comparative dimension to the agrarian discussion by examining the relationship between agrarian political economy developments and social justice. A human rights framework is used to assess the experiences of peasant communities in Mozambique and Angola. These two states have experienced rapid economic growth since the early 2000s, which is attributed to the increased foreign direct investment in the extractive sectors, such as mining and energy (World Bank, 2017). This trend has created new waves of dispossession, which Moyo and Patnaik describe as 'a new scramble over African lands for agriculture, mining, natural resource attraction, entailing a growing East-West-South rivalry to gain footholds on the entire continent' (Moyo and Patnaik, 2011: 73).

Matsinhe details the impact of the dispossession in four peasant communities, highlighting several core arguments related to land development and compensation. The primary one is the necessity of building state capacity to hold all stakeholders accountable in land development regulatory regimes. He shows how both state and private sector actors undermine land-use legislative prescripts in both countries. He attributes this finding to patronage and regulatory incapacity within the state's bureaucracy. He uses Mahmood Mamdani's (1996) seminal citizens/subjects discussion to demonstrate the contemporary state's disregard for rural citizenry rights.

An additional significant finding is the failure of peasant community relocation or resettlement agreements, which exacerbate different feelings of dispossession. These injustices permeate all human development areas: socio-economic, cultural, political, ecological and health. Citizens who are relocated, through both illegitimate and legitimate means, express a deep sense of loss, which exhibits both material (livelihood) and non-material values attached to land ownership. Their accounts nudge stakeholders to rethink land-related compensation processes and community relocations. The peasant communities have sought to reaffirm their citizenship through social justice campaigns aimed at challenging illegal land evictions, weak state regulatory oversight and, in some cases, compensation measures implemented without their consent. Arguments advanced in this chapter support the book's general contention on the importance of land rights-based citizen agency. Land development projects will continue to undermine land tenure in rural communities in the absence of active citizenry, which is required to hold private companies and state authorities accountable. The arguments add more insight into the underlying reasons for social conflict or discontent in land restitution processes. At the heart of the problem are inadequacies in land compensation policies resulting from misconceptions about rural livelihoods and limited investigations into how rural peasant communities relate to land.

In Section III, we explore how the themes emerging from Sections I and II unfold in the following country case studies: Zimbabwe, Brazil and Palestine. These countries share a significant common trait with South Africa: a history of settler colonialism. But the form of settler colonialism in each case is shaped by peculiar historical factors and systems of land dispossessions. Another significant characteristic, which also relates to the South African situation, is the intersection between race, land ownership and nation formation in all countries. The chapters dealing with lessons from international experiences discuss land politics, with an emphasis on citizenship, nation formation, social justice and debates on the agrarian question.

LESSONS FROM INTERNATIONAL EXPERIENCES

In Chapter 9, Zenzo Moyo and Toendepi Shonhe start the discussion on the international experience with an analysis of the radical land reform approach adopted in Zimbabwe from the late 1990s, and the lessons that can be drawn from this. They depart from previous writings on the Zimbabwe land case by providing an account of the underlying class and citizenship agency that pushed the Zimbabwe African National Union-Patriotic Front (ZANU-PF) to adopt the Fast-Track Land Reform Programme (FTLRP). This discussion goes beyond the dominant policy narrative, which reduces all of Zimbabwe's land-related policy agency to ZANU-PF's elite-formation strategy. The authors approach the agrarian policy outcomes analysis differently through an evidence-based market structure assessment. This includes examining how the FTLRP altered Zimbabwe's agrarian political economy value chains, and the effect this had on certain agricultural markets over time. The authors highlight another significant theme missing in other analyses of Zimbabwe's land reform: the citizens' conceptions of land reform and justice, which transcend the narrow national food-production focus.

The authors emphasise points raised earlier regarding state orientation and regulatory capacity. They cite the politicisation of Zimbabwe's FTLRP as one of its major shortcomings. It shifted state intervention in land and agrarian reform towards the narrow economic interests of beneficiaries with close links to the ruling party, including war veterans, rural peasant movements and political elites. This perverse trend excluded many citizens from receiving state support and distorted the initial policy objectives of the FTLRP. It also marginalised the varied class and political interest groups outside ZANU-PF, which advocate for transformed land and agrarian structures.

Moyo and Shonhe argue that land and agrarian reform policies fail if they overemphasise race without seeking to transform class inequality. Their discussion illustrates how systemic class exclusion can persist in land and agrarian markets, even in a context of changing racial ownership patterns. They advocate for efficient citizen oversight to prevent land reform from producing limited race-based transformation. It is equally important to assess how the balance between different farming models shifts as land redistribution proceeds. These points are enunciated in the chapter's in-depth analysis of trends in certain agrarian markets, before and after the FTLRP implementation. It concludes that the FTLRP produced some positive structural crop market changes and productivity gains over time. An additional significant insight in these findings are land reform demands that fall outside food security and productivity concerns; these are connected with deeper cultural and political redress objectives. These demands did not emerge from ruling party ideological policy narratives – calls for land reform pre-dated the ZANU-PF-led FTLRP and different generations of Zimbabweans have sought to elevate land demands using different policy advocacy tactics.

Andrew Bennie develops the argument on land and agrarian policy advocacy further in Chapter 10. His analysis is located in Brazil and traces two prominent civil society land movements: Movimento dos Trabalhadores Rurais Sem Terra (MST) and the *quilombos*. The former is the Rural Landless Workers' Movement and the latter are descendants of runaway slaves fighting for land rights. This chapter is based on literature analysis and the author's ethnographic field research into MST activists in Brazil. There are many lessons for South Africa's land and agrarian policy stakeholders in Bennie's chapter. One of the significant takeaways is the relationship between land advocacy, social cohesion and nation formation. His data illustrate that land struggles are embedded in efforts to transform underlying race and class inequalities in Brazil, which have considerable impacts on nation-building. These efforts are not limited to class or socio-economic factors, as they include cultural rights of marginalised peasants, Afro-Brazilians and indigenous populations. In other words, land is at the heart of Brazilian political discussions on nation formation.

The connections between land and nation formation in Brazil are clearly illustrated in Bennie's discussion on different land-related constitutional amendments during the 19th and 20th centuries. The Brazilian constitution emphasises socio-economic, cultural and ecological factors, which highlight the state's attempts to protect different types of land rights. Bennie uses the concept of territory (in a South American context) to elaborate on the various political identities and meanings associated with Brazilian land. He then illustrates how different governments since the end of the dictatorship have sought to accommodate these land conceptions, using both constitutional law and government development policies. The most important lesson for South Africa is to appreciate the nexus between land law and policy formulation processes which accommodate different dimensions of land rights. Both movements have used this land policy framework to nudge state authorities towards deeper land and agrarian reforms.

The political agency initiated by social movements is cited as an essential aspect in Brazil's agrarian and land policy developments. Bennie's extensive analysis of both civil society groups illustrates how citizen-led movements can attain some policy successes using constitutional provisions; but these policy gains are a product of historical struggles, internal organisational capacity and the ability to adapt in changing political economy contexts. The author argues that South Africa's land and agrarian movements have attained minimal policy gains compared to the Brazilian civil society formations. He attributes these failures to differences in agrarian political economy structures, class political agency and ruling party policy orientation over the last three decades. This finding is important as it relates to ongoing debates about what form of active citizen participation is required to transform unequal land and/or agrarian relations in South Africa. This theme emerges throughout this book in different social contexts.

Class relations also feature in this case study, with an emphasis on how they impact the state's regulatory role in agrarian political economy structures. Bennie explains how Brazil's powerful agricultural business class, which owns most of the country's land, continues to receive substantial state support, despite the policy victories of the MST and the *quilombos*. This is attributed to Brazil's high dependency on commercial agricultural exports to finance its social programmes, especially during the Workers' Party's tenure. However, it is equally important to note Brazil's support for family and small-scale farming through its targeted state-procurement programmes. The successes and shortcomings of these policies are documented elsewhere in other research papers (Rocha et al., 2012). Bennie contends that Brazil's industrial agricultural class still receives more state support than family or small-scale farmers. It also engages in various forms of land dispossessions and the degradation of arable land through over-reliance on chemical inputs (Rocha et al., 2012: 527). This finding highlights the importance of changing the structural make-up in agrarian political economies and addressing unequal class relations.

Quraysha Sooliman concludes the international section with her discussion on citizenship, identity and nation formation in the Occupied Palestinian Territories. She employs a settler-colonial analytical framework to link Palestinian statehood and land advocacy. Sooliman amplifies the historical connections between nation formation, land disputes and citizenship in the Israeli–Palestinian conflict, and argues that Israeli settler colonialism has shaped Palestinian identity, citizenship and nationhood. She positions historical and contemporary land dispossession as the main manifestation of Israel's settler-colonial expansion. This account draws attention to the deeper political, cultural and economic livelihood impacts created by land seizures, forced removals and relocation. These impacts include conflict, human rights violations, and stripping Palestinians of their identity and sense of belonging (UNESCWA, 2017; Greenstein, 2020).

Chapter 11 highlights citizen erasure and the reconstruction of political identities in land disputes. It compares Israel's land settlement programmes with apartheid South Africa's separate development strategies. The author argues that it is essential to understand the underlying political and socio-cultural factors driving settlement creation. Her account points to the Israeli state's political outlook, which attempts to delegitimise indigenous land claims. This approach, according to Sooliman, is a key aspect of the settler-colonial state narrative that legitimises continued land dispossessions and race-based separate development. It also sustains notions of political and race-based superiority embedded in the Israeli state's laws. The chapter highlights a connection between land dispossessions and laws that promote citizen erasure in several ways.

Palestinians have attempted to resist land confiscations, Israeli settlement expansion and forced relocations since the mid-20th century. Sooliman discusses the deeper issues underpinning this resistance, which cut across multiple meanings of land. The primary objective of this resistance is reclaiming identity and historical indigenous land, obscured through systemic dispossession or the ideological views of the Israeli state. An additional aspect is challenging the usurpation of basic human rights associated with citizenship. Sooliman connects this element with discriminatory laws used in justifying land expropriations, and provides additional examples of Palestinian resistance that illustrate connections between political agency, land struggles and redefining citizenship.

These international case studies address the core research questions relating to land and nation formation. All cases bring to the fore, the varied meanings and values associated with land, which encompass political, socio-economic, ecological and cultural dimensions of human development. A society's historical and contemporary contexts determine which of these meanings are elevated. Attempts at building social cohesion need to accommodate these diverse meanings in land regulation and development policies. These case studies reveal how the evolution of nation formation is inextricably connected with land redistribution or restitution. The construction and remaking of national identity hinges on land power relations and their impacts on social inequality. The evidence presented shows how land policy struggles contribute to determining social cohesion and nation formation. Citizen agency is presented as a crucial factor in determining land and agrarian power relations. It is shaped by the strength of civil society movements advancing social transformation in land and agrarian political economies. These organisations have the potential to ensure that policy-making and implementation processes are inclusive, fair and transparent.

CONCLUSION

Overall, this book broadens the scope and approaches to South Africa's unresolved land question. It shifts the debates on land policies and inequalities beyond the narrow productivist lens. The chapters investigate the diverse and contested meanings of land to elevate how South Africans perceive land justice and reform. This discussion on differing relations to land is positioned within a social cohesion and nation-formation conceptual framework. Land power relations and conceptualisations are at the centre of nation-building, as they determine citizenship, political identity, belonging and socio-economic inequalities. This connection between land and nation formation is more pronounced in a society grappling with apartheid socio-economic legacies, which have produced systemic land ownership disparities. This book illustrates that these unequal relations cut across different types of human rights and areas of human development. It therefore proposes several policy options to resolve land disparities that transcend market-centric monetary solutions. These propositions appreciate the depth of the land question in South Africa and its multiple dimensions.

Furthermore, the book's main arguments illustrate the contradictions and shortcomings in existing land policy frameworks.

These pieces of legislation have not achieved the goals set out in the Constitution, neither do they support or complement the historical land governance systems used by South Africa's black majority population. Several chapters emphasise the need to rethink and reformulate land tenure and restitution policy implementation. The authors present insights and proposals on how to approach these areas of land policy differently. Their suggestions rest on deeper understandings of citizens' relationships with land, removing colonial distortions from legislation, and advocating inclusive decision-making.

All these proposals cannot be achieved without political will, active citizenship and efficient state capacity. The lessons from the different country case studies emphasise the centrality of land politics and citizen agency in transforming land and agrarian power relations. Chapters in this book connect transformative land politics with nation formation, political identity and social movement advocacy. They present the various land policy outcomes produced by this political agency and how these intersect with state capacity. The policy orientation, performance and responsiveness of governments in the area of land governance are shaped through engagements with non-state actors. Steven Friedman's (2019) notion of positive liberty or freedom emphasises the necessity of active citizenry from marginalised citizens in holding governments accountable. Civil society action is imperative in debates on the future of land policy in South Africa. This book encourages South Africans to develop different forms of citizen-led oversight to protect and advance land-based rights across the country. This is essential for addressing land inequalities, which determine social cohesion and nation formation.

REFERENCES

Beinart, W., Delius, P. and Hay, M. 2017. *Rights to Land: A guide to tenure upgrading and restitution in South Africa.* Johannesburg: Jacana Media.

Bernstein, H. 2006. 'Is there an agrarian question in the 21st century?'. *Canadian Journal of Development Studies*, 27 (4), 449–460.

Bundy, C. 1988. *The Rise and Fall of the South African Peasantry*. London: James Currey.

Cousins, B. and Walker, C. (eds.) 2015. *Land Divided, Land Restored: Land reform in South Africa for the 21st century.* Johannesburg: Jacana Media.

Department of Arts and Culture (DAC). 2012. 'What is social cohesion and nation-building?', http://www.dac.gov.za/sites/default/files/WHAT%20IS%20SOCIAL%20COHESION%20AND%20NATION%20(3).pdf, accessed 1 August 2019.

Department of Rural Development and Land Reform (DRDLR). 2017. 'Land Audit Report', https://www.gov.za/sites/default/files/gcis_document/201802/landauditreport13feb2018.pdf, accessed 19 August 2020.

Dodson, B., Chiweza, A. and Riley, L. 2012. 'Gender and food insecurity in southern African cities'. Urban Food Security Series No. 10, http://www.afsun.org/wp-content/uploads/2016/06/Afsun10.pdf, accessed 20 May 2020.

Du Plessis, H., Sehume, J. and Martin, L. (eds.) 2014. *The Concept and Application of Transdisciplinary in Intellectual Discourse and Research.* Johannesburg: MISTRA.

Friedman, S. 8 February 2019. 'The problem of leadership in Africa'. Democracy in Africa, http://democracyinafrica.org/problem-leadership-africa/, accessed 9 September 2020.

Goebel, A. 2005. 'Is Zimbabwe the future of South Africa? The implications for land reform in Southern Africa'. *Journal of Contemporary African Studies*, 23 (3), 345–370.

Greenstein, R. 2020. 'New Israeli government finally formed, prepares to annex West Bank territory'. Afro-Middle East Centre, http://www.amec.org.za/israel/item/1659-new-israeli-government-finally-formed-prepares-to-annex-west-bank-territory.html, accessed 20 July 2020.

Hall, R. and Ntsebeza, L. 2007. 'Introduction', in Ntsebeza, L. and Hall, R. (eds.) *The Land Question in South Africa: The challenge of transformation and redistribution*. Cape Town: HSRC Press, 1–28.

Jara, M. K. 2014. 'The solidarity economy response to the agrarian crisis in South Africa', in Satgar, V. (ed.) *The Solidarity Economy Alternative: Emerging theory and practice.* Pietermaritzburg: University of KwaZulu-Natal Press, 227–248.

Kepe, T. and Hall, R. 2016. 'Land redistribution in South Africa', https://

www.parliament.gov.za/storage/app/media/Pages/2017/october/High_Level_Panel/Commissioned_Report_land/Commissioned_Report_on_Land_Redistribution_Kepe_and_Hall.pdf, accessed 12 August 2020.

Kroll, F. 2016. 'Foodways of the poor in South Africa: How value-chain consolidation, poverty and cultures of consumption feed each other'. Working Paper No. 36, PLAAS, University of the Western Cape.

Mafeje, A. 2003. 'The agrarian question, access to land, and peasant responses in sub-Saharan Africa'. Paper No. 6, Civil Society and Social Movements Programme, United Nations Research Institute for Social Development, https://www.unrisd.org/80256B3C005BCCF9/(httpPublications)/A2B577C61B19F92EC1256D56002B5291?OpenDocument, accessed 9 May 2020.

Mamdani, M. 1996. *Citizen and Subject: Contemporary Africa and the legacy of late colonialism*. Princeton, NJ: Princeton University Press.

MISTRA. 2014. *Nation Formation and Social Cohesion: An enquiry into the hopes and aspirations of South Africans*. Johannesburg: MISTRA.

Mkodzongi, G. and Lawrence, P. 2019. 'The fast-track land reform and agrarian change in Zimbabwe'. *Review of African Political Economy*, 48 (159), 1–13.

Mnwana, S., Mtero, F. and Hay, M. 2016. 'Dispossessing the dispossessed? Mining and rural struggles in Mokopane, Limpopo'. Working Paper No. 7, Society, Work and Development Institute, University of the Witwatersrand.

Moyo, S. and Patnaik, U. 2011. *The Agrarian Question in the Neoliberal Era: Primitive accumulation and the peasantry*. Dar es Salaam: Pambazuka Press.

Moyo, S., Jha, P. and Yeros, P. 2013. 'The classical agrarian question: Myth, reality and relevance today'. *Journal of Political Economy*, 2 (1), 93–119.

Neocosmos, M. 1993. 'The agrarian question in southern Africa and accumulation from below: Economics and politics in the struggle for democracy'. Research Report No. 8, Scandinavian Institute of African Studies.

O'Laughlin, B., Bernstein, H., Cousins, B. and Peters, P. E. 2013. 'Introduction: Agrarian change, rural poverty and land reform in South Africa since 1994'. *Journal of Agrarian Change*, 13 (1), 1–15.

Peters, B.L. and Malan, N. 2009. 'Caveats for land reform in South Africa: Lessons from Zimbabwe'. *South African Journal of International Affairs*, 7 (2), 151–161.

Presidential Advisory Panel on Land Reform and Agriculture. 2019. 'Final report of the Presidential Advisory Panel on Land Reform and Agriculture', https://www.gov.za/sites/default/files/gcis_document/201907/panelreportlandreform_0.pdf, accessed 1 August 2020.

Rocha, C., Burlandy, L. and Maluf, R. 2012. 'Small farms and sustainable rural development for food security: The Brazilian experience'. *Development*

Southern Africa, 29 (4), 519–529.

Shisana O., Labadarios D., Rehle T., Simbayi, L., Zuma, K., et al. 2013. *South African National Health and Nutrition Examination Survey (SANHANES-1)*. Cape Town: HSRC Press.

United Nations Economic and Social Commission for Western Asia (UNESCWA). 15 March 2017. 'ESCWA launches report on Israeli practices towards the Palestinian people and the question of apartheid'. UNESCWA, https://www.unescwa.org/news/escwa-launches-report-israeli-practices-towards-palestinian-people-and-question-apartheid, accessed 15 February 2020.

World Bank. July 2017. 'Mozambique economic update: A two-speed economy'. World Bank, https://www.worldbank.org/en/country/mozambique/publication/mozambique-economic-update-a-two-speed-economy, accessed 2 August 2020.

Yeni, S. 2018. 'Traditional leadership, violation of land rights and resistance from below in Makhasaneni village, KwaZulu-Natal', in Buthelezi, M., Skosana, D. and Vale, B. (eds.) *Traditional Leaders in a Democracy: Resources, respect and resistance*. Johannesburg: MISTRA, 153–178.

Legislation

Constitution of the Republic of South Africa (Act No. 108 of 1996).

Communal Land Rights Act (No. 11 of 2004).

Extension of Security of Tenure Act (No. 62 of 1997).

Interim Protection of Informal Land Rights Act (No. 31 of 1996).

Labour Reform (Tenants Act) Act (No. 3 of 1996).

Upgrading of Land Tenure Rights Act (No. 112 of 1991, amended in 1996 and 1998).

Section One

Land, Citizenship and Nation Formation

ONE

Nationalisms and Nation Formation in South Africa

YACOOB ABBA OMAR

INTRODUCTION

The history of South Africa has been shaped by two key nationalist narratives: the 'native question' and the 'national question'. The first phrase refers to the framework that the colonisers used to govern and subjugate the indigenous population, while the second describes the varied responses from the colonised in search of national unity and liberation. These decolonial responses were articulated in inclusive nationalism, non-racialism and, more recently, social cohesion. Land possession and dispossession inform all nationalist narratives that determine essential post-apartheid policy redress discourses. This chapter examines some of the critical concepts around nationalism and their relation to the land question. Using Anthony Smith's (1999) observation that it is rare for only one nationalism to exist in a country, I discuss Afrikaner and Pan-African/Black Consciousness nationalist movements. The latter two movements are associated with the African National Congress (ANC), where they either challenge the non-racialism political principle or find space in its broader conceptualisation.

The Pan-African analysis includes the period before the ANC's formation, as well as the formulation of historical documents such as African Claims (1943), the Freedom Charter (1955) and the ANC's 1989 constitutional guidelines. I also consider the emergence of African nationalism and Black Consciousness in discussing Pan-Africanism. The evolution of Afrikaner nationalism is traced from the Afrikaners' contested roots, which shaped the apartheid state's emergence, and internal debates during the constitutional negotiations, which led to the formal political transition from apartheid.

This chapter specifically explores how the two nationalisms interact with notions of race, ethnicity, history and land in contemporary South Africa. The discussion reveals the extent of social cohesion and social compacting in society, which influences the process of nation formation. At its core, the land question is about the resolution of a great injustice that began when colonialists arrived in South Africa. This injustice was perpetuated over several centuries, up to and including the era of democracy in South Africa. Nationalist rhetoric was used to justify the black majority's dispossession of land by a white minority. This dispossession was used at different points of colonial history as a means to force black people into the labour market to meet the requirements of capital, and it thus required the juridical and violent physical subjugation of the majority indigenous population. On the other hand, the experience of the dispossessed gave rise to a form of nationalism that was encompassing of all the people living in South Africa. This imagination of a nation, to paraphrase Benedict Anderson (1983), went beyond notions of race, colour or ethnicity to provide the impetus for the particular way in which the national question was engendered. It also required the courage to look beyond the jackboot of oppression, brutal wars of conquest and dispossession in order to recognise the humanity within all South Africans. It is this imagination that is once again being marshalled in the face of grinding poverty, gross inequalities, racial tensions and all manner of violence so that social cohesion can be addressed. Thus, the land question is part of a double-barrelled agenda, captured by Cyril Ramaphosa (2018):

> Land is about dignity, identity, security. It is intimately linked to the preservation of culture and heritage, a bridge between the past and the present. We are engaged in this great effort to heal the wounds of the past. We are driven also by an economic imperative. For all its historical, social and political meaning, land is fundamentally an economic resource. And like all other economic resources in this country, it has historically been employed to serve the interests of a narrow section of society.

THE EVOLUTION OF THE NATIONAL QUESTION

Pan-Africanism can be traced back to the early 1800s when American Negroes, as they were then termed, sought refuge from American racism by migrating to the Black Republics – Ethiopia, Liberia, Haiti and Sierra Leone (Ndletyana et al., 2014: 147). This movement continued to develop throughout the 19th and 20th centuries. It culminated in the first Pan-African conference convened by Henry Sylvester Williams in London in 1900, where W. E. B. Du Bois declared: 'The problem of the 20th century is the problem of the colour line – the relation of the darker to the lighter races of men [*sic*] in Asia, Africa, America and the islands of the sea' (cited in Lemelle, 1992: 94). Booker Washington's response to this problem was an ideology of black nationalist entrepreneurship, which argued that the time was not ripe for social equality and integration. It was a philosophy that the first president of the ANC, John Langalibalele Dube, took up with gusto in his beliefs in self-sufficiency. In contrast, African-American intellectuals from the northern states took a more radical perspective, criticising the 'Atlanta Compromise' (Odendaal, 2012: 253). They aimed to get the vote and civil rights within an integrated system and founded the National Association for the Advancement of Colored People in 1910.

Marcus Garvey represented the next generation, which focused especially on the 'Negro' working class and poor. There was a discernible shift in the 1945 Pan-Africanism congress held in London, largely due to the presence of Africans from the continent, who were 'buoyed by the promise of self-determination made by the victors of the Second World War' (Ndletyana et al., 2014: 154). They had felt the devastating effect of racialised colonialism, captured in Frantz Fanon's opening line of *Black Skin, White Masks,* where the writer observes that 'the black man is not a man' (Fanon, 1986: 8). He was commenting on the crushing impact of colonialism that had destroyed black peoples' sense of self-worth. But this self-worth was reasserted in different liberation nationalist movements and the advocacy directed towards challenging colonialism. A clear example is the early African intellectual activism in South Africa, which spoke of a single nation long before the creation of the Union of South Africa in 1910.

Several reasons have been proffered for why national identity issues trumped ethnicity so early on. André Odendaal argues that early nationalists were 'influenced by the trinity of African humanism, or *ubuntu*, the egalitarian message of Christianity and mid-Victorian political liberalism', and that 'they engaged with metropolitan debates ... In the process, their struggles and activities acquired an international dimension, which became a strong feature of 20th-century political resistance in South Africa' (Odendaal, 2012: 241). Garvey's exclusivist Pan-Africanism had also found expression in South Africa, for example, in the political views of the ANC's Western Cape leader, James Thaele, who had spent 10 years in the United States where he came under Garvey's influence. Similarly, Reverend Z.R. Mahabane, the ANC's Western Cape president, and Clements Kadalie, who founded the Industrial and Commercial Workers' Union, supported Garvey's perspective (Ndletyana et al., 2014: 166). Pixley ka Isaka Seme strengthened the emerging Pan-Africanist tradition in his historic speech at Columbia University in 1906, starting with the following words: 'I have chosen to speak to you on this occasion upon "The Regeneration of Africa". I am an African, and I set my pride in my race over against a hostile public opinion' (Seme, 1906).

The Pan-Africanist strand influenced the early founders of the ANC when they formed the organisation in 1912. The organisation's nascent political culture was shaped largely by *amakholwa*, a broad term used to describe Africans who received missionary education and subscribed to Christianity. This culture sought accommodation within the established framework of white domination. However, this began to change in the 1940s due to South Africa's burgeoning urbanisation during the country's second industrial revolution. During this period, a major advance in the ANC's thinking was its push – for the first time – for an unqualified universal franchise. The leadership of Alfred Xuma provided a stimulus to black politics generally and set in place a trend of united radical mass action, which continued well into the 1990s. Just as the ANC and its newly created African National Congress Youth League (ANCYL) were going through a period of radicalisation in the 1940s, so was the South Africa Indian Congress (SAIC) under the leadership of a group of young activists, including Yusuf Dadoo and Monty Naicker. They played a leading role in the creation of the Non-European United Front, which, from 1938 onwards, organised anti-war protests, defended arrested leaders and mounted opposition to Hertzog's 'Native Bills', which in effect created the legal framework for apartheid.

Two major debates occurred at this point, which continue to influence contemporary manifestations of the national question, namely Africanism and non-racial cooperation. The latter was eventually elevated as a principle of the ANC and expressed in the organisation's African Claims document, which was adopted during the 1943 conference. It proclaimed that 'the African people in the Union of South Africa urgently demand the granting of full citizenship rights such as are enjoyed by all Europeans in South Africa' (ANC, 1943). The Bill of Rights contained in African Claims listed the 'Full Citizen Rights and Demands', which called for, inter alia, 'the right of every child to free and compulsory education', and 'the establishment of free medical and health services for all'. The document also called for 'a substantial and immediate improvement in the economic position of the African' (ANC, 1943). This 'profoundly social humanism in the ANC's approach found its way into the Freedom Charter adopted in 1955 and subsequent policy documents' (Netshitenzhe, 2012: 24).

The Africanist emphasis of the 1944 ANCYL manifesto offered a marked contrast to the African Claims document and could be regarded as the first avowedly Africanist document produced by a mainstream South African nationalist organisation. According to Gavin Williams (1988: 77):

> The manifesto saw the ANC as a 'national unity front' through 'which the national liberation of Africans will be achieved by Africans themselves'. In terms of the manifesto, African nationalism had to create a 'united nation out of heterogeneous tribes' and to free Africa from foreign domination and foreign leadership.

By 1944, the ANCYL, under the leadership of Anton Lembede, A. P. Mda, Nelson Mandela, Walter Sisulu and Oliver Tambo introduced a radical form of politics to the ANC. In its 1948 manifesto, the ANCYL envisaged 'South Africa as a country of four chief nationalities, three of which are minorities and three of which suffer national oppression. It also saw the national organisations of Africans, Indians and Coloureds cooperating on common interests.' G. R. D. Halisi describes Lembede's approach as that of a black republican – thinkers who believe that 'African people themselves are the source of all legitimacy ... black republicans see democracy and socialism as inherent in the ways of the African folk' (Halisi, 1988: 132).

Empowered by the ANC's national leadership decision to cooperate with other race groups, Xuma signed a joint declaration of cooperation with Dadoo and Naicker on 9 March 1947. But ANCYL leaders such as Anton Lembede opposed such cooperation. He argued that African leaders were fighting for Africa, while Indians 'are fighting only for their rights to trade and extract as much wealth as possible from Africa' (Lembede, 1945). His untimely death in 1947 saw the ANCYL subsequently reviewing its position, and the organisation concluded in 1948 that Indians 'did not come as conquerors and exploiters, but as the exploited' (Soske, 2012: 182). The Defiance Campaign of 1952, which saw collaboration within what was developing into the Congress Alliance, drew on the success of the passive resistance campaigns initiated by the SAIC. It laid the basis for what ANC leader Albert Luthuli came to call an 'inclusive nationalism' and was captured in the term non-racialism.

David Everatt (2009) argues that the ANC never quite clearly defined non-racialism beyond the notion of equal citizenship, and thus did not address what this meant for national identity and social cohesion – a challenge that persists to this day. The incipient non-racial leanings of the ANC created problems for the more Africanist-oriented youth league leadership. The adoption of the Freedom Charter in 1955, and especially the line proclaiming that South Africa belongs to all who live in it, catalysed the eventual breakaway of the Pan-Africanist Congress (PAC) in 1958, under the leadership of Robert Sobukwe and Potlako Leballo. These leaders also took exception to another Freedom Charter clause: 'The land shall be shared among those who work it! Restrictions on land ownership on a racial basis shall be ended, and all the land re-divided among those who work it, to banish famine and land hunger' (ANC, 1955). The PAC's view was that the land belonged to the indigenous African majority and was captured in the slogan *Izwe Lethu, iAfrika* (Africa Belongs to Us).

Sabelo Ndlovu-Gatsheni (2006) makes a useful observation that Africanism has always been a contradictory phenomenon, with some nationalists learning through the struggle and realising its limits or exclusive tendencies. Other nationalists enthusiastically embraced exclusive black Africanist ideology. Another way to look at the PAC's views on the land question is to cite Nico Vorster, who discusses recent policy debates on expropriation without compensation (EWC). He states that 'South Africans who attach social meanings to land generally tend to consider land as a space of rootedness, a locus of life and a place of history-making where identities are formed' (Vorster, 2019: 4).

I return to the EWC debates later in the chapter, but the critical issue to note here is the way the ANC managed the potential tension between its non-racial position and its commitment to African leadership. The former has been the core policy position of the ANC, especially since the 1950s. In a 1968 interview, then ANC president, Oliver Tambo, explained: 'We fight for a South Africa in which there will be no racial discrimination, no inequalities based on colour, creed, or race – a non-racial democracy which recognizes the essential equality between man and man' (Tambo, 1987: 70).

The ANC's Morogoro conference held in Tanzania in 1969 was significant in that it allowed non-Africans to join the organisation as individuals. Non-Africans were admitted to the national executive at its Kabwe conference in Zambia in 1985. The predominance of non-racialism should not be seen as a defeat of Pan-Africanism. It ensured that Africanism is located within the concept of the South African nation. This is captured eloquently in Luthuli's assertion: 'Somewhere ahead there beckons a civilization which will take its place in God's history with other great human syntheses: Chinese, Egyptian, Jewish, European. It will not necessarily be all black: but it will be African' (cited in Netshitenzhe, 2013). Those very themes would be echoed by Thabo Mbeki 90 years later in his 'I Am an African' speech to mark the adoption of the Constitution in May 1996.

The 1960s saw the roots of the Black Consciousness Movement being laid. Steve Biko led the creation of the South African Students' Organisation (SASO) in 1969 after black students withdrew from the student body of the National Union of South African Students NUSAS). Biko, alongside the black student leadership of the time, such as Barney Pityana and Saths Cooper, are examples of a different set of political entrepreneurs who personified the views of their generation. SASO embodied the principles of Black Consciousness, which sought to imbue black people with a higher degree of confidence, justifying this as an essential step towards democracy. Biko's writings reflect an important dialogue with the thinking of Franz Fanon, Aimé Césaire and Léopold Senghor and the politics of Négritude. In many ways, these were building on the traditions of the early versions of Pan-Africanism, but now in the context of newly independent countries, heightened liberation struggles – often taking the form of armed struggles – and the emergence of the Non-Aligned Movement. This context was giving a new assertiveness to anti-colonialists around the world.

According to Biko, 'Liberation is of paramount importance in the concept of Black Consciousness, for we cannot be conscious of ourselves and yet remain in bondage ... being black is not a matter of pigmentation – being black is a reflection of a mental attitude. Merely by describing yourself as black you have started on a road towards emancipation' (cited in Reddy, 1995: 184). In many ways, the Black Consciousness perspective was influenced by Garvey's emphasis on self-assertion, as well as Frantz Fanon's views on self-identity and revolt. Shortly after the formation of SASO in 1969, the Black People's

Convention was launched in July 1972 in Hammersdale in Natal. Abram Onkgopotse Tiro captured the essence of these movements in a speech delivered during his tenure as president of the Student Representative Council at the University of Turfloop. He criticised Bantu Education and described the system as 'very poisonous' and said: 'The magic story of human achievement gives irrefutable proof that as soon as nationalism is awakened among the intelligentsia it becomes the vanguard in the struggle against alien rule' (Tiro, 1972). He was expelled from the university for his views, sparking nationwide student protests, consolidating SASO as one of the leading organisations of its time.

Strini Moodley, one of the leaders of the Black Consciousness Movement in Natal, explains that they tried to steer a path between the Freedom Charter, 'which did not go far enough ... in the interests of the black people, it was too accommodating', and the PAC, which had a 'too narrow concept of Pan-Africanism ... and failed to embrace the notion of socialism' (Desai and Vahed, 2012: 500). Neville Alexander points out that the Black Consciousness perspective, shared by some tendencies in the PAC, sees the existence of 'two nations' in South Africa, an oppressing white and an oppressed black, sometimes referred to as a 'black nationality' (Alexander, 1986: 81–82). Alexander continues (1986: 81–82):

> Exponents of the Black Consciousness position have tended to conflate 'race' and 'class' to the point that in some versions all whites are projected as capitalists while all blacks are seen as workers ... It seems to assume that all whites in South Africa, because they are not oppressed, cannot identify at a certain unspecifiable deep psychic level with the oppressed and with their struggle.

The 1980s saw the emergence of a plethora of organs of civil society, many of which coalesced in the ANC-aligned United Democratic Front (UDF), while the Congress of South African Trade Unions (COSATU) consolidated a vast array of worker organisations. The debates in the 1980s between the workerists and the ANC-aligned charterists were largely around the question of what was called the National Democratic Revolution (NDR). In Joe Slovo's description (1989: 3):

> The national democratic revolution – the present stage of struggle in our country is a revolution of the whole oppressed people ... The main revolutionary camp in the immediate struggle is made up of different classes and strata (overwhelmingly black) which suffer varying forms and degrees of national oppression and economic exploitation. The camp of those who benefit from, and support, national domination is also divided into classes.

For the workerists, Slovo's and the UDF's conception of people was not helpful because society is composed of diverse interests, and it was not clear how this heterogeneous community would be united behind a common nation-formation vision. According to Ivor Chipkin, 'The NDR presumed that the struggle against racial oppression advanced the interests of the black, coloured and Indian bourgeoisie and petit bourgeoisie at the same time as it satisfied workers' interests' (Chipkin, 2007: 95). This debate continued in the trade union movement throughout the 1980s and still shapes contemporary debates within South Africa's broad left.

EVOLUTION OF THE NATIVE QUESTION

The central concern of the white regimes in South Africa – whether they were Dutch, British or Afrikaner – was the native question in its various forms, which Adam Ashforth describes as 'the intellectual domain in which the knowledge, strategies, policies, and justifications necessary to the maintenance of domination were fashioned' (Ashforth, 1990: 5). Broadly, Afrikaner nationalism can be seen in ethno-symbolist or in constructed terms. The former approach is best explained by Hermann Giliomee (1989), who argues that the early economic and later political developments met diverse psychological needs of the Afrikaners. Dan O'Meara (1996) develops this idea further in describing how economic entrepreneurs, drawn from the embryonic financial and commercial capital sectors, played a leading role in crafting a nationalist project of economic empowerment. The capital used to develop the sectors mentioned above was drawn from the Afrikaner agricultural capitalist class, which had managed to secure state policy support from the early 20th century.

The South African War of 1899–1902 and the eventual creation of the Union of South Africa in 1910 represented an important moment in South African politics. Pieter Duvenage explains that the two Boer Republics accepted a unitary state for several reasons – the most important being that it kept them 'within the Western sphere of influence' (Duvenage, 2014: 85). The South African Native Affairs Commission (SANAC) Report of 1905 laid the basis for the 1920 Native Affairs Act, which established the Native Affairs Commission and extended the Transkei Council System to other reserves. Another major piece of legislation was the 1913 Natives Land Act, which had the effect of forcing African people off the land and pushing them to seek employment in urban areas. They would come in direct competition with Afrikaners, who were also going through their own process of urbanisation, which had reached 41 per cent by 1926, compared to less than 10 per cent in 1900.

During this period, a movement emerged that essentially believed 'only a combination of ethnic mobilisation and *volkskapitalisme* could improve the lot of the economically and politically marginalised Afrikaner' (Davies, 2009: 19). This was the context in which the government set up the Native Economic Commission (NEC) from 1930 to 1932 to look into the socio-economic conditions of the 'natives', especially in the cities. Like the SANAC, the NEC had to deal with the term 'native'. Ashforth explains that 'their objection to the term derives from the fact that it is imbricated within a discourse engaging notions of rights, principally aboriginal rights to land – a matter with important political implications' (Ashforth, 1990: 76). The NEC Report proposed the development of the reserves and a halt to uncontrolled movement of natives into urban areas. Following this report, various pieces of legislation, commonly referred to as the Hertzog Bills, were enacted in 1936. The Native Trust and Land Act was passed in 1936 to carry out the provision of the 1913 Natives Land

Act, which allowed for reserve extension and the creation of a South African Native Trust.

The Tomlinson Commission of 1954 was the next major enquiry into the native question, emphasising the principle of national self-determination, but being careful not to cast any normative judgements on 'Bantu culture', such as being inferior or backward. There was widespread rejection of the commission's proposal of the balkanisation of the African people into bantustans. The government promulgated the Promotion of Bantu Self-Government Act of 1959, which eventually led to the creation of the bantustans of the Transkei, Ciskei, Bophuthatswana, KwaNdebele, Gazankulu, Lebowa, QwaQwa, KaNgwane, KwaZulu and Venda.

Within the Afrikaner nationalist movement, attitudes towards coloured people went through several transformations. Coloureds were perceived as part of the alliance against Africans until the 1930s. In 1936, Prime Minister J.B.M. Hertzog finally had enough support in parliament to change the Constitution and close the common voters' roll to Africans in the Cape. In 1938, the National Party (NP), under D.F. Malan's leadership, advocated scrapping the Cape black franchise and removing coloured people from the common voters' roll. J.G. Strijdom, the hard-line leader from the Transvaal, was opposed to any compromise, even dismissing the notion of native representatives in parliament. The 1951 Separate Representation of Voters Act placed coloured people on different rolls in the Cape and Natal, even though the coloured franchise had been entrenched in the 1909 South Africa Act. The Cape's coloured voters were finally disenfranchised in 1956 (Van der Westhuizen, 2007: 44–50). Sharon Gabie argues that through this 'social and economic materiality both the state and the Coloureds gained an interest in their differentiation. Unbeknown to them this essential difference was to become their Achilles heel post-1994 as it is this very same identity that they now denounce' (Gabie, 2014: 27).

Afrikaner relations with the land in the early stages of this nationalist development plan were informed by classical biblical texts. According to Vorster (2019: 6):

> [M]any Voortrekkers identified closely with ancient Israel and considered themselves as a people elected by God to drive away heathen nations from God's Promised Land. Although these ideas are no longer common among white South Africans, most Christian white farmers still consider land as an inheritance from God and themselves as stewards who received a calling from God to cultivate land.

This religious political base was complemented by deep nationalist cultural beliefs centred on language. Afrikaans as a language emerged from a mixture of Dutch with the various languages spoken in the Cape Colony – especially Malay and Portuguese (as a result of the slaves imported from the Dutch colony of what is today Indonesia and the then Portuguese colony of Mozambique), Khoisan, and a sprinkling of French with the arrival of the French Huguenots in 1688. By the 1890s, efforts to promote Afrikaans seemed to have fizzled out. Kees van der Waal (2012) argues that the creolised version, which coloured people in the Cape had begun using, nevertheless survived. In the aftermath of the South African War, the anglicisation programme of Lord Alfred Milner 'provided the catalyst for the development of the so-called Second Afrikaans Language Movement' (Kriel, 2010: 407) (the more recent Third Afrikaans Language Movement of the 1990s is discussed later). But it was only in the 1930s that South Africa saw the consolidation of a white Afrikaner identity. During this time, historian and filmmaker Gustav S. Preller played a major role in popularising the Afrikaner myth of the Great Trek. According to Mariana Kriel, '[I]t marked the mass spread of national consciousness among Afrikaners [and] culminated in the erection of the Voortrekker Monument' (Kriel, 2010: 408).

The period between 1948 and 1960, which began with victory for the NP under Malan's leadership, is referred to as that of 'low apartheid', when the NP-led government expanded on the existing segregationist policies laid by the British colonialists in areas such as Natal. This became the basis for the later 'high' or 'grand apartheid'. Afrikaner economic empowerment and access to welfare benefits expanded during this period, especially in the form of job reservation in a growing state bureaucracy. By 1960, Afrikaner nationalism was transformed from oppositional nationalism, which saw the British as the enemy, to state nationalism. However, it could not achieve consensus on apartheid because of the irreconcilable needs of the different factions of capital, as well as critiques from the Afrikaner elite themselves.

These voices of disquiet were raised further in the aftermath of the Sharpeville massacre in March 1960, with three ministers asking for the pass system to be scrapped. Verwoerd's successor, B.J. Vorster, began speaking increasingly of a white state within which Afrikaner identity was to be asserted, trying to bring English-speaking whites into its fold. This was opposed by *verkramptes* such as Albert Hertzog and Jaap Marais, who were expelled from the NP in 1969. They went on to establish the Herstigte Nasionale Party. These various dynamics led Christi van der Westhuizen to comment: 'Some South Africans oversimplify the NP's core constituency, the Afrikaners, as a monolithic grouping' (Van der Westhuizen, 2007: 64).

The economy grew between 1964 and 1972, averaging 6 to 8 per cent annually. By the mid-1970s, the NP was becoming a victim of its own success and the Afrikaners were transforming into a predominantly urbanised middle class. White-collar workers constituted 65 per cent of the total economically active population by 1977, compared to about 30 per cent in 1946. Unemployment among Afrikaner men fell to 12 per cent, while their presence in professional and technical categories increased by more than 93 per cent (Van der Westhuizen, 2007: 93). This period also witnessed the rise of an Afrikaner business class, who saw themselves as a politically based class with their own specific interests. Afrikaner capital in finance grew from 5 per cent in 1938/39 to 25 per cent in 1975, while mining grew from 1 per cent to 18 per cent in the same period. The NP ensured that it did not grow too distant from the agricultural sector, with state subsidies representing 20 per cent of an average farmer's income.

South Africa experienced several economic challenges during the late 1970s. The global oil crisis and low domestic demand were the primary causes of the country's economic stagnation during this period. This was the milieu that framed the Wiehahn and Riekert

Commissions of 1977–1981 where, according to Ashforth (1990), the 'native question' came to be couched in terms of race relations. This was also the period when black urban workers were beginning to have their voices heard – either though strike actions, such as the 1973 Durban worker protests, or the militant action of students, which was epitomised by the Soweto uprising of 1976. The use of repressive measures continued to be the hallmark of NP rule and it eventually delegitimised the state. South Africa's economy experienced structural challenges that were exacerbated by political authoritarianism.

The need for political cohesion in a society with a rapidly changing class structure influenced the NP to consider altering the racial composition of the party's support base, and this was spurred on by P. W. Botha's injunction to 'adapt or die'. This came on the back of the realisation that apartheid had spawned an economy that was aimed at meeting the needs of the small, white domestic market. Botha's 'Total Strategy' aimed to create a new national basis of consent, and this created political differences within the NP traditional support base, especially the Afrikaner farmers who became alienated from the state (Davies, 2009: 34). The state enacted a new Constitution in September 1984 that established a Tricameral Parliament, which, with the creation of urban councils, was aimed at drawing Indian, coloured and African elites into its power axis. It was an unpopular decision for various reasons, but the primary one was the exclusion of the majority of South Africans.

The limited reform manoeuvres Botha engaged in had a telling impact on dynamics within the NP, where the *broedertwis* (tensions between brothers) took the form of bitter battles between the *verkrampte* (conservative) and *verligte* (progressive) elements. The NP split once again in March 1982, with the *verkramptes* under the leadership of Andries Treurnicht leaving to form the Conservative Party. The base of the NP had shifted dramatically over the previous couple of decades. Ownership patterns in the agricultural sector had become more concentrated and Afrikaner economic participation in other industries was expanding. The percentage of Afrikaners active in farming dropped from 30 per cent in the 1930s to 8 per cent in 1977. By the 1970s, the Afrikaner presence in manufacturing had risen to 15 per cent, and the group's participation in finance and mining accounted for 25 per cent and 30 per cent, respectively (Davies, 2009: 39).

The NP went into the 6 September 1989 election under the leadership of F.W. de Klerk, and its deviation from its traditional, white, Afrikaner-centric policies took its toll on the party, as it won only 93 of the 166 seats in parliament. The election represented the first time that the NP's base was drawn mainly from English speakers (50 per cent) compared to 46 per cent from Afrikaans speakers. The NP was being punished not only by the right wing – within the broader white community, resistance to military conscription was rising, and other voices emerged from within the Afrikaner community. These included the *Vrye Weekblad*, an alternative weekly newspaper, several white Afrikaner musicians who raised their voices against apartheid, as well as a number of students from the Afrikaans-speaking campuses who joined the fight against apartheid.

On 10 February 1990, De Klerk crossed the Rubicon – where Botha had become stuck – on 15 August 1985. By all accounts, this was a pivotal moment for the NP, the Afrikaner nationalist movement and whites generally, as well as the anti-apartheid forces and the broader disenfranchised community. Within the NP, the struggle between De Klerk and more reform-minded leaders, on the one hand, and the right wing, on the other hand, continued unabated. One of the major issues De Klerk did not shift on in his talks with the ANC and other parties was the notion of group rights, which, in the guise of power-sharing, was nothing but a white veto (Van der Westhuizen, 2007). Formal talks in a negotiation process titled the Convention for a Democratic South Africa (Codesa) began in 1991. A declaration of intent, outlining the principles of the proposed new democratic South Africa, was signed, and five working groups were appointed to look into issues such as the principles of a new Constitution, arrangements for an interim government and the future of the homelands. This process culminated in two pivotal moments in South Africa's democratic transition during the early 1990s: the first democratic elections in 1994 and the formal adoption of a new Constitution in 1996 by the Constitutional Assembly. I now explore how the two nationalisms have been affected by these two significant moments in South African history.

CLASH OF NATIONALISMS TODAY

Afrikaner nationalism

The constitutional negotiations resulted in significant compromises being made in terms of cultural, religious and linguistic communities. The outcome was what Alexander termed the 'constitutionalisation of ethnic politics' (Alexander, 2004: 119). The white trade union movement, Solidarity, encapsulated this by invoking populist sentiments that could threaten the broader objective of the citizenship project. According to Jacob Boersema, 'The public campaign about poor whites aims to undercut the ANC's argument that all whites are rich and privileged. It also reinforces fears that without political power and assistance by the state, Afrikaners might again become impoverished and needy' (Boersema, 2012: 414).

In the post-1994 period, there emerged what has been labelled the Third Afrikaans Language Movement, 'which was an organised response by Afrikaners upset by the loss of protection for Afrikaans by the post-apartheid state' (Van der Waal, 2012: 451). According to Van der Waal (2012), it retained elements of ethno-nationalism, expressed in essentialist notions of language and identity. 'The movement attracted extremely conservative Afrikaner voices, such as the author and activist Dan Roodt and his movement PRAAG (Pro-Afrikaanse Aksiegroep, Pro-Afrikaans Action Group)' (Van der Waal, 2012: 451). A further problem with this movement was that 'there was little room left for the code switching between English and Afrikaans, that coloured Afrikaans speakers preferred' (Van der Waal, 2012: 451). Disparagingly referred to as 'Engifrikaans', Van der Waal explains that 'code-switching was ... a standard practice in the Kaapse Afrikaans of the coloured population where it had a function of expressing social belonging, based on membership in both English-speaking and Afrikaans-speaking social orders' (Van der Waal, 2012: 452).

On the other hand, the attempts by the Groep van 63 (Group of 63) to initiate a cross-race, Afrikaans-speaking movement showed promise, especially when the initial discussions were joined by Afrikaans-speaking coloured people such as Jakes Gerwel, who served as the director-general and cabinet secretary in the Nelson Mandela administration, and Hein Willemse, an anti-apartheid activist and Afrikaans literature academic. According to Rebecca Davies, what was emerging was a 'movement of the "other or new" Afrikaner; post-nationalist Afrikaners with a strong if largely uncritical and ahistorical sense of community ... the label has hardened ... and there is apparently little space in which a more inclusive refashioning of Afrikanerness can resume' (Davies, 2009: 91).

Writing about the contemporary Afrikaans-speaking intellectuals, Duvenage argued that this generation had to establish a 'moral place to stand' in the new South Africa (2014: 110). In 2006, Solidarity set up AfriForum, which campaigns for the protection and consolidation of civil rights and gives the Afrikaner community a voice in a society where minorities are increasingly being ignored. AfriForum works together with Solidarity's new centre on constitutional rights. Boersema (2012: 415) argued:

> In a constitutional democracy like South Africa, it might not be surprising that the ANC's opposition phrases its arguments in a discourse of rights ... Solidarity's trope of rights functions through a series of three oppositions: the domination of (black) majority rule is posited against (white, Afrikaans) minority rights; the gain of blacks' rights comes at the cost of whites' rights; and racial integration threatens the right to be Afrikaans.

African nationalism

In his speech, when parliament debated the Truth and Reconciliation Report in 1998, Mbeki pointed out that through the period of colonial domination and apartheid, South Africans had been carved into two nations (Mbeki, 1998: 71):

> The one black, the other white ... [the latter] is relatively prosperous and has ready access to a developed ... infrastructure ... The second, and larger, nation of South Africa is black and poor, living under conditions of a grossly underdeveloped infrastructure.

Mbeki further argued: 'Neither are we becoming one nation ... we have not made the extra effort to generate the material resources we have to invest to change the condition of the black poor' (Mbeki, 1998: 72). These fault lines of South African society continue to shape discourse today, especially under the question of social cohesion. Part of this discourse has been the relationship between Africans and other formerly oppressed people. This reflects the very same dialogues that were occurring within the ANC in the 1950s and led to the PAC breakaway. Wally Serote (1997) argues:

> With Africans being indigenous to South Africa, their being in the majority and most important, their being the most oppressed in the country, dictates to and seeks a special positioning for them within the liberation process and the resolution of the national question.

Yunus Carrim (1997) suggests:

> This approach of investing a greater African and class content to non-racialism must be distinguished from an exclusive Africanism which serves the interests primarily of an upwardly mobile narrow stratum of Africans rather than the mass of poor people.

The views of Serote and Carrim contrasted with those of former ANCYL President Peter Mokaba, whom Mandela appointed to his first cabinet. Writing in *The Star* of 23 July 1997, Mokaba said: 'The Africans ask themselves ... if 60 per cent of the 62 per cent that voted the ANC into power is African, why is it that the percentages of other national groups in the leadership structures is more than their contribution to the democratic vote?' This rhetoric is part of what Ndlovu-Gatsheni (2009) signals as a rise in nativism in South Africa. He cites Mbembe, who saw the task of nativism as that of creating a common language of grievance through repetition of 'the sorry history it pretends to redress' (Mbembe, 2006). Ndovu-Gatsheni traces its roots to Garvey's slogan, 'Africa for Africans', which the PAC had taken up, arguing that 'African nationalism, that initially assumed the character of developmentalism and a civic conception of the nation, is gradually falling into cultural nationalism, Afro-radicalism, and nativism' (Ndlovu-Gatsheni , 2009: 67).

For example, the redrawing of provincial demarcations saw the strengthening and emergence of 'ethnic entrepreneurs', often with violent consequences. The opposition by residents of Bushbuckridge to being incorporated into Limpopo Province is an early example of this, while the more recent example is that of violence around the incorporation of Vuwani into the Malamulele Municipality. At the heart of the Bushbuckridge tension was the resistance to being governed by faraway Polokwane, the capital of Limpopo, while Mbombela, the capital of Mpumalanga, is closer.

There has been much speculation as to what informs these nativist tendencies. Pallo Jordan posits that under apartheid the revival of African ethnicity had little to do with nostalgia for past greatness on the part of Africans. It was even less about the articulation of a psychological urge, as the theorists of ethnicity claim. He argues that it was encouraged by the state to justify its policy of segregation and discrimination (Jordan, 1997: 10). However, Mukoni Ratshitanga (2016) points out that, notwithstanding the fact that Vuwani and Malamulele were kept apart by apartheid design, to date there has been no acrimony between the Venda- and Tsonga-speaking communities. Ratshitanga is among those who lay the blame for today's rise in ethnic consciousness on deliberate mobilisation, reflected, for instance, in the '100% Zulu Boy' campaign, promoted by Jacob Zuma's backers in the lead-up to the ANC conference in Polokwane in 2007. Zuma was elected as head of the ANC at that conference, which resulted in him becoming president of the country after the 2009 elections. Ratshitanga (2016) notes that after the conference, paraphernalia materialised carrying the slogan *Shumela Venda* (Work for Venda), which was the motto of the Venda bantustan.

David Masondo (2015) builds on the preceding point:

> Yearning for ethnic belonging also enables ethnic political entrepreneurs in our ANC-led movement to make demands for representation in public institutions. They start by supporting or joining ethnic based civil society movements ... translate power

> accumulated within their ethnicised civil society environment into a political society and demand ethnic representation in the name of an ethnic balancing act and addressing the 'national question'. Consequently, nation building simply gets reduced to an ethnic numerical equation.

Another example of the nativist tendency can be seen in the complex notions of coloured identity and how it interacts with the Khoisan identity, among others. Henry C. Jatti Bredekamp (2001) points out that before the 1990s, no coloured South African willingly admitted to being Khoisan, Khoekhoe or San. However, the end of apartheid, and South Africans connecting with global First Peoples' networks, 'saw certain Coloured people warming to the idea of reclaiming an identity linked to indigeneity' (Bredekamp, 2001). It should also be noted that the Khoisan felt they were being discriminated against again. They were excluded from the Restitution of Land Rights Act of 1994 because it recognised only those who were dispossessed after 1913 (Klaasen, 2010: 8). The proponents of the demands of the Khoisan were given a major fillip at the 2001 National Khoisan Consultative Conference, where then Deputy President Zuma said in his address (Zuma, 2001):

> The growing sense of pride amongst people of Khoisan descent about their roots in Southern Africa will bring increased benefits. For centuries people referred to as Basters, Coloureds, 'Hotnots', 'Boesmans', Griquas and Koranas have been made to feel ashamed of their identity.

Anthony Phillip Williams, the national coordinator of the Khoisan Liberation and Mass Movement, argues that land is a prerequisite for cultural identity (Secorun, 2018). Contemporary attitudes towards their demand for land are met largely with derision or the occasional platitudes. Andile Mngxitama, leader of Black First, Land First, states that the Khoisan claims undermine the restitution movement by trying to get special treatment. 'The Khoisan are part of us, and we will take them to freedom even if we need to drag them, screaming and kicking' (Secorun, 2018).

SOCIAL COHESION AND NATION FORMATION

This broad sweep of historical debates around the twin propellers of nationalist narratives discussed earlier find contemporary manifestation in the search for social cohesion in a South African society riven by a range of fault lines. And there is no clearer fulcrum around which these debates revolve than that of the land question. This has been at its sharpest around what is referred to as the 'expropriation without compensation' or EWC debate (see Chapter 7 in this volume). At the core of the debate is section 25 of the Constitution, commonly referred to as the property clause, which was hammered out during the constitutional negotiations. It aims to balance the protection of the property rights of landowners while pursuing the interests of society, thus allowing the state to interfere with the very same property rights. It allows for the state to take away property if it is for a public purpose or interest, as long as the owner is suitably compensated.

The ANC's 54th National Conference held in December 2017 decisively shifted the centre of gravity of the debate when it adopted a resolution calling for EWC. Masondo (2018) sums up the ANC's motivation:

> Uncompensated land expropriation is not only a Constitutional imperative for land reform to redress the historical injustice, but also a necessary condition to increase agricultural production, economic growth and development to reduce the unacceptable levels of inequality, unemployment and poverty in South Africa.

Masondo further claims that opponents to EWC have tended to focus on failed examples, such as the Makgoba Tea Estate and the Zebediela Citrus Estate in Limpopo where farming has collapsed, in order to discredit land reform and uncompensated expropriation. These overlook 'relatively successful land transfer projects such as the Nodunga Communal Property Association in KwaZulu-Natal, which struck a deal with the sugar-producing company Tongaat Hulett, and the Mkhuzane community and Mondi, both of which continue to undertake productive farming' (Masondo, 2018).

Arguing against the need for a constitutional amendment, Advocate Thembeka Ngcukaitobi claims that a unanimous judgment of the Constitutional Court had already affirmed that 'it is permissible for legislation, in the broader public interest, to deprive persons of property without payment of compensation' (Ngcukaitobi, 2018). Other arguments made include the lack of progress in the state's implementation of its own land reform programme, as well as the need to find other ways to address the suffering that arose from dispossession. Ngcukaitobi (2018) continues:

> We should interrogate what precisely was lost by conquest. Land is not the only asset that was lost through colonial occupation. African societies were broken up, their cultures ravaged, and their identities erased. The language of restitution or redistribution is too narrow to capture the scope of the project of restoration. A forward-looking project of reparations is urgently needed ... then reparations through land reform might serve not as colonialism in a different guise, but as an antidote to colonialism. Only then will the land truly be ours.

The EWC debate occurs as the third decade of South Africa's democracy has brought to the fore concern about social cohesion, given the worrisome features of ethnic mobilisation, as well as race, class, gender, urban/rural and generational divides. The pervasive violence that characterises domestic relations, protest actions and the settling of political scores, raises questions about the very foundation of South African society. There have been several initiatives to analyse and understand this phenomenon, and ultimately to develop strategies. These include the National Development Plan, unveiled in 2012, which was meant to set out a vision for the South Africa of 2030, and the Declaration and Programme of Action, which emerged from the National Social Cohesion and Nation Building Summit in 2012, a ritual that was re-enacted in 2020. Both saw the 1996 Constitution as 'a national compact that defines South Africa's common values and identifies our rights and responsibilities as people living together' (NPC, 2012: 458).

Neither of these developments have had the effect of advancing social cohesion. A scenarios exercise, anchored in research by the Mapungubwe Institute for Strategic Reflection (MISTRA), found social cohesion to be the issue of greatest concern impacting on South Africa's future (Indlulamithi South Africa Scenarios, 2018). This led to the identification of three key drivers that will shape the country's future: institutional capacity and leadership; social inequality; and the 'triple R' of reconciliation, resistance and resentment.

The land question and the EWC debate express these three key drivers perfectly. Access to land by the majority of South Africans continues to exacerbate the inequalities between the two nations that Mbeki described. The dearth of bureaucratic and societal leadership, as well as institutional capacity to effect needed reforms, stymie the progress that could have been possible since the 1996 Constitution was adopted. Added to this, resistance by the privileged parts of South African society to adopt the compromises needed, continues to threaten the possibility of reconciliation.

CONCLUSION: WILL THE CENTRE HOLD?

Unlike experiences in other parts of the world, there seems to be little prospect for the separate identities, discussed earlier, to be cemented, to the extent that secession could be on the cards. There are many reasons for this unitary state to endure. According to Daryl Glaser (2001: 154–155), these include:

> The urbanization process has *over the long run* done more to dissolve than reinforce sub-African ethnicity ... the rival magnetic pull of the larger ethnicities of African, black and non-racial identities ... ethnically divided but economically viable states, like Canada, Belgium or Britain, are more likely to hold together [original emphasis].

Furthermore, the concessions made in the drafting of the Constitution have helped to reduce irredentist tendencies. These compromises have included the recognition of a constitutional monarchy in KwaZulu-Natal, advisory Houses of Traditional Leaders in six provinces, the establishment of the Council of Traditional Leaders, and chiefs paid from the state coffers. This has also been a source of major concern in so far as they relate to the rights of women, children and labour, and this is dealt with in other chapters of this volume.

In his 2020 State of the Nation Address, President Ramaphosa called for greater social cohesion. He said that the social compact 'is a covenant rooted in the strategic objective of our National Development Plan, which is to eliminate poverty and reduce inequality by 2030' (Ramaphosa, 2020). Admitting that the government cannot solve economic challenges alone, he pointed out that compacting has been taking the form of the 'mini-compacts' approach, which he had articulated on many occasions before. This signalled the placing of the challenge to achieve social cohesion at front and centre.

This chapter has focused on how African and Afrikaner nationalisms impacted national identity, the land question and social cohesion. The unity of all South Africans and the creation of a democratic society dominated African nationalism's approach to the national question. The control of the land by a small minority and the protection of various economic privileges that accrued from dispossession was the DNA of Afrikaner nationalism.

The armies of these two major forces finally met on the battlefield of the constitutional negotiations. In that rare moment, the key protagonists reached deep into their sense of a common South Africanness and produced one of the most enlightened constitutions in the world. Three decades later, the democratic edifice that was built is beginning to show cracks. Debates around the land question, economic strategies, language policies and the position of minorities, all occur within the enduring framework of the Constitution. Under courageous leadership, that is willing to find the compromises necessary for social cohesion to be achieved, South Africa could reimagine itself as a united community and attain its sense of nationhood.

REFERENCES

African National Congress (ANC). 1943. 'African claims in South Africa by Dr Xuma, 1943'. *South African History Online*, https://www.sahistory.org.za/archive/african-claims-south-afica-dr-xuma-anc-conference-1943, accessed 25 August 2020.

African National Congress (ANC). 1955. 'The Freedom Charter, 1955', http://scnc.ukzn.ac.za/doc/HIST/freedomchart/freedomch.html, accessed 25 August 2020.

Alexander, N. 1986. 'Approaches to the national question in South Africa'. *Transformation*, 1 (1), 63–95.

Alexander, N. 2004. 'The politics of language planning in post-apartheid South Africa'. *Language Problems & Language Planning*, 28 (2), 113–130.

Anderson, B. 1983. *Imagined Communities: Reflections on the origin and spread of nationalism*. London: Verso.

Ashforth, A. 1990. *The Politics of Official Discourse in Twentieth-Century South Africa*. New York: Oxford Press.

Boersema, J. R. 2012. 'Between recognition and resentment: An Afrikaner trade union's brand of post-nationalism'. *African Studies*, 71 (3), 408–425.

Bredekamp, H.C.J. 2001. 'Khoisan revivalism and the indigenous people's issue in post-apartheid South Africa: A question of self-identity?'. Paper presented at the Conference on Africa's Indigenous Peoples: 'First Peoples' or 'Marginalised Minorities'?, Centre of African Studies, University of Edinburgh, 24–25 May.

Carrim, Y. 13 July 1997. 'Africanism and non-racialism'. *Natal Witness*.

Chipkin, I. 2007. *Do South Africans Exist? Nationalism, democracy and the identity of 'the people'*. Johannesburg: Wits University Press.

Davies, R. 2009. *Afrikaners in the New South Africa: Identity politics in a globalised economy.* New York: Tauris.

Desai, A. and Vahed, G. 2010. 'Identity and belonging in post-apartheid South Africa: The case of Indian South Africans', in Uys, T. and Patel, S. (eds.) *Exclusion, Social Capital and Citizenship: Contested transitions in South Africa and India*. New Delhi: Orient Black Swan, 488–508.

Duvenage, P. 2014. 'Afrikaner intellectual history: An interpretation', in Vale, P., Hamilton, L. and Prinsloo, E.H. (eds.) *Intellectual Traditions in South Africa: Ideas, individuals and institutions.* Pietermaritzburg: University of KwaZulu-Natal Press, 73–94.

Everatt, D. 2009. *The Origins of Non-racialism: White opposition to apartheid in the 1950s*. Johannesburg: Wits University Press.

Fanon, F. 1986. *Black Skin, White Masks* (translated from French by Markmann, C.L. 1967) London: Pluto Press.

Gabie, S. 2014. 'Khoisan ancestry and coloured identity: A study of the Korana Royal House under Chief Josiah Kats'. Master's thesis,

University of the Witwatersrand, http://wiredspace.wits.ac.za/bitstream/handle/10539/13968/Combined%20Sub.pdf?sequence=2, accessed 14 August 2020.

Giliomee, H. 1989. 'The communal nature of the South African conflict', in Giliomee, H. and Schlemmer, L. (eds.) *Negotiating South Africa's Future*. Johannesburg: Southern Book Publishers, 114–129.

Glaser, D. 2001. *Politics and Society in South Africa*. London: SAGE Publications.

Halisi, G.R.D. 1988. 'Dividing lines: Black political thought and the politics of liberation in South Africa'. PhD dissertation, University of California.

Indlulamithi South Africa Scenarios. 2018. 'Scenarios 2030', https://sascenarios2030.co.za/.

Jordan, P. 1997. 'The national question in post-1994 South Africa', http://www.anc.org/anc_docs, accessed 1 June 2020.

Klaasen, J. 2018. 'Khoisan identity: A contribution towards reconciliation in post-apartheid South Africa'. *Studia Historiae Ecclesiasticae*, 44 (2), 1–14.

Kriel, M. 2010. 'Culture and power: The rise of Afrikaner nationalism revisited'. *Nations and Nationalism*, 16 (3), 402–422.

Lembede, A. 11 August 1945. 'The fallacy of the Non-European Movement'. *Bantu World*.

Lemelle, S. 1992. *Pan-Africanism for Beginners*. New York: Writers and Readers Publishing.

Masondo, D. 25 March 2015. 'Tribalism, language and the national question in post-apartheid SA'. *Politicsweb*, https://www.politicsweb.co.za/documents/tribalism-language-and-the-national-question-in-po, accessed 1 June 2020.

Masondo, D. 2018. 'Land expropriation as a means to boost agriculture and food security'. *Umrabulo*, https://anc1912.org.za/sites/default/files/umrabulo_43_2018_ebook.pdf, accessed 1 June 2020.

Mbeki, T. 1998. *Africa: The time has come*. Cape Town: Tafelberg.

Mbembe, A. 14 June 2006. 'South Africa's second coming: The Nongqawuse syndrome'. *Open Democracy*, www.opendemocracy.net/en/southafrica_succession_3649jsp/, accessed 17 August 2020.

National Planning Commission (NPC). 2012. 'National Development Plan: Vision 2030', https://www.nationalplanningcommission.org.za/National_Development_Plan, accessed 1 June 2020.

Ndletyana, M., Tchereni, B., Maimela, D. and Lerakong, S. 2014. 'Voting trends twenty years after democracy: Analysis of South Africa's national and provincial elections' (edited by Netshitenzhe, J.). Research Report, http://www.mistra.org.za/Library/Reports/Documents/MISTRA%20ELECTION%20REPORT%202014.pdf, accessed 1 June 2020.

Ndlovu-Gatsheni, S.J. 2006. 'The nativist revolution and the development conundrums in Zimbabwe'. ACCORD, https://www.accord.org.za/

publication/nativist-revolution-development-conundrums-zimbabwe/, accessed 1 June 2020.

Ndlovu-Gatsheni, S. J. 2009. 'Africa for Africans or Africa for "Natives" only? "New nationalism" and nativism in Zimbabwe and South Africa'. *Africa Spectrum*, 44 (1), 61–78.

Netshitenzhe, J. 2012. 'A continuing search for identity: Carrying the burden of history', in Lissoni, A., Soske, J., Erlank, N., Nieftagodien, N. and Badsha, O. (eds.) *One Hundred Years of the ANC: Debating liberation histories today*. Johannesburg: Wits University Press, 13–27, citing Chief Albert Luthuli, ANC President, 1952–1967, in Luthuli, A. 1962. *Let My People Go*. London: Collins, 231.

Netshitenzhe, J. 2013. 'The vision of Seme 107 years on: Is civilization still a dream and is the regeneration of Africa possible?' *Institute of African Studies*, https://www.ias.columbia.edu/blog/vision-seme-107-years-civilization-still-dream-and-regeneration-africa-possible, accessed 20 August 2020.

Ngcukaitobi, T. 2018. 30 August 2018. 'Focus on need-based land redistribution system'. *News24*, https://www.news24.com/news24/columnists/guestcolumn/focus-on-need-based-land-redistribution-system-20180830, accessed 4 August 2020.

Odendaal, A. 2012. *The Founders: The origins of the ANC and the struggle for democracy in South Africa*. Johannesburg: Jacana Media.

O'Meara, D. 1996. *Forty Lost Years: The apartheid state and the politics of the National Party, 1948–1994*. Johannesburg: Ravan Press.

Ramaphosa, C. 2018. 'SA: Cyril Ramaphosa: Address by South Africa's president, during the land ANC workshop, Birchwood Hotel, Ekurhuleni (19/05/2018)'. *Polity*, https://www.polity.org.za/article/sa-cyril-ramaphosa-address-by-south-africas-president-during-the-land-anc-workshop-birchwood-hotel-ekurhuleni-19052018-2018-05-21, accessed 14 August 2020.

Ramaphosa, C. 2020. 'State of the Nation Address', https://www.gov.za/speeches/president-cyril-ramaphosa-2020-state-nation-address-13-feb-2020-0000, accessed 14 August 2020.

Ratshitanga, M. 22 May 2016. 'Vuwani, Malamulele breathe life into Verwoerd's ghost', *Sunday Times*.

Reddy, T. 1995. 'Hegemony and resistance: The construction of subaltern subjects as other in South Africa'. PhD dissertation, University of Washington.

Secorun, L. 19 October 2018. 'South Africa's first nations have been forgotten'. *Foreign Policy*, https://foreignpolicy.com/2018/10/19/south-africas-first-nations-have-been-forgotten-apartheid-khoisan-indigenous-rights-land-reform/, accessed 14 August 2020.

Seme, P. 5 April 1906. 'The regeneration of Africa'. *South African History Online*, https://www.sahistory.org.za/sites/default/files/regeneration_of_

africa_by_Pixley_Seme.pdf, accessed 25 August 2020.
Serote, M.W. 1997. *Freedom Lament and Song*. Cape Town: Mayibuye Books.
Slovo, J. 1989. 'The South African working class and the national democratic revolution'. *Umsebenzi* Discussion Pamphlet, South African Communist Party.
Smith, A.D. 1999. *Myths and Memories of the Nation*. Oxford: Oxford University Press.
Soske, J. 2012. 'Unravelling the 1947 "Doctors' Pact": Race, metonymy and the evasions of nationalist history', in Lissoni, A., Soske, J., Erland, N., Nieftagodien, N. and Badsha, O. (eds.) *One Hundred Years of the ANC: Debating liberation histories today*. Johannesburg: Wits University Press, 163–190.
South African Native Affairs Commission. 1905. *Report of the South African Native Affairs Commission 1903–1905: Report with annexures nos. 1 to 9*. Cape Town: Cape Times Limited.
South African Native Economic Commission. 1932. *Report of the National Economic Commission 1930–1932*. Pretoria: Government Printer.
Tambo, A. 1987. *Preparing for Power: Oliver Tambo speaks*. London: Heinemann.
Tiro, O.A. 1972. 'Turfloop testimony'. *South African History Online*, https://www.sahistory.org.za/people/abram-ramothibi-onkgopotse-tiro, accessed 14 August 2020.
Van der Waal, C. S. 2012. 'Creolisation and purity: Afrikaans language politics in post-apartheid times'. *African Studies*, 71 (3), 446–463.
Van der Westhuizen, C. 2007. *White Power and the Rise and Fall of the National Party*. Cape Town: Zebra Press.
Vorster, N. 2019, 'Land and identity in South Africa: An immanent moral critique of dominant discourses in the debate on expropriation without compensation'. *HTS Theological Studies,* 75 (4), a5290, https://doi.org/10.4102/hts.v75i4.5290.
Williams, G. 1988. 'Celebrating the Freedom Charter'. *Transformation*, 6, 73–86.
Zuma, J. 29 March 2001. 'Opening address at the National Khoisan Consultative Council'. http://www.info.gov.za/speeches/2001/010330145p1006.htm

Legislation

Native Affairs Act (No. 23 of 1920).
Natives Land Act (No. 27 of 1913).
Native Trust and Land Act (No. 18 of 1936).
Promotion of Bantu Self-Government Act (No. 46 of 1959).
Restitution of Land Rights Act (No. 22 of 1994).
Separate Representation of Voters Act (no 46 of 1951).
South African Act of 1909.
South African Act Amendment Act (No. 9 of 1956).

TWO

Decolonising Laws and Policies to Represent the People

BULELWA MABASA

INTRODUCTION

Since its adoption, the South African Constitution has been internationally hailed for its progressive and pragmatic nature. However, 27 years after its promulgation, relentless unemployment, pervasive poverty, widening inequality, and racially skewed, unequal land access and ownership patterns persist. Although there has been a rise in the black middle and upper strata accessing and owning land and property through the market in the constitutional era, and despite efforts at restitution and redistribution, a significant number of the black majority remains largely landless, without legally recognisable rights or secure tenure. According to the 'Land Audit Report' by the Department of Rural Development and Land Reform (2017), 72 per cent of individually owned farms and agricultural holdings are owned by whites, with only 4 per cent owned by black Africans. It states that 49 per cent of individually owned erven are owned by whites and 30 per cent by black Africans. While the accuracy of the 'Land Audit Report' has been questioned, it nevertheless makes it plain that black Africans exist on the periphery of South Africa's property ownership and formal legal system.

This chapter first traces the foundations of South African property law and assesses to what extent these principles continue to be at the centre of the reality of the South African condition, having survived beyond the new constitutional era. As is well documented, South African property law is a product of its Roman-Dutch and English common law heritage (Kleyn and Boraine, 1992: 8). The principle that forms part of this system holds that the highest form of landholding is through a real right held by an individual in respect of an object (Scott, 2011: 23–24). This does not mean that other forms of landholding, other than individual tenure, are not recognised in Roman-Dutch law.

In accordance with the Deeds Registry Act No. 47 of 1937, real rights are protected by way of registration in the Deeds Registry and afford owners formal legal remedies with which they can resist interference in their property. Although this system has been hailed as reliable and among the best in the world, it caters only to a minority of South Africans, leaving the black majority to dwell in the informal sector. I will briefly demonstrate the dominance of Western notions of property law with reference to current legislation that has survived beyond the promulgation of the Constitution. This leads to a closer and deeper review of current property laws that serve to defer the realisation of the goal of attaining access to land and equitable redress.

The manner in which the majority of black South Africans hold and occupy land, with a particular focus on customary property relations, differs vastly from common law in its conception of property and the rights individuals have in relation to real estate. I provide some examples of how notions of landholding vary from the manner in which property is regulated and protected. I describe these nuances with particular reference to traditional notions of rights, traditional leadership, customary expropriation, the status of individual rights in customary law and whether rights are transferrable. To this end, I offer processes and principles to guide future policy-making in relation to customary tenure, which will serve to close the legislative gap between individual tenure, on the one hand, and customary law tenure, on the other hand.

I then turn to the manner in which property and land reform objectives ought to be implemented. The focus on section 25 of the

Constitution is not based on whether the wording is adequate to bring about mass equity in land and property holding. Rather, it focuses on the concepts of the meaning and import of 'property' juxtaposed against 'land reform'. Embedded in the notion of protecting existing property owners against arbitrary deprivation by the state are pre-existing notions of markets, the economy and rights, which on their own exclude the majority of South Africans from the formal property sector. I argue that the continued reluctance, or complicity, of the state to intervene meaningfully to ensure and promote mass participation by the black majority in all levels in the formal property sector, perpetuates exclusion and keeps elusive the goal of nation formation and social cohesion. I engage with relevant policy and legislative proposals to merge land reform objectives within the formal property sector, with particular focus on the role of the state.

Finally, I will demonstrate how policy-makers and various authors have treated land reform and property as dichotomous, and that the latter enjoys elevated legal protection from the former. Property protection dwells in the world of the formal economy, while land reform also exists in the world of informality, with peripheral relevance to the formal economy. Government has also unwittingly perpetuated legislating for the advancement of the black, rural, poor population, while largely ignoring the dispossessed black, urban, poor population. In this regard, I address land reform failures that have resulted from their treatment as a rural, farming and agricultural issue, rather than linked intrinsically with urbanisation, markets and access to housing. The failure to appreciate the linkages between rural and urban realities has culminated in continued inequity and inequality. If there is no focus on transforming markets and access to property for the majority, and if land reform and property continue to be seen as dichotomous concepts, then the reform of South African land patterns will continue to evade us.

The heritage, dignity and identity of the majority of South Africans ought to shape and mirror how we regulate, legislate, protect and enforce our laws. There remains scope to do this in a meaningful way through legislation, policy-making and transforming land markets. Continuing to interpret property and land reform oppositionally, perpetuates the exclusion of the majority. There is a need to explore how the foundations of law, which inform South Africa's current property regime, have embedded a system that perpetuates the widespread landlessness of the majority of South Africans. They remain on the periphery of legal recognition, economic activity and notions of belonging.

This chapter suggests a proactive strategy by government aimed at ensuring that South African identity and heritage, and their interaction with land and resources, begin to shape the manner in which land and property are regulated, governed and enforced. The lived experiences of the majority of South Africans and their relationship with land, property and belonging, must inform our laws and their application, as opposed to a system of laws and property markets that continue to alienate the majority of citizens and frustrate land reform objectives.

South Africa needs land and property laws in general that are fit for purpose and firmly rooted in a broad set of socio-economic, cultural and political rights (Van der Walt, 1990: 43). This proposition is supported by Ting Xu (2015), who indicates that there is a need to recognise access to, use of and management of land resources by indigenous peoples and to secure the land rights of local communities as property rights. The power balance needs to be corrected so that people and their livelihoods can be protected.

THE FOUNDATIONS OF THE SOUTH AFRICAN COMMON LAW PROPERTY SYSTEM

Ownership in Roman law was known as *dominium* and meant the strongest right that an individual could have over an object, or a *res*. A *res* had a wide definition, and included immovable, movable, corporeal and incorporeal property. Ownership, as the strongest real right, was protected by the *rei vindicatio*, an action exercisable by owners in order to regain control over their property, as well as various other remedies (Van der Walt and Dhliwayo, 2017: 45). Ownership included several sub-rights, such as the right to use, possess, alienate, encumber, vindicate or even destroy the property. Ownership is, therefore, best understood as a bundle of rights in relation to an object, which the owner can enforce 'against the whole world'.

This means that an individual could have a real right in respect of a thing, such as land, which gave that individual the strongest and nearly unassailable right to prevent others from interfering with the property. It must be said, however, that Roman law did not regard ownership as being absolute or totally free from restrictions. The Roman conception of ownership can be explained by the maxim *plena in re potestas*, which means that owners have the right to exercise ownership in whichever manner they please, provided that it is exercised within the limits of the law.

South African property law still rests on the foundations of Roman law, even under the democratic Constitution. English common law has also had a considerable influence through case law and legislation. It is well documented that colonial governments and history considerably altered indigenous land systems, not only in South Africa but also throughout Africa. Edward Said observed: 'The nations of contemporary Asia, Latin America, and Africa are politically independent but in many ways are as dominated and dependent as they were when ruled directly by European powers' (Said, 1993: 20). I agree with this observation in so far as current property laws mirror this assertion.

According to Allison Drew, the 'land wars of 1799, 1811, and 1834 ushered in modus for the dispossession of indigenous South Africans by the British' (Drew, 1997: 238). The expropriation was later followed by a plethora of legislation seeking to legitimise prior and subsequent land dispossessions. These included, but are not limited to, the Glen Grey Act of 1894, the Natives Land Act of 1913 and the Native Land and Trust Act of 1936, all of which were aimed at stripping Africans of independence and a sense of autonomy over land, cattle and possessions. Only recently have there been substantial legal developments that might herald a change, and this includes the calculation of compensation. The Draft Constitution Eighteenth Amendment Bill of 2019, for instance, aims to provide for the amendment of section 25(3) of the Constitution to allow expropriation without compensation for land reform purposes.

The 'Final Report of the Presidential Advisory Panel on Land

Reform and Agriculture' provides a brief but useful overview of what constitutes property in South African law. According to the report, the foundations of our property law system have 'historically enabled mass dispossession and conquest' institutionalised under the system of apartheid (Presidential Advisory Panel on Land Reform and Agriculture, 2019: 69). In other words, the law was used by the apartheid government as a central tool to enforce separate development.

As a result of past oppressive and racially discriminatory legislation, millions of South Africans were deprived of their rights, land and dignity. Although our law has undergone a significant degree of transformation, the Presidential Advisory Panel on Land Reform and Agriculture (2019: 69) finds:

> There has been a trend of retaining our common-law heritage and tweaking it almost superficially in order to suit the majority's lived experience, relationship and conception about what constitutes property, and at worst, it has been the persistence of a dichotomous legal system that excludes the majority from legal recognition and protection.

The report shows that 'more than 31 million South Africans hold "property" outside the formal common-law system' (Presidential Advisory Panel on Land Reform and Agriculture, 2019: 69). Most of these landholders live in communal areas, with others living on farms, in informal settlements or in free, low-cost construction houses[1] in urban areas.

HOW PRECOLONIAL CONCEPTIONS OF PROPERTY CONTINUE TO EXCLUDE THE MAJORITY OF SOUTH AFRICANS

According to section 2(1) of the Alienation of Land Act No. 47 of 1937, no one may alienate land unless the sale is recorded in writing in a deed of sale and signed by the parties. It is also a mandatory requirement

1 These are commonly referred to as Reconstruction and Development (RDP) houses.

that the sale must be registered at the Deeds Registry, according to the Deeds Registry Act No. 47 of 1937. The latter is yet another example of how colonial laws continue to inform current laws in the context of property law. Implicit in this law is the notion that registration is key in the recognition and protection of property, a concept that bears little meaning in the contexts in which the majority of South Africans interact with land and/or property.

Common law remedies such as 'the *rei vindicatio* afford owners of property the right to reclaim lost or stolen property by means of a court order, or to interdict others from interfering with their ownership' (Van der Walt and Dhliwayo, 2017: 45). However, these rights are not available to those who hold no formal rights within the formal property system. Registration in the Deeds Office is a mechanism to protect the owners in whose names the rights are registered. Registration constitutes conclusive proof of an individual's real right of ownership in respect of property (*Frye's (Pty) Ltd v Ries*). Only real rights, such as ownership, usufruct rights, mortgages or servitudes, are capable of being registered, although 'there is evidence that a real right does not become unenforceable by the mere fact of it being unregistered' (Brits, 2018: 363).

Notwithstanding that South African law embodies the foregoing notions, modes of landholding and occupation by the black majority, such as a right to occupy land, are not registerable in law. Because millions of South Africans either do not own land, or their holding of land is determined according to customary tenure, they do not meet the requirements of these pieces of legislation and, therefore, are not protected by them. Most 'transactions in the informal or customary sector are not recorded in writing and therefore fall outside the scope of the Alienation of Land Act' (Brits, 2018: 365).

The result is that although the courts have developed constitutional jurisprudence that seeks to promote constitutional imperatives, the property clause fails, on its own, to protect those who hold only informal, unregistered or customary law rights to property, in instances where cases must be brought before the courts to develop the jurisprudence. Kleyn and Boraine (1992: 7) recognise that the task of adapting law to changing economic and social conditions must be shared between the courts and the legislature. In the South African context, the overwhelming majority of South African citizens operate outside of the formal property system. The Presidential Advisory Panel on Land Reform and Agriculture (2019: 87) asserts that 'an estimated 60 per cent of all South Africans hold property outside of the formal property legal system'. The conundrum is as a result of the fact that to date there has not been an intentional and pointed effort to develop and elevate property law beyond its colonial foundations. The objective would be to reflect the values and principles that emanate from indigenous South African systems of tenure in policy and law-making in a deliberate manner. The tendency has been to retain and maintain the property law system with its Western-influenced foundations, without making a meaningful effort to understand the nuances and complexities of the so-called 'customary' laws of tenure in their undiluted forms.

Heinz Klug (2015) indicates that demands for different forms of tenure have become more acute in land debates as opposed to those with colonial and postcolonial biases that still persist.

HOW CUSTOMARY NOTIONS OF LANDHOLDING AND OCCUPATION DIFFER FROM COMMON LAW

It is crucial to preface the discussion on customary tenure with a proper understanding of the way in which indigenous individuals and communities interact with land and other forms of property under customary law. Thomas Bennett states that 'land tenure is perhaps the most problematic topic in customary law' (Bennet, 2015: 374). Concepts such as ownership or trusteeship, as they are commonly understood, are historically and socially defined, and they cannot be transposed to customary tenure. The difficulty in describing customary forms of tenure arises from the tendency to interpret them through a common law lens. Even the concept of ownership is understood in terms of common law.

As stated, the defining aspect of ownership lies in its absoluteness, or in the 'concentration of all entitlements in one person, who is free to use and dispose of the property at will' (Bennett, 2015: 375). It may then be useful to frame a discussion about customary tenure using terms such as 'power', 'right' and 'interest', instead of using terms such as 'ownership' or 'trust' as they are understood in their common law context, viewed through a Western lens.

Viewing customary tenure in this way makes it easier to explain the nature of the rights and obligations vested in landholders and traditional leaders. It is also important to remember that customary law places a higher emphasis on the relationships existing between individuals in respect of objects, rather than the relationships existing between individuals and objects per se. As Bennett (2015: 373) states, rights to property were regarded as 'obligations generated by family relationships', rather than absolute entitlements of owners enforceable by civil remedies, such as the *rei vindicatio*.

Descriptions of tenure during the colonial period fell along one of two misconceptions: the first was that the Western concept of ownership could be applied universally; and the second was that colonised societies were too underdeveloped to apply concepts of ownership to the manner in which they interacted with land. This second concept would allow colonisers to deprive African societies of their land because it was, in effect, an unowned *res nullius*. However, Bennett argues that in their desire to avoid the above two extremes, colonial writers developed 'a misleading, but extraordinarily tenacious idea that customary tenure was "communal"' (Bennett, 2015: 377). This term is correct if it implies that the communities equally share claims to land and that rights to land are based on membership of certain political communities, or that individuals are not at liberty to dispose of property in the same way that a common-law owner is.

Mahmood Mamdani (1996) also asserts that the aim of colonial rule was to distort pre-colonial legal systems, and ensure that new colonial legal frameworks became central to the application of customary law in native courts. It is therefore argued that the description of customary land tenure as 'communal' is misleading in that it suggests that in African societies both labour, such as farming, and the produce is shared in a communal way (see Chapter 3 in this volume). Furthermore, when understood in a legal sense, communality may be understood to mean that a group of people hold a single title in respect of the property, or that each individual in a group has a separate entitlement to the property. Customary tenure is also sometimes likened to the concept of a trust, where a traditional leader (chief) acts as trustee and the members of a tribe enjoy only usufructuary rights. However, this also does not adequately encompass the true nature of customary tenure, partly because landholders would not have the same redress as trust beneficiaries in a situation where the chief abuses his or her powers.

On the other hand, the Presidential Advisory Panel on Land Reform and Agriculture report recognises that as complex as customary tenure is, it is crucial to resist the temptation to assimilate and/or to mould customary tenure into the Roman-Dutch principles that largely favour 'titling' as a solution, without ensuring that there is adequate access to finance, infrastructure and a survey of the land.

Beinart et al. (2017) argue that titling provides the most effective way of securing tenure, and that customary rights that are not legally recognised should be brought progressively within the titling framework. In effect, these researchers argue that the idea of private ownership of land by Africans would eventually have been the general status quo had it not been for the promulgation of apartheid legislation, which effectively disturbed the progression of African land possession and land-use patterns.

To be understood in its complexity and true form, one has to appreciate that in customary law, tenure is different and may be held by multiple persons simultaneously in respect of the same piece of land. For example, although traditional leaders have the power to control how land is allocated to beneficiaries and how it may be used, individuals within those communities have the right to benefit from land that they hold and which was allocated to them. Viewed in this way, customary tenure 'appears as a system of complementary interests held simultaneously' (Bennett, 2015: 381).

Bennett (2015) argues that terminology such as 'right', 'power' and 'interest' is useful in the context of customary tenure as it does not espouse the same connotation and pretext of ownership. Bennett employs an analytical scheme proposed by Antony Allott, which poses three questions. The first concerns the identity of the interest holder, such as a traditional leader or an individual, in their capacity as a member of a ward. The second question concerns the nature and content of the interest, which can be divided into the terms 'benefit' and 'control', where a benefit means a right to use and enjoy land, while control means a power to determine the beneficiaries of a particular piece of land and the time and manner in which that benefit may be exercised. The third question concerns the purpose or use of a particular piece of land, for instance, agricultural or residential. The rights, powers and interests of individuals often have a direct connection to the purpose of the land. This view enables an understanding of customary tenure without reference to the paradigm of either absolutely individual or absolutely communal ownership (Bennett, 2015: 378–381).

To introduce a meaningful shift and to learn lessons from customary notions of property and landholding, the legislature is cautioned to heed the role of family relationships, multiple ownership instruments and a focus on relationships between individuals over objects, as opposed to the object itself.

Expropriation in the context of traditional leadership

Although this section seeks to outline inherent conceptual differences and dichotomies in the manner in which expropriation is understood and carried out in common law and in the context of traditional leadership, it is not intended to assess the merits and/or demerits of the value and status of traditional leadership in South Africa. Rather, it attempts to demonstrate that prevailing laws are yet to encompass the concepts and traditional notions held and deployed by the majority.

It is generally accepted that traditional leaders have the power to allot, regulate, confiscate and expropriate land and common resources. Bennett argues that 'traditional rulers no longer exercise such power to allocate land on a daily basis because most land has already been allotted for decades and chiefdoms are settled' (Bennett, 2015: 383). In reality, contemporary traditional rulers most often simply approve a transfer of land between existing landholders. The decision to allot land, or to approve a transfer of land, happens subject to consultation with elders and the community. Formal registers of allotment are not always kept, but usually a landowner may prove their right over the land by proving effective ownership over a period of time. Rulers also have the power to impose restrictions on the use of common resources, particularly in times of scarcity. This power is exercised as a balance between the needs of society and the protection of the environment.

Rulers have the power to expropriate and/or confiscate land. Where land is expropriated for a public purpose, the landholder will receive redress in the form of another piece of land. However, land may also be expropriated as a penalty for committing a crime, in which case no compensation will be paid. Land may be expropriated where a landholder has more land than necessary for his or her own needs or is not using the land productively. In this way, rulers may encourage their subjects to farm their land productively and then equitably redistribute land among the society. However, the power of expropriation may also be used to remove political dissidents and may be abused by corrupt rulers, particularly because the landholder is not always afforded a right to make representations comparable to the common-law rule of *audi alteram partem* (Bennett, 2015: 386–390). This may also be applied in circumstances where mineral endowments have been identified for extraction.

It is, therefore, clear that in reforming land laws and, in particular, expropriation, lessons may be drawn from customary forms of expropriation, where, for instance, expropriation includes a consultative process involving the community and community needs, and where sometimes expropriation becomes necessitated by scarcity, without compensation. In respect of the current debates on expropriation without compensation and the impending proposed amendment of section 25 of the Constitution, customary law offers lessons on the need to consider balancing community needs over individual interests, for the benefit of the greater community.

The status and rights of individuals under customary law

It is a misnomer that individuals inherently have little to no say or agency in the context of customary law tenure. To the contrary, individuals have the right to request plots of land for residential and pastoral purposes, as well as to graze their stock on communal pastures. This right only vests in those who are associated with a ward head by way of affinity of consanguinity.

The growing scarcity of land means that it is highly unlikely for an outsider to be accepted by a ward head without a pre-existing relation to a ward member. When an applicant requests a plot of land, they will usually be given a residential plot as well as a plot to be used for farming. Landholders exercise exclusive rights over their plots, which can be enforced by traditional authorities. The right to request land, however, does not entitle an individual to accumulate large tracts of land to become a commercial farmer.

In fact, according to Bennett, 'commercial farming tends to be discouraged by a prohibition on accumulation of land' (Bennett, 2015: 393). This right therefore entitles an individual and their family to access sufficient land to meet their subsistence needs. Boundaries may be drawn to prevent others from encroaching on the landowner's plot. The right is vested only in the head of a family, and dependants do not have a direct claim against the traditional authority. However, the head of the family has a duty to provide the dependants, including spouses, divorcees and unmarried daughters, with land for farming and dwelling.

Under common law, all immovable property forms part of the land that it is built on. However, it is not clear how the rights to improvements on land are governed under customary law, as there is no principle comparable to accession as an original mode of the acquisition of ownership[2] under the common law. The courts have also not made a decisive ruling in this regard and prefer to apply regular common law principles in disputes.

In general, the evidence suggests that landowners have the right to harvest the crops they themselves have planted on their plots. However, it does not seem that temporary structures are regarded as acceding to the land on which they are built, which means that there is no change in the ownership or right of control over them. Landholders would, therefore, have the right to remove these structures if the land is expropriated. Considerations of equity may dictate that where permanent structures have been erected on land and resources

2 This describes ownership change that does need consent from previous owners.

have been expended on their construction, there must be clear rules regarding the ownership or right of control over them.

Apart from the right to land to grow crops, common pastures may be used by all individuals to graze their livestock. These areas are accessible to everyone who has membership of a particular ward and may not be used exclusively by one person. Traditional rulers exercise a right of control over common pastures and may restrict access to these during droughts or other scarcities. Other common resources, such as wood, clay, edible plants, wild game and water are freely available to all members of a ward.

The preceding paragraphs must not be construed to mean that the author is not cognisant of existing challenges within the concept of traditional leadership, which have been dealt extensively in a wide range of literature. Delius (2018) observes that colonialists exaggerated the rights of chiefs and understated the rights of their subjects. He argues that in reality, chiefs understood that their power and control were subject to the will of the people.

It is also recognised that while traditional leadership is not inherently unbalanced, unequal power and gender relations are persistent issues that problematise the institution in practice, as detailed in the Presidential Advisory Panel on Land Reform and Agriculture report. Dineo Skosana (2018) also notes that traditional leadership today enjoys a symbiotic relationship with the ruling party, which inclines the ruling party to reinforce and support its powers. The lessons for policy-making in respect of customary law are to take a closer look at the importance of the role of individuals within traditional leadership and to resist the temptation to attribute communal tenure to notions of blanket communalism.

How are rights lost or transferred in customary law?

Where a landholder abandons a plot of land for an unreasonably long period of time, the rights in the plot are lost, and it becomes available to be distributed to a new applicant. Community standards determine what would constitute an unreasonable length of time. Because of land shortages, traditional rulers may have come under increasing pressure to redistribute land that is not being used productively. 'Studies from

Botswana and Lesotho show that land may be deemed abandoned after only two or three years' (Bennett, 2015: 400).

According to the Sesotho proverb *ts'imo hase lefa*, land is not generally regarded as part of an inheritance. Where land does not form part of a deceased estate, customary law dictates that the deceased holder's rights to the land cease to exist upon death. However, in reality, dependants of a deceased often refuse to vacate land and remain in occupation, with the rights de facto passing to the surviving spouse or children.

Pre-colonial customary law dictated that land was inalienable and could neither be bought nor sold, nor could it be exclusively owned by one person. Instead, as explained earlier, a traditional authority exercised the power of control over land and distributed a right to individuals to occupy and use the land. Although this traditional idea is deeply rooted, the scarcity of land and the emergence of a real estate market have led to the erosion of this system. Similar to the developments in the customary law of succession, it has become more common for individuals to assert exclusive rights over land. Where land is transferred between individuals, it would be custom not to demand payment for the land, but contemporary practice is that some form of compensation is paid. In practice, the true nature of such transactions is often deliberately obscured.

There is academic debate about whether the prohibition on the alienation of land is inherent to customary tenure. In *Kweneng Land Board v Matlho & Mothlabane*, the Appeal Court of Botswana held that customary law had developed to a point where interests in land should be regarded as equivalent to common law ownership. However, a dissenting judgment raised the point that because the members of a household exercise the right of benefit in the land jointly, it would be arbitrary to confer a right of ownership to only one of the family members, thereby depriving all others from a legal interest in the land. It is, however, accepted in practice and by courts that traditional rulers' power of control grants them the authority to dispose of land.

In *Rathibe v Reid*, the then appellate division court accepted that traditional rulers could dispose of land but emphasised the importance of a fair and reasonable procedure. However, the traditional rulers' power to do so is not limited, but is subject to consent of the majority of the landholders or a representative portion of the relevant nation. In light of the above, it is incumbent on the legislature to interact meaningfully and intentionally with the complexities and realities of how customary tenure systems work in practice and to resist the temptation to seek to legislate through the lens of Western modes of understanding property.

Given that millions of South Africans' interactions with property are based on customary law models, which are to a large extent not regulated or protected by the Deeds Registries Act, in order for the property clause to conform to the spirit, purport and objects of the Bill of Rights, an alternative solution must be proposed by the legislature.

Legislating for customary tenure

The legislature has been complicit in perpetuating the imposition of common law principles that have little to no value in customary law and, indeed, the lived realities and experiences of the majority of South Africans. The Upgrading of Land Tenure Rights Act No. 112 of 1991 (ULTRA) enables traditional authorities to acquire ownership over land with the consent of a minister and subsequent registration. The traditional authorities acquired the power to alienation of the land, but this power was subject to a 10-year moratorium on alienation to third parties without an authorising court order.

This legislation is premised on a misconception that traditional leaders have underlying powers to acquire land, as opposed to the role of custodianship that they should play. An added impediment is that the former so-called 'independent homelands', namely Transkei, Bophuthatswana, Venda and Ciskei (TBVC) to which ULTRA applies, are typically not surveyed, making it even more difficult to 'upgrade' land to freehold. In other words, ULTRA attributes excessive powers to traditional leaders to acquire land, whereas individuals and families should possess such rights. The colonial conflation of traditional leadership with land title has, therefore, crept into the legislation.

The Interim Protection of Informal Land Rights Act No. 31 of 1996 (IPILRA) provided that holders of informal customary law rights may not be deprived of those rights without their consent.

Where applicable, IPILRA made dispositions of land in respect of which individuals held informal rights, such as use or occupancy rights, dependent on the approval of the holders of those rights. In this regard, IPILRA provides that a decision to dispose any informal right may be taken only by a majority of the holders of such rights present at a meeting. The latter demonstrated a conflation and a misconception of the communality principle dealt with earlier.

Are customary rights registrable?

The issue of the registration of traditional rights was considered by the Gauteng Division of the High Court in *Nedbank Limited v Molebaloa.* This case concerned the execution in sale of a family home for the satisfaction of a debt, which was subject to a mortgage bond. The respondent, Mr Molebaloa, had obtained a loan from the applicant, secured by a mortgage bond. However, the respondent's primary residence was not executable for various reasons. The applicant then wished to attach and execute in respect of a secondary property, which was registered in his name in the Deeds Registry. However, it came to light that the secondary property was, in fact, a family home, and not merely a secondary property owned by the respondent. The 'family home' is a widespread form of residential tenure in urban areas and is used by a significant number of South Africans.

Family members of the respondent were in occupation of the family home. The court held that Mr Molebaloa was not an owner of the family home in the usual sense, but rather that he held ownership as the head of the household in terms of customary indigenous law. Jansen AJ stated that family homes, as a form of tenure, are 'largely invisible to the legal system, as the deeds registry system does not properly cater for this form of ownership' (*Nedbank Limited v Molebaloa*). The judge continued, emphasising that the interaction between the owner and the property is interpreted according to the rules of 'individualised and registered common law ownership, and not in the context of indigenous law'. The respondent agreed that according to indigenous law, he was a nominal owner and that a special relationship of trust existed, in which the owner's duty held the property as a custodian for the benefit of the occupiers of the family home, who are the beneficial owners.

This case has been discussed by Reghard Brits, who explains that our current system of property ownership, which is based on individual ownership, excludes the reality of indigenous law systems. *Nedbank Limited v Molebaloa* illustrates the disconnection between private law property rights and the de facto lived reality of a large segment of South African society (Brits, 2018: 348). The occupiers of the family home effectively exercise the rights of co-owners in customary law, but in private law their rights are made dependant on the wishes of the registered owner. If the occupiers had been registered as co-owners in the Deeds Registry, they would have much stronger rights and would be able to effectively defend against attempts to have them removed from the property by relying on formal legal remedies.

Brits goes on to discuss the possibilities of how such customary rights could be recognised as real rights (Brits, 2018: 363). The Deeds Registry does recognise that real rights can still be enforceable even if they are not recorded. Brits states that real rights can be created or acquired by original modes, such as prescription or marriage in community of property (2018: 363–365). However, if unregistered customary law interests were to be included in this list of unwritten exceptions, the result would be extensive uncertainty, particularly because the family home is such a widespread form of tenure in urban centres. If all these interests were to be formally recognised as real rights, the adverse impact on legal certainty may be severe. It would, therefore, be preferable to initiate reform to enable such customary interests to be registered, rather than attempting to enforce them without being recorded on any title deeds.

This was also a recommendation of the court in *Nedbank Limited v Molebaloa*. Such reform may be bolstered by the constitutional entitlement to secure tenure in terms of section 25(6) of the Constitution, as well as the prohibition on arbitrary evictions as provided in section 26(3) of the Constitution. The *Nedbank Limited v Molebaloa* case, therefore, serves as a good illustration of the incongruity between the manner in which millions of South Africans interact with property every day, and how these rights or entitlements are reflected (or not) in the Deeds Registry.

While this chapter has reflected on some lessons that may be drawn from customary tenure, I also argue for an interventionist approach within the formal property sector to bring it into line with policy-making for the wider majority. I caution against understanding land reform as a concept that exists only informally and suggest that for land reform to be sustainable and effective, attempts must be made to bring it within the formal property sector. An integration of common law and customary law notions is necessary and must begin with dissecting true notions of customary tenure away from the Western lens.

CONCLUSION

Section 25 of the Constitution of South Africa deals with the protection of property owners from arbitrary expropriation by the state and the state's obligation to deliver land reform in the form of restitution of land to those who lost land through conquest, appropriation and dispossession after June 1913. In addition, the clause is aimed at the redistribution of land in an equitable manner, and the protection and security of tenure of those historically or currently deprived of secure tenure rights.

Section 25 presents a unique feature in that it specifically elevates land reform as a matter of public national interest. It underpins a systematic, purpose-driven, constructive, interventionist approach by the state aimed at progressively transforming the formal property sector to ensure that land is made available for productive purposes, with value positioned in proximity to economic opportunities. It also asserts that existing land inequality will persist unless substantial effort and resources are directed at spatially transforming the country. In so doing, the formal property sector, including state-owned and privately owned land, is a potential lever to deal with the scarcity of land and to address the majority of South Africans who are effectively excluded from the ownership and productive use of land.

According to Genesis Analytics (2008), the South African property market operates within an institutional framework defined by political, social, economic and legal rules through which society is organised and markets operate. This includes the constitutionally entrenched property rights that exist within legislative parameters, which give effect to policy and institutions (Genesis Analytics, 2008: 43). Having already demonstrated the peripheral and informal context within which the majority of citizens interact with land and property, land reform objectives continue to elude us, considering that neoclassical economics does not take cognisance of the systematic and general exclusion of the black majority from the property sector.

In this regard, the formal property sector consists of four segments: (1) the user segment; (2) the financial segment; (3) the development segment; and (4) the land market segment. These segments have specific players and interests that are connected in a manner that reflects the socio-political framework in which the property sector operates. The availability of property and land in the formal property sector is based on the surveying of specific erven and land. Once land is surveyed, the rights attached thereto are registered in favour of the land. It is, therefore, the Surveyor General who investigates and approves cadastral surveys and constructs plans that demonstrate the relationship between erven. These transactions are made formally and enjoy legal protection and recognition.

Inherent in the formal property market is the role of government and institutions that either promote or frustrate the aim to ensure that land patterns begin to represent all people in an equitable manner, in a spatial sense. The municipalities' mandates are to guarantee ownership, secure tenure, support property taxation, monitor land markets and improve urban planning and infrastructure development. In practice, however, municipalities bear the obligation of acquiring and disposing of land. While municipal land is an important lever for spatial integration, in reality, municipalities tend to dispose of land on the open market, preferring to sell it to the highest bidder. The reason for this lies in the contradictory imperatives between land reform and legislative requirements, demanding of the state to pursue the best value for land. The Government Immovable Asset Management Act No. 19 of 2007 requires that the best value be obtained for public land. The dynamics in the formal property system are such that municipalities tend to sell off municipal land for purposes that perpetuate spatial disparities, that is, selling well-located land for golf estates and shopping malls, opting to build low-cost housing in the peripheral areas that are remotely placed from economic opportunities and places of work.

The complicity of the state in perpetuating spatial injustice arises partly from the fact that, historically, land reform has been treated by policy-makers as a rural and/or former TBVC issue. This bias has little or no connection to the reality that 65 per cent of the population currently reside in urban areas, where the demand for land is the highest. In order to promote and integrate decisions regarding the national spatial framework, section 13 of the Spatial Planning and Land Use Management Act No. 16 of 2003 contemplates the development and publication of a National Spatial Development Framework (NSDF), aimed at taking into account policies and plans of public and private entities that impact spatial planning and land-use management.

On 20 January 2020, the draft NSDF was published for comment, a process that closed on 19 March 2020. The NSDF is intended to be a guiding programme for the achievement of post-apartheid spatial transformation in order to target all infrastructure investment and spending decisions by all sectors, state-owned enterprises and all arms of government. It is also aimed at guiding planning, budgeting and implementation across all sectors. If implemented with a single-minded focus and intent, the NSDF may lead to a more consolidated and spatially just South African society with quality settlements. Reforming property laws to reflect the lived experiences of the majority of people provides a fertile opportunity to utilise such reforms, not only in rural settings, but also in urban centres. This would give dignity and identity to the millions of landless people who reside on the periphery of urban centres. The linkages between the formal and informal sectors can be bridged in some measure, not only by reformed jurisprudence but equally by the policy decisions made by the state in availing land for land reform purposes.

The nation's commitment to reform land and occupation patterns requires a concerted, proactive and courageous undertaking to reform and undo deeply rooted notions, ideas and principles that have perpetuated exclusion of the heritage, identity and sense of dignity of the African majority. This chapter has traced and identified those elements in our law, policy-making and markets that have exclusionary effects and results. The existence of the constitutional property clause has not on its own resulted in any major changes in land ownership and occupation patterns. Implicit in the protection of property rights is a system of property that is in itself exclusionary. Left untransformed, the market will not, on its own, assist in achieving meaningful land reform objectives.

Similarly, existing laws that are promulgated, based on Roman-Dutch principles, continue to mischaracterise the complexity of customary modes of landholding and occupation. A brave undertaking needs to ensure that African values, heritage and lived realities dominate and shape our laws in the recognition and protection of property. The continued focus on legislating for the former TBVC homelands and treating land reform separately from the formal property sector, as well as resisting the need to transform, presents a major challenge and a barrier to nation formation and social cohesion.

REFERENCES

Beinart, W., Delius, P. and Hay, M. 2017. *Rights in Land: A guide to tenure upgrading and restitution in South Africa.* Johannesburg: Jacana Media.

Bennett, T.W. 2015. *Customary Law in South Africa.* Cape Town: Juta.

Brits, R. 2018. 'Executing a judgment debt against immovable property occupied as a family home in customary law: *Nedbank Limited v Molebaloa*'. *SA Mercantile Law Journal*, 30 (2), 348–367.

Delius, P. 2018. 'Mistaking form over substance: Reflections on the key dynamics of precolonial polities and their implication for the role of chiefs in contemporary South Africa', in Buthelezi, M., Skosana, D. and Vale, B. (eds.) *Traditional Leaders in a Democracy: Resources, respect and resistance*. Johannesburg: MISTRA, 30–45.

Department of Rural Development and Land Reform. 2017. 'Land Audit Report', https://www.gov.za/sites/default/files/gcis_document/201802/landauditreport13feb2018.pdf, accessed 19 August 2020.

Drew, A. 1997. *South Africa's Radical Tradition: A documentary history: Volume 2, 1943–1964.* Cape Town: Buchu, Mayibuye and UCT Press.

Genesis Analytics. 2008. 'The dynamics of the formal urban land market in South Africa'. *Urban LandMark*, http://www.urbanlandmark.org.za/downloads/report_formal_land_market_dynamics.pdf, accessed 28 April 2020.

Kleyn, D.G. and Boraine, A. 1992. 'Silberberg and Schoeman's *The Law of Property*', in Kleyn D.G., Boraine A., Du Plessis, W. and Silberberg, H. (eds.) *Silberman and Schoeman's The Law of Property.* Durban:

Butterworths, 7–8.

Klug, H. 2015. 'In the shadow of Zimbabwe', in Hoops, B., Marais, E.J., Mostert, H., Sluysmans, J.A. and Verstappen, L. (eds.) *Rethinking Expropriation Law I: Public interest in expropriation.* The Hague: Eleven International Publishing, 153–183.

Mamdani, M. 1996. *Citizen and Subject: Contemporary Africa and the legacy of late colonialism.* Princeton, NJ: Princeton University Press.

Presidential Advisory Panel on Land Reform and Agriculture. 2019. 'Final Report of the Presidential Advisory Panel on Land Reform and Agriculture', https://www.gov.za/sites/default/files/gcis_document/201907/panelreportlandreform_0.pdf, accessed 19 August 2020.

Said, E. W. 1993. *Culture and Imperialism.* London: Vintage Books.

Scott, H. 2011. 'Absolute ownership and legal pluralism in Roman law: Two arguments'. *Acta Juridica*, 1, 23–34.

Skosana, D. 2018. 'Traditional leadership and the African National Congress in South Africa: Reflections on a symbiotic relationship', in Buthelezi, M., Skosana, D. and Vale, B. (eds.) *Traditional Leaders in a Democracy: Resources, respect and resistance.* Johannesburg: MISTRA, 356–366.

Van der Walt, A. J. 1990. 'Developments that may change the institution of private ownership so as to meet the needs of a non-racial society in South Africa'. *Stellenbosch Law Review,* 1, 26–48.

Van der Walt, A. J. and Dhliwayo, P. 2017. 'The notion of absolute and exclusive ownership: A doctrinal analysis'. *South African Law Journal,* 134 (1), 34–52.

Xu, T. 2015. 'Hidden expropriation in globalisation and soft law protection of communal property rights', in Hoops, B., Marais, E.J., Mostert, H., Slymans J.A. and Verstappen, L. (eds.) *Rethinking Expropriation Law II: Context, criteria, and consequences of expropriation.* The Hague: Eleven International Publishing, 89–109.

Legislation

Alienation of Land Act (No. 47 of 1937).

Constitution of the Republic of South Africa Act (No. 108 of 1996).

Deeds Registry Act (No. 47 of 1937).

Expropriation Act (No. 63 of 1975).

Interim Protection of Informal Land Rights Act (No. 31 of 1996).

Government Immovable Asset Management Act (No. 19 of 2007).

Glen Grey Act of 1894 .

Natives Land Act of 1913.

Native Land and Trust Act (No. 18 of 1936).

Spatial Planning and Land Use Management Act (No. 16 of 2013).

Upgrading of Land Tenure Rights Act (No. 112 of 1991).

Court cases

Frye's (Pty) Ltd v Ries (1957) 3 SA 557 (A).
Kweneng Land Board v Matlho & Motlhabane (1993) 37 JAL 193.
Nedbank Limited v Molebaloa (37780/2015) [2016] ZAGPPHC 863.
Rathibe v Reid (1926) AD 74.

THREE

Securing the Land: From customary land tenure to registered titled land?

PETER DELIUS AND WILLIAM BEINART

INTRODUCTION

Our aim in this chapter is to contribute to debates about land tenure in South Africa. We will focus largely on one central issue: what is the most secure system of land tenure for those who do not have private, titled land? At present, this debate is polarised among different lobbies and interests: those supporting titles registered in the Deeds Office; those advocating for localised customary tenure with or without some form of registration; and those favouring control by traditional authorities. It is difficult to see common ground, and this inhibits the emergence of consensus areas and potential progress. The South African Constitution provides a clear injunction to equalise rights to land. Section 25(6) states: 'A person or community whose form of tenure of land is legally insecure as a result of past racially discriminatory laws or practices is entitled, to the extent provided by an Act of Parliament, either to tenure which is legally secure or to comparable redress' (South African Constitution, 1996).

But the government has not been able to pass constitutionally acceptable legislation that puts this clause into practice. We analyse the current position and suggest policy paths that might draw on the strengths of at least some of the different perspectives. Our primary questions are whether there should be a single, national system of land tenure in South Africa and whether land held in customary tenure should gradually become part of the system of registered, titled land.

We start with a brief discussion of landholding in the country. This is rooted in the history of segregation and apartheid, which we will not examine here. However, we emphasise that there have been many forms of tenure historically, and it would be mistaken to suppose that these operated simply on a racial basis: that whites had private tenure from the start and that African people have always been locked into systems of communal tenure. We also argue that the primary rights in most forms of customary tenure rested in families. They were not in all respects 'communal' and they were not directly controlled by chiefs.

Evidence suggests that landholdings are under threat, especially in places where demand for land has intensified – around mining developments, peri-urban areas or land that becomes valuable because of its location on transport routes. Our approach is to prioritise the cementing of individual and family land rights to residential, garden and arable sites in the customary areas. All South Africans should hold their land in systems that secure ownership. There are currently signs that momentum is building around the issue of tenure. The government released a draft Communal Land Tenure Bill for comment in 2017. The 'Report of the High-Level Panel on the assessment of key legislation and the acceleration of fundamental change' (Parliament of South Africa, 2017) and the Presidential Advisory Panel on Land Reform and Agriculture (2019) made recommendations on tenure. These documents do not advocate all the same policies, nor do we agree with all the proposals. However, there are some concrete measures on the table; we shall refer especially to the Presidential Advisory Panel report as the latest document. The chapter's discussion commences with an overview on different forms of tenure.

VARIETIES OF LAND TENURE IN SOUTH AFRICA

In South Africa, land registered at the Deeds Office represents over 90 per cent of the area of the country. Most of it is owned privately by individuals, families and companies. This includes the farmlands that were reserved largely for white ownership up to 1991 and the great majority of land in the urban areas. State-owned land is also registered at the Deeds Office: including that owned by specific national departments, provincial governments, municipalities and state-owned enterprises. In 2017, 7,309,243 'land parcels' were registered at the Deeds Office with over nine million owners (DRDLR, 2017: 5).

Registered titled land is regulated under the Deeds Registries Act No. 47 of 1937 and its many amendments. The Deeds Offices and the Offices of the Surveyor General provide the administrative underpinning. Every single piece of such land is surveyed. The land is individually registered so that its area, boundaries and ownership is recorded, as well as the date of the last transaction and the purchase price. This system is digitised for current (but not all historical) landholdings and it is possible for any member of the public to get access to this information from the relevant Deeds Office for a small payment. Overall, this system is effectively administered.

Some black people did own titled land in both towns and the countryside in the late 19th and early 20th centuries. But they were prevented from purchasing such land for much of the 20th century, particularly after the 1936 Native Trust and Land Act. Many were deprived of privately owned land during the apartheid era of 1948–1994, although a limited number managed to access land. This exclusion was a fundamental aspect of racial discrimination and enormously short-sighted.

Since the apartheid land laws were abolished in 1991, and a little earlier in specific areas, there has been rapid expansion of black private land ownership. For example, roughly 50 per cent of the formal sites in Soweto became privately owned between 1984 and 1994 (Guduza, 1997). There has been widespread upgrading of landholding in other townships, where it was only possible to lease land in the apartheid era, and substantial purchase in suburbs formerly reserved for whites.

RDP houses, generally estimated at about three million, are also supposed to come with title. In October 2019, South Africa's Department of Human Settlements estimated that the backlog of title deeds for RDP properties given to beneficiaries was 863,222. A sizeable amount of farmland has also been privately purchased by black South Africans, although this has not been adequately quantified. The figures in the 2017 government land audit are confusing. They suggest that African individuals owned 4 per cent of the agricultural land held by private individuals and black South Africans as a whole owned 24 per cent, but this seems to include only about 40 per cent of agricultural land and excludes that held by companies, trusts, community property associations (CPAs) and other collective groups (DRDLR, 2017). This appears, therefore, to be over and above the 10 per cent transferred through government schemes. According to the audit, black South Africans held 44 per cent of erven, or urban land.

The system of private tenure is strongly protected in law and provides security and certainty if landholders follow the rules in transacting sites and transmitting it between generations; they also have to meet the costs that arise. Titles cover many forms of landholding, by individuals, families, co-owners, corporations and other collectivities; sectional title in various forms is another development. Private ownership has come under indirect pressure through informal settlements and in the debates and legislation on expropriation without compensation, which we will not discuss here. Nationalisation of land is also sometimes proposed, although the chairperson of the Presidential Advisory Panel on Land Reform and Agriculture, Vuyokazi Mahlati, noted that it was not envisaged in the Constitution and it was not evaluated in the report. We are assuming that private tenure will remain intact.

This chapter is focused largely on the areas of the country that comprised the former African bantustans, which are occupied by African people and where customary landholding systems survive. Our evidence suggests that these, along with some informal sites largely in urban and peri-urban areas, are the least secure. It is a little misleading to use 'customary' without some qualification because of its timeless and unchanging connotation. Pre-colonial systems were far from static and they were modified over many years by government proclamations and controls. This happened both before and during the apartheid era when the bantustans were formally demarcated. A system of Permission to Occupy (PTO) was gradually introduced in most of the customary tenure areas. This involved a rough measurement of the land allocated (but not a systematic survey) and a written certificate from the magistrate's office with the occupier's name. It generally covered both residential and arable sites when the latter were available.

Since 1994, this old government system has largely broken down, and there is no clarity on the legal status of this tenure. The term 'off-register' land is also used for these landholdings because they are not formally recorded in the Deeds Office. These areas are often said to comprise 13 per cent of the land of the country, but it is probably a little more, because the state bought land rapidly to expand the bantustans in the 1980s and 1990s, and it also began to acquire land adjacent to the bantustans under the Provision of Certain Land for Settlement Act of 1993. If all this land is included, the areas of the former bantustans is probably 14–15 per cent (given as 14 per cent in the Presidential Advisory Panel report). Not all of this is held in forms of customary tenure.

To complicate matters further, some land within the former Transkei and Ciskei bantustans was held under individual or quitrent tenure, mostly in terms of the old Glen Grey Act of 1894. This land is surveyed and registered in the Deeds Offices at King William's Town and Mthatha. Individual tenure did not amount to full ownership in that land could not generally be bought and sold. Under the Upgrading of Land Tenure Rights Act (ULTRA, No. 112 of 1991, amended in 1996 and 1998), it has been legally possible for these landholders to upgrade their land to an unencumbered title, but this has not been done widely. Roughly one-third of the former Ciskei and 20 per cent of the former Transkei came under this system. In the final years of apartheid, some other homeland governments upgraded tenure in urban settlements that fell within their boundaries.

The Presidential Advisory Panel (2019) recorded that about 8 million hectares of land, or 9 per cent of the agricultural land, had been transferred, roughly 4 per cent (3 million hectares) through restitution and 6 per cent (5 million hectares) through redistribution schemes. This land is held through trusts and CPAs – the latter created by legislation in 1996. Both are forms of collective ownership that differ from the systems of customary tenure in that the landholders generally have title to the land, recorded in the Deeds Office. But the CPA retains some similar elements to the customary areas in that individuals and families do not own their holdings. Members of the CPA have a right to land only through the collectivity.

In some cases, CPAs have taken ownership – through restitution awards – of existing, well-capitalised land, such as fruit plantations in Limpopo, wildlife farms like Mala Mala in Mpumalanga, or, in the case of the Wild Coast Sun, a hotel and casino. In many of these contexts, the members of the CPA realise their rights not as occupiers of the land, but as beneficiaries of income that accrues to the CPA through these enterprises, or as workers. Initially the state gave ownership to the beneficiaries of redistribution, but since 2011 it has stopped giving land purchase grants (Presidential Advisory Panel, 2019: 12), and under the Proactive Land Acquisition Strategy, which became the main focus of the redistribution programme, land has been given initially in leasehold.

A fifth important category of land comprises informal settlements, mostly in the urban and peri-urban zones of the country. The number of people in such settlements, sometimes estimated at seven million in 1994, may have declined through massive construction of RDP houses; it has recently been estimated at around three million (Hornby et al., 2017: 8) or perhaps one million structures. These landholders have no formal rights to land, but they are protected by legislation that restricts their removal. Some of these areas fall within the former homelands, and thus they may also overlap with customary systems.

Many of the figures given here are estimates and the categories are not hard and fast; it is difficult to get an overview of the changing position on the ground. The great majority of land by area is registered in around seven million active titles and there may be as many as five to six million landholdings that are off-register. The average size of titled landholding is much larger than that of off-register holdings, which comprise perhaps three to four million residential and garden sites in the customary or communal areas, about one million informal landholdings, largely in the urban areas, and perhaps a similar number of untitled RDP houses. Thus, any attempt to extend titling to all the land in South Africa would be a major and long-term exercise, involving millions of families. In the next sections, we examine customary tenure and how it has been weakened by various land policy stakeholders.

CUSTOMARY TENURE: IS IT SECURE?

At present, there is little certainty respecting who has rights to the land in the customary or communal tenure areas of the former African homelands of South Africa. Are these rights held by family heads, families as a whole, local communities, chiefs and traditional councils or the state? Do they amount to a form of ownership and how do the layers of landholding and authority in these areas interlink? As noted, there is a good deal of evidence suggesting that landholdings are under threat, especially in places where demand for land has intensified.

Land held in customary tenure or in areas under traditional councils has been alienated in a number of places, such as the platinum belt of North West Province, at the Anglo American Mogalakwena platinum mine in Limpopo and at Somkhele coal mine in KwaZulu-Natal (KZN). A community at Xolobeni in the Eastern Cape has been threatened with removal for titanium mining. In all these cases, mining licences have been approved by the state and local chiefs have agreed to transfer land. Mining companies, which must allocate 26 per cent of their shares in new enterprises to black economic empowerment (BEE) beneficiaries, often choose to negotiate with chiefs when the mineral-rich sites fall within the former homelands. In the case of Bafokeng and Bapo, chiefs have benefited directly by controlling enterprises on the land over which they claim authority (Capps and Malindi, 2017). Some chiefs and traditional councils are asserting control over land and development initiatives on behalf of communities, while overriding the interests and consent of landholding families.

More broadly, the Ingonyama Trust Act (No. 3KZ of 1994) effectively grants control over all the customary land in KZN to the Zulu king (see Chapter 4 in this volume). The Trust's Board has been attempting to change some of the customary landholdings into leaseholds, which require payments and imply that the land is owned by the king or Ingonyama Trust. The Traditional and Khoisan Leadership Act (No. 3 of 2019) enables traditional councils to establish partnerships with external agencies for the purposes of development. These require consultation with the affected community and a majority vote, but not consent by the specific landholders who may be affected. An attempt by the Western Mpondo king to enter such a partnership with a Chinese company, including the leasing of an estimated 10,000 hectares of coastal land, has been widely publicised (Bloom, 2019).

These examples suggest that when there is competition for land, the benefits tend to go to a limited elite. Comparative examples in Africa reinforce this view (Peters, 2013). Kojo Amanor (2008) argues that there has been a commoditisation of land in the hands of chiefs in Ghana over the last few decades. Even though chiefs appeal to tradition, there has, in effect, been a process of privatisation from above. Janine Ubink (2008), writing about the peri-urban areas around Kumasi, Ghana's second-largest city, shows that chiefs have redefined customary tenure in a way that enables them to sell peri-urban land at the cost of rural landholders.

The Presidential Advisory Panel (2019: 34) states:

> Traditional communal land administration systems … are under the jurisdiction and control of Amakhosi and their traditional councils … the traditional leaders argue that the current Western-imposed legislative framework fails to appreciate the interplay of individual and group rights; how these live side by side in a mutually beneficial, inclusive and harmonious fashion rather than in a competitive manner.

The panel therefore suggested that land tenure reform should build on African traditional systems. This section of the report is, however, immediately juxtaposed with that on gender, which begins (Presidential Advisory Panel, 2019: 36–37):

> Rights to control and use land are central to the lives of rural

> women, whose lives and livelihoods are derived from the land and its natural resources. The lack of land rights for women and girls threatens their living conditions, their economic empowerment, their physical well-being and their struggle for equality within a patriarchal society ... Rules of access and inheritance in rural societies favour men over women and women with children over those without.

Representations by women to the panel were quite clear in seeing the Amakhosi and 'the oppressive hand of patriarchy' as the main problem. One woman spoke of the 'daily torment of women at the hands of traditional leaders' in a number of spheres, but especially in respect of land rights where women were 'compromised not only legally but through systemic unequal power relations in rural communities' (Presidential Advisory Panel, 2019: 37; see Mnisi Weeks, 2018).

The Presidential Advisory Panel does not resolve this contradictory evidence and we shall try to illustrate that the position presented by the chiefs, glosses over both historical and current realities. As court cases and succession disputes indicate, their role has not always been to create harmony. The Constitution and the 2003 Framework Act do not give authority over land, as suggested here. Although these Acts recognise traditional leaders, the 2003 Act specifies that powers are not carried over from the homeland era; they must be devolved explicitly in legislation. The government passed the Communal Land Rights Act (CLARA, No. 11 of 2004), which may have moved in this direction, but was invalidated by the Constitutional Court in 2010. The Constitutional Court decided that it had not been through an adequate procedure and that it did not guarantee the rights laid down in section 25(6) of the Constitution.

This formulation in the Presidential Advisory Panel report fails to recognise adequately either the history of customary systems or the interests of the most vulnerable rural landholders. Customary land law gave very strong rights to families; their residential and arable land, once granted, could not be removed, except in highly restricted circumstances. In a key legal text on customary immovable property, Alastair Kerr (1953; 1990) argued that in pre-colonial times, land was sometimes associated with a particular chief, who had political authority but that 'the chief is not considered as the owner of the allotted land' (Kerr, 1953: 17). He used the term ownership to describe these African customary rights to homestead sites and arable fields.

This form of tenure was sometimes called communal tenure, but Kerr was clear that, on the basis of legal sources and court judgments, 'arable and residential land is not held in common' (Kerr, 1953: 25). Rights to occupy and use the allotted land were exclusive. Such sites were handed down from generation to generation without interference of the chiefs. This allocated land was heritable within the family, according to the rules for succession. In his reviews of ethnographic studies of southern Africa as a whole, Peter Delius emphasised that 'household rights to arable and residential land were strong in pre-colonial systems of land tenure' (Delius, 2008: 221). In parts of South Africa where there had been no strong chieftaincies, at least in the second half of the 19th century, land allocation and administration was localised (Ntsebeza, 2005; Beinart et al., 2017). We recognise that in parts of the customary tenure areas, where there has been a legacy of more powerful chieftaincy, reinforced during the bantustan era, traditional leaders play a role in allocating and administering land, and may sometimes claim strong authority or even ownership. But even in such areas in the Eastern Cape and KZN, they are sometimes challenged by communities and individuals who assert their rights to their land (Bennett et al., 2013; Yeni, 2019).

Interviews in uMgungundlovu Administrative Area in KZN, and in Bizana (Alfred Nzo District Municipality) in the Eastern Cape Province in 2011–2012 confirmed that landholders, who in these areas did not have PTOs, administered their land at a local level and considered their land grants permanent: 'Mpondo custom is that once granted land, the family have it forever' (Beinart and Wotshela, 2011–2012). Anthropologist Monica Wilson Hunter ([1936] 1964) recorded similar evidence some 90 years ago. Informants said that land was heritable within families, although it could not be bequeathed to individuals. The Constitution provides that where customary law applies, it should be considered by the courts. The Constitutional Court has also allowed for flexibility in interpretation of customary law, accepting 'living customary law' as currently practised (Claassens and Budlender, 2016). Both historical examples and recent expressions of living customary law affirm the rights of landholders in customary systems. To varying degrees, these are respected in practice, but they are not secure in law.

As noted, customary land rights were overlaid in many districts by government proclamations and PTOs. Nicholas Kassier (2019) discusses a judgment in the KZN High Court in 2017 that gave an occupier, whose rights were based on a prior PTO, precedence over another group who claimed the site on the basis of a subsequent Ingonyama Trust lease. He suggests that a PTO 'is still a valid right' (Kassier, 2019). However, this was a complex case, where the PTO was held by a church and not by individual landholders and its broader legal force is uncertain. In an Eastern Cape case, the rights of a descendant of the holder of a PTO was considered by the judge to be protected by the Constitution and the Interim Protection of Informal Land Rights Act (IPILRA, No. 31 of 1996), even though the PTO had not been formally renewed (*Nandipha NO v. Irfani Traders cc*). Thus, some judgments appear to be protecting historical PTOs. But PTOs were not issued in all districts and they have not generally been formally issued since the 1990s, so that many local land grants do not have such certification. The written records, to the extent that they survive, are likely to be very uneven.

Since the invalidation of CLARA, the African National Congress (ANC) government has been unable to legislate on this issue. A new Bill was circulated for comment in 2017 but has not yet been reintroduced to parliament. The land rights of millions of South Africans, who hold their land in the former homelands, remain legally uncertain. In practice, most are probably fairly secure under local customary arrangements; but there are a number of examples where these have not provided adequate protection. These African landholders are located in some of the poorest parts of the country and land is an important asset for such families. Their rights should be secure. We explore several cases in the following sections, amplifying the uncertainty over how to apply customary tenure.

ROUTES TO INCREASING SECURITY: IPILRA AND THE COURTS

In 1996, the ANC government passed three Acts of importance in protecting the land rights of those who did not have formal titles. IPILRA was aimed especially at the former homelands. With respect to labour tenancy, which survived notably in KZN and Mpumalanga, the Extension of Security of Tenure Act (No. 62 of 1997) potentially provided security. The Prevention of Illegal Eviction Act (No. 19 of 1998) was designed to ensure that those who occupied land informally in urban areas had some protection from removal. IPILRA is valuable and has acted as a disincentive to undermining informal land rights. But it has rarely been enforced, or tested in the courts, and is seldom backed up by administrative support. It also reflects communalist approaches adopted in the 1990s. Under the Act, communities have the right to deprive families of their holdings by a majority vote 'in accordance with the custom and usage of that community' with only limited rights to compensation. In cases about mining at Mogalakwena (*Machoga v. Potgietersrus Platinum*) and Somkhele (*Global Environmental Trust and Others v. Tendele Coal Mining*), judges ruled in favour of larger traditional communities, led by the local chiefs, who supported mining, and bypassed the claims of the smaller groups of landholders who actually lost their land. This is a potential weakness of IPILRA and points to confusion over the meaning of community – a term that is used in IPILRA (Beinart et al., 2017: 100–102).

Two landmark judgments in 2018, *Maledu and Others v. Itereleng Bakgatla Mineral Resources (Pty) Limited and Another* and *Baleni, D and 128 Others v. Minister of Mineral Resources and Others*, potentially strengthened IPILRA, at least in respect of landholders being able to defend themselves from removal for the purposes of mining. In the Maledu case in the North West Province, the descendants of a group of African land purchasers, who had been required in 1919 to register their farm in the name of the Minister of Native Affairs, were defending their right to stop mining operations on this land without their consent. This Lesetlheng community claimed that they were the owners, and that the land had not been subsumed under the Bakgatla ba Kgafela

Tribal Authority, whose successor had consented to mining. They also had to show that a licence held under the Mineral and Petroleum Resources Development Act (MPRDA, No. 28 of 2002) did not override their rights as land occupiers. The High Court found against them and ordered their eviction. In respect of IPILRA, specifically section 2 (*Maledu and Others v. Itereleng Bakgatla Mineral Resources (Pty) Limited and Another*):

> The High Court found that this provision does not contemplate that each person who is a holder of informal rights to land should be consulted. It found that section 2(4) makes plain that when land is held on a communal basis [as the Court accepted in relation to this land] it suffices that a decision was taken by a majority of the affected persons.

This court judged the affected persons to be a 'community' comprising the whole of the area claimed by the Bakgatla ba Kgafela, which agreed to the mining lease in 2008. During the appeal, the Constitutional Court decided that it did not have to rule on the ownership of the farm, for which the descendants had applied, but that it had to take into account that they were occupiers and may be confirmed as owners. They found that the MPRDA had to be read in conjunction with the IPILRA and its 'underlying purpose ... to provide security of tenure for the historically disadvantaged and vulnerable' (*Maledu and Others v. Itereleng Bakgatla Mineral Resources (Pty) Limited and Another*). This, in turn, connected with the constitutional provision to strengthen tenure for those who had been disadvantaged by past racially discriminatory laws and practices. The procedures under the MPRDA to consult the landholders had not been exhausted. The appeal was upheld and the rights of the affected landholders recognised.

Xolobeni is a coastal customary tenure area in the former Transkei. A mining company with a licence under the MPRDA planned to extract titanium; they were supported by the Department of Mineral Resources, the ANC, as well as the Amadiba chief, who became a BEE beneficiary. The threatened landholders were not, as in the Maledu case, potentially private owners but customary landholders without PTOs. The Legal Resources Centre and Richard Spoor Attorneys, working with Advocate Tembeka Ngcukaitobi, took up the case on behalf of Duduzile Baleni, the local headwoman, and 128 community members. Xolobeni became a national and international issue, with political support mobilised by the Amadiba Crisis Committee.

When the case came to court in 2018, the lawyers prioritised a defence of community land rights based on IPILRA. They defined the community involved as the landholders and not the chieftaincy. The wording in IPILRA is 'any group or portion of a group of persons whose rights to land are derived from shared rules determining access to land held in common by such group' (*Maledu and Others v. Itereleng Bakgatla Mineral Resources (Pty) Limited and Another*). This could potentially refer either to a local community or to a broader area under a traditional council. Judge Basson accepted that the 128 landholders were the relevant 'portion of a group' that constituted the community for the purposes of the Act. The support of the local headwoman, who also contested the authority of the chief and traditional council in this matter, was important.

In this case, too, the issue arose as to whether the MPRDA – which gives the holders of mining licences, together with the state, powers to override the interests of landowners – trumped the IPILRA. This provision in the MPRDA was intended to give the state more control over mineral deposits and facilitate new entrants into the mining economy. The post-apartheid state did not want black-owned mining companies to be hamstrung by existing white or corporate landowners. Judge Basson agreed that the broader intent of both IPILRA and this section of the MPRDA was to support those who had been most disadvantaged under apartheid. She concluded that the protections offered by the IPILRA, read together with the Constitution, outweighed the relevant section of the MPRDA. Any mining development in customary areas required the free, prior and informed consent of affected landholders. These two judgments have important implications with respect to who must be consulted and who must give full consent when landholders who have customary or informal rights are threatened. In this case, consent was required by those who would experience deprivation.

The question of family land tenure was raised in the Xolobeni court papers (Beinart, 2018). The expert witness on customary law for the state argued that the traditional council of Amadiba as a whole was the appropriate authority to be consulted and to make decisions about land, and that the landholders of Xolobeni held their land from the chief and traditional council as 'lawful occupiers'. The lawyers for the 128 applicants disputed these formulations and argued that the families held their land as customary owners. This judgment did not directly address the strength of individual or family ownership. The judgment was made in favour of a collectivity, as provided for in the IPILRA. This Act does not distinguish between customary rights, which should, under the Constitution, be recognised as positive legal rights, and informal landholding. The IPLRA only provides a defensive remedy against deprivation of land rights. Nevertheless, the Act, bolstered by these recent judgments, is important. It should be made permanent and provided with administrative back-up.

The Xolobeni case illustrates some key issues with respect to customary land rights. There have been earlier cases that throw light on this question. In *Alexkor v. Richtersveld Community*, the Constitutional Court accepted the restitution claim by the community over an area in the Northern Cape that had been appropriated for mining in the 1920s. It also described the nature of the community's rights to that land. The court specified the significance of 'indigenous' or customary law, as recognised by the Constitution, and the judgment talked of community land rights as being 'akin to that held under common-law ownership' (*Alexkor v. Richtersveld Community*). Elsewhere, the judgment talked of 'ownership of the subject land under indigenous law'.

This was a positive statement of rights, with implications for other areas of customary tenure, but the court dealt only with collective customary ownership. In the Hlolweni restitution case, Fikile Bam, Chief Justice of the Land Claims Court, took the Richtersveld judgment as a precedent, but went further and ruled that the chiefs and former tribal authorities did not have the legal power to alienate land without the consent of those who had customary rights (*Hlolweni,*

Mfolozi and Etyeni Communities v. North Pondoland Sugar (Pty) and 2 Others). Claimant families collectively had a form of ownership over the land – this did not rest on being part of a traditional community under a chief. The award was made to a collectivity of those who lost land; they and the Department of Mineral Resources were directed by the court to form a CPA. Again, there was no clear statement in the judgment that cemented ownership of specific holdings by families or individuals. The judgment did not say that families could go back to the lands from which they had been forcibly removed for a sugar scheme 30 years before. The award was to the community collectively and there was subsequently a conflict between the claimant CPA and the local chief, both of whom claimed the land in the name of different communities. In 2019, however, the CPA was given a title over some of the land.

These issues came up again in the uMgungundlovu restitution case of 2014, initially contested by Sun International, for ownership of the land on which the Wild Coast Sun was sited. Again, the case was based on the collective right of the 106 claimants to the land and the chieftaincy was excluded. However, in this case, affidavits more clearly stated the significance of family ownership of land as a basis for the claim. These ideas were not tested in court because Sun International settled before court case proceedings started. The successful claimants for the Wild Coast Sun site were largely content to accept a settlement that disallowed their movement back onto their former land. Their rights were realised through a generous cash payment and membership of a CPA that became owner of the site and would receive annual rental payments. The courts have not yet – to our knowledge – expressed any clear detailed view concerning the nature of customary land tenure. The Constitutional Court has likened it to ownership, and this is an important concept that potentially gives the strongest possible collective rights to landholders. However, we do not know of a ruling that specifies the customary land rights of families or individuals. The following sections discuss possible legislative interventions to address this gap.

LEGISLATION FOR UPGRADING TENURE: ULTRA

Legislation is also potentially a route to enhance land rights and the ULTRA enabled certain surveyed sites in the former townships and homelands to be converted into privately held titles. These included lands held in surveyed individual tenure in the former Transkei and Ciskei. It also applied to deeds of grant issued for some townships and, for example, certificates of occupation given by the Bophuthatswana government in urban areas.

The Act has not been extensively implemented, except in a few major urban townships such as Mdantsane, part of East London, which formerly fell within the Ciskei, and in Thaba 'Nchu, which was placed for a limited period within Bophuthatswana (Umhlaba Rural Services, 2009). The ULTRA is potentially applicable to PTOs in the communal areas, and to traditional councils seeking collective, titled ownership over customary land, except for the former Transkei, Bophuthatswana, Venda and the Ciskei. The government has generally not extended the Act in non-surveyed customary areas, but has planned alternative legislation, notably the invalidated CLARA and its still-pending successor.

Opponents of the ULTRA argued that any exercise in titling may result in land being registered in the name of an individual, which might make it difficult for other family members, especially women, to realise their rights. Some of the older township sites, as well as PTOs, were held largely by men and upgrading could extend the exclusion of women. A Constitutional Court judgment in 2017 declared a section of the ULTRA unconstitutional for this reason (*Mary Rahube v. Hedsrine Rahube and Others*). The land had been upgraded and registered in the name of a male member of the family who attempted to sell it without the consent of a woman family member who lived there. The court recognised her interest in the site, annulled the sale and declared the relevant clauses in the ULTRA unconstitutional. Parliament was given the opportunity to amend the legislation and a draft Bill (Minister of Agriculture, Land Reform and Rural Development, 2020) has gone to the Portfolio Committee on Agriculture, Land Reform and Rural Development. This envisages that there will be no automatic upgrading; applications will be needed, and procedures to allow full scope for women to become owners and for other family members to participate. If these amendments are passed, it is also likely to become nationally applicable to a wider range of tenure types.

Could the ULTRA – if successfully amended – be more widely applied? Chiefs are opposed to the extension of family or individually based private tenure within the customary areas. There are also strong lobbies, growing out of anti-apartheid struggles and NGOs, that have consistently opposed chiefly assertions over land but have also been opposed to privatisation, which they see as disadvantaging poorer people. Some, but not all, sections of the Presidential Advisory Panel embrace this view: 'We are faced with a situation where communalism is at the centre of African lived experience, therefore necessitating a different approach to the land tenure question' (Presidential Advisory Panel, 2019: 44).

A more nuanced analysis is developed in a recent collection titled *Untitled*, where the editors argue that 'the relationships through which many South Africans gain access to land and housing are messy, complex, multi-layered and poorly understood' (Hornby et al., 2017: 3). Donna Hornby and colleagues argue that some of the systems that have evolved outside of formal tenure arrangements are relatively well organised and operate according to a set of rules that are largely accepted locally; intervention should identify, and work from, the 'social tenures' on the ground. They do not see these simply as 'communalism', but they also mount a multifaceted argument against titled, private tenure and they ask who might lose rights in such a process? Titles, it is also argued, cannot easily cope with the layered rights that characterise customary systems, where landholders have access to commonage, as well as stronger family rights on residential and arable plots.

We have discussed some of the arguments for and against extending the system of titling in South Africa elsewhere (Beinart et al., 2017). We take cognisance of these and related points but believe that the evidence and arguments for a gradual movement towards a single national system of land tenure are stronger. The Presidential Advisory Panel was clearly divided on this issue. For us, as historians, it is valuable to note that private titled tenure is not foreign to black South Africans. It was permitted on a non-racial basis in the Cape Colony in the 19th century. Following the 1905 Tsewu judgment, a spate of rural land purchases took place in the Transvaal. In both provinces, these continued beyond the Natives Land Act of 1913, although, by the 1920s, the government insisted that these should take place through traditional leaders or the state (Beinart and Delius, 2014).

The purchase of farmland by Africans was finally halted after 1936. Although the bantustans were predominantly held in customary systems of tenure, there were significant pockets of private, titled landownership in districts such as Umzimkhulu and in Bophuthatswana. Ownership was permitted in a number of cities, including Johannesburg suburbs such as Sophiatown and Alexandra, as well as in Evaton until the Group Areas Act. And elsewhere, many in the African elite, both chiefs and people, aspired to own land when this was possible. If they had not been curtailed by segregation and apartheid for many decades, more would have purchased land and the picture by 1994 would have been different. The scale of black-owned private property has increased rapidly in a relatively short period since it has been possible. Most people's lives are more commoditised and, following rapid urbanisation from the 1980s when the apartheid laws were loosened, perhaps 65 per cent live in urban or peri-urban areas.

Historical processes are also changing in the former homelands. Over the last 50 years, the percentage of people living in peri-urban contexts, or dense settlements within these areas, has greatly increased. At the same time, many people have stopped farming arable lands, though most still have gardens next to their homesteads. A minority own livestock, often wealthier people. Residential and garden sites are the major focus of investment for many families in the former homelands. We cannot give a percentage but perhaps over a third of the estimated 17–18 million people, who still live within the boundaries of the former homelands, are in dense settlements and peri-urban zones.

The question is, where do the greater dangers lie for those with off-register rights? Is this in upgrading? Or is it in customary systems? Evidence increasingly points to examples where customary owners have found it difficult to defend land against those with local political power, allied to external investors. The social geography of mining has changed in the country and it is no longer concentrated in the old centres of the Witwatersrand. Other investment opportunities have arisen along transport routes near towns and cities on the coast. There is no simple answer and much depends on specific local contexts and the resources at stake. But markets in land are spreading. We would rather see landholders getting clear rights and being able to decide on, and benefit from, development, or to sell, rather than being sidestepped.

Upgraded private tenure with title registered in the Deeds Office is a secure system of land rights at present. Local intermediaries or collectivities, such as government officials, chiefs, CPA committees or communities, would not have discretion to remove land from individuals or families with title, except in clearly defined laws where compensation is payable. Intermediary control of land seems to provide rent-seeking opportunities that disadvantage poorer or less influential people. Gradual movement towards a single system would end the dualism in tenure that has so long been highlighted by those critical of segregation and apartheid.

The prohibition on African land ownership during most of the apartheid era had devastating results for the personal wealth of many African families – a hidden aspect of racial discrimination that inhibited accumulation and social mobility. It has been removed in the cities, but it remains intact in the former homelands and on CPA land. One reason for the relative economic security of most white South Africans is that they accumulated through property holdings over more than one generation. Strategies to counter this legacy must be inclusive and ensure that the rights of all existing customary and informal landholders are recognised. This includes emphasising that allocations are still possible on the remaining commonage, which is still the largest area of land within the former homelands. In this way, land ownership will be very widespread. Interviews in rural districts suggest that people believe they 'own' their land and use local vernacular words with something like that meaning.

We will leave aside the issue of smallholder production in this chapter; there is a large and complex literature on the relationship between tenure and production that we cannot review here. But it is important to think creatively about unlocking the productive potential of the former homelands, which remain some of the poorest parts of South Africa. The traditionalist and communitarian approaches may continue to provide some rural people with varied access to land, but we suggest that policy should move on. Traditional authorities have been an important pole of power in the countryside for more than 60 years since the Bantu Authorities programme was introduced. Their involvement as claimants for land and power may not only ignite ethnicity and conflicting claims – as seen recently in Limpopo Province – but also facilitate elite capture of land and rural resources.

TENURE AND LAND ADMINISTRATION: A HYBRID ROUTE?

In 1999, Martin Adams, who worked in President Nelson Mandela's Department of Land Affairs, together with Ben Cousins and Siyabulela Manona, remarked that the existing land administration system was breaking down: 'This collapse includes loss of records, doubts as to which laws apply and the unauthorised issue of permits and other documents' (Adams et al., 1999: 15). The Presidential Advisory Panel found that little had changed: 'The state land administration system is excessively fragmented and disjointed, and in some contexts broken down completely' (Presidential Advisory Panel, 2019: 86). Local customary arrangements, chiefs and headmen, and sometimes local PTOs, continue to operate but generally without formal authority. There is evidence of localised systems of record keeping, from Monwabisi Park informal settlement in Cape Town (Barry and Kingwill, 2020), to rural areas such as Xolobeni in the Eastern Cape. These have a degree of local acceptance and may have weight as evidence of 'living customary law' in a court case, but their status in law is uncertain. Insecurity of tenure is thus compounded by the post-1994 weakness of land administration.

Siyabulela Manona and Rosalie Kingwill (2016) suggest a new system of land administration that gives strong rights to families who hold off-register land. They argue that titles are unsuitable and that attempts to legislate for communal land rights have failed or tend to favour traditional authorities. They believe that major legislation is required in the shape of a Land Records Act or similar measures. This suggestion has been taken up both by the High-Level Panel (Parliament of South Africa, 2017) and the Presidential Advisory Panel (2019). The proposed land records system should be parallel to Deeds Registry, located in the same government department and articulate with it. Landholders should be able to upgrade to title if families agree. The Act should provide for clarifying and recording rights as a first step and for an administrative system that includes all sites that are currently off-register. The Presidential Advisory Panel does not see the lack of detailed survey in such areas as a central problem, but we suggest that it should be an element in the recordal of rights.

The development of an effective system of adjudication with trained officials would be necessary. A Land Records Act would work with legislation such as the IPILRA, but it would provide a positive statement of rights for families or individuals and would not be limited, as in the case of these Acts, to a defensive approach for broader collectivities. If such legislation is to be passed, then other Acts such as the IPILRA and ULTRA may need to be amended so that all can be complementary. In our arguments for a single national system of landholding, we are not suggesting a sudden, national process of titling. The state does not have the capacity and it may trigger political opposition. Providing families who live on customary land with security of tenure in the form of ownership is likely to be seen by most chiefs as a direct threat to their political authority. This cannot be overlooked in attempts to reform the tenure system, and policy recommendations will have to take this into account.

A slow process of the kind, which has been happening to a limited extent under the ULTRA, and is envisaged under a Land Records Act, is a possible route. It would start in the urban and peri-urban areas, and with RDP houses, where there is less complexity in relation to collective rights over common land. However, some important issues must be adequately thought through before this path is taken. The state would have to develop major new administrative capacity and pay the costs of research and first registration at a time of great financial stringency. Education and publicity will be needed as it is vital that people understand what is being done. As we have noted, the area of land involved is probably less than 15 per cent, but the number of landholdings is large, maybe around five to six million if untitled RDP houses are included. The process needs to be scrupulously fair and free of corruption.

Although Manona and Kingwill are advocating a recordal of existing rights, and cementing them, rather than upgrading to title, we see the potential for this programme to be part of a longer-term movement, over a few decades, towards a single national system of landholding. The Deeds Office and Surveyor General Offices are well established, with clear processes and experienced officials. It is vital that the state ensures that these institutions have the capacity to expand and innovate as new technology becomes available. This may greatly reduce costs of recordal, registration and transactions. It would be possible to expand title to specific components of rural residential landholdings and fields without threatening other rights. Commonages were attached to private property settlements in the 19th-century Eastern Cape for white and black people. Alternatively, experiments could be developed to subdivide commonages (Beinart et al., 2017). The Presidential Advisory Panel (2019), among other sources, suggests that consolidated smallholder sites are likely to be most successful. Upgrading and registration need not preclude further allocation of residential sites on the commonages, which are probably still the largest areas of land in the former homelands. This would be important in ensuring that some land remains accessible at low cost.

REFERENCES

Adams, M., Cousins, B. and Manona, S. 1999. 'Land tenure and economic development in rural South Africa: Constraints and opportunities'. Working Paper No. 125, Overseas Development Institute, http://dlc.dlib.indiana.edu/dlc/bitstream/handle/10535/4077/Adams%26Cousins-et_al-land_tenure_and_economic_development_in_rural_south_africa_costraints_and_opportunities.pdf?sequence=1, accessed 20 August 2020.

Amanor, K. 2008. 'The changing face of customary land tenure', in Ubink, J. M. and Amanor, K. (eds.) *Contesting Land and Custom in Ghana: State, chief and the citizen*. Leiden: Leiden University Press, 55–81.

Barry, M. and Kingwill, R. 2020. 'Evaluating the community land record system in Monwabisi Park informal settlement in the context of hybrid governance and organisational culture'. *Land*, 9 (124), 1–34.

Beinart, W. 2018. Supporting affidavit, heads of argument bundle, *Baleni, D and 128 Others v Minister of Mineral Resources and Others.*

Beinart, W. and Delius, P. 2014. 'The historical context and legacy of the Natives Land Act of 1913'. *Journal of Southern African Studies,* 40 (4), 667–688.

Beinart, W., Delius, P. and Hay, M. 2017. *Rights to Land: A guide to tenure upgrading and restitution in South Africa.* Johannesburg: Jacana Media.

Beinart, W. and Wotshela, L. 2011–2012. Unpublished interviews in preparation for the uMgungundlovu (Wild Coast Sun) restitution case.

Bennett, J., Ainslie, A. and Davis, J. 2013. 'Contested institutions? Traditional leaders and land access and control in communal areas of Eastern Cape Province, South Africa'. *Land Use Policy*, 32, 27–38.

Bloom, K. 26 March 2019. 'China, the Pondo king and Namaqualand: In pursuit of the "Disney playground" deal'. *Daily Maverick,* https://www.google.com/amp/s/www.dailymaverick.co.za/article/2019-03-26-china-the-pondo-king-and-namaqualand-in-pursuit-of-the-disney-playground-deal/amp/, accessed 9 June 2020.

Capps, G. and Malindi, S. 2017. 'Dealing with the tribe: The politics of the Bapo/Lonmin royalty to-equity conversion'. Working Paper No. 8, Society, Work and Development Institute (SWOP), University of the Witwatersrand.

Claassens, A. and Budlender, G. 2016. 'Transformative constitutionalism and customary law'. *Constitutional Court Review*, 6, 75–105.

Delius, P. 2008. 'Contested terrain: Land rights and chiefly power in historical perspective', in Claassens, A. and Cousins, B. (eds.) *Land, Power and Custom: Controversies generated by South Africa's Communal Land Rights Act.* Cape Town: University of Cape Town Press, 211–237.

Department of Rural Development and Land Reform (DRDLR). 2007. 'Land audit report: Phase II: Private land ownership by race, gender and nationality', https://www.gov.za/sites/default/files/gcis_document/201802/landauditreport13feb2018.pdf, accessed 20 May 2020.

Guduza, C.M. 1997. 'Housing markets in Greater Soweto'. PhD dissertation, London School of Economics and Political Science, University of London.

Hornby, D., Kingwill, R., Royston, L. and Cousins, B. 2017. *Untitled: Securing land tenure in urban and rural South Africa.* Pietermaritzburg: University of KwaZulu-Natal Press.

Hunter, M. [1936] 1964. *Reaction to Conquest.* London: Oxford University Press.

Kassier, N. 2019. 'Current status of permission to occupy'. *Go Legal*, https://www.golegal.co.za/pto-rural-land-occupation/, accessed 9 June 2020.

Kerr, A.J. 1953. *The Native Common Law of Immovable Property in South Africa.* Durban: Butterworth.

Kerr, A. J. 1990. *The Customary Law of Immovable Property and of Succession.*

Grahamstown: Grocott & Sherry.
Manona, S. and Kingwill, R. 2016. 'Land Records Act: Proposals at a glance'. Unpublished paper prepared for the High-Level Panel, Cape Town.
Minisi Weeks, S. 2019. *Access to Justice and Human Security: Cultural contradictions in rural South Africa*. London Routledge.
Minister of Agriculture, Land Reform and Rural Development. 2020. 'Upgrading of Land Tenure Rights Amendment Bill', https://www.parliament.gov.za/storage/app/media/Bills/2020/B6_2020_Upgrading_of_Land_Tenure_Rights/b6-2020-upgrading-of-land-tenure-rights.pdf, accessed 20 August 2020.
Ntsebeza, L. 2005. *Democracy Compromised: Chiefs and the politics of land in South Africa*. Leiden: Brill.
Parliament of South Africa. 2017. 'Report of the High-Level Panel on the assessment of key legislation and the acceleration of fundamental change'. Parliamentary Monitoring Group, https://www.parliament.gov.za/storage/app/media/Pages/2017/october/High_Level_Panel/HLP_Report/HLP_report.pdf, accessed 20 August 2020.
Peters, P.E. 2013. 'Land appropriation, surplus people and a battle over visions of agrarian futures in Africa'. *Journal of Peasant Studies*, 40 (3), 537–562.
Presidential Advisory Panel on Land Reform and Agriculture. 2019. 'Final Report of the Presidential Advisory Panel on Land Reform and Agriculture', https://www.gov.za/sites/default/files/gcis_document/201907/panelreportlandreform_0.pdf, accessed 19 August 2020.
South African Constitution. 1996. 'Section 25 Amendment: Expert opinion', https://pmg.org.za/committee-meeting/28079/, accessed 26 August 2020.
Ubink, J.M. 2008. 'Struggles for land in peri-urban Kumasi and their effect on popular perceptions of chiefs and chieftancy', in Ubink, J.M. and Amanor, K. (eds.) *Contesting Land and Custom in Ghana: State, chief and the citizen*. Leiden: Leiden University Press, 155–182.
Umhlaba Rural Services. 2009. 'Situational analysis of the upgrading of Land Tenure Rights Act (ULTRA)'. Umhlaba Rural Services, East London.
Yeni, S. 2019. 'Traditional leadership, violation of land rights and resistance from below in Makhaseni village, KwaZulu-Natal', in Buthelezi, M., Skosana, D. and Vale B. (eds.) *Traditional Leaders in a Democracy: Resources, respect and resistance*. Johannesburg: MISTRA, 129–153.

Legislation

Communal Land Rights Act (CLARA, No. 11 of 2004).
Deeds Registries Act (No. 47 of 1937).
Extension of Security of Tenure Act (No. 62 of 1997)
Ingonyama Trust Act (No. 3KZ of 1994).
Interim Protection of Informal Land Rights Act (IPILRA, No. 31 of 1996).
Mineral and Petroleum Resources Development Act (MPRDA, No.

28 of 2002).
Natives Land Act (No. 27 of 1913).
Native Trust and Land Act (No. 18 of 1936).
Prevention of Illegal Eviction Act (No. 19 of 1998).
Provision of Certain Land for Settlement Act (No. 126 of 1993).
Traditional and Khoisan Leadership Act (No. 3 of 2019).
Upgrading of Land Tenure Rights Act (ULTRA, No. 112 of 1991).

Court cases

Alexkor Ltd and Another v. Richtersveld Community and Others (CCT19/03) [2003] ZACC 18, 2004 (5) SA 460 (CC); 2003 (12) BCLR 1301 (CC).
Baleni, D and 128 Others v. Minister of Mineral Resources and Others (2018) (73768/2016).
Global Environmental Trust and Others v. Tendele Coal Mining (11488/17P) [2018] ZAKZPHC 62; [2019] 1 All SA 176 (KZP).
Hlolweni, Mfolozi and Etyeni Communities v. North Pondoland Sugar (Pty) and 2 Others (2010) LCC41/03.
Madumetsa, *Machoga v. Potgietersrus Platinum* (2006) 1(3498/06).
Maledu and Others v. Itereleng Bakgatla Mineral Resources (Pty) Limited and Another (CCT265/17) [2018] ZACC 41; 2019.
Mary Rahube v. Hedsrine Rahube and Others (2017), 101250/2015.
Nandipha NO v. Irfani Traders cc (2018) 4654/2017.
Mgungundlovu Community v. Minister of Rural Development and Land Reform, Transkei Sun International Limited et al., (2014) (LCC 10/2011).

FOUR

Traditional Leaders' Conceptions of Land Reform and Rural Citizens' Identities

Fani Ncapayi

INTRODUCTION

South African traditional authorities' conceptions of land reform impact rural residents' identities and livelihoods. The ownership claims over communal land by some traditional authorities amounts to the denial of citizenship rights to residents under their jurisdiction (Claassens et al., 2016). Both High and Constitutional Court judgments reining in traditional authorities for handling land in communal areas as their own, confirm contestations over land control in these locations. Politicians and state officials equally contribute to this perception about traditional authorities owning land in communal areas. The South African government's policy approach to communal tenure grants ownership of the outer boundaries of communal land to traditional authorities (Department of Rural Development and Land Reform, 2014). This is tantamount to handing over the land of whole villages to traditional authorities.

Yet, access to property, especially land, gives people a sense of belonging (Lund, 2011). At the same time, citizenship affords a country's population rights to participate in public affairs (Jones and Gaventa, 2002). Deborah James (2013) emphasises that citizens' rights include access and control over land. Transforming land-ownership patterns was an integral component of the liberation struggle, highlighting strong links between land access and control, on the one hand, and citizenship, on the other hand. This is what James calls 'land-based citizenship' (James, 2013: 29). Another form of citizenship relates to rights determined by segregated spatial development in South Africa. For instance, the land rights of people in communal areas are viewed as very precarious (James, 2013; Human Rights Commission, 2018). According to the Human Rights Commission (2018), residents in communal areas are vulnerable as they can lose their land at any time, due to the unresolved issue of land tenure in communal areas. In turn, the precarity of land tenure of residents in communal areas makes their livelihoods precarious too (Adams et al., 1999b; see chapters 2 and 3 in this volume).

I argue that giving land ownership and control to traditional authorities renders people in communal areas non-citizens, and this impacts on the dignity, identity and livelihoods of residents in communal areas. These residents' relationships with the land is weakened without a sense of belonging and identity, and this negatively affects their livelihoods. This approach to communal tenure undermines the political agency of rural citizens in defending land rights and creates conducive conditions for external parties to exploit them. This chapter advocates for an alternative policy approach in communal tenure, which restores community control over land ownership and development. The first section discusses land reform, with a specific focus on traditional authorities' views on how land acquired through reform policies should be registered. A case study is examined in Nombanjana village – an area located within the jurisdiction of King Sigcawu of the amaXhosa kingdom. It highlights how these citizens understand and engage with land tenure debates in these communities.

LAND REFORM, CITIZENSHIP, IDENTITY AND LIVELIHOODS

Land has various meanings in the lives of Africans. It gives them identity, dignity and citizenship (Jones and Gaventa, 2002; Lund, 2011; Bruchhausen and Naicker, 2018). Similarly, land dispossession due to colonial conquest and apartheid laws impacted various aspects of the lives of Africans. For instance, the removal of communities from land identified for mining means that the residents do not only lose their land, but also the graves of their relatives and forebears are also affected (see Chapter 5 in this volume). The depth of Africans' relationships with the land is elevated in Judge Basson's 2016 High Court judgment on the Xolobeni case, which was initiated by residents opposing commercial mining on their land. *Baleni and Others v. Minister of Mineral Resources and Others* contained the following words of one applicant, who is an older Xolobeni community member:

> The land! Our purpose is the land; that is what we must achieve. The land is our lives: we plough it for food; we build our houses from the soil; we live on it; and we are buried on it. When the whites took our land away from us, we lost the dignity of our lives: we could no longer feed our children; we were forced to become servants; we were treated like animals …

This quote indicates that land provides a sense of identity to people in communal areas. Bruchhaussen and Naicker (2018) draw links between the land and citizenship. They explain that citizenship is about participation, rights and obligations. According to Emma Jones and John Gaventa, citizenship is also about 'the act of taking part in public affairs' (2002: 1). Implied here is the right of African people in communal areas to participate in decision-making processes, including decisions about their land; non-participation in decision-making results in policies that have negative effects on the livelihoods of rural residents. This is exacerbated by land tenure insecurity in communal areas. Martin Adams and colleagues (1999a) show that insecure tenure means rural residents cannot have sustainable livelihoods.

To address the legacies of colonial conquest and apartheid land dispossession, the South African democratic government adopted a three-pronged land reform policy approach in 1994. Essentially, the policy's aim has not only been about returning the land to African people, but also to restore their citizenship and dignity (see Buthelezi et al., 2019). The report of the South African Human Rights Commission (2018: 3) aptly captures the sentiment and hopes of many Africans about land reform:

> For the dispossessed in South Africa and elsewhere across the world, land is both material and symbolic, a factor of production and a site of belonging and identity. Not surprisingly, return of the land was a rallying cry of the anti-apartheid struggles, and in the 1990s, as the transition was made towards a democratic South Africa, hopes were high that dispossessed lands would be returned.

However, the land reform policy, which should contribute to addressing the issues of belonging and identity for landless citizens, has failed in many respects to fulfil the dream of millions of landless people. According to Aninka Claassens, laws passed post-1994 advance 'the interests of a small elite at the expense of the property and citizenship rights of 17 million South Africans living in the former homelands' (Claassens, 2019: 75). The clearest area where land reform has failed to fulfil the dreams of many South Africans is with respect to customary tenure reform in rural areas under traditional authorities (Brandt and Mkodzongi, 2018).

Customary tenure reform has constantly faced, and still faces, serious challenges from a section of traditional authorities who claim ownership of the land in rural areas. Although there is no unanimity among traditional authorities on the issue of communal land ownership and control, the dominant view among them is that they own communal land – this is certainly the presiding view of those that fall under the Eastern Cape House of Traditional Leaders. For instance, the current chairperson of the provincial house of traditional authorities, Chief Mwelo Nonkonyana, believes that they own and control land in rural areas. He stated: 'The reason why I think they [traditional authorities in KwaZulu] were in a better position than all of us is because of that dispensation; to actually put the land of the Zulu people in a trust. And the only trust that is legitimate is the Ingonyama Trust.'[1]

Chief Nonkonyana supports the land arrangement under the Ingonyama Trust (Lamani, 2020). According to section 2A (2) of the KwaZulu-Natal Ingonyama Trust Act (No. 3KZ of 1994, 3), the Ingonyama Trust Board:

> Shall administer the affairs of the Trust and the trust land and without detracting from the generality of the foregoing the Board may decide on and implement any encumbrance, pledge, lease, alienation or other disposal of any trust land, or of any interest or real right in such land.

Importantly, the board is chaired by either King Goodwill Zwelithini or his nominee. The four other board members are nominees of the minister in the Department of Rural Development and Land Reform, who must consult the king about the nominees. This means that the king is in control of the board and, by extension, he is also in control of the land the board administers. In his June 2018 article in the *Daily Dispatch*, the chief of amaHegebe and a member of the national parliament, Chief Phathekile Holomisa, called for the registration of communal land in the name of traditional authorities (Holomisa, 2018). He holds similar views to those of Chief Nonkonyana. These are prominent members of the Congress of Traditional Leaders of South Africa, whose views cannot be dismissed easily as they have a strong influence over the organisation's members.

The Eastern Cape traditional authorities' views are similar to those of King Zwelithini and the Ingonyama Trust. Rural land in KwaZulu-Natal is held in trust by the Ingonyama Trust, with King Zwelithini being the sole trustee. Consequently, the residents lease the land from the trust for a fee. This means that King Zwelithini and his chiefs have effectively stripped rural residents of their land rights, using the

1 Chief Nonkonyana speaking on eNCA on 31 January 2020.

Ingonyama Trust as their instrument.

The example of Chief Zulu of the Entembeni Traditional Council in KwaZulu-Natal, who unilaterally gave a mining company access to land in Makhasaneni, confirms this point. Jaconia Dludla, a 97-year-old induna or 'headman' of Makhasaneni who grew up in the area, says that the mining situation threatens his access and rights to the land. Sithandiwe Yeni (2019: 161) explains Jaconia's story:

> As a young boy during the 1930s, his family and neighbours were forcibly removed from their homes in eMagogogweni near Melmoth by the colonial government to make way for tree plantations. They were dumped in Makhasaneni village. In 1998, when the South African government opened the call for people to lodge land claims under the land restitution programme, many of Makhasaneni did so … While reflecting on the painful experience of being forcibly removed, he speaks fondly of his current home, Makhasaneni, and promises that he will not be forcibly removed again.

However, in 2015 there was another threat of forced removal for Jaconia and his community from Jindal Africa (Pty) Ltd. This mining company first arrived in the community in 2011 'and began prospecting in people's fields, without consulting the community or the people who depended on the produce grown on the fields' (Yeni, 2019: 162). Chief Zulu had taken the decision to allow the company to start prospecting in the village, without consulting Jaconia, the 'headman' of the area. This prospecting poisoned the water and fields for crops, and resulted in the death of cattle and goats. The damage even extended to family graves. These examples epitomise the gravity of the situation regarding tenure in rural areas and the position of influential traditional leaders on the issue. Ultimately, the laws and developments flowing from them negatively impact on the identity of rural residents such as Jaconia.

Some traditional authorities are against the establishment of communal property associations (CPAs) (Africa Research Institute, 2016). CPAs are landholding legal entities established in terms of the Communal Property Association Act (No. 28 of 1996). The Act was formulated to facilitate the transfer and registration of land acquired through land reform to groups. According to the Africa Research Institute (2016), traditional authorities believe the CPAs undermine their authority and control over land. However, it is important to point out that there is no unanimity among traditional authorities in the Eastern Cape House of Traditional Leaders regarding communal land ownership. Prince Zolile Burns-Ncamashe, former deputy chairperson of this provincial House of Traditional Leaders, holds a different view. Burns-Ncamashe (2016) argued:

> Land is not an exclusive Pty Ltd asset on the basis of a feudal-vassalage structural arrangement but an asset of the nation, communally owned by the nation … Thus, any notion that the land belongs to traditional leaders is historically flawed, politically distorted, and academically unsustainable. The land belongs to the communities.

Burns-Ncamashe's view on traditional authorities and land ownership is not unique and is mirrored in other land literature and policy debates (Ntsebeza, 2006; Ncapayi, 2018; Claassens, 2019; Mnwana, 2019).

However, while the view that traditional authorities own communal land has been challenged by various scholars, it still prevails. Sonwabile Mnwana correctly states that traditional authorities aim to control land and mineral resources: 'Chiefs currently enjoy an advantageous position, especially on the platinum belt, where they control and distribute vast mining revenues and act as custodians of community property' (Mnwana, 2019: 131). There are many instances where traditional authorities believe that they should benefit from the land reform policies. Some have even submitted land claims in their own names as though they were the rightful owners of communal land from which communities were removed in the past. All these points highlight the extent to which current land reform legislation has completely failed to resolve the vexed issue of land tenure in communal areas.

This belief that traditional authorities own and control land in communal areas receives support from some senior politicians in the ruling party, who support the idea that traditional authorities should be beneficiaries of land reform. For instance, when the restitution claims were reopened, some politicians actively promoted the submission of claims by traditional authorities. Indeed, in opening the National House of Traditional Leaders in 2014, former president Jacob Zuma stated that he has 'advised traditional leaders that they must appoint a firm of attorneys to handle the issues of land and they indicated that the National House was engaging the Black Lawyers Association to assist' (Zuma, 2017).

This approach is alluded to in national legislation. The Communal Land Tenure Policy of 2014, which aims to provide tenure security and clarify land allocations in communal areas, ensures that traditional authorities will be the beneficiaries of communal land tenure reform (Department of Rural Development and Land Reform, 2014). According to this policy, the outer boundaries of communal land must be registered in the name of traditional councils, which are controlled mostly by traditional leaders – unelected royal family members or those appointed by the chiefs – raising concerns about the lack of accountability (Ntsebeza, 2006).This policy does not make provision for individuals and households to hold these traditional councils accountable. Similarly, the recently promulgated Traditional and Khoisan Leadership Act (No. 3 of 2019) also perpetuates the situation. This Act advantages traditional authorities regarding land control in communal areas. For instance, section 24 empowers traditional authorities to enter into partnership agreements with municipalities, government departments, other persons and institutions. Although this section proposes consultation with communities, it still gives land ownership and control to an undemocratic structure in rural areas: 60 per cent of the members of traditional councils are unelected. As in the case of the Ingonyama Trust, section 24 creates conditions conducive for land rights violations and rural citizens have minimal recourse when traditional leaders undermine their land tenure security.

TRADITIONAL AUTHORITIES AND LAND CONTROL IN CENTANE

This section reflects on how the confusion around land ownership in communal areas due to poor governance by traditional authorities is experienced in the rural areas of Centane. Rural residents who look up to traditional authorities for governance are left unable to protect their land rights. In the Centane area, a Gauteng-based agri-business exploited this lack of clarity about land ownership and approached the local traditional authorities for access and control over vast tracts of communal land.

Centane is a small town about 31 kilometres south-east of Butterworth in the Eastern Cape Province and is surrounded by several villages. AmaGcaleka, the great house of the amaXhosa kingdom under the Sigcawu family, occupies this portion of land (Nhlapho Commission, 2014; Mvenene, 2014). Since the reconstruction of local government in 2000, the area has been placed under the Mbashe Local Municipality within the Amathole District Municipality.

In the following sections I use evidence from interviews with landholders and participant observation during community meetings in the Nombanjana and Thuthurh villages of Centane, between 2017 and 2019, to explore the relationships between the traditional authority, business and citizens. I interviewed several stakeholders, including two representatives of the Women Investment Portfolio Holding Limited (WIPHOLD) in May 2020.[2]

According to one of the executive members of WIPHOLD, Debra Marsden, the company has been working in the Mnquma and Mbashe local municipalities since 2006. In an interview, Marsden revealed that the company worked closely with traditional authorities 'in exploring ways of developing the agricultural land' in the villages of Centane. The initial exploratory phase of 2006 was followed by a more focused intervention in 2007, when the founder and chief executive officer

2 WIPHOLD is a South African women-led empowerment company based in Johannesburg. In partnership with the Eastern Cape provincial government, WIPHOLD spearheads the initiative. Old Mutual and Nedbank have partnered WIPHOLD in the initiative since 2015.

of WIPHOLD approached 13 traditional authorities in Centane for access to agricultural land. Indeed, WIPHOLD reached an agreement with the traditional authorities, thus gaining access to both communal grazing and arable land in the area, but the traditional authorities neglected to consult the landholders beforehand. One of the chiefs who committed the land under his jurisdiction to the Centane Agricultural Initiative was Chief Zonwabele Dyantyi (Ngcukana, 2015).

WIPHOLD's approach of negotiating with the traditional authorities before engaging with the affected community landowners, reinforces the view that traditional authorities are the owners of land in communal areas. Marsden's explanation justifies this view. Traditional authorities also became central in the operations of the scheme and, according to Marsden, they play a leadership role in the business operations. For instance, they participated in meetings with WIPHOLD before the community meetings and played a supportive role in the project. After winning the confidence of traditional authorities, the company persuaded individual landholders in the 13 villages to offer their arable land to the initiative (Phillips, 2015). Bringing the fields under collective production was aimed at aggregating them, according to Marsden. This marked the birth of the Centane Agricultural Initiative, which aimed to facilitate the development of a model for the profitable and sustainable farming of communally owned land (WIPHOLD, 2017b).

As Marsden (quoted in Ngcukana, 2015) puts it:

> [T]he initiative recognises the inherent potential of the Eastern Cape's vast tracts of arable land, and that the proper use of land resources in South Africa by small-scale farmers has the potential to play a significant role in enhancing food security, particularly in poor communities.

To achieve this, WIPHOLD had to facilitate food security, micro-agriculture, dipping tank restoration and micro-enterprises such as fence-making (Pinyana, 2008). The company committed to ensuring that 'all residents of Centane benefit materially and financially' from the project (Phillips, 2015). The initiative included residents who did not have arable land as members. Marsden explains that this strategy was aimed at preventing hostility towards the project as a result of some community members feeling excluded. The agricultural initiative is structured in the following way: the company owns 40 per cent of the shares while 60 per cent is allocated to the participating residents (WIPHOLD, 2017a). According to Marsden, each participating village had to establish a committee to ensure accountability and their involvement in managing the project.

Every participating household gets 10 40-kilogram bags of maize annually as payment for using their land. This benefit was received irrespective of whether production was successful or not. Where production is unsuccessful, the company purchases the maize to honour the annual land-use payment agreement. The members also benefit from an annual cash distribution that ranges between R3,000 and R4,000 per household, which is paid from funds raised. Additionally, dividends were promised to all project members. However, there has been no declaration of dividends as yet because the project has not broken even, according to Marsden. Project members are expected to provide labour to erect and maintain field fencing, guard against livestock theft, monitor crops against diseases, recruit tractor drivers and other workers, as well as identify individuals to be trained. The members also contribute labour during harvesting (WIPHOLD, 2017a).

Participants who achieve good produce are viewed as displaying good management of their production processes. Having fewer incidents of theft is also considered an indication of good governance. The penalty fee for mismanagement in the project can reach 30 per cent of the shares. The agricultural initiative has grown from 13 villages in 2007 to 34 villages in 2016, which has resulted in a drastic increase in the cultivated land from 673 to 2,500 hectares during this period (WIPHOLD, 2017a). The Department of Rural Development and Agrarian Reform (DRDAR) is supportive of the initiative. Addressing the landholders in a ceremony to hand over tractors and other equipment in Ngqamakhwe on 31 January 2018, the former minister of the Department of Rural Development and Agrarian Reform, Gugile Nkwinti, stated (Amatole District Municality, n.d.):

> You know when one of WIPHOLD's founding members, Mrs Gloria Serobe said she wanted to start this community project a few years back, I was sceptical. However, looking at the end product now, I couldn't be happier. Knowing that the communities have been enabled to get into the market with good returns is what our Agriparks initiative is about.

Agriparks consists of coordinated initiatives that combine 'agro-production, processing, logistics, marketing, training, and extension services located in District Municipalities. As a network, it enables a market-driven combination and integration of various agricultural activities and rural transformation services' (Heimann, 2017: 6).

Chief Zonwabele, who is from the area in which the initiative started, states: 'Everyone is happy in our villages. We are united because our stomachs are full, and we are confident that we are going to make this project sustainable and provide a lot of our people with opportunities´(Ngcukana, 2015).

Good maize production in the 2012/13 season made the chief and those who benefit from the initiative happy. There was also distribution of payments to the community members who had provided communal land for the maize crops (Phillips, 2015). Consequently, following the payments, more community members offered their land to the scheme. By 2015, the cultivated land in Centane included Thuthurha, Khobonqaba, Nxaxho and Nombanjana villages. According to a local leader, Harvey Ntshoko, landholders in the latter three villages approached the leader of WIPHOLD for assistance after seeing the developments in other areas.[3]

THE CENTANE AGRICULTURAL INITIATIVE IN NOMBANJANE

Nombanjan village is located in Ward 28 of the Mnquma Local

3 Harvey Ntshoko is one of the local leaders of Coastal Links – an organisation of small fishers – in Nombanjana village. The discussions with him and other leaders of Coastal Links were held in Nombanjana, 4 October 2018.

Municipality and is about 5 kilometres from the Wavecrest Hotel on the Centane coast. The village consists of the sub-villages of Nxaxho, Ngcizele, Ngcotyeni and Khobonqaba. This case study shows that while the leader of the Eastern Cape House of Traditional Leaders maintains that traditional authorities own and control the land in communal areas, the chief of Nombanjana's role in the ownership and governance of land is unclear. At the same time, the landholders are unable to take measures to protect their land as they look to the chief for governance. Thus, a state of ambiguous governance is created at Nombanjana, leaving the land rights of landholders vulnerable and their dignity negatively impacted. This is reflected in the unhappiness and a sense of powerlessness among some landholders as they struggle to deal with the governance of their land.

Marsden states that regular reports are provided through the village committees set up to manage the project in each village. But this has not led to consensus in communities and many of the landholders complain about the lack of transparency in the project and the alleged failure of WIPHOLD to implement its promises. In an interview in 2018, Mrs Mdukiswa summarised the feelings of the group regarding Mrs Serobe – the leader of the company:

> She came as somebody who would assist to plough. We continued working together, with the company ploughing for us. However, we realised at some point that there were issues and we became unhappy about the company. The director promised that her company would plant maize for us, and we would either sell or share it among ourselves. She took the maize over to sell it for us when we were unable to sell it. Three big trucks were filled with maize from our fields and transported to the markets. Each household was given 10 bags of maize in the first season.

The complaint in the extract displays weak transparency about the agricultural produce and its marketing. Although trucks leave their fields with tons of maize, very little goes to the households. Payment for the use of land is another source of concern for the landholders, who complain about a lack of consistency in the amount paid by WIPHOLD. Mr Mgcadiya, for instance, reported to have received nothing from the agricultural initiative in the first season, except for the 10 bags of maize. He got R4,900 in the second season, R3,000 in the third season and R2,000 in 2017. Consequently, 'we told her [the WIPHOLD director] to stop using our fields', Mgcadiya said. Participants in two community meetings of about 100 unhappy villagers on 3 and 5 October 2018 confirmed these views. Landholders in the meeting agreed that this project should be stopped, and that the land should be released from the agricultural initiative.

The landholders are also unhappy that their livestock is prevented from accessing grazing land, which is now fenced off and reserved for WIPHOLD's livestock. In the community meeting on 5 October 2018, the landholders complained about the company's operations on their land. They claimed that their livestock was dying because of starvation and they argued that fencing off the commonage land prevented their livestock from accessing the best grazing land. The residents also complained about the tensions and divisions the project has caused at Nombanjana.[4] Harvey Ntshoko (2019) concurs with the views of the participants in the meeting concerning cattle in Nombanjana. Ntshoko (2019) explains:

> In 2014, Mrs Serobe introduced another project for livestock where she came with 80 cows. She promised that the project aims to boost the local economy. She further indicated that some of the cattle will be handed over to members of the new livestock project, which she called the Ikhobonqaba Project. The cattle used the commonage land for grazing. She sells the cattle without consulting anyone.

Marsden confirmed the presence of cattle in Nombanjana and explained that this was Serobe's independent initiative. In other words, WIPHOLD is not involved. According to Marsden, Serobe introduced the cattle into the community as an experiment to assess

4 Personal notes of the author taken during the meetings at Nombanjana on 3 and 5 October 2018.

the potential for livestock farming in the area. Her explanation shows that some landholders involved in the agricultural initiative have not been provided with sufficient information to distinguish between the activities of WIPHOLD and Serobe's private projects. The confusion emanates from the fact that the landholders have no signed contract with either the company or with Serobe. This information gap is created by the nature of WIPHOLD's operations and ambiguous partnership terms. The most vivid example is the confusion surrounding the landholder benefits. Marsden states that the partnership has the following benefits:

- Ten 40-kilogram bags per household distributed as a land-use fee. These bags are distributed annually, irrespective of the amount of production in a season. WIPHOLD even buys maize when necessary.
- An annual cash distribution, which ranges from R3,000 to R4,000 per household. The cash distribution fluctuates because it is dependent on the availability of funds in the project.
- The company has convened regular consultative meetings with the village committees and other community members since 2014.

The information about the benefits did not filter down to all the affected landholders. Serobe confirmed that she is the owner of the livestock and she further explained that she also gave some livestock to the landholders of Nxaxho and Ngcotyeni. Therefore, the fenced-off land kept her livestock together with the ones she donated to the landholders.[5] According to Serobe, the landholders later requested her to buy their cattle back after there were differences among the members about the management of the cattle. She bought them back and thus she is the sole owner of the livestock. She also acknowledged that fields have been fenced off for the cattle 'to keep it separately from the cattle of the villagers'. According to her, the soil in the fenced fields had been tested and found unsuitable for maize production. These are fields for 72 households.

5 During the interview, Serobe could not remember the number of cattle she had brought to Nombanjana. Similarly, she could not tell the number of cattle she had in the village currently.

The fact that some landholders thought the cattle belongs to WIPHOLD indicates a lack of information among the landholders about the partnership. A central issue is the nature of the agreements between the parties involved in the agricultural initiative. The regional director declared the existence of a contract between the DRDAR and WIPHOLD to help the landholders plough and plant crops in Centane, including Nombanjana.[6] This was confirmed in a multi-stakeholder meeting held on 9 October 2018 between the executive mayor of Mnquma, the regional director and the concerned landholders of Nombanjana and other surrounding villages. Loyiso Mpalantshane (2018) of the Mnquma Municipality confirms the agreement between WIPHOLD and the DRDAR:

> As part of implementing the Agricultural Economic Transformation Strategy aimed at commercialising agriculture production, creating jobs through partnerships with farmers and commodity groups to upscale production, maize was planted on about 2,000 hectares through a partnership between the department and [a] black women-owned investment company, Women Investment Portfolio Holdings (WIPHOLD) and DRDAR. About 22,038 farmers from 32 villages participated in the programme wherein DRDAR invested R6.4 million to produce maize on 2,000 hectares, with WHIPHOLD investing R20 million.

However, both Serobe and Marsden refute the existence of a contract. According to Marsden, WIPHOLD's involvement in preparing and planting fields is paid through the grant of R3,200 per hectare, which DRDAR provides to each household for these activities. At the same time, there is no signed agreement between WIPHOLD and Serobe, on the one hand, and the landholders, on the other hand. This emerged in a meeting of the concerned landholders on 5 October 2018, who indicated that Serobe had discouraged the drawing of a formal document regarding the partnership between

6 Personal notes of the author taken in the community meeting at Nombanjana on 9 October 2018.

them and WIPHOLD. According to the landholders, Serobe argued that the use of formal documents had led to the loss of land by Africans historically.[7] Marsden confirmed the absence of a formal agreement. Serobe concurred and reiterated her opposition to the use of formal documents in the partnership in our interview with her: 'Precisely because land is a sensitive matter, we decided to make the partnership the isiXhosa way. We act this way so that if I am ordered to get out of the area, I should get out without any hiccups.' According to Serobe, 'The partnership is based on trust.'

The absence of contractual agreements in the partnership is at the centre of the tensions in the agricultural initiative. This ambiguity opens the terms of the partnership to different interpretations, as illustrated in the interview responses. The situation is worsened by the local chief's lack of intervention in problems arising between landholders and WHIPHOLD, despite the landholders calling for his involvement. He is expected to take an active interest in how land development partnerships work in areas under his jurisdiction, but we see an unclear situation regarding land ownership and governance in Nombanjana. This chief's non-interventionist approach contradicts the claims by the leader of the Eastern Cape House of Traditional Leaders, Chief Nonkonyana, about responsible chiefly ownership and governance of land in areas under their jurisdiction.

This case study shows that the dissatisfied landholders in Nombanjana are unable to enforce their land rights. Their unsuccessful attempts to secure the local chief's intervention also points to their lack of clarity about their land rights. They approached the mayor of the Mbashe Local Municipality to intervene in October 2018, but the mayor has not dealt with their concerns. This means that the local chief is the last available option within local authority structures to address their challenges with WHIPHOLD. Lungisile Ntsebeza (2006) makes a similar point with regard to rural residents in the former Xhalanga magisterial district. He points out that the unresolved issue of land governance and allocation in rural areas, combined with the failures of

7 Personal notes of the author take in the meeting of the concerned landholders on 5 October 2018.

local government to deliver on their promises, forces the residents to turn to traditional authorities for assistance. Because the local chief in Nombanjana has not intervened, the issue of land administration is in a state of flux.

The Food and Agriculture Organization (2002) shows a close correlation between secure tenure and the ability of people to protect their land rights:

> In many cases, responses to concerns of environmental sustainability, social conflicts, and food security of the vulnerable are affected by land tenure and have an impact on land tenure … In some cases, it may even worsen the situation, for example by inadvertently dispossessing people of their rights to land.

The experience of the Xolobeni landholders in Mbizana shows that landholders strongly identify with the land if local traditional authorities acknowledge the community members' land rights. This example also shows preparedness of the landholders to defend their land from outsiders, such as the Xolobeni Mine Sands Project, which seeks to mine titanium along the Wild Coast (see Ledwaba, 2019). The views of a female community member expressed during a meeting in Xolobeni epitomises this point: 'My tears won't fall on the ground for nothing. You can bring your machine guns. I am prepared to die for my land; I am not going anywhere' (*Mail & Guardian*, 2016). The residents of Xolobeni know that they control their land, hence their ability to protect it from outside interests, such as the mining companies. A 23-year-old member of the community captures what land means to him (*Mail&Guardian*, 2016).

> I am a black man, fourth generation of the Pondo tribe; my umbilical cord is here. For 23 years the only life I know is here in Amadiba. I feel the land belongs to me. It should not be assumed because I am a new generation, I want to change my way of life. Traditional healers from the area use the trees to cure our ailments; we have cemeteries at home where we worship our ancestors.

These powerful statements illustrate the deeper meanings associated with land in the Xolobeni community. Some residents state that they are prepared to sacrifice their lives in defending community land rights. Landholders of Nombanjana do not show a similar passion. Instead, they expect their chief to intervene and resolve their land disputes with WIPHOLD. This approach reflects one main challenge affecting communal tenure: a flawed perception that traditional authorities own the land and rural citizens' land rights are subject to this authority.

CONCLUSION

This chapter shows how the continued perception that traditional authorities own the land in rural areas, negatively affects the identities and livelihoods of rural residents. In the Nombanjana case study, unresolved land tenure causes confusion and creates an ambiguous state of governance, with the local chief adopting a hands-off approach. The landholders in this area expect the chief's intervention because they believe traditional authorities own the land in communal areas. This confused state of land governance creates opportunities for outside agents and individuals to exploit the situation in their favour.

Additionally, the forceful approach and attitude of the leaders of traditional authorities at a provincial level and the non-partisan attitude of the local authority exacerbates the situation for the landholders, leaving them unable to protect their land rights. Claims by some traditional authorities about their ownership of communal land, which is supported by various politicians and government officials, creates uncertainty among rural residents about their rights to the land they utilise – as seen in Nombanjana, where citizens' relationship with the land is weakened.

The challenges highlighted in Nombanjana point to the importance of formal agreements. It shows the dangers of basing land transactions on trust. Even though the representatives of WIPHOLD indicated that there had been regular meetings with village committees and the communities, it is clear that there was an information gap between the company and the landholders. This lack of clarity about the terms of the agreement has resulted in the disagreements and dissatisfaction of the landholders. It is clear that a formal document, capturing the terms of the agreement, is needed in the partnership in Nombanjana.

Lastly, the government needs to resolve the issue of tenure in areas under the jurisdiction of traditional authorities. To avoid the confusion outlined in this chapter, the government needs to make it clear that the ownership of land in communal areas is vested in the landholders and not the traditional authorities, and it needs to assure the landholders of their tenure. As shown in the case of Xolobeni, under the leadership of the Amadiba Crisis Committee, where the local chief acknowledges that the ownership of land rests with the residents, the landholders are more likely to protect their land.

REFERENCES

Adams, M., Cousins, B. and Manona, S. 1999a. 'Land tenure and economic development in rural South Africa: Constraints and opportunities'. Working Paper No. 125, Overseas Development Institute, http://dlc.dlib.indiana.edu/dlc/bitstream/handle/10535/4077/Adams%26Cousins-et_al-land_tenure_and_economic_development_in_rural_south_africa_costraints_and_opportunities.pdf?sequence=1, accessed 20 August 2020.

Adams, M., Sibanda, S. and Turner, S. 1999b. 'Land tenure reform and rural livelihoods in southern Africa'. *Natural Resource Perspectives*, No. 39, Overseas Development Institute, https://www.odi.org/sites/odi.org.uk/files/odi-assets/publications-opinion-files/2883.pdf, accessed 20 July 2020.

Africa Research Institute. 2016. 'Land, law and traditional leadership in South Africa'. Africa Research Institute, https://www.africaresearchinstitute.org/newsite/publications/briefing-notes/land-law-and-traditional-leadership-in-south-africa/, accessed 3 August 2020.

Amathole District Municipality. n.d. 'Amathole District Municipality farming co-operatives to receive major boost with the handover of tractors from Department of Rural Development and Land Reform', http://www.amathole.gov.za/index.php/portfolio/843-adm-farming-co-operatives-to-receive-major-boost-with-the-handover-of-tractors-from-department-of-rural-development-and-land-reform, accessed 12 March 2019.

Brandt, F. and Mkodzongi, G. 2018. 'Revisiting South Africa's land reform and agrarian questions', in Brandt, F. and Mkondzongi, G. (eds.) 2018. *Land Reform Revisited: Democracy, state making and agrarian transformation in post-apartheid South Africa*. Leiden: Brill, 17–37.

Bruchhausen, S. and Naicker, C. 2018. 'Broadening conceptions of democracy and citizenship: The subaltern histories of rural resistance in Mpondoland and Marikana', in Brandt, F. and Mkondzongi, G. (eds.) *Land Reform Revisited: Democracy, state making and agrarian transformation in post-apartheid South Africa*. Leiden: Brill, 4–17.

Burns-Ncamashe, Z. 14 May 2016. 'African royalty must lead as change agents, says Zolile Burns-Ncamashe'. *Daily Dispatch*, https://www.dispatchlive.co.za/news/opinion/2016-05-14-african-royalty-must-lead-as-change-agents-says-zolile-burns-ncamashe/, accessed 4 June 2020.

Buthelezi, M., Skosana, D. and Vale, B. 2019. 'Collisions, collusions and coalescences: New takes on traditional leadership in democratic South Africa: An introduction', in Buthelezi, M., Skosana, D. and Vale, B. (eds.) *Traditional Leaders in a Democracy: Resources, respect and resistance*. Johannesburg: MISTRA, 1–20.

Claassens, A. 2019. 'Mining magnates and traditional leaders: The role of law in elevating elite interests and deepening exclusion, 2008–2018', in Buthelezi, M., Skosana, D. and Vale, B. (eds.) *Traditional Leaders in a Democracy: Resources, respect and resistance*. Johannesburg: MISTRA, 51–75.

Claassens, A., Clark, M., Dasnois, A., De Souza, M. and Duda, T. 2016. 'Rural land justice'. *People's Law Journal* (Special edition). Land and Accountability Research Centre, http://www.larc.uct.ac.za/sites/default/files/image_tool/images/347/NewsStories/Peoples-Law-Journal-vol-IV-Digital-2.pdf, accessed 20 July 2020.

Department of Rural Development and Land Reform. 2014. 'Communal land tenure policy framework', http://www.rebosa.co.za/wpcontent/uploads/2014/09/Communal_Land_Tenure_Policy_Framework.pdf, accessed 4 June 2020.

Food and Agriculture Organization. 2002. 'Land tenure and rural development'. Land Tenure Studies No. 3, http://www.fao.org/3/a-y4307e.pdf, accessed 13 March 2020.

Heimann, C. 2017. 'Towards inclusive economic development: Agri-parks programme as a response'. Presentation at the National Local Economic Development Conference, Pretoria, http://www.cogta.gov.za/cgta_2016/wp-content/uploads/2017/11/Clinton.Heimann.Agri-Parks-LED-Conference-9-November-2017.pdf, accessed 20 July 2020.

Holomisa, P. 6 June 2018. 'Communal land is private property'. *Daily Dispatch*, https://www.pressreader.com/south-africa/daily-dispatch/20180606/281681140568610, accessed 4 June 2020.

Human Rights Commission. 2018. 'Report on the high level public inquiry on the impact of rural land use and ownership patterns on human rights', https://www.sahrc.org.za/home/21/files/SAHRC%20Land%20Hearing%20Report%20FINAL%20WEB%20READY.pdf, accessed 1 May 2020.

James, D. 2013. 'Citizenship and land in South Africa: From rights to responsibilities'. *Critique of Anthropology*, 33 (1), 26–46.

Jones, E. and Gaventa, J. 2002. 'Concepts of citizenship: A review'. Development Bibliography No. 19, Institute of Development Studies, Brighton, https://opendocs.ids.ac.uk/opendocs/bitstream/handle/20.500.12413/12081/Db19.pdf?sequence=1&isAllowed=y, accessed 28 August 2020.

Lamani, L. 31 January 2020. 'Land reform: EC House of Traditional Leaders back amaZulu king'. *eNCA*, https://www.msn.com/en-za/news/national/land-reform-ec-house-of-traditional-leaders-back-amazulu-king/ar-BBZwqhN, accessed 21 February 2020.

Ledwaba, L. 14 February 2019. 'Xolobeni judders as mining hovers'. *Mail&Guardian,* https://mg.co.za/article/2019-02-15-00-xolobeni-judders-as-mining-hovers/, accessed 21 July 2020.

Lund, C. 2011. 'Land rights and citizenship in Africa'. Discussion Paper No. 65, Nordiska Afrikainstitutet, Uppsala, http://nai.diva-portal.org/smash/get/diva2:460067/FULLTEXT01.pdf, accessed 20 July 2020.

Mail&Guardian. 12 February 2016. 'We will die for our land, say angry Xolobeni villagers as dune mining looms'. *Mail&Guardian*, https://mg.co.za/article/2016-02-12-we-will-die-for-our-land-say-angry-xolobeni-villagers-as-dune-mining-looms-1/, accessed 29 March 2020.

Mnwana, S. 2019. 'Chiefs, land and distributive struggles on the platinum belt, South Africa', in Buthelezi, M., Skosana, D. and Vale, B. (eds.) *Traditional Leaders in a Democracy: Resources, respect and resistance*. Johannesburg: MISTRA, 128–152.

Mpalantshane, L. 2018. 'Centane reaps fruits of hard labour', http://www.mnquma.gov.za/NewsView.aspx?pageid=130&id=33, accessed 4 June 2020.

Mvenene, J. 2014. 'A social and economic history of the African people of Gcalekaland, 1830–1913'. *Historia,* 59 (1), 59–71.

Ncapayi, F. 10 July 2018. 'Who owns land in South Africa's communal areas?'. *Daily Dispatch*, https://www.dispatchlive.co.za/news/opinion/2018-07-09-opinion--motlanthes-finding-on-rural-land-is-correct/, accessed 4 June 2020.

Ngcukana, L. 18 May 2015. 'Land focus: Community makes mealie magic'. *City Press,* https://city-press.news24.com/News/Land-Focus-Community-makes-mealie-magic-20150518, accessed 4 June 2020.

Nhlapho Commission. 2014. 'Determination on amaRharhabe and amaGcaleka paramountcies', https://www.gov.za/sites/default/files/gcis_document/201409/determinaion-amarharhabe-and-amagcaleka-paramountcies.pdf, accessed 29 July 2020.

Ntsebeza, L. 2006. *Democracy Compromised: Chiefs and the politics of land in South Africa*. Leiden: Brill.

Ntshoko, H. March 2019. 'Concerns of residents of the Nombanjana village against Mrs Gloria Serobe'. Unpublished statement written for the Legal

Resources Centre.
Phillips, L. 19 July 2015. 'Private-sector help for an impoverished community'. *Farmer's Weekly*, https://www.farmersweekly.co.za/agri-business/empowerment/private-sector-help-for-an-impoverished-community/, accessed 3 August 2020.
Pinyana, N. 2008. 'Launch of a public–private partnership at Centane Thusong Service Centre'. Centane Thusong Service Centre (Eastern Cape), http://www.thusong,gov.za/news/success/centane.htm, accessed 6 March 2019.
WIPHOLD. 2017a. 'Agri initiative boosts Eastern Cape rural economy', https://www.wiphold.com/Home/AgriInitiative, accessed 23 February 2020.
WIPHOLD. 2017b. 'Centane and Mbashe agricultural initiative', https://www.wiphold.com/assets/docs/WIPHOLD%20Centane%20Mbashe%20Agricultural%20Initiative%20Case%20Study.pdf, accessed 23 February 2020.
Yeni, S. 2019. 'Traditional leadership, violation of land rights and resistance from below in Makhasaneni village, KwaZulu-Natal', in Buthelezi, M., Skosana, D. and Vale, B. (eds.) *Traditional Leaders in a Democracy: Resources, respect and resistance.* Johannesburg: MISTRA, 129–153.
Zuma, J. 2017. 'Opening of National House of Traditional Leaders: Address by President Jacob Zuma', https://pmg.org.za/page/Opening%20of%20National?via=homepage-feature-card, accessed 24 February 2020.

Legislation

Communal Property Association Act (No. 28 of 1996).
KwaZulu-Natal Ingonyama Trust Act (No. 3KZ of 1994).
Traditional and Khoisan Leadership Act (No. 3 of 2019).

Case

Baleni and Others v. Minister of Mineral Resources and Others (2016) 73768/2016.

Interviews

Ms Marsden, D. 28 May 2020. Interview with author, Eastern Cape.
Mrs Mdukiswa, 4 October 2018. Interview with author, Nombanjana.
Mr Mgcadiya, 4 October 2018. Interview with author, Nombanjana.
Mrs Serobe, 1 June 2020. Interview with author, Eastern Cape.

FIVE

Magic Mountain: The spiritual meaning of land to South Africa's rural dispossessed, past and present

DAVID COPLAN AND
KEARABETSWE MOOPELO

INTRODUCTION

In the south-west of the province of Limpopo in South Africa, there is a crescent-shaped ridge of rounded, verdant mountains, rising above the montane grasslands, yet of a human scale and supportive of occupation and productive purpose. To varying degrees, many of the mountains in this region contain major deposits of iron ore. Since at least the 16th century, local inhabitants have smelted iron ore, dug with hand tools from the mountain slopes, to forge tools, weapons of war and the hunt, ornaments, symbols of political rank, and artefacts of sacred ritual often used in Batswana and Bapedi 'cleromancy' or divination (Leslie and Maggs, 2000; Huffman, 2007).

At the base of Meletse (place of waters) Mountain, the tallest peak in this range, is a rugged, winding cave known as Madimatle, which penetrates deep into the interior. Mountains and caves have played an important role in the history of group interaction in South Africa, both peaceful and violent. The mountains and the caves on their slopes have provided refuges and rallying points for both people and domestic animals under attack during the many wars of the 18th and 19th centuries, which involved both African and European invaders. This explains why traditional healers and African Christian 'prophets' who conduct ceremonies of healing at Madimatle, spoke to us, the authors, of honouring the graves of the ancestors who had died on the mountain, whether or not there are actual known graves there.

The spirits of great chiefs and their diviners, who rallied their people in times of conflict, are still believed to inhabit the vastness of certain caves and mountains. This makes these mountain caves 'sacred' (inhabited by the presence of the divine and, therefore, deserving of veneration) and constitutive of the present collective identity of their descendants. It is the 'blood' of legendary ancestors that gives power, solace and meaning to African communities and to traditional health practitioners, who revere Madimatle. Its significance is due partly to the history of conquest and its loss to the white invaders. The name Madimatle means 'beautiful, or royal blood', and refers to the blood that was shed on the mountain by ancestors who died in the caves and on the hills during times of war, including colonial raids in the 19th century.

This chapter is admittedly a departure from the conventional study, as it is an account of the authors' roles as expert consultants in an ongoing legal case, and not an academic project. As such, we seek to provide an alternative perspective and a different form of narrative altogether from a research study, in the hope of enriching the broader understanding of what the loss of their land has *meant,* in the deepest sense, to community in this area.

Mining companies have had a licence since 2014 to construct an opencast iron mine that would remove the upper 40 per cent of the mountain. Local interests, which we shall discuss, have for the past six years carried forward a legal effort to prevent mining and preserve the peak. The case, presented before the South African Heritage Resources Agency (SAHRA), is based on the identity of the cave and adjacent mountain as a site sacred to, and preserving the heritage of, the people and practitioners of indigenous African religion of the Bakgatla ba Bagkafela, a Setswana-speaking people, and their neighbours.

Our research has been both documentary and ethnographic in method, which was specifically in line with the wishes of our clients and the requirements of SAHRA. Archival, scholarly and even popular media sources are, of course, essential in providing the context and facts to support our case. Ethnography was the only viable choice among methods for study in the field. The people and communities to whom the cave and mountain are sacred have been approached many times by agents of the mining companies, their opponents, experts and 'interested parties' of many kinds. They are suspicious of 'researchers' and 'Greeks bearing gifts' and are worried about somehow making difficulties for themselves. Only long hours spent in their company, at their homes and speaking their languages could persuade them at length to share their genuine experiences and views.

The people engaged ('interviewed' is rather too formal or structured) include those who grew up in the immediate area, with ancestral graves on the mountain, those who work on the land within the mining right or close by, and those dispossessed and removed to neighbouring townships and settlements by the closure of other nearby mines and by the mining company involved in the present case. Additionally, we spoke at length to traditional healers, diviners and African Christian clergy (prophets) who practise their medical and religious rites at or around the cave. All have been and will be profoundly affected by the plans to mine the mountain. We are grateful for the trust they ultimately extended to us during our visits in August 2019 and June to July 2020.

In presenting this case, we must acknowledge that standards in legal anthropology call for case-based evidence: citations, references, actual quotations from litigants, witnesses and from the judgment, all of which clarify the reasoning and argumentation, as well as the processes and problematics. Currently, our account cannot simply present evidence submitted in the case, due to the requirements of confidentiality and the fact that the litigation of this case is currently before SAHRA and the courts for final determination. We do not wish to prejudice the status of SAHRA's process or of long-standing court proceedings. Those who spoke to us trusted our assurances that no negative personal consequences would result from their testimony and cooperation. Nevertheless, we argue that the case should be presented here while it is still topical, and while the immediate issues it illustrates are hotly contested in the domain of law and society in South Africa. This explains why our chapter is admittedly more essay than article, and reliant on our own compressed narrative, summations and interpretations. We offer it to readers only for what it may be worth to them.

Our objectives then are first to argue for the protection of the cave and mountain from destruction by mining; and second, to bring into the debates over land a first-hand expression of the meaning of lost land. It is drawn from spiritual and culturally philosophical views held by black South Africans who are landless but lifetime residents of the district. The body of the chapter is an explanation of what our interlocutors meant by the 'sacredness' of the cave and mountain, and a narrative account of how these concepts of religious value, as protected in the Constitution, have been deployed or disputed in this case. Lastly, we argue that this religious or spiritual value must be considered in the legal sector as an important part of once landed but now landless people's fervent desire to re-establish their rights to, and material embeddedness in, this historical patrimony.

TECHNICIANS OF THE SACRED

Our field research, following that of Chris van Vuuren (2014; 2019), documents how traditional healers (Setswana: *dingaka*) and, more recently, Afro-Christian pilgrims and prophets have come to regard such caves and the mountains that 'guard' them as abodes of the ancestors, or meeting points between living and ancestral worlds. Citizens who suffer from a host of misfortunes consult there with healers and prophets. These clairvoyants direct them, through dreams and divination, to seek holistic restoration through rituals, medicines, sacred waters, holes and caves that connect to the subterranean 'villages' of the ancestors. Furthermore, caves in Setswana folk stories are said to be sites where creation took place, where the god of creation,

Modimo, emerged with the Batswana people and brought them to this world of the living as we know it (Malebye, 1997). Ancient tales about mountains transmogrified into living giants are now, with the revitalised longing for the 'lost' land in the post-apartheid period, told with a special longing to return to the caves (Malebye, 1997). 'Mountains are viewed as meeting points between the visible and the invisible worlds, and between heaven and earth' (Matsepe and Madise, 2005: 361). These spiritual as well as social connections are vitally at issue in the role of mines and mining in the context of colonial and, indeed, postcolonial dispossession. Anything that interferes with natural places evokes resentment and may produce a hostile reaction from the people concerned. Whatever takes place on the mountain or in the cave has special meaning to the people participating in those rituals and holding such beliefs.

The independent or indigenous African churches that worship at Madimatle combine a continued faith in their ancestors with a belief in the blessed working of an almighty God. As David Chidester describes it, indigenous African Christianity involves 'complex strategic negotiations in which symbolic forms are formulated, appropriated, manipulated, and mobilized to carve out a human identity and a place for that human to stand and to act as a human being' (cited in Masondo, 2014: 1).

Theologian and biblical scholar Itumeleng Mosala, in commenting on the topic of reconciliation, points out that Africans were not 'alienated' from white people but rather from their land, their livestock and themselves. The indigenous churches, therefore, provide an avenue for African self-definition by highlighting what is good about being African and inculcating a sense of pride in that identity (Mosala, 1985). For philosopher Gabriel Setiloane, land is holy property, as it does not belong to any individual but to the ancestors. Even chiefs do not own the land but are trustees who distribute it to people in order for them to be able to make a living (Setiloane, 1991: 32). Land is not considered wealth as is livestock since no one can possess it and exclude others within the polity from benefiting from its fruits. Prior to colonial expropriation, even the loss of territory through armed attack and expulsion by more powerful neighbours did not end this sense of group identification. People's ancestral land still 'belonged' to them through their ancestors.

In urban black townships, people may not know the names and histories of their families beyond their grandparents. This is why sacred cave shrines such as Madimatle have special settings reserved for the divination of the celebrants' family tree, lineage, clan names and praises (see Coplan, 2003). Today, Madimatle is a resource for people whose roots in the land and its associated culture were torn out by colonial and apartheid dispossession. 'The place is not sacred purely because it is a mountain, but rather for its rich history,' explains Bakgatla ba Bakgafela community elder and activist, Grace Masuku. 'In my culture, if a person wants to destroy you, they only need to destroy your roots, and thus your identity is destroyed,' Masuku explains. 'Without your identity, you simply have no value as a person. Once our identity is lost and our ancestors have retreated, we shall no longer enjoy protection by the ancestors. This is frightening' (Masuku quoted in Bega, 2015).

In a more fundamental sense, we must consider what sites such as Madimatle and its associated mountain, called Meletse, mean for the cohesive self-definition of the local community. At some sacred sites in South Africa, such as the famous Mautse, Matuoleng and Modderpoort caves and mountains in the Free State, 'ownership' is ascribed to the ancestors and, by extension, to the religious communities who perform rituals and healing at the sites (Coplan, 2003). This is not so much a formal or legal 'land claim' as an attempt to replant the uprooted roots of historically resident, indigenous communities or polities in the land. It is this 'identity function' that makes sites such as Madimatle the only appropriate location to practise ancestral rituals, apart from family homes.

Struggles over conquest, exclusion and appropriation are thus intrinsic to sacred space (Chidester, 1994: 229). The conquerors can erase sacredness, but the former inhabitants and holders of the land will continue to claim and retain it from a position of decentred exile. Sacred sites such as Madimatle are vectors of disalienation, particularly important in 21st-century South Africa, where historically and socially grounded perceptions of alienation from the land are so prevalent and powerful. Sacredness is thus about power relations and the sacred site is a place where one is truly 'at home' in this world, as well as in the previous one, and the next (Chidester, 1994: 226–229). Deeply involved in these power relations is the problematic role of government, specifically the national and provincial mining authorities, which in this case issued mining licences to outside companies without consultation with the local black communities (see chapters 3 and 4 in this volume). At Meletse Mountain, a central vector of the underlying conflict is that between broad-based black economic empowerment (BBBEE) imperatives, which favour the interests of an already empowered elite, above those of these local communities. There is a lack of policy coherence and failure to recognise indigenous, cultural, intangible knowledge within our formal systems of law and policy-making (Tlale, 2020). Just who is being empowered, and how does this imbalance affect the vital relationship between South African people and the land?

GODS OF IRON

The mountain that is our subject conceals many millions of tons of iron ore beneath its summit. Until 2014, the mountain was the legal property of local Afrikaner farmers, whose forebears had expropriated the area from Batswana clans during the 19th century. But the mountain is not suited for cultivation or stock-raising, and it was left to shelter workers on the farms, small farmers who gardened at its base and many species of wild game. The two farms within which the mountain and its cave are situated were ultimately sold to an Australian mining company. Application for a mining licence was made to the provincial authorities and prospecting began in 2014. Ultimately, the plan projected the total removal of the upper 40 per cent of the peak by means of opencast mining (Shangoni Management Services, 2014). This plan was not without precedent. Only 30 kilometres away stood the iron mining town of Thabazimbi, where a similar opencast mine had been in operation for 84 years. Then in 2015, the collapse of the main retaining wall sent an avalanche of debris down into the outskirts of the town below. The mine was closed and sold as a loss, 1,160 miners were retrenched, and none of the promises to rehabilitate the landscape were ever kept. We have visited Thabazimbi, and we can testify that the site is an appalling disaster, and the future of the town of 26,000 people is in doubt (*Die* Kwêvoël, 2015). Recently, ArcelorMittal, which bought the mine for a nominal sum, has reconsidered reopening some operations at Thabazimbi. This latest investment may not improve the employment prospects of local people since the majority of the mine workers were migrants brought in from mining operations in other parts of the country (Shangoni Management Services, 2014; Seccombe, 2018).

Returning to our own case, local land and business owners began efforts to oppose the construction of the mine as soon as prospecting and feasibility operations became evident on the mountain in 2014. Indeed, the mining company commissioned socio-economic and environmental impact studies, and met with representatives of local businesses (Shangoni Management Services, 2014). But local residents from the area presented other concerns, which fall outside these regulatory compliance investigations. They complained that the sacred cave site would be compromised or even destroyed by mining operations. The mine, they argued, would destroy Madimatle Cave as a centre for herbal, religious, ceremonial and divinatory ritual, involving direct communication with the spirits of the ancestors. These residents highlighted that healers take their patients there for treatment, with herbal medicines gathered from the mountain slopes. And prophets or pastors visit the sacred site regularly with their followers for days of prayer and ceremony. Unaffiliated individuals also use Madimatle for healing, supplication and communication with the ancestors.

Additionally, the healers, prophets and their legal advisers argued that the noise, heavy lorry traffic, pollution, waste processing, storage and other mining-related construction work would make the cave unusable, while destroying its sacred atmosphere and status. The ancestors, who were said to occupy an entire village underneath the mountain and cave, would not be able to communicate with their living descendants and would be driven away from the site. Activists from within the Bakgafela chieftaincy, within whose district the mountain and cave were located, stated that the cave was sacred for religious beliefs, historical rootedness and cultural identity. The caves and mountains are historically significant sites for supplication. Indigenous communities used these locations to ask for favours, such as rain for their crops and livestock, fertility and regeneration among the people (Bega, 2015).

The chiefs testified that disturbing the physical or even non-physical environment of the cave would destroy its usefulness and status, its sacrality. It would 'suffocate' sounds of the ancestors' villages. There would be no privacy for the healers, and herbal medicine plants would be destroyed (Van Vuuren, 2014: 11–12). Words and phrases such as terrified, hopelessness, 'destroying our soul' and losing identity were used to describe the future dangers of mining activity at these sacred sites. These included the likelihood of forced entry by disgruntled pilgrims once access has – inevitably, informants thought – been physically closed off. The Traditional Healers Organisation (THO) argued that mining the mountain would cause 'spiritual genocide', since the umbilical link between the landmark mountain and its intricate cave system – and the wildlife they support – hold 'special healing power' (THO, 2014).

Pauline Maomi, a professional healer, says the mountain heals and provides herbal medicines and sacred water, both used in healing, hence the name for the mountain, Meletse. Understandably, she is, like other healers, worried about being put out of business by the mine. She says God (Modimo) is on the mountain and will attack the mine. She is one of many commentators who believe that restrictions on entry and the eventual construction of the mine will cause natural disasters, injuries and deaths among the mine workers. As her colleague Bernard Msomi commented, 'We need the mountain because no one else helps the people' (THO, 2014). This prescient observation points to the reality that, if they wish to protect Meletse, local black communities have no alternative course of action but to petition SAHRA to declare the mountain an official heritage site.

Organisations such as the THO, the Kara Heritage Institute, African church prophets and social advocates like Grace Masuku of the Bakgala ba Bakgafela, filed a suit against the Australian mining company for violating constitutional and legislative protections regulating religious rights and cultural heritage. The Australian investors were not prepared for the costly delay and negative publicity, and they subsequently sold the mine site to a local black empowerment consortium, with black ownership and management. The province approved licences for prospecting and feasibility work. The new owners, however, had not reckoned with a range of well-resourced local business interests. These interests opposed the construction of the mine, and the resources they could deploy were formidable and diverse.

In the original court application to interdict the mine, the mining company argued in reply that the cave was a full three kilometres distant from the mining site, that the mountain itself could not be shown to have any sacred or religious status in connection to the cave, and that, if necessary, the cave site could be sequestered and protected from damage or interference from mining operations. Many millions of rand were at stake. The company argued that the local population stood to gain employment and that government would make significant revenues. Business, including tourism, would supposedly thrive. Black empowerment goals would be furthered, and 'development' would arrive, bringing a better life for all.

The THO, and other interested parties supporting them, engaged one of Johannesburg's most prominent law firms to submit an application before SAHRA for the protection of the cave and the mountain as a recognised national heritage site for its religious and cultural significance. The mining company hired an equally large and prestigious firm to oppose them. Even a short, superficial visit to the area makes apparent the destruction that an iron mine, involving the removal of the upper half of the mountain, would cause. The nominators argued that the natural beauty and tranquillity of the mountain chain and valley would disappear, the surrounding ecology would be destroyed, local residents would be forcibly removed, wild game would be driven out, water sources, the land and the air would be polluted, the tourism industry would be ruined, and landscape rehabilitation would never be implemented. Not least, the mine would make religious activity and sanctuary impossible.

The disappearance of the peak as a beacon, the noise, the dust, the mountain roads and erosion of the lower slopes, the destruction of the vegetation, the processing and waste management activity: all would turn the sacred into the appallingly profane. Business and landowners are not mentioned as applicants in the case. Instead, it is the disempowered traditional healers, prophets and pilgrims who are formally pitted against the politically and financially empowered black corporate sector and government. That said, our investigations lead us to argue that this is a case of local people, both black and white, with local common interests, uniting to protect their land and its inherent value from the earth mover of outside interests that would lay waste to it.

Revealingly, the National Heritage Resources Act (NHRA No. 25 of 1999), under which SAHRA operates, contains no definition of the concept of the 'sacred'. Indeed, SAHRA's own mission statement and associated publications make no mention of the sacred either. Instead, both emphasise the notion of 'heritage'. With relevance to Madimatle, the NHRA only notes: (1) places; (2) oral traditions; (3) living heritage; (4) landscapes of cultural significance; (5) importance in the community; (6) understanding of South Africa's cultural heritage; and (7) strong association with a particular community or cultural group (Van Vuuren, 2014: 13).

The Constitution protects freedom of religious practice and both tangible and 'intangible' cultural heritage in South Africa. The NHRA is the enabling legislation specifying these protections. In addition, the Recognition of Traditional Marriages Act (No. 120 of 1998) and other legislation imply, more broadly, the equality of African law and custom and the existing corpus of civil law. Yet, however difficult to define, specify and institute in practice, heritage and its rights and protections are paid far more than lip service in a country that is especially sensitive to the wholesale dismissal of traditional law and the dispossession of millions of black South Africans decreed by colonial and apartheid laws prior to the 1990s.

Since the democratic transition to majority government, land restitution and reform have remained an important government policy goal and, indeed, an audible emotional political issue in South Africa. The debate over the success, or lack thereof, and even over the proper definition of both restitution and reform efforts, continues. A BBBEE policy was implemented during the administration of President Thabo Mbeki (1999–2008), which had the practical effect of transferring shares in existing JSE-listed companies to black individual entrepreneurs and empowerment consortiums. The institutionalisation of this policy has brought into serious question, the state's commitment to righting past oppression, expropriation and apartheid's destructive reformulation of identity, broadly among ordinary citizens, and not merely among the already 'empowered' officials and clients of the new ruling party. In the domain of traditional and customary law, thought to be a repository of the rightful claims for restitution and upliftment for the disempowered majority, elite empowerment has, in practice, displayed its heavy hand. Further, the lack of specificity in the recognition, promulgation and application of indigenous African law in the post-1994 legislation provides a wide field for legal contestation and for the employment of legal advocates on every side. This is the road that led to our involvement in the Madimatle heritage case as 'expert' authorities, recognised by SAHRA and the courts, on religious and heritage designations.

AFRICAN CUSTOMARY LAW?

With the legal revalorisation of indigenous principles of dispute resolution, there arose the problem of finding a mechanism for ascertaining what had once been, what was and what was not 'traditional' or 'customary' African law. African polities before, parallel to and since the imposition of promulgated colonial law had elaborate legal and bureaucratic systems of justice and adjudication. But their written codification had been undertaken only under the colonial government and tended strongly to institutionalise colonial policy and principles of overrule. Many issues more domestic to African community life and law were not codified but left in the official limbo of oral contestation. Since 1994 as well, there have been widespread efforts to contest colonial and apartheid-era laws, rulings and precedents. Among these, in many instances, are cases of legal marriage and divorce, descent, inheritance, succession to high office, chieftaincy, land tenure and, most recently, religious freedom and protection of sometimes inchoate 'heritage'.

In our present case, the mining company commissioned a lengthy report by independent consultants (Shangoni Management Services, 2014), which included a section by a senior anthropologist, to research the cultural and heritage value of the cave and mountain, and its relevance to African users and residents. The company hoped to use the anthropologist's findings to argue that the mine would not destroy the cave shrine or make it unusable. Further, they wanted support for their contention that the mountain to be mined had no religious, heritage or ecological connection to the cave. The anthropologist argued, in his initial report, that the cave shrine was not directly connected to the mountain, and that controlled access, proper oversight and maintenance could protect and facilitate the religious uses of the site. His report also provided copious survey testimony from traditional healers and prophets, and other local residents involved with the shrine (Van Vuuren, 2014). There were other subsidiary reports from an archaeologist and an ecologist (Miller, 2011; Almond, 2012). Ultimately, SAHRA declared that only the cave was a level 2 (provincial) protected site, one that must not be compromised by mining activities. Permission was granted to construct a limited roadway of three kilometres for prospecting and preparation for the mine on the mountain, and the company began physical operations on the slopes.

This result, of course, was not satisfactory to the nominators, the opponents of the mine, whose backers had hoped to secure protected status for the mountain itself. They argued that the planned fencing and controlled entrance to the cave site and the construction of visitor facilities would violate the religious traditions of open access, prohibition of physical modification or commercial development, and absolute tranquillity in which the ancestors could dwell undisturbed. Preventing the mine from removing the mountain was, after all, more the point of the application than preserving the hardly noticeable cave shrine. Legal contestation has continued up to the present, and currently there is a second case pending before SAHRA, seeking level 1 (national and international) protection for the cave and mountain as a unitary religious and heritage site. This time, the opponents of the mine engaged the authors' services to bear expert witness to the violation of religious freedom and the irreparable destruction mining would cause.

INSIGHTS FROM MADIMATLE

As stated earlier, our brief was to refute the arguments and proposals the mining company was making in favour of their application to resume mining on Meletse. Yes, the mine would provide millions of rand in tax revenue and local development, but it would also destroy the natural beauty and ecological system of the entire area. Not only the ancestors but also their descendants would be driven from the land. Indeed, residents whose homesteads were located within the actual mining concession and land now owned by the mining company, had already been removed to a nearby black township, where neither horticulture nor stock-raising is possible. They were not compensated and currently they are without employment (Van Vuuren, 2014: 11–15). Only 446 jobs would be created, while 105 existing posts would likely disappear (Shangoni Management Services, 2014: 179). In violation of the conditions under which prospecting rights had been granted, 11 times the allowed length of exploratory roads had been constructed (33 kilometres), visibly scarring the mountain slopes. The cave shrine had been fenced off from the road, and an entrance gate, albeit unlocked, was constructed. A steel signboard stating rules and conditions for visiting the cave now greeted the pilgrims' arrival. An employee of the new mining company sat near the entrance all day, making visitors write down their personal details, place of origin and reasons for visiting. Knocked down by the new owners, the remains of a brick shed, which had once served as a storage place for healers' paraphernalia, littered the margin.

Among the many documentary sources that we excavated, few were as useful as the first report by our anthropological colleague (Van Vuuren, 2014), and a second report addendum he submitted at the behest of the new owners (Van Vuuren, 2019). He had included not only original informants' testimony, but also expressed his own misgivings about the effect of the mine on the cave shrine, the mountain and the people, who for so many generations had farmed the area before colonial expropriation. The testimony rang out with distress, fear, warning and horror of the cultural destruction, which they believed would be sure to accompany the detonation of explosives, and the cacophony of earth movers and lorries shifting crushed rock and decapitating the landscape forever. The ancestors, as well as their descendants, would be driven from their homes below and above ground and into the wilderness to plot revenge. Community roots would be torn up, identity would be lost, souls destroyed or made vagabond. Sickness and misfortune would reign and plagues descend upon the unknowing miners. The sacred order of nature, established over centuries, would become, quite literally, an unholy mess.

Equally persuasive were the objections to the fencing off and policing of the site, the imposition of rules and regulation, and the proposed facilities for religious tourism. Our colleague had written of these controls and developments as positive, a form of recognition and upgrading. Littering and ecological damage would be controlled, ceremonies would be orderly and uncompetitive, charlatanism challenged, and refreshment and resting places provided. Almost without exception, our colleague's informants objected to these 'improvements'. The shrine should be accessible to all who came, whatever they were seeking. Permission to enter could be granted only by the ancestors and other resident spirits. Only God could say who was a charlatan. The ancestors did not like modification of holy ground by the living and would retreat forever from their supplicants. The cave was among those few sacred places visualised in dreams and prescribed by traditional healers, where sufferers might be 'cured', and where essential personal, family and communal rituals could be carried out. The clearly audible sounds of life from the subterranean villages of the ancestors would cease or be drowned out. Most tellingly, cave and mountain – as at other sacred sites in South Africa – were inseparably linked as an enspirited whole. The mine would permanently destroy the existing game farming and tourism industry in the area. The Shangoni Management Services report had actually stated that the area made 'irredeemable' would include 'the Madimatle Cave hub of the indigenous religious shrine as well as the associated Meletse Mountain within a perimeter of eight kilometres around the mine and beyond'

(Shangoni Management Services, 2014: 178). The cave itself, the report stated, 'would no longer be viable for purposes of praying and connecting to God and the ancestors' (Shangoni Management Services, 2014: 181).

Testimony from Bakgafela residents in the vicinity, which we collected ourselves, was even more telling. One man, who works for the mining company as a caretaker emphasised (TM, 2020):

> Nothing should be forced; it should all take place through the ancestors. Traditionally speaking, you do not abandon the land from which you were born, you in fact notify the land when you leave so as to cut your ties to the land in a conducive manner. People are lost, the ancestors are looking for them and they do not know where their children have gone. This is a serious crisis of identity for a lot of African people everywhere who are not connected to their ancestors. People come here looking to find themselves ... A lot of them do not know their own parents nor their bloodline and they come searching for them here ...
>
> The ancestors must have shown you in a dream while lying on your bed in your home, that you must come and see us here; we have work for you. They will invite you to come to the cave to come collect your blessings, healing and gift of their powers. This place is no joke. When you are divinely ordained to be here your ancestors will pinpoint you out of the crowd, you will hear them call you by your name to say [whistles instructively] 'you come here!' and you will not get lost in there to wherever they lead you within the cave. People who come to communicate with the ancestors in the cave sleep there.

A report for NGT Management Services by heritage specialist Sibongile Masuku (2019) recommends moving and relocating the ancestral graves that we were shown on the slopes of the mountain. Masuku seems to suggest that the ancestors can be removed from their emplacement. This is, in fact, confusing a homestead practice with a remote communal sacred site. She contends that an ancient sanctuary of the ancestors can and should now change location on the basis of the prospective mine. In Setswana religion, homesteads can be moved, but the ancestors residing in their caves and mountains cannot. The ancestors cannot be relocated. One head of a family, who took us to visit their ancestors' graves, explained this religious problematic (JM, 2020):

> This entire land belongs to the ancestors, the mountain and cave are of the same area geographically and spiritually because they are both the dwelling place of the ancestors and they own it. This place is ancestral and has a rich cultural history of our people. They cannot be removed from this place because they choose it; it is theirs and their people, us. The rivers demarcate this area that belongs to *badimo* (ancestors).

This family is still very angry about the loss of their original land rights and forced removal from these lands by the white colonial/apartheid authorities and land speculators. Powerless to gain redress or repossession of their land, they take refuge in stories or predictions of the terrible fates that have befallen – and will befall – anyone who attempts to mine, develop or further 'desecrate' (in their view) these lands of their ancestors.

A member of the independent Zion Christian Church, whom we met with fellow congregants at the cave, was even more forceful (Name withheld, 2020):

> But why is it when it comes to our matters as Africans, we also must justify them for the European outlook? Explain to me why, when one goes to Germany there are places which have been kept in their natural state due to their historical significance and these places attract many tourists. These places are often vacant land that have no developments and you will hear them say this is where the king was killed, or they show the old Catholic church which remains unchanged and undisturbed. Why is it that we have to justify ourselves and change our ways of living or the things we hold dear as heritage and history? In Europe you can still visit the first and oldest buildings; they renovate

them, but they do not change things that are historical to them. Why is our history irrelevant?

Batswana religious belief and practice requires that the natural settings in which the ancestors reside as a place of interaction with their descendants be left unmodified and undisturbed. A religious site of the nature of Madimatle, like the Mautse and Matuoleng caves in the Free State, is incompatible with visits or usage by groups of tourists, nature lovers and hikers, students, or even educators and researchers in any significant numbers, and religious pilgrims to all the sites have often told us so (Coplan, 2003).

CONCLUSION: LAND AND BLACK EMPOWERMENT?

Back in Johannesburg, the CEO of the mining company was making much of the claim that it was 'rich whites' who were behind a grand plan to obstruct black empowerment – in the form of his company – and the economic upliftment of the area and its black, mostly poor and landless population. It must be noted that it is not only the local indigenous community that seeks to defend against the construction of the mine, as land-based business and property owners of diverse racial groups are also collaborating with the healers, prophets and their adherents to prevent the construction of the mine. Black empowerment, be it said, has been famously shown as an often unequally distributed resource. The most famous instance in the domain of mining is, of course, that of the Royal Bafokeng platinum mines near Rustenburg in the North West Province, but that is far from being the only one (Comaroff and Comaroff, 2011). There are many recent cases, such as at Xolobeni in the Eastern Cape, where mining has been successfully (or not) ruled illegal on the basis of non-consultation and exclusion of the affected community members (Mitchley, 2018). This occurs most often through private concessions granted to mining interests by senior traditional leaders, who stand to benefit hugely and improperly from such agreements. The signing into law on 20 November of the Traditional and Khoisan Leadership Act (No. 3 of 2019) demonstrates the backing that the ruling African National Congress is giving this process (Heywood, 2019).

With the black-empowered mine company and revenue-hungry provincial government against the opponents of the mine, they had only SAHRA and, if that appeal failed, the courts to rely on. We argued before SAHRA that, with regard to the land, exploitation, destruction and dispossession have continued over the past 25 years under new political arrangements (Coplan and Moopelo, 2019). How long, we asked rhetorically, would our democratic, constitutional legal system allow this to continue? In other countries, such an argument might not have carried much weight. In South Africa, however, issues of the land – and who has which rights to benefit from it – are of the greatest import. This was demonstrated by the Xolobeni case, where the judgment against the miners threw the Minister of Mineral Resources and Energy into a fury (Matya, 2018).

Amidst the current debate over land reform and even expropriation, there is a widespread yearning that goes far beyond the demand for land for productive purposes (see Chapter 7 in this volume). The African value of *ubuntu-botho* (humanism) includes historical placement in the earth that long precedes claims of material residence and possession (Mazamisa, 1993: 5). Even the loss of territory through armed attack and expulsion, or colonial conquest, did not obliterate this deeper understanding of land. People's ancestral land still 'belonged' to them, they maintained, through their ancestors. That is why it is no coincidence that Basotho sacred sites, including Mautse and Matouleng, are located in the 'conquered territory', lost to the Orange Free State in the wars of the 1860s. At these shrines, the pilgrims' insistence that 'these caves belong to the ancestors' appears to be an unacknowledged strategy for reclaiming the land; the ancestors reconquering their territory when other means are unavailable (Coplan, 2003).

Among Africans, land has not been traditionally conceived as real estate that can be bought and sold (Coplan, 2001, 2003). It is a source of being and a basis of identity because it is where their ancestors are buried. In the KwaZulu-Natal townships, when asked where they come from, people would say, for example: '*Ngokuhlalangise Mlazi, kodwa inkaba yami iseNkandla*', which means: 'I live at Umlazi, but my umbilical cord is at Nkandla' (Silitsena, 1990: 151). The umbilical cord that had tied the baby to its mother now symbolically unites or binds a person to a piece of ground. If this piece of land were sold, it would mean that the person would be rootless. The architects of apartheid understood this, driving black people from their lands and its livelihoods into reserves and 'locations' where they had no connection to the soil. There, like livestock, African people could be herded and kraaled wherever and for whatever purpose the white rulers advanced. Over a century since the infamous Natives Land Act of 1913, such rootlessness remains an obstacle to national and community identification and social improvement.

The rather imprecise concept of black empowerment requires ongoing redefinition and reformulation. Of course, the provincial and national government are most interested in the revenue and development that flow from economic investment in the land and the exploitation of its natural resources. When a black-owned and managed company applies to pursue such an enterprise, it is seen by the wealthier and better-resourced class of society as black empowerment. For the black former peasantry and rural workers, however, so many of whom are landless and unemployed, black-owned enterprise in this form has offered little empowerment. Whether or not the promise of temporary and even longer-term employment for some is fulfilled, we argue here that the longer-term vision of life on the land, which pre-dated dispossession, is of importance in the debate over this crucial issue. To begin with, the existing economy of tourism, game farming and the numerous local businesses does provide a great many jobs for black people in the area of Madimatle. Those jobs will continue to exist in the indefinite future and increase as local tourism in Limpopo increases without the mine. With the mine proposed to operate for only 18 years, the existing local economy will die (Shangoni Management Services, 2014: 179–181). Further, the local economy preserves rather than destroys the natural beauty, tranquillity and cultural heritage of the area. The vaunted spiritual and historical (heritage) value that people placed on the cave and mountain are really a symbolic expression of a longing for re-emplacement and re-identification with the land as home – as a place where one can always claim to belong, with or without a cave. Yet, it is the cave and mountain, in this case, in which the spiritual and emotional attachment to the land is genuinely represented and embodied.

The identification of black people with their places of origin may not mean much to government and mining companies amidst the overriding need for economic development. But we argue that social progress in South Africa must also address the need for rootedness, which has been so severely compromised. It follows that our legal system must determine the role and prominence of African indigenous knowledge systems into the national agenda and identity. These include the right of Africans to perform rituals and cultural practices linked to sites popularly identified as 'sacred'. We argue that the cultural as well as natural environmental rights are part of the restitution equation and merit protection. The activity at sacred sites is a small means available to displaced African people to grow the sense of social rootedness and national common destiny, which colonialism and apartheid systematically destroyed. The Meletse Mountain is just such a site. To allow it to be decapitated and hollowed out would visibly demonstrate a willingness to continue 'selling off' South Africa's patrimony, both tangible and intangible, today, just as it was by an illegitimate governmental and legal system in the past. Protecting Madimatle is one small step towards resolving the land problem in the interests of nation-building. This will remain unstable until there is not only material restitution on the land but also a genuine sense of it among all affected parties. The preservation of the Madimatle sacred site, in line with constitutional rights, will be a step towards this. Lastly, this narrative is a useful contribution, we suggest, to the need to incorporate spiritual, historical and, yes, affective identification with the land, and the demand for landedness among the majority, still-dispossessed black population.

REFERENCES

Almond, J.E. 2012. 'Gatkop Cave on farm Randstephane 415 KQ near Thabazimbi, Limpopo Province'. Palaeontological Assessment: Site Visit Report. Natura Viva, Cape Town.

Bega, S. 17 January 2015. 'Grace Masuku: Our spirituality will move mountains'. *Saturday Star*, https://www.pressreader.com/south-africa/saturday-star-south-africa/20150117/283463549693970, accessed 8 September 2020.

Chidester, D. 1994. 'Sacred space and power', in Tymieniecka, A.T. (ed.) *From the Sacred to the Divine: A new phenomenological approach*. New York: Springer, 214–233.

Comaroff, J.L. and Comaroff, J. 2011. *Ethnicity Inc.* Chicago, IL: University of Chicago Press.

Coplan, D.B. 2001. 'A river runs through it: The meaning of the Lesotho-Free State border'. *African Affairs,* 100 (398), 81–116.

Coplan, D.B. 2003. 'Land from the ancestors : Popular religious pilgrimage along the Lesotho-South African border'. *Journal of Southern African Studies,* 29 (4), 977–993.

Coplan, D.B. and Moopelo, K.I. 2019. 'Report on the sacred site status of Madimatle caves and Meletse Mountain in Thabazimbi district, Limpopo'.

Heywood, M. 29 November 2019. 'The Traditional Khoisan Leadership Bill: President signs away rural people's rights'. *Daily Maverick,* https://www.dailymaverick.co.za/article/2019-11-29-the-traditional-khoisan-leadership-bill-president-signs-away-rural-peoples-rights/amp, accessed 8 September 2020.

Huffman, T.N. 2007. *Handbook of the Iron Age: The archaeology of pre-colonial farming societies in southern Africa.* Pietermaritzburg: University of KwaZulu-Natal Press.

Die Kwêvoël. 18 June 2015. 'Massive slope failure at mine'. Die Kwêvoël, https://www.kwevoel.co.za/2015/06/18/massive-slope-failure-at-mine/, accessed 8 September 2020.

Leslie, M. and Maggs, T. (eds.) 2000. *African Naissance: The Limpopo Valley 1000 years ago*. Goodwin Series, 8. Cape Town: South African Archaeology Society.

Malebye, T.K. 1997. *Madimatle*. Pretoria: J.L. van Schaik.

Masondo, S.T. 2014. 'The African indigenous churches' spiritual resources for democracy and social cohesion'. *Verbum et Ecclesia* 35 (3), 1–8.

Masuku, S. 2019. 'An assessment of the heritage significance of Madimatle Cave and Gatkop Mountain through an environmental and indigenous knowledge lens'. NGT Management Services.

Matsepe, S.S. and Madise, J. S. 2005. 'A new phenomenon in the Zionist churches of Botswana: The use of divination bones and sacred places'. *Studia Historica Ecclesiasticae*, 31 (2), 353–375.

Matya, L. 22 November 2018. 'Mantashe expresses concern at the Xolobeni mining rights judgment'. *SABC News,* https://www.sabcnews.com/sabcnews/mantashe-expresses-concern-at-the-xolobeni-mining-rights-judgment/, accessed 8 September 2020.

Mazamisa, W.L. 1993. '*Umhlaba* and the ethics of reparation'. Paper presented at African Studies Seminar Programme, University of Cape Town.

Miller, S. 2011. '1st phase cultural heritage resources assay for the farms Donkerpoort 448 KQ, Randstephane 455 KQ and Waterval 443 KQ, Thabazimbi, Limpopo Province'. African Heritage Consultants cc,

Magalieskruin.
Mitchley, A. 22 November 2018. 'High Court rules in favour of Xolobeni community in historic mining rights case'. *Mail&Guardian,* https://www.google.com/amp/s/mg.co.za/article/2018-11-22-high-court-rules-in-favour-of-xolobeni-community-in-historic-mining-rights-case/%3Famp, accessed 8 September 2020.
Mosala, I. 1985. 'African Independent Churches: A study of socio-theological protest', in De Gruchy, J.W. and Villa-Vicencio, C. (eds.) *Resistance and Hope: South African essays in honour of Beyers Naudé.* Grand Rapids, MN: W. B. Eerdmans, 103–111.
Seccombe, A. 15 October 2018. 'ArcelorMittal sees strategic value in mothballed Thabazimbi mine: Steelmaker mulls reopening operations after taking full control of the asset'. *Business Live,* https://www.businesslive.co.za/bd/companies/mining/2018-10-15-arcelormittal-sees-strategic-value-in-mothballed-thabazimbi-mine/, accessed 8 September 2020.
Setiloane, G.M. 1991, 'Land in the negotiations chamber: An Afro-centric approach'. *Journal of Black Theology in South Africa,* 5 (2), 29–39.
Shangoni Management Services, 26 March 2014. 'Environmental management programme under the MPRDA, 2002: Locality: Remainder of the farm Donkerpoort 448 KQ and remainder of the farm Randstephne 455 KQ, Thabazimbi, Limpopo'. Pretoria.
Silitsena, R. 1990. 'Impact of colonialism on land use in central and southern Africa', in Olson. P.A. (ed.) *The Struggle for Land: Indigenous insight and industrial empire in the semiarid world.* Lincoln, NE: University of Nebraska Press, 146–170.
Tlale, M.T. 2020. 'Xolobeni: Protecting vulnerable people's land against mineral rights grabs'. *Potchefstroom Electronic Law Journal,* 23, 1–32.
Traditional Healers Organisation (THO). August 2014. 'A statement of significance of Madimatle Mountain'. Annexure S.3.
Van Vuuren, C.J. 2014. 'Cultural heritage of the Madimatla Cave and surrounding area: An anthropological perspective'. Shangoni Management Services, Pretoria.
Van Vuuren, C. J. 2019. 'Summative report on the cultural heritage of Madimatle Cave'. NGT Management Services, Pretoria.

Legislation

National Heritage Resources Act (NHRA, No. 26 of 1999).
Natives Land Act (No. 27 of 1913).
Recognition of Traditional Marriages Act (No. 120 of 1998).

Interviews

TM. 26 June 2020. Interview with author, Madimatle.
JM. 26 June 2020. Interview with author, Madimatle.
Name withheld. 25 June 2020. Interview with author, Madimatle.

Section II

Agrarian Reform and Social justice

SIX

Abafazi Bayazbambela:[1] A gendered response to South Africa's agrarian question

KHWEZI MABASA

INTRODUCTION

South Africa's post-apartheid agrarian reform debates focus mainly on the formal agricultural sector (Bernstein, 1994; Makhaya and Roberts, 2013). The analyses examine the relationship between macroeconomic trends and developments in commercial agriculture, drawing attention to pertinent developmental indicators such as national food security, commodity prices, trade volumes and technological change (Kirsten, 2006; DAFF, 2014; Sihlobo and Kirsten, 2018). Some of the studies explore how state policy shifts since 1994 have altered market structures across the agricultural value chains (Makhaya and Roberts, 2013; Greenberg, 2015). All these themes feature prominently in ongoing public policy debates on land and agrarian reform, which have

1 This is a Zulu phrase used by one of the interview participants to explain that African women can engage in subsistence farming without male or state assistance. The direct translation in English is 'they hold their own'.

influenced the recently published report by the Presidential Advisory Panel on Land Reform and Agriculture (2019).

There are several researched positions on the policy proposals for future developments in formal commercial agriculture, which are well documented elsewhere and will likely shape the future of agrarian relations in South Africa (Greenberg, 2013; Sihlobo and Kirsten, 2018). However, the contributions are limited because they place emphasis on two main approaches in agrarian policy debates: the market-oriented productivist paradigm and the neo-Marxist political economy. The first prioritises market-led interventions, while the second shows that markets are imbued with structural class inequalities. Both approaches present policy solutions that reproduce and overlook gender inequalities in the agrarian political economy. They perpetuate the gendered disparities discussed in feminist agrarian literature in several ways (O'Laughlin, 2007; Razavi, 2011; Park et al., 2013; Tsikata, 2015).

South Africa is the most food secure country on the African continent, with a ranking of 48 out of 113 countries assessed in the Global Food Security Index (2019). The country exports valuable agricultural commodities to different global markets and is lauded for maintaining national food security (TRADE, 2013; Global Food Security Index, 2019). But several reports point out that household food insecurity persists (50 per cent), especially in low-income communities in rural and urban areas (Shisana et al., 2013). The disaggregated data indicate that race, class, gender and spatial development inequalities determine levels of food security (Shisana et al, 2013; Oxfam, 2014). Hunger is most prevalent in black African low-income communities and, in most cases, women experience more food insecurity than male counterparts (Moletsane and Reddy, 2011; Dodson et al., 2012; Oxfam, 2014). This trend raises several important questions regarding the relationship between South Africa's agrarian political economy and food security. For example, why does a country with an industrialised agricultural system fail to feed all its citizens? How does the race-class-gender inequality dynamic influence agrarian relations in post-apartheid South Africa? And, more importantly, what policy interventions are required to transform the country's agrarian structure?

These questions are debated largely within the confines of existing commercial agrarian market structures. I add a slightly different dimension to contemporary debates on agrarian reform in South Africa by examining the experiences of black African women in low-income, peri-urban areas. This gendered approach differs from previous South African agrarian policy debates, which are concerned primarily with transforming race and class power relations. The following discussion addresses this shortcoming by purposefully adopting a gendered analysis.

I argue that South Africa's agrarian development literature and state policies underestimate gender differences. Crucial social reproduction factors, such as the reproductive labour of women, the gendered nature of food insecurity, land access and women-led, informal food production, receive minimal attention. In the post-apartheid era, emphasis has been placed on a limited notion of agrarian transformation that privileges race relations in the commercial sector (Hart, 2008; Hart and Aliber, 2012; Cousins, 2019). This has subsequently led to the preservation of an agrarian structure that reinforces gendered socio-economic inequalities (Walker, 2002). The post-apartheid agrarian political economy favours large-scale commercial farming, dominated by males, as the main source of food security and agrarian development (Sihlobo and Nel, 2016: 66).

This policy bias within the agrarian political economy is gendered because most small-scale subsistence farmers are women (Walker, 2002; O'Laughlin, 2007; CWGL, 2011). Black African women in low-income areas have responded to this structural challenge in dynamic ways, and they still maintain their small-scale food production within this unfavourable policy environment. This farming is a central part of their broader livelihood strategy, which includes several sources of income. The women use these multiple livelihoods strategies to reassert their economic agency and citizenship. This chapter goes further than existing studies on food security, which focus mainly on access to food without interrogating the role of working-class women in food production systems in any depth, and the different meanings associated with participation in agrarian development. These studies ignore the socio-economic value of active, women-led agrarian citizenship.

The chapter commences with a brief description on methodology. I then outline the main arguments presented in gendered analyses of the agrarian question, which illustrate how market-oriented productivist and neo-Marxian critical political economy approaches underestimate gender differences. This shortcoming is discussed using literature from feminist and neo-Marxist agrarian debates. The focus is on small-scale food production and the livelihood strategies employed by African women from low-income communities in peri-urban areas. The chapter conclude with four main policy insights emerging from the literature analysis and fieldwork evidence. Overall, I attempt to address the following core questions:

- What policy lessons can we learn from informal food systems led by women in African low-income communities?
- What forms of women-led, agrarian citizenship and development agency emerge from participating in these informal local food systems?
- How can the state support small-scale localised food systems?

METHODOLOGY

The methodology is based, first, on qualitative research because it places emphasis on comprehending 'social interaction from the perspectives of insiders and participants in the interaction' (Roberts et al., 2003: 49). Qualitative methods are more suitable for exploring research themes from a different perspective, while considering the broader sociological context within which social relations take place (Roberts et al., 2003; Burawoy, 2009). Second, an examination of relevant literature and policy documents on South Africa's agrarian question is used. This includes primary and secondary information obtained from academic articles, state policies, financial media reports and books. Content analysis is important for situating the chapter's discussion within contemporary agrarian public policy debates. It also allows the researcher to compare people's lived experiences with government policy orientation and goals (Roberts et al., 2003: 66).

Third, I use data obtained from interviews conducted with 40 participants between 2017 and 2018 in my ongoing study on South Africa's post-apartheid agrarian question. These semi-structured interviews included both individual and focus group interviews with African women involved in small-scale food production in households and community gardens.

The women reside in Ermelo, which is a peri-urban area situated in Mpumalanga Province. It is part of the Msukaligwa Municipality, which has 164,608 residents. Africans make up 91 per cent of the population, white people 6 per cent, coloured people less than 1 per cent and Indians also less than 1 per cent. Women make up 49 per cent of the total population while males account for 51 per cent (Mskaligwa IDP, 2017: 66) The municipal survey data indicates that women-headed households account for 37 per cent of homes in Msukaligwa (Msukaligwa IDP, 2017: 62). A purposive sampling technique was used to identify the participants. It is suitable because the research theme focuses on the experiences, perceptions and agency of a particular social group (Palys, 2008).

GENDERING THE AGRARIAN QUESTION

Gendered agrarian literature draws our attention to important oversights in market-oriented, productivist and neo-Marxian approaches. These authors agree with market structure and class inequality criticisms raised in neo-Marxist critiques of neoliberal agrarian policies (Hall, 2011; Makhaya and Roberts, 2013; Greenberg, 2015). But they highlight how both approaches focus on a limited conception of social reproduction in agrarian reforms, which pays insufficient attention to gendered social relations underpinning agrarian structural transformation (O'Laughlin, 2007; Razavi, 2011; Park et al., 2013; Tsikata, 2015). The gender dimension is underestimated in historical and contemporary debates on South Africa's agrarian question (Cousins, 2007; Bundy, 1988; Mtero, 2012; O'Meara, 1983). This explains why the contribution of reproductive labour, which supported capitalist development within and outside commercial agriculture, is omitted in this literature (Bradford, 2000; O' Laughlin, 2007; Tsikata, 2015). The unpaid reproductive labour includes child rearing, food preparation, cleaning, home-based healthcare provision and household farming (Bradford, 2000; Razavi, 2011; Cock, 2016).

Shahra Razavi contends that 'the unpaid (non-commodified) provisioning of household members has been invisible to political economists of agrarian change and continues to be invisible in research on livelihoods' (Razavi, 2009: 200). Black African women's agricultural production in South Africa supplemented migrant workers' low wages throughout various historical periods. These women's agrarian agency sustained both informal and formal economies (Wolpe, 1972; Walker, 1982). Cherryl Walker explains this trend: 'As more and more men were sucked into the labour migrant machine, the women left behind came to play an increasingly important part in keeping the subsistence economies of the reserves functioning and, thereby, reproducing the supply of migrant workers' (Walker, 1982: 6).

This statement highlights the importance of factoring black African women's unpaid household labour into South Africa's political economy. It played an essential role in developing both mining and agricultural sectors (Bradford, 2000; Benya, 2015). Belinda Bozzoli's (1991) study, *Women of Phokeng*, also reveals black African women's roles in agricultural production during the early 20th century. Her account details a history of women's participation in agricultural production across different generations (Bozzoli, 1991: 44). One cannot comprehend this trend with an analytical framework that limits social reproduction to formal economy labour relations (Davis, 1981; Collins, 2000). This critique is important for contemporary agrarian policy debates. It widens society's conception of labour when examining the post-apartheid agrarian political economy structure. Agrarian policy-makers are encouraged to observe the historical and contemporary value of black African, women-led, subsistence agriculture and unpaid labour (Razavi, 2009; 2011).

Gendered analyses also criticise the state and market relations reductionism in agrarian studies and policy paradigms (Tsikata, 2015). They argue that existing literature sources reduce agrarian political economy institutional analysis to the national state and markets. This approach has neglected social relations in other institutions that shape resource allocations in agri-food systems. Agrarian feminist writers cite several institutions, such as households, the local state, traditional authorities and community organisations, in their analyses

(O'Laughlin, 2007; Park et al., 2013; Rakolojane, 2015). All these social institutions shape agrarian reforms, but the nature of this influence is determined by the sociological context. They emphasise linking national-level trends to sociological interactions in the local state, households and communities. This approach facilitates a deeper and more meaningful exploration of social relations. Dzodzi Tsikata (2015: 6) defines social relations as:

> the structured and systemic interactions of different social groups and individuals within those groups for production, exchange, consumption and reproduction, which are governed by institutions such as markets, states, civil society and households. The key social relations within the agrarian political economies of sub-Saharan Africa are class, patron–client, gender, kinship and generation, as well as the host–stranger relations of race, nationality and local citizenship.

It is important to emphasise the household in gendered agrarian studies and social relations. Razavi (2009: 200) explains this observation:

> Bringing the domestic arena into the analytical framework thus demands not only that we scrutinise what goes on inside domestic institutions – cooperation and conflict, pooling/sharing and inequality in resource allocation and in the division of unpaid work necessary to sustain the members of the household – but also that we tease out the interconnections between domestic structures and broader economic and political processes.

Most of the data and statistical analysis on agricultural production uses the household as the primary analytical unit (Aliber and Mdoda, 2015; Stats SA, 2020). These studies disaggregate the household information by employing several variables such as geographic location, type of farming, access to water and gender (Stats SA, 2016; 2019). According to Stats SA, 'More than half (52.8 per cent) of the households involved in agricultural activities were headed by women whereas just below a half (47.2 per cent) were headed by males' (Stats

SA, 2019: 10). This statistic informs us that more women-headed households are participating in household agricultural production. But the report does not discuss how this participation is impacted by broader structural factors in the agrarian political economy. It does, however, reveal that most households in the study farm for subsistence or additional income generation. 'The main source of income in these households is social transfers, followed by wages and then lastly farming activity' (Stats SA, 2019: 13).

The Stats SA (2019) report does not provide an in-depth gendered analysis beyond this demographic data. Nonetheless, it is important to note that women-headed households are more susceptible to hunger (Shisano et al., 2013; Oxfam, 2014; Stats SA, 2019). There is no account of the gender dynamics in the male-headed households involved in agriculture. An in-depth gendered view on both types of households is required in agrarian studies. It must place household dynamics within a broader context of social reproduction (Davis, 1981; Collins, 1998). This necessitates a shift in conventional household analyses in food and agrarian policy literature. Households exist within a sociological milieu characterised by unequal social relations based on race, class and gender (Rakolojane, 2015: 144). There are three central policy lessons in this critique on state and market reductionism:

1. Gendered agrarian analyses must link national and household trends.
2. Women-headed households are more involved in agricultural activities than their male counterparts.
3. Subsistence farming is essential for women's social reproduction and livelihood strategies.

Gendered agrarian literature supports the neo-Marxian critique of large-scale commercial agriculture. But it transcends market structure analysis and amplifies gender dimensions overlooked in critical agrarian political economy (Walker, 2002; Hart, 2008). Policies shaping post-apartheid state intervention have prioritised large commercial production while regarding 'subsistence farmers as relics of the era of deliberate under-development' (Cousins, 2007: 7). Transformation in agrarian structures focuses on integrating commercial black farmers into existing market structures (Cousins, 2007; Hart, 2008). This policy orientation reproduces unequal gender relations with the agrarian structures in several ways. Most black African women practise subsistence farming for household consumption or small-scale trade in the informal economy (Walker, 2002; Hart, 2008; Stats SA, 2019). They fall within the country's two-and-half million small-scale black households farming in South Africa. This group comprises two million subsistence farming households and 167,000 households that use farming as a main or extra source of income; 80 per cent of these farming households are in the former bantustans and 13 per cent in urban areas (Aliber and Mdoda, 2015). Their main aim is to ensure household food security and obtain some additional income. This trend is in line with developments in sub-Saharan Africa, with black African women mostly engaged in subsistence and small-scale farming (Walker, 2002; O'Laughlin, 2007; CWGL, 2011).

The prioritisation of a male-dominated commercial sector underestimates the gender differentiation within agricultural production. It also influences state policy orientation and public resource allocation (Greenberg, 2015). This ultimately leads to the introduction of agricultural support programmes that 'tend to be gender blind and are often biased in favour of large farms' (CWGL, 2011: 10). South Africa's commercial agriculture is capital intensive and requires access to industrial inputs. Black African women experience greater challenges when trying to access finance, land and other productive resources (Njobe and Kaaria, 2015: 9). Inequitable access to land is important because it determines access to resources and other support measures in commercial agriculture (CWGL, 2011). This is a substantial challenge in the South African context, where gender inequalities in land ownership persist. Black African women's access to land is limited by the following factors: patriarchal family structures; systemic dispossession (including land grabs); unjust land governance by traditional authorities; and flaws in the Restitution of Land Rights Act 1994 (Claassens, 2014; Yeni, 2018; Presidential Advisory Panel on Land Reform and Agriculture, 2019). These factors are shaped by various institutions in the agrarian political economy, such as traditional authorities, the local state, private companies and family structures.

Greenberg (2015) and Cousins (2007) argue that South Africa's agrarian policies see 'only commercial agriculture as real agriculture' (Cousins, 2007: 7). This policy paradigm relegates small-scale farming to welfare provision and food security, with a few black small-scale commercial farmers integrated into existing market structures in the agrarian system (Greenberg, 2015). There are three major problems with this policy orientation. First, it ignores the concentrated ownership in various segments of the agricultural value chain. There are several market barriers that stymie the increased participation of black-owned small, medium and micro enterprises (SMMEs) in the agri-food system (Makhaya and Roberts, 2013; Jara, 2014; Greenberg, 2015). Second, non-commercial small-scale farming, involving mostly women, is reduced to household food security. This limits the economic agency of black African women participating in agricultural production and determines the policy support they receive. Third, commercial neoliberal economic policies are a clear example of the 'free' market-based paradigm, which promotes deregulation and liberalisation with a minimal role for the state. South Africa's post-apartheid agrarian reforms emerged in a largely neoliberal context and emphasised market-based agrarian reforms as opposed to a greater role for the state (with the state seen by advocates of market-friendly policies as inefficient). The liberalisation and deregulation of the agricultural sector – through the removal of credit and input subsidies, dismantling of single marketing channels and privatising agricultural cooperatives – are all part of these so-called market-friendly policies. Small farmers, the majority of whom are women, struggle to survive without significant state support in agriculture.

This policy approach minimises the real value and socio-economic impact of black African, women-led subsistence farming. It is reduced to a survivalist food security strategy that can develop only as part of the state's social development programme. Yet, evidence from literature and the interview sources discussed in the following sections counters this narrative. The value of this subsistence farming in the informal agrarian economy transcends formal economy market indicators. It reasserts these women's agency in dynamic ways and provides some insights on how to approach agrarian social reproduction differently.

The pessimism and policy biases discussed earlier reflect flawed presuppositions regarding gendered divisions of labour in agrarian political economy relations.

Feminist theorists argue that women's marginalisation in economic, political and social spheres does not reduce them to passive prisoners or recipients of structural marginalisation. Rather, it provides opportunities to resist or develop collective responses in different ways.

ABAFAZI BAYAZBAMBELA: WOMEN-LED RESPONSES TO CONTEMPORARY AGRARIAN QUESTIONS

The discussion on black African women's subsistence farming is organised around the gendered political economy agrarian literature discussed earlier. Two themes are identified for this section: (1) households and social reproduction; and (2) women and agrarian citizenship. The social reproduction concept developed in this political economy theoretical framework is employed.

Households and social reproduction

The literature on household social reproduction points to several forms of unpaid labour performed by black African women. This labour comprises social reproduction activities such as child rearing, cleaning, healthcare and food production. Several policy and research literature sources argue that the responsibility for food security in low-income households is gendered. Women are expected to grow and prepare food for other family members (Dodson et al., 2012; Oxfam, 2014). Their reproductive labour is an essential part of household farming and food preparation. A black African woman participant, who has a food garden in her household, captured this point (Interview 7, 2017):

> Everybody looks at the woman in the house when there is no food on the table. It does not matter whether she is employed or not. But a woman must always make a plan to get something on the table for the night. A strong and hardworking black woman always makes sure that everyone is fed.

The gendered nature of household food security responsibility is not reduced to consumption in the formal retail sector and food preparation. The ability of black African women to develop and nurture a food garden, which supplements food obtained from retailers, is important. It is part of a broader household food security strategy that cushions these women from high food prices. Research reports on post-apartheid agrarian developments attribute price increases to financialisation, market collusion, food miles (the distance from production to consumer) and rising input costs. All these factors are caused by market structure consolidation and restructuring since 1994 (Makhaya and Roberts, 2013; Greenberg, 2015). So, it is evident that the formal agrarian markets impact low-income household's food security strategies. Participants also highlight the household garden's nutritional value because the crops are produced differently from those in commercial industrial agriculture. One participant emphasised the value of women-led household farming (Interview 13, 2017):

> Women in rural areas and townships cannot buy all their household food items from retailers. They do not have enough money to do that and food is very expensive these days. Another problem is the quality of food because some retailers keep the food for long periods. A clever and industrious black woman starts her own garden to avoid the high prices and protect family members from possible health risks.

Household, women-led, subsistence farming also provides some level of economic independence. It ensures that women are not dependent on male partners for food security, and it supplements the monthly social transfer income in some cases. The idea of not depending on males for food security featured prominently in these discussions. It is informed by the prevalence of gendered violence within this community and past trauma from experiences with male partners. This observation is expressed in these succinct words (Interview 20, 2017):

> I do not want to depend on a man for feeding my kids and grandchildren. There are many women in the community who

> have been abandoned by their partners. Some women also rely on financial resources from abusive partners to feed their families. I know that hunger is a big problem in this community, but this is not right.

Additionally, household farming is perceived as a form of self-employment in an economy with minimal or short-term precarious employment for black African women. This is an interesting observation because most studies assume that citizens engaged in informal economic activity do not value their work. This is based on a belief that formality is the most suitable development pathway for all entrepreneurs and workers in the informal economy (Dooms, 2020). Yet, these women value their self-employment in the informal sector because it produces several socio-economic benefits. They produce food for household consumption and generating extra income in some cases. A statement uttered in an interview with a black African woman household farmer confirmed this perspective (Interview 10, 2017):

> Most women are sitting at home waiting for some form of employment in the mines, farms or Transnet. This will not succeed because all these employers prefer to hire men. You are also expected to give more than a man when looking for a job. For example, a sexual favour. I always tell women that the most valuable employment, which gives life, is self-employment in your own garden. You produce food for your family and make extra money from selling the extra food. There is no one exploiting you.

The value attached to agrarian self-employment in the household is expressed in discussions on the future. Wage employment in the formal economy is presented as the panacea for gendered socio-economic inequality in most studies. This makes sense when one considers the disaggregated data on unemployment in households. It illustrates that unemployment is more prevalent among black African women in low-income communities. Government's solution to this trend has been to introduce several interventions, which can rapidly increase wage employment for black African women. A prominent example is the Community Works Programme (CWP), which guarantees some part-time employment for citizens who are unemployed. Several black African women in low-income communities participate in this programme. Themba Masondo's (2018) comprehensive study on the CWP reveals how important it is for livelihood strategies in black African, women-headed households. Another policy proposition from government is supporting formal SMMEs led by black African women.

Household women farmers in this study hold a slightly different perspective on wage employment. They acknowledge the importance of addressing the general community unemployment issue, especially for youths. However, they insist that the ultimate solution for their socio-economic livelihood challenges is not wage employment. This belief was expressed in a debate on what measures government should take to support their future social and economic development. The group discussion concluded (Focus group 1, 2018):

> We do not want government to organise wage employment for us in the mines or farms. Many males who work in the mines receive very little money and they always end up sick. Women who obtain part-time seasonal employment on farms also complain about low wages and bad treatment. So, for us, the future is in our own household and community farming. We do not want the exploitation, ill health or stress that comes with working on the mines or farms. Government must just support our current self-employment.

The discussion on household social reproduction and women-led home garden farming reveals some important insights. The first is the gendered nature of food production and preparation within low-income households. It is clear that the black African women's reproductive labour is still significant for securing food security and additional household income. The historical agrarian agency, discussed earlier in this chapter, is still prevalent in the post-apartheid era. It is taking place within a different sociological context, with fewer low-income households relying on formal wages or remittances (Hall, 2011). There are multiple sources of income and livelihood strategies in households (Scully, 2016; Masondo, 2018). Food production is an essential part of these livelihood strategies because it ameliorates the negative effects of poverty or inequality.

Another insight is the impact of the post-apartheid agrarian structure on livelihood strategies in low-income households. Food prices and health practices in formal retail compel these women to seek alternative livelihood strategies so they are not over-reliant on formal markets. Agrarian relations on the national level, centred on state-market relations, also affect meso- and micro-level social institutions such as households. Therefore, policy-makers and stakeholders should not limit their analyses to the macro institutions.

The most important lesson is the conception and value attached to household and community agrarian labour. Participants do not reduce household/community farming to a welfare or poverty reduction strategy like mainstream policy-makers (Cousins, 2007; Greenberg, 2015; Hart, 2008). They perceive this labour as a form of self-employment, which increases their economic autonomy and agency. It also saves them from what they see as unjust exploitation in formal wage employment. This explains their preference for a post-formal, wage labour socio-economic intervention, which is built around their existing farming livelihood strategy.

Women and agrarian citizenship

The women-led agrarian agency discussed above is not confined to the household. It also influences social reproduction patterns and politics in communities. In this section, the discussion is broadened by exploring agricultural production in a collective garden led by black African women. It is important to note that I discuss both the collective farming and political agency required to sustain this production. This political agency cannot be reduced to productivist views on land and agrarian reform (see Chapter 7 in this volume). These views assess only output while ignoring the other meanings or uses associated with agrarian and land livelihoods (Ferguson, 2013). James Ferguson explains: 'Attention to the broader question of land's multiple uses and meanings can help to explain why land is valued and desired in ways that agricultural utility alone cannot' (Ferguson, 2013: 168).

The notion of women-led agrarian citizenship is used in this section to show the deeper social meanings associated with the women's farming. It is drawn from the work of Hannah Wittman, who argues that active citizenship from the marginalised in rural and peri-urban societies drives structural reforms in agrarian political economies (Wittman, 2009: 806). The 'ability of a diverse array of rural actors to articulate and act on political demands constitutes an active citizenship that provides the foundation for improved access to material and ecological resources' (Wittman, 2009: 811). I provide a gendered analysis of the agrarian citizenship in the following sections using the women's community garden farming and organising strategies.

The women who farm in the collective gardens generate more income from agricultural production than those who rely solely on household production. The variety and volume of production in the community garden exceeds household agricultural production. Women who farm in collective gardens also benefit from the combined labour power and historical agricultural knowledge in the group. The farming skills and knowledge are not obtained from formal training in agricultural colleges or previous formal wage employment. Most of the women performed agricultural labour during their early childhood years in family households. This provided them with opportunities to obtain organic knowledge on farming, nutrition and ecological trends from mothers, aunts or grandmothers. Ugandan scholar Dani Nabudere (2011) argues that indigenous farming knowledge systems produce minimal ecological degradation. He believes that 'they have enabled millions of people to subsist for thousands of years in some of the most hostile environments all over the world' (Nabudere, 2011: 143).

Black African women have used this agrarian knowledge to respond to gendered inequalities within and outside agricultural market structures. This knowledge has improved food security within individual households and several social institutions. It is more impactful when it is shared and used for agricultural production in collective food gardens. The value of this knowledge is summarised by a collective food garden member (Interview 18, 2018):

> No one here went to agricultural school or worked for a white farmer. But we all have sufficient knowledge on crop farming, livestock breeding and ecological issues. This knowledge comes from our childhood days when we used to farm with our mothers and grandmothers. You would wake up and head to the family or community field early in the morning with no complaints. People always ask: who taught these women to farm and produce crops? They forget that we come from families with a peasant history.

The women have used this knowledge to build economic and political solidarity. The production system, knowledge-sharing, rules and use of the produce is not based on individualism or self-interest. Rather, it builds on the women's collective labour power and ideas on how to manage production within this communal space. The agricultural production relations among these women are organised around various solidarity economy principles (Bennie, 2014; Williams, 2014; Jara, 2019). Beyond sharing knowledge, farmers also share access to crucial inputs such as seeds, tools and fertiliser. They pool resources to deal with the perennial challenge of access to inputs. One collective garden sells its produce to self-employed women who sell cooked meals in public areas such as taxi ranks. This provides these women with an alternative source to obtain vegetables at a lower price than formal markets (Interview 16, 2018).

Another aspect of the solidarity economy is the approach to distributing crop production and income from crop sales. There is a crop basket quota for weekly household consumption and rules on how to share income from sales among individuals or micro-enterprises. Participants also state that they provide some crops to households in the community that experience high levels of food insecurity. All these practices signify how some solidarity economy principles are applied in organising production in the collective garden. However, this does not mean that there is no conflict or disagreement among members on certain issues. For example, one of the contentious matters is managing water use and infrastructure in the collective garden. Limited water access and dysfunctional water purification systems exacerbate this conflict. But the women have attempted, with some level of success, to address this through a coordinated collective garden governance structure. It is convened weekly to discuss various issues related to the collective garden. The emphasis on solidarity and coordination was described (Interview 18, 2018):

> We have attempted to create a system of sharing seeds, tools, water, income and crops. This coordination only works when everyone follows the rules and understands that farming in this garden is about serving the group's interests. I like that fact that we also learn and teach each other different methods of producing and managing crops. It is nice that women are helping each other to make a living through agricultural production. There will always be some conflict because we are human, and some members do not always follow the rules. But at least we are given the opportunity to discuss and fix our issues in the weekly meeting.

The emphasis on organising around women-led agricultural production is important from a gendered perspective. Participants emphasised that some males lead collective/communal gardens in the community. This point also features prominently in Brittany Kesselman's (2017) study on food gardens in Johannesburg. Her work proves how broader gender roles and power relations in society shaped gender interactions within communal gardens (Kesselman, 2017: 228–229). Women from this collective garden are proud that they do not rely on male labour or leadership to sustain their agricultural production. The Zulu phrase *Abafazi bayazbambela* was repeated throughout the discussions. According to the women, males in the community do not have the work ethic or patience to succeed in agricultural production. They also criticise men for being obsessed with waged labour in the mines. This criticism is outlined in this statement (Focus group 1, 2018):

> Most men are untrustworthy and controlling. They want instant gratification when it comes to economic or money issues. This is why they only perceive mine wages and formal employment as the best source of livelihood. They cannot see the potential

> provided by producing and selling your own crops. They become so stressed when they lose their mine employment. I am also happy that we do not have men in our garden because they will want to take over and control everything that happens here.

The discussion on collective or community gardens highlights how women-led agrarian citizenship operates in a collective production setting. It shows us the embedded knowledge on farming that these women possess. This is an important point because the legitimacy and credibility of women-led farming is always questioned. There is an implicit assumption in policy debates that presents subsistence farmers, especially women, as people with very little knowledge of farming or natural-resource management. These women counter this narrative. The attempts to coordinate and build economic relations, underpinned by some aspects of solidarity economy principles, is also noticeable. We see some evidence of how to think about localised food system value chains that can address gendered socio-economic inequalities.

Furthermore, the collective garden experience provides some insights into how to manage agricultural production in communal settings. Women-led agrarian citizenship is also reaffirmed through focusing on the strengths of collective women agricultural production.

CONCLUSION: STATE POLICY INTERVENTIONS

Black African women who farm in the informal economy encounter several systemic challenges. These structural impediments cannot be separated from broader trends in South Africa's post-apartheid agrarian structure. The discussion in previous sections emphasises how participants value their self-employment and agricultural production. They do not want it replaced by formal wage labour or alternative formal livelihood strategies. Rather, state intervention must support them to develop their subsistence farming in different ways. The first intervention should focus on access to land and supporting infrastructure (especially fencing) for sustainable agricultural production. As argued earlier, gender inequalities are still prevalent in land access and ownership patterns in South Africa. The state has focused largely on land reforms within the confines of market relations in the formal commercial agrarian economy. It is essential to factor in the land and infrastructure needs of small-scale black African women farmers in the informal economy. As one participant from the collective garden explains (Interview 23, 2018):

> We could really improve our agricultural production if government provided us with more land and suitable fencing. Our current land is not enough because more women want to join us. We also need proper fencing because animals always come in and eat or destroy our crops. They have promised to give us unused municipal land and we are still waiting.

The second intervention relates to the point made in earlier sections about the solidarity economy. This development paradigm is encouraging society to design local economic systems, which focus on linking social enterprises or cooperatives through 'forward and backward linkages' (Williams, 2014: 52). The discussions in previous sections illustrates that the women farmers are already establishing localised value-chain links with other actors in the food system. Government should support the growth and development of these food system linkages through localised farmers' markets. This strategy has produced positive results for small growers in countries such as the United States of America, India and Brazil. The process does not have to be driven by government only. There are several non-governmental organisations working on food systems within local municipalities that can provide valuable advice on how to connect with informal economy farmers and other SMMEs in the food system.

Another crucial form of state support is public procurement through the provincial government's nutrition programme. It should be decentralised so that local women producers can access demand for their produce. One participant described her future vision (Interview 6, 2017):

> We want our produce to be bought by the government one day, so people eat our crops in schools, hospitals and day-care

> centres. But it is very difficult because the system works with formal agricultural businesses which have access to land, finance, inputs and information.

Third, it is essential to place gender differences at the centre of agrarian policy development and food systems planning. But the approach to gender inequality must be based on an appreciation of race, class, sector and geographical differences. A blanket approach to gender transformation, which ignores intersectional inequalities among women participating in the agrarian political economy, is not useful. It will intra-gender inequality in the agrarian structure while integrating a few black African middle- and upper-class women. The gendered agrarian approach must consider food security and agricultural household production data, which specify women households who should be targeted beneficiaries of a gender-sensitive agrarian strategy. The reformed strategy must also consider other livelihood sources that maintain social reproduction in households. There must be policy coordination between this gender-sensitive agrarian strategy and the national policies governing other livelihood sources.

Fourth, the approach to dualism in South Africa's agrarian policy frameworks needs to be reconsidered. Previous attempts to address this challenge have focused on integrating some black farmers into existing market-value chains. This chapter has highlighted the major shortcomings of this approach and highlighted the inherent gendered policy bias contained in its logic. I suggest that the most sustainable policy solution to dualism is the reconstruction of agrarian value-market structures through industrial, competition and land reform policies. This requires effective policy coordination across several departments and a holistic development paradigm. Policy-makers cannot implement this recommendation successfully if they favour the current model, with its concentrated patterns of ownership and gender inequalities across the value chain.

REFERENCES

Aliber, M. and Mdoda, L. 2015. 'The direct and indirect economic contribution of small-scale black agriculture in South Africa'. *Agrekon*, 54 (2), 18–37.

Atkinson, D. 2007. *Going for Broke: The fare of farm workers in arid South Africa*. Cape Town: Human Sciences Research Council.

Bennie, A. 2014. 'Linking food sovereignty and the solidarity economy in South African townships', in Satgar, V. (ed.) *The Solidarity Economy Alternative: Emerging theory and practice*. Pietermaritzburg: University of KwaZulu-Natal Press, 249–278.

Benya, A. 2015. 'The invisible hands: Women in Marikana'. *Review of African Political Economy*, 42 (146), 545–560.

Bernstein, H. 1994. 'Food security in a democratic South Africa'. *Transformation*, 24, http://transformationjournal.org.za/wp-content/uploads/2017/03/tran024002.pdf, accessed 30 May 2020.

Bozzoli, B. 1991. *Women of Phokeng: Consciousness, life strategy and migrancy in South Africa, 1900–1983*. Oxford: James Currey.

Bradford, H. 2000. 'Peasants, historians, and gender: A South African case study revisited, 1850–1886'. *History and Theory*, 39 (4), 86—110.

Bundy, C. 1988. *The Rise and Fall of the South African Peasantry*. Oxford: James Currey.

Burawoy, M. 2009. *The Extended Case Method: Four countries, four decades, four great transformations, and one theoretical tradition*. Berkeley, CA: University of California Press.

Centre for Women's Global Leadership (CWGL). 2011. 'The right to food, gender equality and economic policy'. Meeting Report, Rutgers University, https://www.cwgl.rutgers.edu/docman/economic-and-social-rights-publications/361-righttofood-pdf/file, accessed 20 July 2020.

Claassens, A. 2014. '"Communal land", property rights and traditional leadership'. Centre for Law and Society, University of Cape Town.

Cock, J. 2016. 'Marxism and feminism: "Unhappy marriage" or creative partnership', https://www.womin.org.za/images/the-alternatives/ecofeminism-social-reproduction-theory/J%20Cock%20-%20Marxism%20and%20Feminism.pdf, accessed 30 May 2020.

Collins, P.H. 1998. 'It is all in the family: Intersections of gender, race and nation'. *Hypatia*, 13 (3), 62–82.

Collins, P.H. 2000. 'Gender, black feminism, and black political economy'. *Annals of the American Academy and Social Science*, 568, 41–53.

Cousins, B. 2007. 'Agrarian reform and the 'two economies': Transforming South Africa's countryside', in Ntsebeza, L. and Hall, R. (eds.) *The Land Question in South Africa: The challenge of transformation and redistribution*. Cape Town: HSRC Press, 220–245.

Cousins, B. 2019. 'Land policy must change South Africa's agrarian structure'.

PLAAS, University of the Western Cape, https://www.plaas.org.za/land-policy-must-change-south-africas-agrarian-structure/, accessed 27 May 2020.

Davis, A. 1981. *Women, Race and Class.* New York: Random House.

Department of Agriculture, Forestry and Fisheries (DAFF). 2013. 'National policy on food and nutrition security', https://www.nda.agric.za/docs/media/NATIONAL%20POLICYon%20food%20and%20nutririition%20security.pdf, accessed 22 May 2020.

Dodson, B., Chiweza, A. and Riley, L. 2012. 'Gender and food insecurity in southern African cities'. Urban Food Security Series No. 10, http://www.afsun.org/wp-content/uploads/2016/06/Afsun10.pdf, accessed 20 May 2020.

Dooms, T. 2020. 'Informalising black economic empowerment: A citizen-centred development approach', in Cawe, A. and Mabasa, K. (eds.) *Beyond Tenderpreneurship: Rethinking black business and economic development.* Johannesburg: MISTRA, pp. 256–277.

Ferguson, J. 2013. 'How to do things with land: A distributive perspective on rural livelihoods in southern Africa'. *Journal of Agrarian Change*, 13 (1), 166–174.

Global Food Security Index. 2019. 'Strengthening food systems and the environment through innovation and investment'. The Economist Intelligence Unit, London.

Greenberg, S. 2013. 'The disjunctures of land and agriculture reform in South Africa: Implications for the agri-food system', Working Paper No. 26, PLAAS, University of the Western Cape.

Greenberg, S. 2015. 'Agrarian reform and South Africa's agro-food system'. *Journal of Peasant Studies*, 42 (2), 957–979.

Hall, R. 2011. 'Revisiting unresolved questions: Land, food and agriculture'. *Transformation*, 75, http://transformationjournal.org.za/wp-content/uploads/2017/04/T75_Part10.pdf, accessed 9 May 2020.

Hart, T. 2008. 'The ignorance of gender in agrarian livelihoods in rural South Africa'. *Agenda*, 22 (78), 144–155.

Hart, T. and Aliber, M. 2012. 'Inequalities in agricultural support for women in South Africa'. Policy Brief, Human Sciences Research Council, Pretoria.

Jara, M.K. 2014. 'The solidarity economy response to the agrarian crisis in South Africa', in Satgar, V. (ed.) *The Solidarity Economy Alternative: Emerging theory and practice.* Pietermaritzburg: University of KwaZulu-Natal Press, 227–248.

Jara, M.K. 2019. 'Land redistribution in South Africa: Pondering the solidarity economy alternative'. Paper presented at the Conference on Land Redistribution for Equitable Access to Land in South Africa, Cape Town, 4–5 February.

Kesselman, B. 2017. 'Sowing the seeds of food sovereignty or cultivating consent? The potential and limitations of Johannesburg's community gardens'. PhD dissertation, University of KwaZulu-Natal.

Kirsten, J. 2006. 'Socio-economic dynamics of the South African agricultural sector'. Trade Policy Briefing No. 10, South African Institute for International Affairs, https://media.africaportal.org/documents/Socio-Economic_Dynamics_Of_The_South_African_Agricultural_Sector.pdf, accessed 10 May 2020.

Makhaya, G. and Roberts, S. 2013. 'Expectations and outcomes: Considering competition and corporate power in South Africa under democracy'. *Review of African Political Economy*, 40 (138), 537–555.

Masondo, T. 2018. 'Protecting and promoting livelihoods of the excluded through the community work programme: A comparative case study of Munsieville and Bekkersdal'. PhD dissertation, University of the Witwatersrand.

Mnisi Weeks, S. 2018. 'The violence of the harmony model: Common narratives between women and lower-level traditional leaders', in Buthelezi, M., Skosana, D. and Vale, B. (eds.) *Traditional Leaders in a Democracy: Resources, respect and resistance.* Johannesburg: MISTRA, 182–223.

Moletsane, R. and Reddy, V. 2011. 'The gendered dimensions of food security in South Africa: A review of the literature'. Policy Brief, Human Sciences Research Council, Pretoria.

Mtero, F. 2012. 'Commercialisation, deagrarianisation and the accumulation/reproduction dynamic: Massive maize production schemes in the Eastern Cape, South Africa'. Working Paper No. 23, PLAAS, University of the Western Cape, https://media.africaportal.org/documents/PLAAS_WorkingPaper23Mtero.pdf, accessed 18 June 2020.

Msukaligwa Integrated Development Plan (IDP). 2017. 'Msukaligwa Local Municipality: 2017–2022 Draft IDP', http://www.msukaligwa.gov.za/msukweb/documents/reports/IDP/2017%202022%20Msukaligwa%20Draft%20IDP.pdf, accessed 2 September 2020.

Nabudere, D.W. 2011. *From Agriculture to Agricology: Towards a global circular economy*. Johannesburg: MISTRA.

Njobe, B. and Kaaria, S. 2015. 'Women and agriculture: The untapped opportunity in the wave of transformation'. Background paper, https://www.afdb.org/fileadmin/uploads/afdb/Documents/Events/DakAgri2015/Women_and_Agriculture_The_Untapped_Opportunity_in_the_Wave_of_Transformation.pdf, accessed 10 September 2020.

O'Laughlin, B. 2007. 'Widow's weeds: Gender, AIDS and the agrarian question in southern Africa'. IESE Inaugural Conference on the Challenges for Social and Economic Research in Mozambique, Conference Paper No. 59, Maputo, 19 September.

O'Meara, D. 1983. *Volkskapitalisme: Class, capital and ideology in the development of Afrikaner nationalism, 1934–1948*. Cambridge: Cambridge

University Press.
Oxfam, 2014. 'Hidden hunger in South Africa', https://www.oxfam.org/en/research/hidden-hunger-south-africa, accessed 10 June 2020.
Palys, T. 2008. 'Purposive sampling', in Given, L.M. (ed.) *The Sage Encyclopedia of Qualitative Research Methods*, Volume 2. New York: SAGE Publications, 627–628.
Park, C.M.M., White, B. and Julia. 2013. 'We are not all the same: Taking gender seriously in food sovereignty discourse'. *Third World Quarterly*, 36 (3), 584–599.
Presidential Advisory Panel on Land Reform and Agriculture. 2019. 'Final report of the Presidential Advisory Panel on Land Reform and Agriculture', https://www.gov.za/sites/default/files/gcis_document/201907/panelreportlandreform_0.pdf, accessed 20 August 2020.
Rakolojane, M.J. 2015. 'The gender dimensions of land reform in South Africa: A case study of Daggakraal rural housing and resettlement project'. PhD dissertation, University of South Africa.
Razavi, S. 2009. 'Engendering the political economy of agrarian change'. *Journal of Peasant Studies*, 36 (1), 197–226.
Razavi, S. 2011. 'Agrarian debates and gender relations: "Now you see them, now you don't"', in Verschuur, C. (ed.) *Du grain à moudre: Genre, développement rural et alimentation.* Genève: Graduate Institute Publications, 47–58.
Roberts, B., Sitas, A. and Greenstein, R. 2003. 'Research methods training manual', https://www.academia.edu/3198713/Research_Methods_Training_Manual, accessed 28 May 2020.
Scully, B. 2016. 'From the shop floor to the kitchen table: The shifting centre of precarious workers' politics in South Africa'. *Review of African Political Economy*, 43 (148), 295–311.
Shisana O., Labadarios D., Rehle T., Simbayi, L., Zuma, K., et al. 2013. *South African National Health and Nutrition Examination Survey (SANHANES-1).* Cape Town: HSRC Press.
Sihlobo, W. and Kirsten, J. 2018. 'A compendium of essays on land reform in South Africa', https://agbiz.co.za/uploads/AgbizNews18/181207_Land%20Reform%20Essays%20Final.pdf, accessed 27 May 2020.
Sihlobo, W. and Nel, L. 2016. 'Is South Africa's agricultural sector addressing inclusive socio-economic development?', in Qobo, M. and Hofmeyr, J. (eds.) *Opportunity for Change: The private sector's role in inclusive development.* Cape Town: Institution for Justice and Reconciliation, 65–81.
Statistics South Africa (Stats SA). 2016. 'Community survey 2016: Agricultural households', http://www.statssa.gov.za/publications/03-01-05/Presentation_CS2016_Agricultural_Households.pdf, accessed 20 August 2020.
Statistics South Africa (Stats SA). 2019. 'Towards measuring the extent

of food security in South Africa: An examination of hunger and food inadequacy'. Report 03-0014, http://www.statssa.gov.za/publications/03-00-14/03-00-142017.pdf, accessed 20 August 2020.

Statistics South Africa (Stats SA). 2020. 'Census of commercial agriculture, 2017'. Report 11-02-01, http://www.statssa.gov.za/publications/Report-11-02-01/Report-11-02-012017.pdf, accessed 20 August 2020.

TRADE. 2013. 'South Africa's agricultural trade competitiveness'. North West University, Potchefstroom.

Tsikata, D. 2015. 'The social relations of agrarian change'. Working Paper, Institute of Development Studies, https://pubs.iied.org/pdfs/17278IIED.pdf, accessed 20 August 2020.

Walker, C. 1982. *Women and Resistance in South Africa.* Cape Town: David Philip.

Walker, C. 2002. 'Agrarian change, gender and land reform: A South African case study'. Social Policy and Development Programme Paper, United Nations Research Institute for Social Development, Geneva.

Williams, M. 2014. 'The solidarity economy and social transformation', in Satgar, V. (ed.) *The Solidarity Economy Alternative: Emerging theory and practice.* Pietermaritzburg: University of KwaZulu-Natal Press, 37–63.

Wittman, H. 2009. 'Reworking the metabolic rift: La Via Campesina, agrarian citizenship, and food sovereignty'. *Journal of Peasant Studies*, 36 (4), 805–826.

Wolpe, H. 1972. 'Capitalism and cheap labour-power in South Africa: From segregation to apartheid'. *Economy and Society*, 1 (4), 425–456.

Yeni, S. 2018. 'Traditional leadership, violence of land rights, and resistance from below', in Buthelezi, M., Skosana, D. and Vale, B. (eds.) *Traditional Leaders in a Democracy: Resources, respect and resistance.* Johannesburg: MISTRA, 153–178.

Legislation

Restitution of Land Rights Act (No. 22 of 1994).

Interviews

Anon. Interview 6. July 2017. Interview with author, Ermelo.

Anon. Interview 7. 26 July 2017. Interview with author, Ermelo.

Anon. Interview 10. August 2017. Interview with author, Ermelo.

Anon. Interview 13. August 2017. Interview with author, Ermelo.

Anon. Interview 16. March 2018. Interview with author, Ermelo.

Anon. Interview 18. March 2018. Interview with author, Ermelo.

Anon. Interview 20. September 2017. Interview with author, Ermelo.

Anon. Interview 23. September 2018. Interview with author, Ermelo.

Focus group 1. 23 February 2018. Ermelo.

SEVEN

Land is More than Farming: Former labour tenants' views on land expropriation without compensation

Sithandiwe Yeni

INTRODUCTION

One hundred former labour tenants and their descendants from uMgungundlovu district in KwaZulu-Natal filled the Constitutional Court for their court case hearing on 23 May 2019. They were represented by the Legal Resource Centre (LRC) and supported by the Association for Rural Advancement (AFRA). The former labour tenants and their descendants applied to have a special master appointed to oversee the processing of about 11,000 land claims, which had not been implemented since their lodgement in 2001. On 20 August 2019, the court ruled in favour of the labour tenants and a special master was appointed. This ground-breaking constitutional ruling provides important insights into the post-apartheid government's failure to implement a pro-poor land reform policy.[1] The former labour tenants' preferences for a time-consuming and costly legal strategy to settle their claims points to institutional weaknesses in the government's land policy regulatory regime.

South Africans from rural and urban areas emphasised land reform policy failures throughout the public hearings, organised by the constitutional review committee on amending section 25 of the Constitution.[2] Politicians, academics, commercial agriculture organisations and civil society commentators have dominated these public debates. Views from land claimants, such as the former labour tenants, are largely overlooked in public discourses on land expropriation without compensation. This chapter aims to fill this gap by bringing the views of former labour tenants into these debates.

The former labour tenants argue that black land claimants who were forcibly dispossessed of land, and continue to experience socio-economic exclusion, must get their land back and receive compensation for their suffering. They unreservedly reject the idea of the state paying compensation, particularly to the white farmers who currently own the land, which the former labour tenants and their descendants claim. Their land needs and uses are not limited to farming – reclaiming their dispossessed land will also allow them to live freely where they belong. The dominant framing of the land public discourse is based on agricultural production or food security considerations. It marginalises discussions on the divergent meanings and uses of land connected to nation formation and belonging (see Chapter 1 in this volume). This chapter focuses on the voices of these land claimants and their views on expropriation of land without compensation. These voices illuminate the contested meanings of land that challenge the conventional commercial land approach. The views of former labour tenants presented in this chapter were obtained through a series of

1 *Mwelase and Others v Director-General for the Department of Rural Development and Land Reform and Another*, http://www.saflii.org/za/cases/ZACC/2019/30.html, accessed 20 August 2020.

2 In February 2018, the majority of the members of South Africa's National Assembly adopted a motion to start the process to amend the Constitution to clarify the powers of the state to expropriate land without compensation.

focus group discussions.[3]

In this chapter I provide a brief history of land dispossession and labour tenancy in the then Natal Province, which resulted in a racially skewed agrarian structure, a process central to the arguments of the former labour tenants. I proceed to look at contemporary attempts by the democratic government to give land back to those who were historically dispossessed, such as the former labour tenants, paying attention to prospects and disappointments. This is followed by a closer look at section 25 of the Constitution and the debates around it, including uses and meanings of land, such as belonging, which are of importance to the former labour tenants and have been on the periphery in the public discourse. The chapter then returns to the views of the former labour tenants and their descendants from uMgungundlovu on why they believe the Constitution should be amended and land be expropriated without compensation. My concluding remarks suggest other mechanisms to address land and agrarian reform beyond amending the Constitution.

LAND DISPOSSESSION AND NATAL'S LABOUR TENANCY SYSTEM

African land dispossession and the destruction of the African peasantry in South Africa date back to colonial periods. On settling in Natal, the British colonists dispossessed Africans and allocated themselves Crown lands (land belonging to the monarch). They established their own private farms and created reserves for the Africans (Welsh, 1971). Not all Africans resided in these reserves, as some continued to live

3 The former labour tenants were from Mshwathi, Richmond, Mpofana, Mngeni, Mpendle, Gongolo, Muden and Mkhambathini in KwaZulu-Natal – all were concerned with unresolved land claims, lack of service delivery on the farms and threats of evictions. Collectively, they organised themselves into a forum called Siyanqoba, where they come together to learn, strategise and campaign around challenges they face on the farms. They requested that pseudonyms be used. I convened and facilitated focus group discussions in my then capacity as the national coordinator of Tshintsha Amakhaya, a network of NGOs and their constituencies working on land and agrarian transformation issues.

or farm on what became private farms on Crown lands, occasionally providing cheap labour for the white settlers (Welsh, 1971). Natal officially became a British colony in 1843 and the colonists complained that there was an acute or even chronic shortage of labour. The colonial state subsequently attempted to constrain economic development in reserves and destroy the African peasantry. The reserve economy was a threat because it enabled Africans to subsist without having to take up employment as labourers for the white settlers (Welsh, 1971). Despite these attempts, economic livelihood activities continued in the reserves and, in some cases, the African peasantry produced more than their white counterparts. Africans who did not move to the reserves but remained on the newly white-owned farms had an obligation to provide only labour. However, rentals were imposed as the number of Africans on these farms increased beyond the labour needs of the white farmers. Two systems of tenancy on the farms prevailed: (1) cash rents but no labour obligations; and (2) no rents but only the provision of labour. Rentals became too high, forcing Africans to leave the farms and move to the overcrowded reserves. Those who resisted the rent increases had their huts burnt and were evicted. In addition to land shortages, the African peasant farmers were hit hard by drought and pests, which led to crop failure in the 1870s. The state provided drought relief measures only to white farmers and not Africans (Williams, 1996).

By 1880, Crown lands became available for sale, and Africans were promised they would receive prior notification, but this did not happen and many were evicted. Some resisted the evictions, saying that the colonists had found them there. The Natives Land Act was passed in 1913 to restrict Africans from purchasing land outside of the reserves and, likewise, prohibit whites from obtaining land in African areas. It also contained other provisions to meet the demands of white farmers for more cheap African labour, particularly in the then Transvaal and Orange Free State Provinces, where sharecroppers were transformed into farm labourers or servants (Feinberg, 1993).

The labour tenancy system

A labour tenant refers to a black person living on a white-owned farm who undertook work for the landowner for part of the year in exchange for the right to use a small portion of the land for their own purposes, such as grazing, growing crops and housing (Hathorn and Hutchinson, 1990). White farmers created this system with state support to enable them to expand their farms, increase production and have access to cheap or free labour (Williams, 1996). Its origin was a consequence of land dispossession and forced removals attributed to state-driven colonial conquest and capitalist development (Bundy, 1990).

Gender and generational dynamics within African homesteads are crucial for understanding how the labour tenancy system operated (McClendon, 2002). The system was reliant on the relationship between patriarchal white farmers and African homesteads. It depended on the homestead head's (male) ability to secure labour from his homestead, which entailed committing the labour of wives, sons and daughters to meet the demands of white (male) landowners. In return, they regained access to their land to grow crops for subsistence and engage in livestock grazing. These tasks were primarily performed by wives and children (see Chapter 6 in this volume).

With industrialisation, more young men (and a few young women) left the farms in search of better-paying jobs in the cities. The male migrant labourers sought employment in the mines around the 1930s and later other industries (Morris, 1977). This created a labour crisis on the farms and resulted in struggles between sons and fathers over generational authority (McClendon, 2002). The burden on women was heavy because of the gendered labour divisions on white landowners' farms. African women (wives/daughters) were responsible for crop production in farmers' fields and social reproduction within homesteads. The consequences of labour crises on the farms were evictions, as sons often refused to return to provide labour (McClendon, 2002). According to Mike Morris (1977), white commercial farmers and landowners viewed labour tenancy as an impediment to the development of more efficient agricultural production by the 1940s.

The advocacy urging state authorities to phase out the labour tenant system increased gradually during this period. A significant number of labour tenants were evicted from farms because of state policies or farm owners' decisions (Williams, 1996). The evicted labour tenants had limited alternative livelihood options due to restrictive migrant laws, unemployment in towns and overcrowding in the reserves. These factors coincided with a decrease in employment in commercial farming and subsequently led to former tenants returning to the farms as 'illegal' squatters (Williams, 1996). Despite measures by the state to abolish labour tenancy, the number of labour tenants continued to increase through the 1970s. While labour tenancy no longer exists as a system, the former labour tenants and their descendants continue to live under harsh conditions as second-class citizens at the mercy of, predominantly white, farm owners. These people want their land back, not as a favour from the government but because this is a matter of justice. This demand must be contextualised within ongoing debates on post-apartheid land and agrarian reform policies – examined in the following sections.

LAND AND AGRARIAN REFORM PROGRAMMES IN POST-APARTHEID SOUTH AFRICA

In the first few years after coming into power in 1994, the African National Congress (ANC)-led government embarked on a market-based land reform programme constituting three tiers: restitution; redistribution; and tenure reform (Hall and Cliffe, 2009). Land reform is entrenched in section 25 of the Constitution, which makes provisions with regard to the eligibility of beneficiaries, land expropriation and its conditions. The section provides additional legislative measures necessary to ensure redress and equitable land access by all citizens. For the first time since the end of colonial and apartheid rule, land and agrarian reforms in South Africa entrenched equal rights to land as provided in the Constitution of the Republic of South Africa (Act No. 108 of 1996) (Hebinck, 2013). While the Constitution provided the legal basis for land and agrarian reform, the designated state departments developed policy instruments.

According to Ruth Hall, the World Bank was instrumental and influential in shaping the land reform policy direction, which resulted in the state adopting a market-based land reform policy (Hall, 2011). She explains that World Bank economist Hans Binswanger led the World Banks' mission to South Africa on land and agricultural policy in the 1990s. He proposed three options for land redistribution: (1) a 'willing buyer, willing seller' approach, which would be supported by state land purchase through grants; (2) expropriation of land with compensation at market price; or (3) expropriation of land with compensation just below market prices, taking into consideration past state subsidies that were provided to white farmers and thereby eliminating distortions. Hall (2011) explains that arguments against expropriation included the cost of political opposition and lengthy legal processes. The drafters of the Constitution anticipated appeals from landowners through the courts, which could lead to delays and high administrative costs for the state.

Between 1994 and 1996, the first policy initiative of the Nelson Mandela administration was the Reconstruction and Development Programme (RDP), which aimed to redress the injustices of the past, including transforming racially skewed land ownership and discriminatory laws. The purpose of land and agrarian reforms was to correct and transform the agrarian structure (DLA, 1997). During the RDP phase, the state made available a Settlement/Land Acquisition Grant of R16,000 to black people with a monthly income below R1,500 to enable access to land (Lahiff, 2007). The class orientation of this policy was pro-poor and the state prioritised redistributing land for multiple livelihood uses (Hall, 2004; Lahiff, 2007). This is articulated in the White Paper on South African Land Policy of 1997, which lists urban and rural poor people, former labour tenants, farm workers and small-scale farmers as the targeted beneficiaries of land redistribution to support varied livelihoods (DLA, 1997). The period that followed under President Thabo Mbeki (2000–2010) saw a shift to the Growth, Employment and Redistribution (GEAR) policy, which placed more emphasis on a market-oriented land development strategy (Cousins, 2013).

GEAR came with the introduction of the Land Redistribution for Agricultural Development programme, which demanded contributions from land reform beneficiaries, while the type of land use prioritised agriculture (Hebinck, 2013). The beneficiary target orientation shifted from the broad segments of the working class to emerging black capitalist farmers (Hall and Kepe, 2017). The state primarily focused on supporting a large-scale commercial agriculture model, with the gradual integration of black farmers into established commercial markets (DOA, 2001). Since 2006, the state has introduced the Proactive Land Acquisition Strategy, still premised on the willing buyer, willing seller model. But the grant system was discontinued, so state officials buy commercial land in open markets and then redistribute it to the beneficiaries. In this model, the land use is biased towards commercial agriculture and prioritises black, small-scale farmers who compete in formal markets (Hall and Kepe, 2017).

The big winners of the market-led policy approach were the willing sellers, that is, the white landowners who acquired millions from the post-apartheid state land reform programmes. One of the ways that the willing sellers became the winners was through joint ventures. These are partnerships between black people acquiring land and commercial farmers or private companies (Hall and Cliffe, 2009). They usually occur in sectors where production is capital-intensive and in regions with high land prices, such as the wine farms in the Western Cape. Critics of joint ventures highlight that they are a new form of exploitation, a mechanism through which white commercial farmers spread the risk of being part of a capital-intensive sector while enjoying market and political credibility (Hall and Cliffe, 2009). Some researchers add that high-risk and high-cost farming seldom declares profits, and members may have little say over how much should be reinvested in the business. Other controversies came from disputes over whether joint ventures contributed to tenure security, which is one of the objectives of land reform (Hall and Cliffe, 2009).

Some researchers have critiqued this approach, citing high costs and dysfunctional farming projects. They attribute the failures to imposed land uses with no proper support, which ultimately leads to conflicts among beneficiaries (Lahiff, 2007; Hall, 2009). In reviewing the evolution of land and agrarian reform policy and practice from 1995 onwards, Ruth Hall and Thembela Kepe conclude that 'the policy principles of tenure security, poverty reduction, gender equity, sustainable land use, and resilient rural livelihoods appear to have foundered in practice' (Hall and Kepe, 2017: 126). The former labour tenants are undoubtedly among those who have been excluded and who have felt the impacts of weak land policy implementation.

LABOUR TENANTS' EXPERIENCES AND LAND COMPENSATION SINCE 1994

The post-apartheid government introduced the Labour Tenants Act (LTA, No. 3 of 1996) to improve labour tenants' living conditions and address historical land injustices. Former labour tenants and their descendants expected the new government to restore their land rights and give them access to the farms from which they were evicted. Prior to the passing of this law, during the early 1990s, there had been a rise in evictions as conflicts arose between white farmers and African labour tenants, particularly in areas in the Weenen and Colenso districts in KwaZulu-Natal (Williams, 1996). Farmers evicted tenants, burnt their houses and impounded their cattle. This called for a legislative intervention in the form of the LTA, which was enacted to prevent arbitrary evictions and ensure that labour tenants benefit from land reform policies.

The Nkuzi Development Association conducted a survey on post-apartheid farm evictions. The findings highlighted that the number of farm evictions between 1994 and 2004 was greater than it had been in the last decade of apartheid, despite the laws and the Constitution which were meant to prevent evictions (Wagerif et al., 2005). Since the passing of the LTA, the process of settling the land claims has been slow and bureaucratic, with officials seemingly not playing their part in informing landowners about the claims or intervening to ensure that labour tenants have their tenure secured (Lahiff, 2009). By March 2001, about 19,416 labour tenants' land claims had been lodged, largely from KwaZulu-Natal and Mpumalanga provinces. But it is unknown what proportion of the total number of labour tenants this figure represents (Lahiff, 2009). The uMgungundlovu district former labour tenants and their descendants were among the thousands that lodged land claims when the government passed the LTA. However, these claims still remain unsettled.

Dissatisfied with the slowness of the land claims process, and having been sent from pillar to post each time they followed up on the status, the former labour tenants of uMgungundlovu district approached AFRA for assistance. AFRA and the LRC first brought the case to the Land Claims Court (LCC) in 2013 as a class action case on behalf of the former labour tenants, arguing that the court should appoint a special master to deal with settling these land claims. The court ruled in favour of the former labour tenants. The Department of Rural Development and Land Reform opposed the judgment, stating that it was their function and not the courts to deliver on land reform. Yet, the experiences of most labour tenant land claimants were that the state had proved to be incompetent in settling land claims.

Some claimants were even told that their claims were missing from the files and that they had to resubmit their applications. In 2018, the Supreme Court of Appeal (SCA) set aside the LCC judgment, which then led to AFRA and the LRC taking the matter to the Constitutional Court in May 2019. While preparations for the SCA hearing were underway in 2018, debates on whether to amend the Constitution to allow for land expropriation without compensation dominated the media, academic and civil society platforms. There is consensus among land researchers and stakeholders that land reform has failed to redress the injustices of land dispossession. However, there are different views on why it has failed and how it should be fixed. Notably, some land and agrarian scholars have argued that it is a lack of political will that is a hindrance to the delivery of a transformative and pro-poor land reform (Hall, 2004), while others attribute the failures to 'the property clause' (section 25) of the Constitution (Ntsebeza, 2007).

Section 25 of the Constitution has been at the centre of the land reform debates in South Africa since the beginning of 2018. Powerful interests in society played a central role in framing the debate on land expropriation without compensation. Some key discussions on the possible impacts of expropriation cite national food security, export earnings and economic growth as salient considerations. The media presented scenarios of possible economic collapse if land reform proceeded based on populist considerations. While the argument to revise the property clause is not new, as Lungisile Ntsebeza advanced in 2007, 2018 heightened the discourse between those in favour and those against its amendment.

For Hall (2004), the Constitution, as it stands, is not a hindrance to land reform. South Africa's current Constitution already gives the state sufficient mechanisms to expropriate land in pursuit of land reforms. However, the state has not sufficiently exercised its powers to expropriate land for land redress purposes. This is often attributed to the lack of political will. Hall's view is supported by academics such as Professor Ben Cousins, lawyer activists in the LRC and Advocate Tembeka Ngcukaitobi. Their opposition to amending the Constitution suggests that the problem with the property clause rests on how it is interpreted. They argue that state authorities and legal precedents emphasise market value of land when determining compensation. Section 25 of the Constitution provides more than 'the market value of the property' and includes other conditions such as 'the history of the acquisition and use of property' and 'the purpose of the expropriation' (Mabasa, 2020).

Ntsebeza (2007), on the other hand, argues that the property clause in the Constitution protects the rights of private property owners while also recognising and protecting the rights to land of the dispossessed. Therefore, it is a hindrance to land reform because it protects the same land that must be redistributed to those who were dispossessed (Ntsebeza, 2007). The problem is beyond mere interpretations, but the actual protection of private property. Ntsebeza (2007) suggests that those that acquired property through land dispossession and state support have a right to such property, the same way as those who were dispossessed and displaced. Some legal scholars take Ntsebeza's (2007) argument further, bringing our attention to the fragility of the South African Constitution in its totality, and not just the property clause.

Tshepo Madlingozi (2018) suggests that the Constitution in its current form does not provide a thorough framework to redress the injustices suffered by black people under apartheid and colonial rule. While amending the property clause for expropriation without compensation is necessary for land acquisition, Madlingozi (2018) calls for an entire remaking of a 'post-conquest constitution' that starts with the recognition of the crimes exerted against the humanity of black people by the racist colonial regimes and is explicit about reparations. This is particularly crucial in a settler colony like South Africa, in which land dispossession of black 'natives' by white settlers was central to colonial conquest and later advanced by the apartheid state. Having said this, the scope of this chapter is limited to the debates about amending the property clause.

Ntsebeza's (2007) argument exposes a dilemma: attempting to address the land question using the Constitution, which gives all, the dispossessed and beneficiaries of that dispossession, equal rights will keep leading to an impasse. A classic example of when the land reform programme reached a dead end was with the implementation of the willing buyer, willing seller policy, a political position adopted by the post-apartheid government for land reform in 1995, as discussed earlier. While land reform is embedded in the Constitution, the willing buyer, willing seller mechanism was a policy choice of government and is not enshrined in the Constitution (Lahiff, 2007). This policy choice did not produce success, as many farmers were unwilling to sell, and the government could not afford the market prices. This partly explains why there are over 11,000 labour tenant claims that have not been settled yet. A different approach is required in all areas of land reform, and it must consider the deeper meanings associated with land. The following sections present some ideas on how to discuss this wider conception of land, using both literature debates and views from the former labour tenants of the uMgungundlovu district.

CONTESTED LAND MEANINGS

While the dominant debates on land and agrarian reform have focused largely on the agricultural aspects of land, some scholars have highlighted other aspects that are equally important. Sam Moyo, Praveen Jha and Paris Yeros (2013) critique a view of the classical agrarian question in Marxian political economy that focuses solely on capital accumulation through capitalist agriculture. They argue that agrarian and land reform debates are naturally connected to the national question in societies with a colonial history (Moyo et al., 2013). Similar views are shared by Ntsebeza (2007), who states that even though the liberation struggle in South Africa was not fought explicitly around the land question, there was always an expectation that addressing centuries of land dispossession and oppression of black people by white settlers would be among the priorities of a democratic South Africa. There are cases where land was returned through the land reform programme, where beneficiaries were expected to continue with the agricultural business operations, yet they opted to use the land for settlement (Hall and Cliffe, 2009).

The unplanned uses of land led to relevant authorities disengaging from projects (Hall and Cliffe, 2009). This use of land, which does not fall within a commercially oriented land development paradigm, needs further attention. The land question is still not addressed, and the public interest in the debates about the amendment of the Constitution and land expropriation without compensation indicates this.

What seems to be neglected in the dominant competing views for addressing land and agrarian reforms are the non-productionist functions of land. These go beyond agricultural production or housing and are concerned with other land uses and meanings associated with people's notions of belonging. Notions of belonging are concerned with discourses, social practices and institutional arrangements through which people make claims for resources and rights, the ways through which they become 'incorporated' in particular places (Rutherford, 2008). This aspect of land use and meaning is important for rural black people, such as the former labour tenants and their descendants. They experienced land dispossession during the colonial and apartheid periods, which violated their citizenship and property rights. Such dispossession processes and outcomes are referred to by Bernadette Atuahene (2011) as 'dignity takings', as they occur when a state confiscates land and property rights from owners it deems to be subhuman, without any compensation for all that is lost. 'Dignity taking' was not a one-off event, but a process that continues to shape the livelihood options and life opportunities of those who were dispossessed and their descendants (Fay and James, 2010). Land is not limited to farming. Cross et al. (1996: 122) argue:

> Land includes savings in cattle, income in cash and in kind from production, growing demand for small business sites, rights to water, energy and other basic needs taken from a natural resource base, it also relates to land-based social networks as mechanisms for insurance and livelihoods security, and these need to be fully recognised.

This shows the diverse demands for land one could find in one locality. Drawing on their research on social reproduction on a former labour tenant's farm and communal land in KwaZulu-Natal, Cousins et al. (2018) emphasise that land and property rights are significant in different ways, even when their contribution to agriculture is limited. They further highlight how 'land is pivotal for the establishment of a homestead, the locus of daily and generational reproduction, which is why customary norms and practices offering guaranteed and free access to land to accepted community members remain important' (Cousins et al., 2018: 22). Jocelyn Alexander (2007) uses her research on Zimbabwe to explain that land is about identity, alongside production and class formation. It is equally about varied meanings and values that landowners or occupants attach to it. Such meanings are contested and not fixed (Alexander, 2007).

For a long time, the former labour tenants in KwaZulu-Natal demanded land for agricultural production, particularly cultivation, grazing and tenure security (Marcus et al., 1996). A need for security of tenure goes beyond farming but includes secured land rights to live with no fear of evictions. This security preserves dignity and secures land or homes for the future generation as well. My work with former labour tenants in uMgungundlovu district and northern KwaZulu-Natal illustrates how the demands for land are still the same. I have observed that while some aspire to be small-scale commercial farmers, and others do not, the common assertion is that they belong to the land, referring to the private farms they live on, which are also their homes. Cross et al. (1996) suggest that land rights, natural resources, self-determination, preservation of sacred sites and customs are among the pressing problems facing postcolonial societies today.

State-driven land reforms are an attempt to respond to such problems. Cross et al. (1996) elaborate that people claim belonging in varied, complex and often contradictory ways. These claims do not allow for a simple analysis or definition; they can be expressed in different ways, ranging from how people habitually use the land to its political value. The cultural meanings contained in naming land and a community's legal perspective also reveal claims for belonging (Cross et al., 1996). These aspects of land are important to black South

Africans such as the former labour tenants.

The following sections surface the forgotten voices of former labour tenants, who represent one of the most marginalised social groups in South Africa, and whose views were often peripheral in the public discourse. These are essentially the voices of ordinary black South Africans who still have fresh scars and memories of forced removals. The violent dispossession included white farmers taking their cattle away from them, burning their houses, displacing them from their land and forcing them into labour tenancy (Williams, 1996). Today, they continue to live in inhumane conditions in their homes that became privately owned farms as a result of land dispossession.

VIEWS FROM THE 'RIGHTFUL OWNERS' OF LAND

The group of former labour tenants, who participated in the debate about amending the Constitution, came under the banner of Siyanqoba. Siyanqoba was set up by its members as a forum to fight for land, better working conditions, humane living conditions, access to basic services and livelihood opportunities. Established in 2017, Siyanqoba brings together women and men, aged between 20 and 60 years. They were all born on commercial farms around uMgungundlovu district and they still reside in the area. Some of the members worked as labour tenants when they were young, while others shared experiences of their parents and grandparents who were labour tenants. The livelihood strategies of Siyanqoba members vary. Some derive income from seasonal jobs in the local municipality, commercial farms and in public employment programmes such as the Expanded Public Works Programme (EPWP) offered by the Department of Public Works. In these EPWP jobs they clean and repair roads. Others engage in informal businesses, such as selling refreshments and airtime vouchers in their local communities, or they engage in small-scale agriculture, mainly for subsistence. These are often combined with remittances from relatives and government social grants. These precarious livelihood strategies are common in rural South Africa today and can be explained by the agrarian changes that have unfolded over time (Neves and Du Toit, 2013).

The challenges of the former labour tenants living on commercial farms are often tied to property and power relations (Brandt, 2018). Some of the violations that the former labour tenants continue to endure on the farms include being prohibited from keeping livestock. In some cases, farm owners do not allow them to keep dogs and walk freely on the farm (Ms Mkhize, 2018). These restrictions on private farms highlight the powers of private property holders and demonstrate the contradictions of the property clause emphasised by Ntsebeza (2007). The private property rights of farmers, clash with those of former labour tenants, who have an equal claim to the land; this then becomes a hindrance to land reform policy implementation (Ntsebeza, 2007).

Siyanqoba has repeatedly challenged the local municipality over poor service delivery on the farms and has urged the officials to implement the provisions of the LTA to secure tenure and prevent evictions. These engagements with the municipality have sometimes included pickets and marches as well as court cases (Ms Zuma, 2018). Members of Siyanqoba participated in a series of discussions in preparation for the public hearings to voice their views on the question of whether the Constitution should be amended and if land should be expropriated without compensation. Their historical frustration was captured in the following words: 'Stop calling us farm dwellers, we are the rightful owners of this land, these were our homes before they became private farms and we were forced into labour tenancy' (Mr Dlamini, 2018).

Who should get which land and why? Should the Constitution be amended to allow for land expropriation without compensation and why? These questions framed the debate among the 40 former labour tenants and their descendants who participated. I have organised responses to these questions into the following sections. All interviewees have been allocated pseudonyms to maintain their anonymity.

Who should benefit from land expropriation?

One of the labour tenant land claimants criticised those who refer to former labour tenants as farm dwellers. He explained that this is dangerous, incorrect and dilutes their history, resulting in former labour tenants being seen by white farm owners and the state as having weaker rights to claim back the land (Mr Dlamini, 2018). The term farm dweller is used to describe farm workers, ex-workers and other citizens residing on farms that they do not own. Many farm dwellers are long-term residents, tracing their occupation back through generations. Under apartheid, farmworkers were tied, by law, into highly subservient relationships with white landowners, severely restricting their rights to change jobs or move off a farm (Lahiff, 2009).

Today, farm dwellers are constantly fighting against evictions from the farm and they often fail. The Extension of Security of Tenure Act (ESTA) of 1997, which was meant to protect farm dwellers from farm evictions and give them tenure security, has been challenged by academics, civil society and land rights activists for being too lenient on white farmers (Lahiff, 2009). In ESTA, farm evictions are allowed on condition that the farm owner follows legal procedure. In reality, most farm evictions occur illegally and, since ESTA was enacted, no single white farmer has been charged for any illegal farm eviction (Tshintsha Amakhaya Workshop, 2018). A significant feature of former labour tenants is that they experienced land dispossession and were forced to provide free and/or cheap labour for white farmers. It is this historical fact that gives them entitlement to getting their land back through the LTA.

The land claimant further elaborated that, as descendants of labour tenants, they are actually the 'rightful owners' of the land because had it not been for colonial conquest and apartheid, which saw their land and homes forcibly turned into private property, the country would not be having debates about who should get the land. His views were held by many who participated in the debate. They were against reducing labour tenants and their history to a mere loss of land through some unknown process. This view resonates with Madlingozi's (2018) argument on the fragility of the Constitution: that if we do not name colonialism and apartheid as crimes against humanity and are not explicit about who was responsible, who benefited and continues to benefit, then our work on restitution and reparations becomes untenable. All labour tenants across gender and age affirmed that they are the 'rightful owners' in the discussions. There was broad consensus among participants that former labour tenants and their descendants must get their land back as a matter of priority.

What do former labour tenants want land for and what does land mean?

Some want ownership of homes and small fields that they already live in. They also want the land portions that are currently utilised by white farmers to be expropriated and redistributed among them (the 'rightful owners') for commercial agriculture (Mr Khumalo, 2018). The former labour tenants can succeed in small-scale commercial agriculture with proper state support, especially if it includes the policy support measures provided to white commercial farmers during apartheid. Tessa Marcus, Kathy Eales and Adele Wildschut (1996) remind us that the former labour tenants in KwaZulu-Natal demanded land for agricultural production, particularly cultivation and grazing.

Not all the former labour tenant land claimants want to pursue small-scale commercial agriculture or any form of agricultural production for that matter. Some emphasised that land meant dignity, belonging, housing and other livelihood opportunities (Ms Mkhize, 2018). One of the land claimants shared a story of how the white farm owner, who owns the property on which she resides with her grandfather, shot and killed her dog for loitering. She recalled several occasions when family relatives, friends or AFRA staff members were aggressively questioned when they visited her homestead. Mrs Mkhize (2018) added:

> We can't live like we are in prison. There are many South Africans who travel on the N3 over there, all they see are large farms with high fencing, they do not know these are actually prisons to us. We want our land back because we belong here and have every right to live freely, with our dogs, cats or whoever we like.

Her views resonated with many who shared similar experiences about their visitors being interrogated whenever they were seen on the farm. When asked what land meant to them as former labour tenant land claimants, Ms Msomi (2018) explained:

> Land means everything to us here, you can come to the farms and ask each person there, they will tell you the same thing. Land means having a home for you and your children, and their

> children to come, it means food, it is where our ancestors were buried and where we also shall be buried. The problem with government and all these delays with the processing of our land claims is that they think land is only a farm. Yes, we farm on the land, but that's not the only thing it is used for.

These material and symbolic meanings of land often determine how people use the land. I have observed this in my family homestead, but also through my work in rural South Africa over the years. This ranges from the kinds of crops people grow, the structures they construct in the homestead, the position of the sites for graves and the kraals for livestock. There was no single person in the room that disputed the take on the meaning of land shared by the land claimant above; instead there was a big round of applause after she spoke, which I took as agreement. However, there were tensions and points of disagreement on some issues that emerged during the debate.

Imagining the future

Disagreements in the debate hinged on two issues: (1) should the current white farmers operating on the farms leave when land claims are settled? and (2) should the former labour tenants that do not live on the farms for a range of reasons come back when the land is returned to the claimants? Some claimants expressed the view that the white farmers would have to go, and that those former labour tenants who want to increase their farming production would share the land accordingly. One of the land claimants, Mr Luthuli (2018), explained this position:

> I think it is obvious that the white farm owners will have to go. I am just thinking about the white farmer on our farm. He simply hates us and does not see us as humans. Now tell me how can we share that land with the same person when we finally get our homes and land back? I say no, they must go, and they must not be compensated.

Another land claimant, Mr Khumalo (2018), held a slightly different view:

> On the question of compensation, I fully agree that the government must not pay them. Where I differ is on the issue of whether they must stop farming and leave the property. I think those who want to use some parts of the land to continue with agricultural production should do so, but not on their terms. The problem is that they have land ownership papers and so they also treat us like they own us. Once those papers become invalid, then we can talk.

There was no consensus on this subject, and those who felt strongly about the white farmers leaving concluded by suggesting that more debates on this point were crucial, perhaps drawing on experiences from other areas. Indeed, this is an issue that the land claimants on each farm will have to grapple with, especially because some of them are employed by the production side of the farm, and not all of them want to pursue small-scale commercial agriculture. This, however, does not change their position regarding transferring land ownership to them. How will the land be shared among the claimants and governed once the claims are settled? This is a separate question from the one about acquiring land through expropriation without compensation. Although they are closely related, the two issues need to be dealt with separately.

The second point of disagreement during the debate was about whether those that had left the farms should be allowed to return once the land claims were settled. A distinction was made between those who had left because they were evicted by farm owners and those who had volunteered to leave. One of the land claimants felt strongly that those who had volunteered to leave must not come back. His reason was that 'we are fighting alone here, even going to courts, where are they? They can't only come in the end when our claims are settled' (Mr Mpungose, 2018). Another land claimant, Ms Zuma (2018), swiftly responded:

> Let us hang on a bit, we know what happens on these farms, people are forced to leave because of hardships, so we can't say they volunteered as if it was a happy choice. You know when a white farmer does not want you on the farm, they make it very difficult, like cutting your water and threaten to beat up your

> children. There are many people who left the farms, yet their parents are buried on the farms. They also belong with us.

A land claimant emphasised that all those people who lodged land claims, and do not live on the farms for whatever reasons, have the same rights to claim the land as everyone else in the room. He said that 'those are our allies' (Mr Khumalo, 2018). This is another issue that the former labour tenants of Siyanqoba must discuss further because it could potentially cause conflict among land claimants in the future.

On the amendment of the Constitution and expropriation without compensation

Atuahene (2011) describes historical land dispossession and the development of the labour tenancy system as the 'dignity takings', as discussed earlier. This violent appropriation informs former labour tenants' views on justice, which, according to them, is expressed in expropriation and redistribution of land without compensating white farmers. They argue that they must get their land back and any form of compensation should be directed towards them. This position is based on all the cheap labour provided to white farmers by different generations of labour tenants, and other forms of suffering they endured since experiencing dispossession. As one of the land claimants, Ms Ngcobo (2018), elaborated:

> Why was the word compensation in the property clause in the first place? Who put it there? I ask this because I can see that this compensation is only intended for white farmers, they are promised to be paid for returning the land that belonged to us in the first place and was taken by force and black people died in the process. Is this what the government means by land reform?

Responding to these questions and views, another former labour tenant, Mr Luthuli (2018), nodded in agreement, adding:

> As a young boy it was very painful to see my father cry as the white man confiscated about 30 of his cattle; we never saw those

> cattle again, in fact if you need a cow for *umsebenzi* [traditional ceremony] today, you buy it from a white man.

The views expressed were challenging and questioned the foundation of the property clause, and the purpose of land reform broadly and whether it is really about redressing the injustices of the past or merely a perfunctory exercise that is far from dismantling inequality, as Ntsebeza (2007) observes. A claimant, Ms Mgoma (2018), emphasised:

> As long as white farmers are private owners, even if we get access to bigger portions of land for our own production, we will never live freely, they must not be the owners period. In other words, land must be returned to its rightful owner.

Many agreed that the racially skewed and unequal property relations on the farms caused and exacerbated the harsh living conditions. This included the ruthless treatment that most of them received from the white farmers on a regular basis. Therefore, returning the land to its rightful owners through settling pending land claims is non-negotiable. One of the land claimants, Ms Maphumulo (2018), sealed the two-hour vigorous debate by asking:

> If the government pays white farmers for our land (that they now call theirs), where will the money come from? Will it come from everybody's tax? How can my land be taken away and then later my tax be used to pay the white farmer who took my land compensation? We are being fooled here. They must remove that compensation thing from the Constitution. In a nutshell, the Constitution must be amended.

There were no objections from anyone else in the room. The members of Siyanqoba gave a round of applause, one member shouted '*Amandla*' (Power), to which everyone replied, '*Awethu*' (It's Ours/ To the People).

Conclusion

It is clear from the views of the former labour tenants of uMgungundlovu, who are also land claimants, that no compensation should be paid to white farmers who currently own the land for which they have lodged claims. If the Constitution is not explicit enough on the matter of expropriation without compensation, the former labour tenants argue, it must be amended (Siyanqoba members, 2018). I have outlined the reasons for their position on the matter. Central to their argument is a history of land dispossession and the development of capitalist agriculture, which occurred through displacing the black peasantry, forced removals and the exploitation of black people's labour – all of which unfolded over generations (Morris, 1977; Williams, 1996). According to the Siyanqoba members, nothing will ever compensate for the historical dispossession and vicious cycle of poverty resulting from landlessness. They argue that any compensation should be paid to them, and many other former labour tenant land claimants, as reparations for colonial and apartheid land dispossession rather than the state compensating white landowners.

This chapter has also discussed the democratic government's failure to address the racial injustices suffered by former labour tenants and their descendants, and how the latter have responded to these disappointments through protests and court actions. The disconnection between the state's land reform model and the needs of those it is supposed to benefit comes out clearly in the focus group discussions and existing land reform literature (Hall and Kepe, 2017). Former labour tenants and their descendants need land because they belong to it. Land is not just a commodity, it is also a place of belonging and this is expressed in different ways (Bundy, 1990; Alexander, 2007). The state has put little emphasis on other land demands and uses that are not productivist in nature. Yet, for black people, such as the former labour tenants who were dispossessed of their land, symbolic dimensions of land, such as belonging, are crucial. Belonging is an important dimension of the ongoing work of transformation in South Africa, where capitalist development was premised largely on racial segregation and the economic exploitation of black people (Morris, 1977).

Overwhelming numbers of ordinary South Africans attended the public hearings on the constitutional amendment. This indicates the importance of the land question and how land reform programmes have not brought about desirable redress for many black South Africans. Even if the Constitution is amended and explicitly provides for land to be expropriated without compensation, the political will of the state will still be crucial for the implementation. The evolution of land reform programmes articulated in this chapter provides little hope on the political will of the state to deliver on pro-poor land reform. What these observations suggest is that there is an urgent need for many black people, such as the former labour tenants, farm workers, small-scale farmers, rural and urban landless people, to use their agency to organise and strengthen their power to put pressure on the state. The ugly picture of structural poverty and inequality must be challenged, and radical land redistribution that addresses colonial and apartheid ills is a good place to start. This requires laws and policies informed by the experiences of the marginalised, such as the former labour tenants of uMgungundlovu.

REFERENCES

Alexander, J. 2007, 'The historiography of land in Zimbabwe: Strengths, silences, and questions'. *Safundi,* 8 (2), 183–198.

Atuahene, B. 2011. 'Paying for the past: Redressing the legacy of land dispossession in South Africa'. *Law & Society Review,* 45 (4), 955–989.

Brandt, F. 2018. 'South Africa's dangerous game: Re-configuring power and belonging on Karoo trophy-hunting farms', in Brandt, F. and Mkodzongi, G. (eds.) *Land Reform Revisited.* Leiden: Brill, 58–77.

Bundy, C. 1990. 'Land, law and power: Forced removals in historical context', in Murray, C. and O'Regan, C. (eds.) *No Place to Rest: Forced removals and the law in South Africa.* Cape Town: Oxford University Press, 3–12.

Cousins, B. 2013, 'Land reform and agriculture uncoupled: The political economy of rural reform in post-apartheid South Africa', in Cousin, B. and Hebinck, P. (eds.) *The Shadow of Policy: Everyday practices in South Africa's land and agrarian reform.* Johannesburg: Wits University Press, 47–62.

Cousins, B., Dubb, A., Hornby, D. and Mtero, F. 2018. 'Social reproduction of "classes of labour" in the rural areas of South Africa: Contradictions and contestations'. *Journal of Peasant Studies,* 45 (5–6), 1060–1085.

Cross, C., Mngadi, T., Sibanda, S. and Jama, V. 1996, 'Making a living under land reform: Weighing up the chances in KwaZulu-Natal', in Lipton, M., Ellis, F. and Lipton, M. (eds.) *Land, Labour and Livelihoods in Rural South Africa, Volume 2: KwaZulu-Natal and Northern Province*. Durban: Indicator Press, 121–172.

Department of Agriculture (DOA). 2001. 'Land redistribution for agricultural development', https://www.daff.gov.za/docs/Policy/redistribution.htm, accessed 20 August 2020.

Department of Land Affairs (DLA). 1997. 'White Paper on South African land policy', http://www.ruraldevelopment.gov.za/phocadownload/White-Papers/whitepaperlandreform.pdf, accessed 6 August 2020.

Fay, D. and James, D. 2010. 'Giving land back or righting wrongs', in Walker, C., Bohlin, A., Hall, R. and Kepe, T. (eds.) *Land, Memory, Reconstruction, and Justice: Perspectives on land claims in South Africa.* Athens, OH: Ohio University Press, 41–61.

Feinberg, H.M. 1993. 'The 1913 Natives Land Act in South Africa: Politics, race, and segregation in the early 20th century'. *International Journal of African Historical Studies,* 26 (1), 65–109.

Hall, R. 2004. 'Restitution and the politics of land reform: Stepping outside the box'. Paper presented at the Conference on Ten Years of Democracy in Southern Africa, Queens University, Kingston, 2–5 May.

Hall, R. 2009. 'Land reform for what? Land use, production and livelihoods', in Hall, R. (ed.) *Another Countryside: Policy options for land and agrarian reform in South Africa*. Cape Town: PLAAS, 23–62.

Hall, R. 2011. 'The politics of land reform in post-apartheid South Africa, 1990 to 2004: A shifting terrain of power, actors and discourses'. D.Phil. thesis, University of Oxford.

Hall, R. and Cliffe, L. 2009. 'Introduction', in Hall, R. (ed.) *Another Countryside: Policy options for land and agrarian reform in South Africa.* Cape Town: PLAAS, 1–22.

Hall, R. and Kepe, T. 2017, 'Elite capture and state neglect: New evidence on South Africa's land reform'. *Review of African Political Economy,* 44 (151), 122–130.

Hathorn, M. and Hutchinson, D. 1990. 'Labour tenants and the law', in Murray, C. and O'Regan, C. (eds.) *No Place to Rest: Forced removals and the law in South Africa.* Cape Town: Oxford University Press, 194–213.

Hebinck, P. 2013, 'Land and agrarian reform policies from a historical perspective', in Hebinck, P. and Cousins, B. (eds.) *In the Shadow of Policy: Everyday practices in South Africa's land and agrarian reform.* Johannesburg: Wits University Press, 29–47.

Lahiff, E. 2007. '"Willing buyer, willing seller": South Africa's failed experiment in market-led agrarian reform'. *Third World Quarterly,* 28 (8), 1577–1597.

Lahiff, E. 2009. 'With what land rights? Tenure arrangements and support', in Hall, R. (ed.) *Another Countryside: Policy options for land and agrarian reform in South Africa*. Cape Town: PLAAS, 93–117.

Mabasa, B. 14 February 2020. 'The lay of the land'. *Werkmans*, https://www.werkmans.com/legal-updates-and-opinions/the-lay-of-the-land/, accessed 24 August 2020.

Madlingozi, T. 6 April 2018. 'The proposed amendment to the South African Constitution: Finishing the unfinished business of decolonisation?' *Critical Legal Thinking*, https//criticallegalthinking.com/2018/04/06/the-proposed-amendment-to-the-south-african-constitution/, accessed 10 June 2020.

Marcus, T., Eales, K. and Wildschut, A. 1996. *Down to Earth: Land demand in the new South Africa*. Durban: Indicator Press.

McClendon, T.V. 2002. *Genders and Generations Apart: Labour tenants and customary law in segregation-era South Africa, 1920s to 1940s*. Portsmouth: Heinemann.

Morris, M. 1977. 'Apartheid, agriculture and the state: The farm labour question'. Saldru Working Paper No. 8, http://opensaldru.uct.ac.za/bitstream/handle/11090/524/1977_morris_swp8.pdf?sequence=1, accessed 18 August 2020.

Moyo, S., Jha, P. and Yeros, P. 2013. 'The classical agrarian question: Myth, reality and relevance today'. *Agrarian South: Journal of Political Economy*, 2 (1), 93–119.

Neves, D. and Du Toit, A. 2013. 'Rural livelihoods in South Africa: Complexity, vulnerability and differentiation'. *Journal of Agrarian Change*, 13 (1), 93–115.

Ntsebeza, L. 2007. 'Land redistribution in South Africa: The property clause revisited', in Ntsebeza, L. and Hall, R. (eds.) *The Land Question in South Africa: The challenge of transformation and redistribution*. Cape Town: HSRC Press, 107–131.

Rutherford, B. 2008. 'An unsettled belonging: Zimbabwean farm workers in Limpopo Province, South Africa'. *Journal of Contemporary African Studies*, 26 (4), 401–415.

Wagerif, M., Russell, B. and Grundling, I. 2005. *Still Searching for Security: The reality of farm dweller evictions in South Africa*. Polokwane: Nkuzi Development Association.

Welsh, D. 1971. *The Roots of Segregation: Native policy in colonial Natal, 1845–1910*. London: Oxford University Press.

Williams, G. 1996. 'Transforming labour tenants', in Lipton, M., Ellis, F. and Lipton, M. (eds.) *Land, Labour and Livelihoods in Rural South Africa, Volume 2: KwaZulu-Natal and Northern Province*. Durban: Indicator Press, 215–238.

Legislation

Constitution of the Republic of South Africa (Act No. 108 of 1996).
Extension of Security of Tenure Act (ESTA, No. 62 of 1997).
Labour Tenants Act (LTA, No. 3 of 1996).

Interviews (All interviewees have been allocated pseudonyms)

Mr Dlamini. 2018. Interview with author, Pietermaritzburg.
Mr Khumalo. 2018. Interview with author, Pietermaritzburg.
Mr Luthuli. 2018. Interview with author, Pietermaritzburg.
Mr Mpungose. 2018. Interview with author, Pietermaritzburg.
Ms Maphumulo. 2018. Interview with author, Pietermaritzburg.
Ms Mkhize. 2018. Interview with author, Pietermaritzburg.
Ms Mngoma. 2018. Interview with author, Pietermaritzburg.
Ms Msomi. 2018. Interview with author, Pietermaritzburg.
Ms Ngcobo. 2018. Interview with author, Pietermaritzburg.
Ms Zuma. 2018. Interview with author, Pietermaritzburg.
Ms Zuma. 2018. Interview with author, Pietermaritzburg.
Siyanqoba members. 2018. Interview with author, Pietermaritzburg.
Statement made by an attorney of the Legal Resource Centre at a Tshintsha Amakhaya Workshop, 2018.

EIGHT

Dispossession and Displacement: Land, rights and dignity in rural Mozambique and Angola

DAVID MATSINHE

Our ancestors have always used this land as a reserve for grazing cattle. In difficult times people have always come from as far as 150km with their cattle. They still do. This place was always a miracle that saved lives from time immemorial. Then the Portuguese came and took the land and pushed our ancestors out. We fought for independence and got our land back only to have our own people become the colonisers, taking our land and pushing us out again. This time the colonisers are our people who have influential positions in the government. They are the ones exploiting us.[1]

1 Words of a traditional pastoralist in southern Angola, quoted in Amnesty International (2019).

INTRODUCTION

This chapter documents the dispossession and displacement of rural communities in Mozambique and Angola to make room for mining and agribusiness projects. This phenomenon has been one of the most visible economic, social and topographic transformations in the countryside since the end of the civil wars in both countries. Like elsewhere in Africa, foreign direct investment-friendly policies were promoted to attract foreign companies looking for land, natural resources, cheap labour and higher profits (World Bank, 2009; 2010). Driven by the dominant belief that stimulating a scramble for land would fuel much-needed economic growth, job creation and development, the countries opened the floodgates for land acquisition for mining, logging and the production of cash crops for export (McKenzie, 2006; Chanda, 2010; Richardson, 2010). In this manner, remote rural lands and communities became increasingly absorbed into the global economy, as the case studies in this chapter demonstrate.

However, these developments were problematic because, since independence in 1975, the Mozambican and Angolan governments had failed to build basic infrastructure for education, healthcare, transportation, telecommunications, water and sanitation in the countryside, leaving rural and isolated populations almost entirely dependent on the land for their livelihoods and ways of life (Nabudere, 2001; Moyo, 2003; Clover, 2005; Foley, 2007; De Oliveira, 2015; Filipe and Norfolk, 2017). This meant that, rather than creating the coveted opportunities and prosperity, large-scale land acquisition for mining and agribusiness dispossessed already marginalised communities without offering them viable livelihood alternatives in exchange.

While the problem under consideration is widespread in these countries, the chapter focuses only on two cases per country as entry points into the problem. In Mozambique, the first case study is the dispossession and displacement of peasants to make room for coal mining in Tete Province, and the second is the clearance of peasant and fishing communities on the coast of Cabo Delgado Province in favour of liquefied natural gas (LNG) exploration. In Angola, the first study is the dispossession and displacement of pastoralists and peasants in the municipality of Curoca, Cunene Province, and the second is the expropriation and dislocation in the municipality of Gambos, Huila Province.

Taking a human rights approach for each country, the chapter introduces the land tenure legal context before documenting the cases. In so doing, it situates the reader in relation to the cases within the legal parameters of what is admissible and inadmissible in Mozambican and Angolan legislations. The content makes explicit the legal assignment of roles, responsibilities and rights between the actors – governments, companies and communities – showing how the relationships between them are, or should be, configured.

METHODOLOGY

Under the auspices of Amnesty International, a global human rights organisation of which I am part, this study spins off field research on economic, social and cultural rights in communities dispossessed and displaced by mining and commercial farming operations in Mozambique and Angola between 2016 and 2019, the results of which have been published elsewhere (Amnesty International, 2018; 2019). In Mozambique, my field research has focused on the central and northern regions where this dispossession has been taking place. In Angola, my fieldwork focused on the southern region in the provinces of Cunene and Huila where the government and local and international investors have been occupying communal grazing land for commercial ranching.

I conducted in-depth interviews with dispossessed and displaced families, government officials, civil society representatives, journalists, human rights defenders and activists in both countries (65 in Angola and 75 in Mozambique). For both countries, I analysed legislative and policy frameworks on land rights and security of tenure; and I conducted documentary analysis of campaign and advocacy literature from international human rights organisations, local civil society organisations, journalists and human rights defenders. By comparing the findings of my fieldwork and those of other researchers who had conducted civic research and education, a pattern became evident of rural communities thrown off balance due to dispossession and dislocation, invariably through deception and aggression by government officials working hand in glove with company representatives (Amnesty International, 2018; 2019).

I have drawn from the civic research and education material as well as campaign and advocacy documents produced by partner human rights organisations, including Amnesty International, Human Rights Watch (HRW), the Angolan Working Group on Human Rights Monitoring (GTMDH), Rede Terra Viva (RTV), the Centre for Studies in Communication and Development (SEKELEKANI) and the Civil Society News Agency (CIVILINFO).

The legal land tenures in Mozambique and Angola[2]

The Constitution of the Republic of Mozambique (Article 29) and the Land Law (Article 10) declare land as state property, which cannot be sold, traded or mortgaged. Rather than granting the land itself to interested parties, the government grants only the right to use and develop the land. This right is guaranteed with the issuance of the certificate of the right of land use and development, locally known as the Direito de Uso e Aproveitamento da Terra (DUAT). However, the national legislation recognises the DUAT of rural residents and communities without the need for the DUAT certificate if such residents and communities have been living and using the land for a minimum of 10 years.

The DUAT, not the land itself, can be transferred from one holder to another. Depending on the circumstances, the transfer can be as simple as an agreement between two parties or as complex as a multi-staged process involving community consultations, environmental impact assessments, resettlement of communities and annual environmental auditing. In the cases described here, the DUAT transfer requires all the last-mentioned processes.

Community consultations were required in compliance with the right to free, prior and informed consent of the residents.

2 A detailed exegesis of the Mozambican land tenure system in the context of business and human rights is available (Amnesty International, 2018). So is a detailed analysis of the Angolan land tenure system in the context of business and human rights (Amnesty International, 2019).

Regulamento Ambiental para Actividade Mineira, Decreto n° 26/2004 (Environmental Regulation for Mining Activities, Decree No. 26/2004) sets out the necessary procedures on community consultations. It states in Article 27:

> (1) Local communities must be consulted regarding the attribution of the rights to land use and development for mining activities, in terms stipulated in the land and mining legislation; (2) The proponent of a mining project must facilitate the participation of local communities of the site of the project in the making of decisions that might directly affect their rights; (3) The public must have access to the summaries of the project, environmental reports and any other documents relevant to the environmental and social management of the project; (4) The public must be informed ahead of time of any presentations or public hearings related to the project, being the responsibility of the project proponent to facilitate the public's presence in the meetings; (5) The public presentations and hearings at the site of the project must be conducted in Portuguese and the local language.

Environmental and social impact assessments are required for all mining projects to identify, anticipate, mitigate and remedy negative impacts on the environment and affected communities. This requirement is governed by Regulamento sobre o Processo de Avaliação do Impacto Ambiental, Decreto n° 45/2004 de 29 de Setembro (Regulation on the Process of Environmental Impact Assessment, Decree No. 45/2004). This process is linked to the resettlement process as it constitutes the basis on which the decision is made on whether communities should be resettled. Regulamento sobre o Processo de Reassentamento Resultante das Actividades Económicas, Decreto n° 31/2012 (Regulation on the Resettlement Process as a Result of Economic Activities, Decree No. 31/2012) states in Article 15:3: 'The Resettlement Plan is an integral part of the Environmental Impact Assessment Process, according to the Annex 1 of the Decree 45/2004, of 29 September, on Environmental Impact Assessment Process.'

The standards and procedures for community resettlement are set out in Regulamento sobre o Processo de Reassentamento Resultante das Actividades Económicas, Decreto n° 31/2012 (Regulation on the Resettlement Process as a Result of Economic Activities, Decree No. 31/2012). The resettlement provisions include (Article 4):

- Ensuring social integration and restoring the standard of living of the affected people to a superior level.
- Restoration or creation of living conditions equal or greater than the previous standard of living.
- Public participation which requires all those affected by the activity to be heard in the resettlement process.
- The principle of environmental accountability according to which whosoever pollutes or in any other shape or form degrades the environment, has always the obligation to repair, or compensate for, the damage thereof.

The implementation of this legislative framework must be undertaken, monitored, supervised and enforced by the Ministry of Mineral Resources and the Ministry of Land, Environment and Rural Development. Local government officials in these ministries have the responsibility to ensure that community consultations, environmental and social impact assessments, community resettlement and environmental audits are conducted within the parameters of this legal framework. In other words, beyond legislating, the government must implement and enforce.

This legislative framework on land tenure and DUAT transfer regulates all the mining projects in Mozambique. Therefore, the Tete and Cabo Delgado cases as presented below must be considered with this land tenure and DUAT transfer framework in mind, given the fact that the mining companies under consideration occupied lands that been inhabited by local communities. In other words, for the mining companies to set up their operations, they needed the affected communities to agree to transfer their DUATs through free, prior and informed consent.

Now let us consider the main characteristic features of the Angolan land tenure system and process of land rights transfer. As in

Mozambique, the Constitution of the Angolan Republic (Article 15) regards the land natural property of the state that may be transmitted to natural or legal persons for rational and effective use in compliance with the law. The Constitution grants land use to communities, although it reserves the state right to land expropriation for public utility, through fair compensation, according to the law (Article 37).

The Land Law recognises the rights of rural communities to own and use land. That is, the Land Law respects customary land tenure and categorises collectively held and used rural land as 'rural communal land'. Lei de Terras de Angola, Lei n° 9/04 (Land Law) states: 'The State respects and protects the land rights of rural communities, including those based on use or custom' (Article 9). The land shall change hands conditional to 'fair compensations to the holder of extinct rights' (Article 12).

Lei de Bases do Ambiente, Lei n° 5/98 (Environmental Law) sets conditions for land rights transfer upon community consultations, without which companies cannot legally occupy rural communal lands. Even where communal rural lands are not involved, community consultations are imperative for projects that can potentially interfere with 'the interests of the communities, interfere with the ecological balance and use of natural resources to the detriment of third parties' (Article 10). In its preamble, Decreto sobre a Avaliação de Impacte Ambiental n° 51/04 (Decree on Environmental Impact Assessment No. 51/04) describes community consultations as follows:

> The consultation of the citizens concerned, residents in the area concerned or affected by the project, their representative associations, in particular, those in the field of environmental protection and local authority bodies in the territorial area concerned, as well as representatives of institutions if the project has an impact on rural communities.

Community consultations must be undertaken side by side with the environmental and social impact assessment. For companies to implement projects with potential environment and social implications, the Angolan law imposes the requirement for environmental and social impact assessment. Lei de Bases do Ambiente, Lei n° 5/98, requires this for any project, 'which by its size, nature or location, has a significant negative impact on the natural or social environment' or which 'may have implications for environmental and social balance and harmony' (Article 16). The objective of the environmental and social impact assessment is to 'determine its social, environmental, economic viability, and the methods for neutralising or minimizing its effects' (Article 15). According to Article 16, the environmental and social impact assessment must be case specific and must include, among other things:

> (a) a non-technical summary of the project; (b) a description of the activities to be carried out; (c) a general description of the environmental situation of the place of implementation of the activity; (d) a summary of the opinions and criticisms resulting from the public consultations; (e) a description of the possible environmental and social changes brought about by the project; (f) indication of the measures envisaged to eliminate or minimize negative social and environmental effects; (g) an indication of the systems planned for the control and monitoring of the activity..

It is crucial that this legal framework on land tenure should foreground the consideration and appreciation of the cases in Cunene and Huila as presented below. That is to say, the legal land tenure framework provides the necessary instruments to measure the depth and breadth to which the protagonists succeeded or failed to comply with the laws of the land.

Dispossession and displacement in Mozambique

In 2012, the United Nations Conference on Trade and Development (UNCTAD) reported that, from the end of the 1990s decade, Mozambique began to attract big foreign direct investment, and by the year 2000 the country was attracting $179 million per year, $258 million per year in the mid-2000s and $890 million in 2009 (UNCTAD, 2012: 15). Large proportions of these investments were for the extractives industry and, to some extent, the aluminium smelter mega-project in Matola (UNCTAD, 2012). According to the World Bank, since 2010, Mozambique has absorbed about 15 per cent of all foreign direct investment inflows in sub-Saharan Africa, and in 2013 to 2015 foreign direct investment accounted for 70 per cent of the country's gross domestic product (GDP), the highest proportion in sub-Saharan Africa (World Bank, 2017: 3). Large proportions of these funds went to resource extraction and agribusinesses that require large tracts of land in rural areas. The intensity of these investments has been such that, despite the ongoing economic crisis which began in 2016, 'the extractive sector has been a pocket of resilience and a driver of the recent improvement in growth', whereby 'extractives maintained double-digit output growth' (World Bank, 2017: 3).

In Mozambique, foreign direct investment in the mining sector circulates in opaque spaces reminiscent of the colonial frontier, characterised by secrecy, poor regulation, human rights abuses and environmental destruction (Omar, 2019; Salimo and Macuane, 2019). As the evidence will show, often the government facilitates unjust processes of land expropriation, resulting in further impoverishment of rural communities. Once mining operations begin, the communities must deal with pollutants released into the air, soil and water. The following sections analyse these processes in Tete and Cabo Delgado provinces.

THE CASE OF COAL MINING IN TETE

Tete Province is made up of 98,500 square kilometres, over half of which contains coal. Since 2007, the Mozambican government has been issuing mining licences to various companies, including Rio Tinto, Vale and Jindal, among others. The province is home to almost three million people, most of whom live in rural areas and depend entirely on the land for subsistence. Their interaction with the land and the local natural ecosystem fulfils their basic needs. In Figure 8.1, the map of coal mining projects in Tete shows the entire province covered in mining concessions, leaving nearly no land for people to produce and collect food, graze cattle, fetch firewood, gather medicinal plants and collect water, or undertake other land-based subsistence activities.

According to Environmental Justice Atlas, 60,000 square kilometres – that is, 61 per cent of Tete Province – sits on coal, and the Mozambican government has issued licences for all the land containing coal. This means 'more than half of the area of Tete province [is] covered by coal mining concessions' (Environmental Justice Atlas, 2013).

Figure 8.1: Map of mining licences in Tete Province, Mozambique

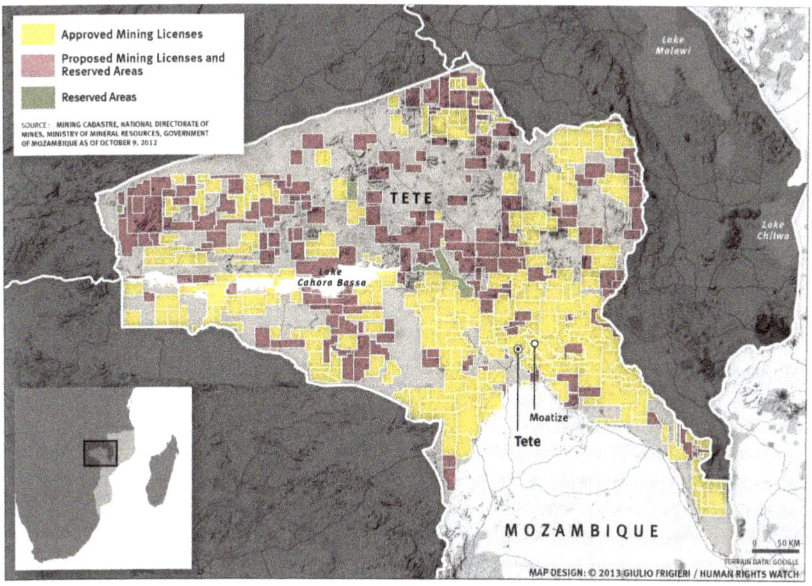

Source: Environnemental Justice Atlas, https://ejatlas.org/conflict/resettlements-for-mining-projects-in-tete-province.

In order to license 61 per cent of the province to mining companies, the government needed to dispossess and displace thousands of people living in these areas. By 2013, there were 10 companies with some form of coal mining operations in Tete, namely Vale S.A. (Brazilian), Rio Tinto (British/Australian), Beacon Hill Resources PLC (British), Nkondezi Coal (South African), Minas de Revuboé Limitada (Mozambican), Jindal Africa (Indian), Eurasian Natural Resources Corporation (Kazakhstan), Mozambi Coal Limited (Australian), Coal India Africana Limitada (Indian) and Essar (Indian) (HRW, 2013: 108). The process of land expropriation from local populations to make room for these companies was not undertaken with human rights due diligence – in other words, largely in violation of the letter and the spirit of existing legislation. The expropriation disregarded the economic, social and cultural rights, and the human dignity of the affected people. As a result, the dispossession and displacement and the mining operations aggravated the impoverishment of affected communities (HRW, 2013; De Matos and Medeiro, 2015; CIVILINFO, 2016a; SEKELEKANI, 2017).

Jindal, Rio Tinto and Vale concessions

HRW (2013) and SEKELEKANI (2016) interviewed community residents affected by Jindal, Rio Tinto and Vale mining operations. The Indian company Jindal Steel and Power Limited obtained the Chirodzi mining concession in 2011 and began operations in 2012. Here, Jindal would resettle the communities of Cassoca and Nhomadzinedzani, consisting of 484 families with 2,050 people in total, into a newly constructed resettlement village. In fact, Jindal's Chirodzi mining operations affected 968 more families comprising about 4,000 people in Chirodzi, Chirodzi-Ponte and Nhatsanga-Ponte through the loss of farmland (HRW, 2013: 47). In the end, however, Jindal resettled none of these affected communities, preferring instead to enclose the concession area with a metallic fence, which kept the communities locked inside the enclosure with restricted movements (SEKELEKANI, 2016: 12).

In 2011, Rio Tinto, the Anglo-Australian mining company, bought Riversdale Mining, an Australian company. The acquisition included all of Riversdale concessions in Tete, namely Zambeze, Tete East and Benga projects. Riversdale had begun resettling communities in 2011. The Benga project, 35 per cent of which belonged to Tata Steel, an Indian company, resettled 679 families living in the Capanga and Benga communities. Most of these families were resettled in the newly constructed Mwaladzi village, adjacent to Vale's Cateme resettlement village. In 2012, Rio Tinto began its mining operations in Benga mine (HWR, 2013; CIVILINFO, 2016b; SKELEKANI, 2016).

The Brazilian mining company, Vale S.A., began exploring for coal in 2004, built its mine in 2008 and resettled communities in 2009 in Moatize district. Vale displaced 1,365 families comprising 6,000 people from the Bagamoyo, Chipanga, Malabwe and Mithete communities, and either resettled them to 25 de Setembro and Cateme resettlements or provided them with some type of compensation. The 25 de Setembro resettlement, in Moatize town, housed 289 families, whereas the rural resettlement in Cateme housed 716 families. In the former, the resettled families who depended entirely on subsistence agriculture were not allotted farmland, whereas in the latter the resettled families, who also depended entirely on subsistence agriculture, were allotted two hectares of farmland (HWR, 2013; CIVILINFO, 2016b; SEKLEKANI, 2016).

The dispossession and dislocation to make room for these and other mining operations in Tete Province have resulted in further impoverishment and immiseration of the affected communities. Whether the communities were resettled in the newly build resettlement villages, as was the case with Rio and Vale, or whether they were simply caged like zoo animals in the enclosures of mining concessions, as was the case with Jindal, this does not account for much difference in the erosion of economic, social and cultural rights and negation of human dignity. The expropriation robbed the communities of their way of life and means of subsistence. This condition found expression in Rio Tinto's Resettlement Action Plan, which said (HRW, 2013: 55–56):

> Wild fruit trees are by far the most important natural resource in the project area, with more than 90 per cent of households reporting that they use this resource. Other important natural resources include firewood and construction materials, which correlates with the use of these materials in housing and structures. Approximately 90 per cent of households in both Benga Sede and Capanga villages have a cash income, whether it is regular, occasional or seasonal income. Selling vegetables, retailing home goods and selling firewood are the most common sources of cash income.

As we shall see, the mining operations also made the environmental conditions unbearable as food, water, vegetation and air carried highly toxic pollutants from the mining operations.

Food and water

Both the resettled and the iron-caged communities experienced severe food and water shortages. The communities resettled by Rio Tinto and Vale in 25 de Setembro, Cateme and Mwaladzi resettlement villages expressed their dissatisfaction with their new living conditions in relation to food and water. When HRW visited these communities in 2012, the residents complained of severe food and water shortage, which led to the publication of the seminal report, *What Is a House without Food?* As the title suggests, the communities would rather return to live in their stick and mud houses with food to eat, as it was before coal mining, than to starve while living in brick and cement houses.

When asked about the new living conditions, Malosa who had been resettled in Mwaladzi in 2011, had this to say (HRW, 2013: 50):

> We are suffering a lot. We had a meeting with the company and told them that if you can't supply us with food and water, it is better that you take us back to the place where we used to live, and we will produce our own food and we will continue our life without depending on you.

Similarly, another Mwaladzi resident, Eulália, echoed the sentiment: 'We are just suffering here. Where they moved us from – there we had enough food to eat and here we do not. There we could do something to earn money and here we can do nothing' (HRW, 2013: 48).

The lack of food was directly related to the poor quality of the allocated farmland or the lack of farmland. The resettled communities either were not allocated farmland to produce their food or they were allocated unsuitable farmland. Elena, a Mwaladzi resident, indicated that one of the major problems in the settlement was the poor quality of land (HRW, 2013: 50):

> We used to produce enough food to keep in storage ... The [plot of] land here is bigger; the problem is the land is not good ... the land is not good. We grew beans, only beans. You can check our storage, there is nothing there ... All the food we are eating, we are buying.

Likewise, Fatima of Mwaladzi said (HRW, 2013: 52):

> We didn't produce anything last year or this year. This land does not grow anything, we produced from other land we borrowed so we could grow maize. Most of our food we depend on buying from the market. We do not produce enough to last a month.

Senolia, a Cateme resident, had no farmland to produce food (HRW, 2013: 54):

> I grew maize the first year [2010]. The second year, people came and said the land belonged to them. I left the maize that I had already planted. I went to Vale and told them the land you gave me belongs to another. They said they would give me more land. It has now been two years.

With no more farmland to allocate to resettled communities, the government decided that the Cateme residents should be given financial compensation, which proved to be unsustainable as people used the money to buy food. Eventually people ran of food and money (HRW, 2013: 54). A Vale official told HRW (2013: 54–55) that financial compensation 'was the decision of the government. We are very worried about this approach. It can generate kind of a fake upgrade in terms of income that is not sustainable.'

In 2015 and 2016, SEKELEKANI visited the same communities and found that the situation had deteriorated. Duzélia explained to SEKELEKANI that her life 'had come to a standstill' since she was resettled to 25 de Setembro village in Moatize town. 'It is as if I am in prison,' she said. Lack of farmland was among her afflictions (SEKELEKANI, 2016: 14):

> In Chipanda life was good because I had farmland where I produced food. When I wanted to make bricks, I did it right there in my yard because I had a big yard. I made bricks and burned them right there. I used the bricks to build my house; I sold others; I bought corrugated metal sheets; and I paid for school fees for the children.

As compensation for her land, Vale paid her MZN119,000 (about $1,800), which did not last because her expenses multiplied when she moved to 25 de Setembro resettlement, as she explains (SEKELEKANI, 2016: 16):

> The amount is not enough to buy land, clear it, start tilling, and buy cement. Farming land is 40 km away and to get there I need transportation. I had to buy maize meal for the family for some months to feed my family. The money was not enough. It is finished now. Here in Moatize we cannot find farmland because everything is fenced off.

Fortunato of Bagamoyo indicated that the arrival of Vale in the area had changed their lives for the worse (SEKELEKANI, 2016: 20):

> The animals have no pastures or water anymore. The fencing occupied the land where we got our clay to make bricks for our subsistence ... we are used to producing almost everything in the farmland, but now we have to buy everything.

Joice of Cassoca explained that her community was locked inside Jindal's fenced concession, which restricted the residents' movements. The community had lived in such conditions since 2013, when Jindal began its mining operations. 'Cassoca is like another country, like a military barrack,' she said. Visitors are not allowed in the community; they must disguise themselves as local villagers in order to enter the village (SEKELEKANI, 2016: 12). In her words to SEKELEKANI (2016: 12), she continued:

> You cannot come here looking clean and well dressed. You must wear dirty, torn, clothes; you must have uncombed hair, looking peasant and poor, and you must arrange with the residents to testify to the guards that you are their family member. Otherwise you cannot get in here.

However, according to Joice, that is not even the worse part SEKELEKANI (2016: 12):

> The worst thing about it are the constant dynamite explosions because they happen right next to people's homes, since the mine works exactly like that – inside the village, among people. Jindal did not resettle anyone.

Further, when the explosions are more intense, Jindal orders community leaders to temporarily remove the people from the village to conduct the blasts: 'Imagine! People must leave their homes and stay in uncertain places the whole afternoon … when they return, they find their food and water covered in black dust from the coal.' Joice (SEKELEKANI, 2016: 13) recounted an incident in which the provincial governor abandoned the area due to Jindal's dynamite explosions:

> The man himself, the governor of Tete province, came here to visit the community but was forced to interrupt the visit and abandon this place, because of the explosions and dust. He fled, to be honest. The community suffers because of the explosions, noise, dust, and barbed wire.

SEKELEKANI (2015: 14) offers a vivid description of the wretchedness inside Jindal's enclosure:

> The 500 families that live inside the enclosure are deprived of access to water. On the other hand, with the construction of Vale's railroad, the residents of Catete were also deprived of access to water, because the construction of this new infrastructure closed the water wells where the residents collected their water. Therefore, access to water became more distant, with direct impact on women who now have enormous difficulties to collect water from the rivers. Consequently, the women are forced to wait for hours on the sides of the railroad while the cargo trains are roaring through, so that they can cross to where they can find water. This exercise is heartbreaking for pregnant women.

Even though Jindal had not complied with human rights standards, and had not conducted any human rights due diligence to identify, prevent, mitigate and remedy adverse human rights impacts on the community, the president of Mozambique at the time, Armando Guebuza, formally inaugurated the mine in August 2013, giving Jindal public endorsement. However, Jindal had started mining in Cassoca months before and the negative impact on the communities must have been self-evident.

THE CASE OF NATURAL GAS IN CABO DELGADO

Cabo Delgado Province is naturally endowed with large deposits of mineral resources, some of which are currently being exploited by various multinational corporations. The most well-known among these are (1) the ruby mining in Montepuez district, and (2) the natural gas explorations in Palma district, near the border with Tanzania. The exploration of rubies in Montepuez and natural gas in Palma brought radical life disruptions to the local communities, including land dispossession, dislocation and loss of the means of subsistence.

Anadarko and dispossession in Palma

Palma is the northernmost district in Cabo Delgado Province on the border with Tanzania. About 44 kilometres north of the town of Palma, the seat of Palma district government, the Rovuma River flows north-east into the Indian Ocean, forming the natural separation between Mozambique and Tanzania.

About 40 kilometres south of the town of Palma lies the Afungi Peninsula, home to farming and fishing villages. But it is also here where Anadarko (now Total) has been building infrastructure for the transformation of offshore natural gas into liquified natural gas (the LNG project), for housing company employees and for the storage, logistics and transportation of the liquefied gas. This whole operation required 7,000 hectares of land, nearly the entire Afungi Peninsula. In addition, the offshore gas pumping operations would require a network of underwater gas pipelines to transport the natural gas into the gas liquification plant (the LNG plant) on land. This means the constant movement of company ships travelling between the offshore gas wells and the natural gas liquification plant on land. As seen in Figure 8.2, the entire Afungi Peninsula coastal area, all the way down to Mocímboa da Praia district in the south, would be off-limits to the villagers, who, for centuries, relied on fishing as a livelihood. Anadarko (2014: 4–1) summarises the project:

The project is designed to collect, transport, process and export in liquified form natural gas in northern Mozambique. This process begins offshore, where natural gas will be extracted from gas reservoirs below the seafloor via subsea wells. The gas will be collected and transported to the onshore LNG Facility by pipelines. Once onshore, the gas will be processed, converted to liquid (through cooling the gas) and stored in storage tanks. The liquefied gas will then be transported through insulated pipelines to one of two export jetties, where it will be loaded into LNG vessels to be transported to international markets. These specially designed ships maintain the LNG in a liquified state for sea voyages of several thousand kilometers.

Figure 8.2: Total's Mozambique LNG project in Cabo Delgado Province

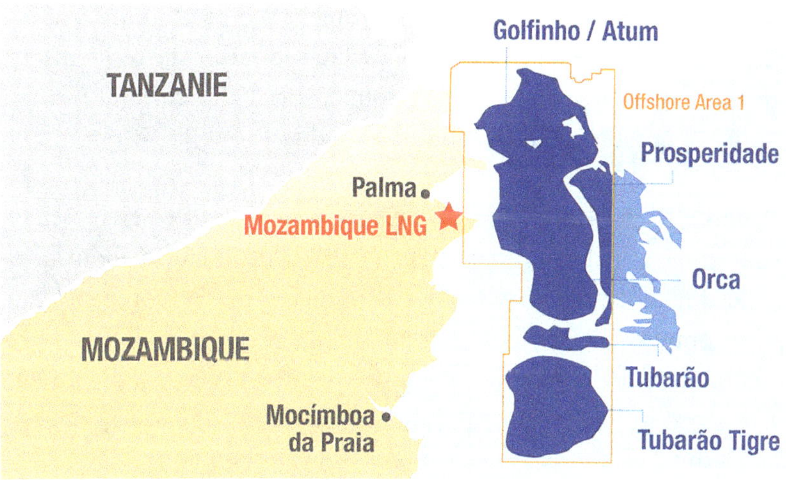

Source: Total, https://www.total.com/media/news/communiques/total-signs-agreement-with-the-government-of-mozambique-regarding-the.

The expropriation of the Afungi Peninsula and surrounding areas to make room for the LNG project violated national, as well as regional and international human rights standards. The land acquisition occurred through deception, lies, intimidation and aggression on the part of the government and the company (Mário and Bila, 2013). There were no community consultations as required by Mozambican legislation. Without free, prior and informed consent, unsuspecting illiterate peasants and community leaders were hoodwinked into signing the forfeiture of their land and rights, only to learn much later what they had signed. By then it was too late. Local government officials working with, and on behalf of, Anadarko cornered village leaders and asked them: 'Do you agree that the government should bring foreign investors to implant development projects in your region, projects which will bring you jobs, big hospitals and schools for your children?' (Mário and Bila, 2013: 8). According to Tomas Mário and Iracema Bila (2013: 9):

> This practice continued, and the government officials presented the village leader with a paper and pen to sign, and ... that was it! In a click of fingers, was accomplished one of the most important phases in the transfer of community land rights to the foreign investor ... from that moment the community was deprived of its most precious asset, which connects the residents to their ancestors, and deep economic, social and cultural ties, without any information about their rights.

Responding to the requests for help from communities, civil society organisations asked the government to share information about how the transfer of land rights from communities to the company had been accomplished. The government simply responded: 'There were community consultations in which the community granted consent, and this was registered in the minutes signed by the village leader, in conformity with the relevant regulations pertaining to land rights transfer' (Mário and Bila, 2013: 9). When asked to produce the legally required evidence for such consultations – consultation meeting minutes signed by all attendees, a list of all attendees, a public announcement calling for the consultation meeting at least 15 days ahead of time – the government could not provide any of these evidentiary documents.

Consequently, the villagers in the entire Afungi Peninsula and the rest of Palma Bay were profoundly affected. Anadarko occupied the

Agungi Peninsula and resettled the communities in places where they would have no access to their means of subsistence. The 750 families would also lose their economic, social and cultural means and ways of life. In meetings with civil society organisations, the Afungi Peninsula residents protested their loss. Assane, a local resident decried to Mário and Bila (2013: 26):

> Many of us are so afraid of what is going to happen ... because the project started very badly: they started with the invasion of our farmlands; cutting down our coconut trees, digging on our cemeteries without a warning ... none! The forests they have destroyed had our medicines ... They say we will have development, but what they have done so far sows in us deep distrust and suspicion. Maybe they think we are idiots. We know our rights. We know what the Constitution of the Republic says.

Another resident, Mbaluka, described the raw deal in this manner: 'First, Anadarko took the sea. Then they took the land, too. We are hungry already. We are hungry!' (Mário & Bila, 2013: 27). Similarly, another resident, Amina, said (Mário & Bila, 2013: 27):

> We used to grow food in our farmlands in the Chii area. Now I am worried. Our farmlands are two hours away from our village. That is why we sleep there during tillage and harvest. If we cannot live there anymore because of the company, where will we spend the nights during tillage and harvest? Will we have transport from the company so that we can go and come back on the same day?

Mazela also said: 'The whole situation is very suspicious because of the way they are handling our property. Will they really compensate us? I think the government has received its money from the companies and now we are being sent to hell.' The like-minded Issa agreed and went further: 'What will we bequeath our future generations, because we live on what our ancestors bequeathed us? Will our descendants feel that they are benefiting from the project?' In the same vain, Esha weighed in: 'I am hearing that we will be removed from here. We have been living here for centuries. Our ancestors were buried here. Their graves are here. So now I ask, what is going to happen to our ancestors' graveyards?' (Mário and Bila, 2013: 27).

RESISTANCE TO LAND DISPOSSESSION

Having considered the subjection of these communities to expropriation and dislocation, it is crucial to turn our attention to their agency lest they appear to be passive victims of oppression. With the support of local civil society organisations, the communities in Tete and Cabo Delgado attempted to organise resistance with some degree of success. However, it is prudent to be cautious about categorising the results of the resistance purely as successful. In Tete, five years after waiting for Jindal to fulfil its obligations, the residents enclosed in Jindal's mining concession organised a demonstration, barricading all the roads to and from the company. The protest, which coincided with a workers' strike inside Jindal, paralysed the company's operations for three weeks. Juvêncio Jeque, the local community leader, is quoted by Arcénio Sebastião (2018a):

> The people of Cassoca decided to paralyse the mine because we are losing our brothers and sisters who are dying because diarrhoea and other illnesses we cannot even tell what they are. So far, we have lost 17 people because of these unknown illnesses; one of them survived after being operated in town.

In tandem with these developments, the Mozambican Bar Association (OAM) litigated against Jindal on behalf of the community of Cassoca for failing to comply with the resettlement obligation (OAM, 2019b). The Provincial Administrative Court in Tete ordered Jindal to compensate Cassoca families for an amount of MZN400,000,000 (about US$5,700,000), although OAM considered the court's decision as deeply disappointing (Zacarias, 2018). Although Jindal agreed to pay the compensations and resettle more than 300 families (Sebastião, 2018b), there has been no further information as to what has transpired since.

In 2017, OAM visited the communities resettled by Vale in Cateme, 25 de Setembro and Bagamoio and found (Carlos, 2019):

> The land assigned to the affected families is full of stones and unsuitable for farming, in addition to the communities facing serious problems of hunger, access to water and sources of income. In general, the mining of coal has had a negative impact on their living conditions.

In the same year, OAM assisted these communities to litigate against Vale and the government on the grounds that the resettlement had been 'unjust and therefore needed to be restructured and the owed compensations paid to the residents' (OAM quoted in Zacarias, 2018). In 2019, the Provincial Administrative Court in Tete ruled against Vale and the government. In the ruling, the court ordered Vale 'to rebuild all the faulty resettlement houses ... in compliance with the standards set out in the model house presented to the affected communities', and the government 'to transfer the revenue generated to the state through coal mining to the communities located in the exploration areas' (OAM, 2019a).

In Cabo Delgado, the Palma communities affected by Anadarko's LNG project relied chiefly on two civil society organisations to articulate their grievances and claim their rights, namely SEKELEKANI and Rede Terra Viva (RTV). Both organisations held community meetings and capacity-building workshops in villages to inform the residents about their rights enshrined in the Constitution and the Land Law. They explained to the communities how the process of DUAT transfer should work if implemented within the legal parameters. The work of these organisations incensed the district and provincial governments who had counted on the villagers' inability to read and write and their lack of knowledge of technical legal issues. The RTV issued a strongly worded critique of the ways in which the government and the company had driven the DUAT transfer process (Manuel, 2015: 8):

> Taking advantage of people's ignorance and poverty to manipulate, entice and deceive them, and to distract them from the attention they must pay to the crucial issues of survival and sustainability of their lives, today and in the future, it must be a crime! Certainly, from a moral and ethical point of view, that is so.

The struggle for human rights and dignity on the part of the Palma communities and civil society organisations eventually resulted in the government and the company agreeing to reduce the land to be occupied by 45 per cent and families to be resettled by 36 per cent (Mário, n.d.).

Writing about the unjust ways in which the government and companies expropriated land in rural Mozambique in 2016, SEKELEKANI could not have been more accurate in titling its report, 'A Minha Voz: Narração de sofrimento ou como se incubam novos conflitos em Moçambique' (My Voice: A tale of suffering or how new conflicts are incubated in Mozambique), notwithstanding the organisation could not have anticipated the ongoing conflict in Cabo Delgado. The most salient exercise of agency, as vicious and destructive as it may be, has been the ongoing armed violence attributed to northern Cabo Delgado youths, locally known as Al-Shabaab. They began their military operations in October 2017 in Mocimboa da Praia, a district adjacent to Palma district. These violent activities have been making sensational news headlines, and, by April 2020, more than 1,000 people were estimated to have been killed. At the core of this conflict, researchers and analysts point to the economic and social marginalisation of local populations, notably the expulsion from their land and natural resources (Pirio et al., 2018; Matsinhe and Valoi, 2019). In 2018, some local authorities in Cabo Delagado informed Amnesty International that, by licensing the land to mining companies leaving little space for people to grow their food, the central government was fanning political disaffection in the area (Matsinhe, 2020). In May 2018, about 100 young people protested in Palma district against what they perceived as exclusion from employment opportunities in Anadarko's LNG projects and spin-off companies (CIVILINFO, 2018).

Dispossession of peasants in Angola

As in rural Mozambique, the large-scale expropriation of land and the displacement of peasants constitute perhaps the most conspicuous topographical transformations that cut deep into the economic and social fabric of rural Angola. There is an unforgiving offensive against rural communities who eat what they produce, drink the water they collect from natural sources, treat themselves with medicinal plants they collect from forests, construct their houses with the material they collect from the forests, and consume dairy products derived from their livestock. Their self-sufficiency is under ruthless attack through dispossession and dislocation (Foley, 2007; Lundström, 2014; De Morais, 2015; De Grassi and Ovadia, 2017; Tump, 2019; Amnesty International, 2019).

While the problem under consideration is widespread in the country, this chapter focuses only on two case studies as a premise to understand the problem. The first is the dispossession and displacement of peasants in the municipality of Curoca, Cunene Province. The second is the expropriation and dislocation in the municipality of Gambos, Huila Province. These municipalities are part of the pastoralist region of southern Angola, dubbed the 'milk region' due to its reliance on traditional cattle breeding. The milk region comprises three provinces of southern Angola, namely Cunene (which borders Namibia), Huila Province to the north of Cunene Province, and Namibe Province, which borders Namibia on the Atlantic Ocean. In these provinces, people rely almost exclusively on the land for their survival. The pastoralist communities who populate this region are economically, socially, culturally and politically marginalised and isolated. A large proportion of the population in this region does not have birth registrations. Since they are not officially counted, they do not matter as people, and do not count as citizens. This administrative oblivion renders them invisible to the government (Fingo, 2018; Wakussanga, 2018b; Amnesty International, 2019).

The case of land invasion in Cunene

In the southernmost end of Cunene Province, along the border with Namibia, lies the municipality of Curoca comprising 7,998 square kilometres. The area is home to Ovaherero and Vanyaneka pastoralists, who for centuries have cultivated and perfected the traditional science of cattle breeding and subsistence agriculture in dry, semi-arid climatic conditions. These pastoralists practise transhumance, the seasonal livestock migration in search of pastures and water. Over the centuries, these pastoralists have developed their traditional cattle-breeding science and built a body of indigenous knowledge within the typical twists, turns and vicissitudes of the local climate. They have adapted their mode of production to the rhythms of the local environment, and they have adapted their lives to the characteristic behaviour of the surrounding natural ecosystem. In the past, they cultivated practices and habits that have enabled them to survive (Urquhart, 1963; De Carvalho, 1974; De Carvalho and Da Silva 1973). However, this economic, social, cultural and epistemological order is increasingly coming under attack through large-scale land expropriation for private commercial interests.[3]

At the beginning of 2016, unbeknown to the residents, a group of strangers entered Curoca municipality to claim 3,200 square kilometres of land for themselves. The outsiders came with heavy machines (bulldozers and diggers) to clear and burn the vegetation and trees from the land. They brought fencing material and began to build an enclosure around the land. The residents – among them the Ovahimba, Ovangabwes, Ovahumbi, Ovandimba and Ovandongona – were scandalised because as far as they were concerned the land was theirs. Their ancestors before them had lived, died and been laid to eternal rest there. For centuries they had hunted, grazed cattle, produced grains, harvested medicinal and cosmetic plants, and collected wild fruit for consumption and the production of cooking oil and traditional beers and spirits. In the early 1900s, their ancestors had fought and died to defend the land during Portuguese colonial occupation. In the 1950s

3 The erosion of this way of life began with the intensification of colonisation in southern Angola in the early 1900s. In their wars to occupy and control southern Angola, the Portuguese expropriated land and cattle, which significantly transformed the way of life among the indigenous people in the region. De Carvalho (1974) makes a compelling case on how the introduction of commercial ranching eroded pastoralism in this region.

and 1960s, they had fought for independence to free the land from the Portuguese (GTMDH, 2016).

Unwilling to lose the land once again, they approached the newcomers to inquire about the movements and noise of the bulldozers and diggers, and to ask them to stop the activities. The newcomers refused, telling them, 'We are preparing a communal farm to benefit your community.' Speaking with the human rights monitors, the residents explained: 'We told them to suspend the activities because the communities had no prior knowledge and had not been consulted for an eventual negotiation' (GTMDH, 2016: 5). That was the beginning of the conflict that saw the involvement of members of the political establishment, including the governor and vice-governor of Cunene Province, the governor of Huambo Province and his nephew, one member of parliament and the Minister of Agriculture. From these people, the residents asked for an explanation [of] why their land was being invaded. When the invaders responded that they were prepared to negotiate, the residents retorted that they were not interested in negotiating with invaders. To this, the governor of Huambo reportedly took offence and responded: 'I don't see anyone worthy of my respect in your community or anyone who can challenge me; you should know that this land does not belong to your mothers; and that whoever tries to challenge me will see what will happen to him' (GTMDH, 2016: 6).

The invaded area was home to 39 communities, comprising 2,129 families, 10,675 children, and 22 chapels and churches of various denominations.[4] According to the testimonies of the residents who spoke with the Angolan Human Rights Monitoring Working Group (GTMDH), during the conflict the government brought in the police to intimidate the residents and protect the land invaders: 'The invasion of our land is guarded by the heavily armed police force whose mission

4 The communities were Kavango, Milenda, Kandjove, Ovipaka, Eyawo, Okatewe, Namatanga, Hano, Kaoloka, Mayova, Kanuambandje, Kamukúwa, Tchitapawa, Kambelona, Nombelo, Noholongo, Kahalala, Mulavi, Tyiheke-Tchomokati, Mukekete, Eume, Kitetembo, Konongunga, Komudi, Námbua, Ngeyaúla, Munhandi, Mutily, Luenge, Mundingalala, Tyiolofeu, Oufina, Komikambo, Viwayanga, Haykoty, Kononkhanga, Tchikuahepo, Tyiakiti and Tyikoto (GDMDH, 2016: 12).

is to threaten, maltreat and intimidate the population' (GTMDH, 2016: 6). The local government threatened community representatives and their families, as one community representative, Yeunique, indicated to GTMDH (2016: 9):

> I responded to the Governor of Huambo saying that if the community is objecting, you cannot continue with the project. We do not want to see the police in our communities making our lives unbearable. For having said this, my family members were called for questioning by the Ombanja Municipal Administrator, just because of my complaint. During the interrogation by the Administrator, I was mentioned as [a] UNITA member. I am sad because in Angola you cannot complain about anything without being labelled a member of the opposition. It is so sad.

The residents also expressed their concern with the government's lack of consideration, respect, humanity and common decency by not consulting and communicating with them prior to the implementation of the project. As Cosseka explained to the GTMDH (2016: 9):

> Even though I am not learned, I can see that the objective of the invaders is to take all our land. I am worried with the Administrator of Chitalo. He does not speak with the communities, does not consult, he has no contact with the people. He went to bring the police to protect the destruction of our cemetery. The Administrator accuses us of starting a conflict with the authorities. I am also worried because the Governor of Huambo said, 'If a child plays with a knife holding it by the blade, the knife must be yanked from him to cut his hand and teach him never to play with it again.'

Similarly, Cosseka, another local resident, reiterated (GTMDH, 2016: 9–10):

> Despite the threats, we are not interested in leaving our land. We prefer to die here rather than abandoning our land. We cannot even sleep because we are trying to imagine how we would

> live without grazing and farming land. We are waiting for the President to put an end to these abuses. We prefer to die. We will not allow any government official to simply show up and occupy our land on which we completely depend. At least we prefer that they kill us than to forcibly expel us from the land we inherited from our ancestors.

Curoca residents objected to the invasion because it threatened their livelihoods, notably the survival of their livestock. Another community representative, Isaias T., used community statistics to explain to the human rights monitors how the communities would be devastated should the project continue (GTMDH, 2016: 9):

> We defend our land because if the invasion and expropriation of 32,000km^2 of land continues, it will affect 1,129 families, 10,675 children, 22 chapels, 7 traditional chiefs, 255,480 heads of bovine cattle, 319,350 goats, 31,935 sheep, 6,387 donkeys, 2,129 horses and 6,387 pigs. So where are we going to live, we and our animals? We must make efforts to stop our eviction and destruction of our property.

Had the newcomers been interested in conducting human rights due diligence before the implementation of their project, they would have known of these statistics and what they meant from the point of view of economic, social and cultural rights of the 39 communities. And the project continued.

In order to claim and defend their rights, the communities in Curoca sought the assistance of Angolan human rights organisations. The GTMDH responded to the request with a fact-finding mission to Curoca, where public meetings were held with the residents and local authorities to understand the roots of the conflict. Following this mission, the GTMDH issued a report and embarked on a campaign at the central government in Luanda and the African Commission on Human and People's Rights. The GTMDH called for support from international human rights organisations, including Amnesty

International and the German Catholic Bishops' Organization for Development Cooperation (MISEREOR). In addition to their own campaign and advocacy, Amnesty International and MISEREOR assisted GTMDH to submit shadow human rights reports to counter the Angolan government's human rights report during the Universal Periodic Reviews of the United Nations Human Rights Council. Campaigns and advocacy in Germany forced the German development finance institution to re-evaluate its financial commitment to the agribusiness client at the heart of land conflict in Curoca.[5]

The case of land invasion in Huíla

In the southern end of Huíla Province lies the Gambos municipality, also home to the Ovaherero and Vanyaneka pastoralist groups. Gambos, which gets its name from the Ovamgambwe people, is divided in two parts by the north–south national highway, the EN-105, which connects Angola and Namibia. On the west side of the highway the pastoralist communities are scattered over the rocky and hard-to-cultivate land. On the east side of the highway is the traditional/communal grazing reserve, which, for centuries, has attracted pastoralists from the entire milk region of southern Angola. The area is a refuge and sanctuary for the pastoralists and their livestock during dry seasons and droughts. In prolonged and severe droughts, such as in 2017, 2018 and 2019, pastoralists from as far as northern Namibia came with their livestock to sit out the drought.

This communal grazing area is itself divided into two parts – one called Tunda dos Gambos, and the other Vale de Chimbolelo or Mulola de Chimbolelo. Tunda is 'a dry, sandy, slightly elevated plain which occupies the "top" position within the catena, relative to the "bottom" position occupied by the river valleys' (De Carvalho, 1974: 210). Mulola, on the other hand, consists of 'intermittent tributaries, channelised to some extent, which flood during the wet season', and 'due to the extreme flatness of the terrain, much of the water seems to be lost by evaporation rather than by drainage' (De Carvalho, 1974:

5 I, the author of this text, led Amnesty International's initiative to support GTMDH to defend the land rights of Curoca communities.

211). Since the Tunda and Mulola areas are reserved for communal grazing, there are fewer pastoralists settled there. Therefore, the areas have always appeared unoccupied to uninformed onlookers. For the invaders, this meant that the land was open for the taking, and that is precisely what happened.

When Angola became independent in 1975, most of the land in Gambos, which had been occupied by the Portuguese, was returned to the original owners, the Ovaherero and Vanyaneka pastoralists. However, since the end of the civil war in 2002, the Angolan political elite have been grabbing the grazing commons of Tunda and Mulola for themselves piece by piece. According to the government records analysed by Amnesty International, the entire area of these communal grazing commons was estimated as follows: Tunda's surface area, 3,609 square kilometres; and Mulola's surface area, 319 square kilometres. Combined, Tunda and Mulola have an estimated surface area of 3,928 square kilometres. By 2018, the invaders had grabbed and enclosed 2,629 square kilometres – that is, 67 per cent – of the traditional grazing commons for private commercial ranching (Amnesty International, 2019: 38).

When I arrived in Gambos in March 2018 and March 2019, I found pastoralist families and their livestock starved, malnourished and emaciated. Some people and cattle had died and the mood was heavy and sombre. The people's demeanour emitted an ambiance of despair and hopelessness, which, at the time, moved me to write (Amnesty International, 2019: 20):

> The ambiance in the homesteads felt sombre and gloomy as if death or some other tragedy had just occurred. The kimbos looked neglected and abandoned. People, both young and old, looked thin, pale, and exhausted from their constant battle with hunger. Although there were many children in the homesteads, there were no sounds of children playing and screaming and they looked exhausted and subdued. Except for a few kimbos, there were no visible signs of food or means for its production. Perhaps the most striking aspect of all this is that the dogs and cattle looked so visibly thin and emaciated that one could count their ribs from a distance.

As in Curoca, in Gambos, prior to occupying the land, the commercial interests conducted no consultations with the pastoralists, provided no compensation to the pastoralists, and undertook no environmental and social impact assessment to determine any possible negative impact on the pastoralist communities, despite the fact that all these processes are legally required, as outlined earlier. Most importantly, the commercial farmers undertook no human rights due diligence to identify and assess possible adverse impacts on the economic, social and cultural rights and human dignity in the communities, even though these undertakings are mandatory international human rights standards. As a result, many residents in these pastoralist communities and their animals were hungry, malnourished and facing death. In what mirrored the governor of Huambo's sentiment about Curoca residents, the commercial farmers in Gambos considered the residents unworthy of respect, and hence there was no consultation, communication, negotiation or compensation (Amnesty International, 2019; Cortez and Matsinhe, 2019).

When requested, the government failed to provide evidence that studies were undertaken to assess the social, spiritual, cultural and environmental impact of commercial livestock farming on the Gambos residents (Amnesty International, 2019). There was no evidence that the government and/or the land grabbers had paid any consideration to the economic, social, cultural and spiritual values of Gambos residents concerning their relationship with Tunda and Mulola. There was no evidence that the government had considered pastoralism as an indigenous mode of economic production and social reproduction in this area (Amnesty International, 2019).

There was also no evidence that the government had ensured that land granting for commercial livestock farming was done within the bounds of free, prior and informed consent principles. In this case, the pastoralists were not passive victims of unwanted attention and aggression from the provincial government and the commercial farmers. It is important to highlight their agency to act on their own behalf, to claim and defend their rights. The land expropriation plans in Gambos included the invasion of the Tyihepepe natural water fountain, which, for centuries, the pastoralists had used for their livestock and for themselves. In 2018, without conducting any environmental, social and human rights due diligence as required by the law, the provincial government and the commercial farmers began their water pipeline construction work at the Tyihepepe fountain.

Enraged communities organised themselves and resisted, barricading the road used by the contractor to build the water distribution network of pipelines (Fingo, 2018; Wakussanga, 2018a). This water pipeline network would divert large quantities of water from the fountain to the commercial farmers located 14 kilometres away (Governo da Huíla, 2017). The pastoralists called for support from the Catholic Church, the GTMDH and Amnesty International. Again, in March 2018, GTMDH and Amnesty International undertook fact-finding missions to the pastoralist communities clustered around the water fountain and held meetings with the residents. They launched a campaign and advocacy nationally and internationally, which eventually saw the Huila provincial governor removed from office and the water distribution project stalled.[6]

Cultural and identity implications

The continuing forced occupation of communal grazing commons in Curoca and Gambos without the legally mandatory due diligence and community consultation, just compensation or environmental impact assessments to at least determine the possible adverse impact on the pastoralist communities has had a heavy toll on the culture of the communities. This has created material conditions in which it is increasingly difficult for the pastoralists to transmit their indigenous and cultural knowledge to future generations. Father Jacinto Pio Wakussanga (2018a) underscores this point:

> All the community life rotates around pastoralism. Their day-to-day life, their habits, the way they live, their culture, their songs, the way they dance, their language, their proverbs, the way they move, their performance, I mean, everything is permeated by the pastoralist lifestyle. They are not nomadic,

6 I, the author of this text, led the Amnesty International's research, campaign and advocacy efforts on this case.

but sometimes the men go looking for pastures, but they return when rainfall comes.

The pastoralist way of life is choking under the ongoing change of land use in Gambos. The fall in milk yield meant that the community needed to make changes to their way of life. Dairy fat is a significant component in their diet, attire and identity. Pastoralist community members were unanimous in their view that their way of life was under threat, as was the case with Madalena (2019), who said:

> I remain dressed in traditional attire because my ancestors bequeathed me this culture; they taught me this culture as a way of life, and I won't give it up. Now I don't use milk fat because the cows no longer produce enough milk, so when I get some money, I buy Vaseline at the shops, but it's very expensive. I must remain this way so that our culture is respected.

In agreement, Mantemba (2019) said:

> We wore beads and covered the whole neck and applied milk fat. But now we use a bit of oil from the shop because there is no more milk to make milk fat. It is an old tradition practised by our ancestors. Nowadays we wear a few beads without covering the neck, unlike in the past when we covered the whole neck.

Similarly, Fatima (2019) told the author:

> We are not wearing our beads because we do not have the cow milk. You cannot wear the beads without the milk fat. We use milk fat to maintain our tradition. The milk fat makes us shine; it makes us beautiful. What I am wearing comes from a tree called mumbili. We grind it into powder. We mix the powder with cow milk. We take the paste and apply it on the head. It is good for growing hair. It keeps the hair healthy. It also protects against lightning storm. But without the milk, it is becoming less and less possible to make this.

The right to participation in one's culture is an integral element of being human, and of human dignity, and is interrelated and embodied in all human rights. The right to participate and preserve one's culture is enshrined in international human rights law. The Universal Declaration of Human Rights declares in Articles 22 and 27:

> Everyone is entitled to the realisation, through national effort and international cooperation, of the cultural rights, indispensable for his or her dignity and the free development of his or her personality ... Everyone has the right freely to participate in the cultural life of the community ...

In the General Comment No. 21 on the right to participation in cultural life, the Committee on Economic, Social and Cultural Rights provides a comprehensive understanding of culture. For the implementation of Article 15.1, the General Comment No. 21 (Article 13) considers culture as encompassing, among other things:

> Ways of life, language, oral and written literature, music and song, non-verbal communication, religion or belief systems, rites and ceremonies, sport and games, methods of production or technology, natural and man-made environments, food, clothing and shelter and the arts, customs and traditions through which individuals, groups of individuals and communities express their humanity and the meaning they give to their existence, and build their world view representing their encounter with the external forces affecting their lives. Culture shapes and mirrors the values of well-being and the economic, social and political life of individuals, groups of individuals and communities.

The committee further explains that the conditions for the full realisation of the right to participation in cultural life include availability, accessibility, acceptability, adaptability and appropriateness of cultural elements such as, but not limited to (Article 16):

> Of cultural goods and services that are open for everyone to enjoy and benefit from, including libraries, museums, theatres,

> cinemas and sports stadiums; literature, including folklore, and the arts in all forms; the shared open spaces essential to cultural interaction, such as parks, squares, avenues and streets; nature's gifts, such as seas, lakes, rivers, mountains, forests and nature reserves, including the flora and fauna found there, which give nations their character and biodiversity; intangible cultural goods, such as languages, customs, traditions, beliefs, knowledge and history, as well as values, which make up identity and contribute to the cultural diversity of individuals and communities.

In Curoca and Gambos, the government failed on both negative and positive obligations, and violated the pastoralists' rights to participate in their cultural life. By expropriating the customary grazing land of the pastoralists without consultation, compensation, alternative grazing land, or social and environmental impact assessments, the government interfered with the pastoralists' right to preserve and participate in their cultural life and identity.

DISCUSSION AND CONCLUSIONS

To explain the lack of law enforcement against businesses in the countryside, government officials and civil society often cite the lack of resources to conduct inspections and poorly trained government inspectors. In fact, it is common practice for companies to fund government monitoring and inspection missions – transportation, accommodation and per diems of government inspectors – which compromises the credibility of these missions. This issue emerged in the interviews with government officials and civil society. However, this issue is only a symptom of a deeper problem.

While Mozambique and Angola have some of the world's most progressive laws to administer justice and protect human rights, both countries fail abysmally in their duty to do so. The reason for this failure is the existence of *sociedade dos patrões* (the boss society) in a bifurcated legal system, which renders the law futile. According to Mahmood Mamdani (1996), in a bifurcated governance system, two unequal forms of subjectivity co-exist: *citizens and subjects*, as his book title proposes. On the one hand, the citizens at the centre of the system enjoy all the rights and dignity enshrined in the laws of the land. The subjects, on the other hand, are considered to be of a lower status and their rights and dignity are not contemplated in the implementation of the law – these are the peasants in the rural areas. In Mozambique and Angola, there are vestiges of this colonial system of governance, most visible in the relations between senior government officials and ordinary citizens, notably peasants and pastoralists who depend on the land as a means and way of life.

At the heart of the disregard of the law in rural areas, resulting in gross violations of the rights of peasants and pastoralists, is the popular figure of *Patrão* or *Chefe* – that is, *The Boss* or *The Master* – which personifies the senior government official, invariably a man. Together, senior government officials form a *sociedade dos patrões* – the boss society and the untouchables, whose everyday lives exist above, or on the margins, of the law. This social form has characteristic structural features similar to those of another social form, the Junkers, members of the landed nobility in 19th-century Prussia (Elias, 1989). According to Norbert Elias (1989), in the power struggle between the landed nobility and the middle class, members of the former not only positioned themselves as superior to members of the latter, but also above and beyond the law, having developed their own code of conduct – the honour code or the warrior code as opposed to the moral code of the middle class – to regulate their lives and relations among themselves. The highest expression of the honour code was the practice of the duel, the extrajudicial institution through which members of the landed nobility settled their differences, that is, to demand and give satisfaction in battle.

In Mozambique and Angola, the *sociedade dos patrões* makes and applies the law; however, it exists above and beyond the law. Not only is it common practice, but it is also expected, for mining projects and other businesses of significant import to be god-fathered by members of the *sociedade dos patrões*, outside the bounds of the law. With these godfathers on their side, companies have the doors open to establish themselves and operate *em belo prazer* (in good pleasure) on the margins of the law, most notably in remote and rural areas. Affected communities may have their rights violated and dignity defiled and the country may lose tax revenues, but if the godfathers accrue benefits, then all is well. The law applies, often harshly, to discipline and punish the ordinary citizen, the worker, the peasant and the petty offender.

The expropriation, dispossession and displacement of communities who have always depended on the land to satisfy their economic, social and cultural necessities and preserve their human dignity, continue to drive poverty, misery and strife in the rural areas of Mozambique and Angola. We have seen how government officials working on behalf of, or in collaboration with, private companies have used deception, threats, intimidation and often violence against those populations who attempt to put up any form of resistance against these occupations. Even in instances where individual government functionaries may want to follow the letter of the law, state incapacity and neglect make this impossible: as indicated above, inspectors rely on the same commercial 'invaders' to conduct the monitoring.

The communities losing their land to private companies and political elites are based in remote rural areas characterised by the state vacuum or government absence. The communities were marginalised during the colonial era and have been forgotten under the postcolonial dispensation. The postcolonial government failed to build infrastructure for education, healthcare, water and sanitation, transportation and telecommunications. For economy subsistence and social reproduction, the communities relied on the land to survive. In other words, the communities were self-reliant. The appearance of the government in these communities did not bring the much-needed public services to improve their well-being but took away their most valuable economic, social and cultural asset – their land.

International human rights law and countless nation-founding documents invariably define human rights as inherent, inalienable and indivisible prerogatives that every human being enjoys by virtue of being human. This could only mean that human rights are the necessary conditions for, and elements of, human dignity, of a life worthy of regard, respect, elevation and honour. As we have seen, in rural Mozambique and Angola human rights are realised through the interaction between human beings and the land and surrounding ecosystem. Expropriation, dispossession and displacement of rural communities without providing alternatives, without human rights due diligence, without free, prior and informed consent, negate human rights and attack human dignity. To the extent that people have lost their land, they have also lost their economic, social and cultural rights. To the extent that governments and capitalists deprive human beings of their land, they reduce them to bare existence as lowly brutes unworthy of regard, respect, elevation and honour. This is bound to generate social conflict in many localities in these countries.

REFERENCES

Amnesty International. 2018. *'Our Lives Mean Nothing': The human cost of Chinese mining in Nagonha*. London: Amnesty International.

Amnesty International. 2019. *The End of Cattle's Paradise: How land diversion for ranches eroded food security in the Gambos, Angola*. London: Amnesty International.

Anadarko. 2014. 'Environmental impact assessment, Volume I: Introduction, project description and baseline, Chapter 4: Project description', http://www.mzlng.com/Responsibility/Environmental-Social-Management/Environmental-Impact-Assessment, accessed 14 February 2020.

Carlos, R. 17 October 2019. 'Mineradora Vale e Estado Moçambicano condenados'. *O Pais*, http://opais.sapo.mz/mineradora-vale-e-estado-mocambicano-condenados, accessed 25 April 2020.

Chanda, S. 2010. 'Reflections on conflicts related to land and resource rights in Angola'. Presentation at the Regional Workshop on Commercialisation of Land and 'Land Grabbing' in Southern Africa, PLAAS, University of the Western Cape, 24–25 March.

CIVILINFO. 2016a. 'Comunidades reassentadas em Tete: Narração de sofrimento', https://www.youtube.com/watch?v=xGDb05ETyHo, accessed 30 April 2020.

CIVILINFO. 2016b. *A Minha Voz: Narração de sofrimento de comunidades reassentadas ou como se incubam novos conflitos em Moçambique*. Maputo: SEKELEKANI.

CIVILINFO. 24 May 2018. 'Mozambique: Youths demonstrate in Palma, Cabo Delgado, against alleged exclusion'. *Club of Mozambique*, https://clubofmozambique.com/news/mozambique-youths-demonstrate-in-palma-against-alleged-exclusion, accessed 20 March 2020.

Clover, J. 2005. 'Land reform in Angola: Establishing the ground rules', in Huggins, C. and Clover, J. (eds.) *From the Ground Up: Land rights, conflict and peace in sub-Saharan Africa.* Pretoria: Institute for Security Studies, 347–380.

Cortez, C. and Matsinhe, D. 2019. *Angola's Disappearing Livelihoods for Pastoralists in the Gambos.* New York: Amnesty International.

De Carvalho, E.C. 1974. '"Traditional" and "modern" patterns of cattle raising in southwestern Angola: A critical evaluation of change from pastoralism to ranching'. *Journal of Developing Areas,* 8 (2), 199–226.

De Carvalho, E.C. and Da Silva, J.V. 1973. 'The Cunene region: Ecological analysis of an African agropastoral system', in Heimer, F-W. (ed.) *Social Change in Angola.* Munich: Weltforum Verlag, 145–192.

De Grassi, A. and Ovadia, J. S. 2017. 'Trajectories of large-scale land acquisition dynamics in Angola: Diversity, histories, and implications for the political economy of development in Africa'. *Land Use Policy,* 67, 115–125.

De Matos, E. and Medeiro, R. 2015. 'Exploração do carvão mineral de Benga em Moçambique e a expropriação da terra dos nativos: Alguns apontamentos referentes à acumulação por espoliação'. *Revista NERA,* 18 (28), 106–131.

De Morais, R.M. 9 February 2015. 'Rafael Marques denuncia expropriação de terras em Angola'. *Deutsche Welle,* https://www.dw.com/pt-002/rafael-marques-denuncia-expropria%C3%A7%C3%A3o-de-terras-em-angola/a-18246521, accessed 10 February 2020.

De Oliveira, E. 2015. *Magnificent and Beggar Land: Angola since the civil war.* London: Hurst.

Elias, N. 1989. *The Germans: Power struggles and the development of habitus in the nineteenth and twentieth centuries.* New York: Columbia University Press.

Environmental Justice Atlas. 2013. *Coal Mining in Tete Province by Vale and other Companies,* https://ejatlas.org/conflict/resettlements-for-mining-projects-in-tete-province, accessed 29 September 2020

Filipe, E. and Norfolk, S. 2017. *Understanding Changing Land Issues for the Rural Poor in Mozambique.* London: International Institute for Environment and Development.

Foley, C. 2007. 'Land rights in Angola: Poverty and plenty'. Humanitarian Policy Group (HPG) Working Paper, London.

Governo da Huíla. 2017. *Projecto de Transumancia of Municipio dos Gambos.* Lubango: Governo da Província da Huíla.

GTMDH. 2016. *Relatório de atividades realizadas no Kalueque, Município do Curoca, Província do Cunene.* Luanda: Grupo de Trabalho de Monitoria dos Direitos Humanos.

Human Rights Watch (HRW). 2013. *What is a House without Food? Mozambique's coal mining boom and resettlements.* New York: Human Rights Watch.

Lundström, K. 6 November 2014. 'Who owns Angola's land? A problem that needs quick resolution'. *The Guardian*, https://www.theguardian.com/global-development/2014/nov/06/angola-land-rights-civil-war, accessed 22 April 2020.

Mamdani, M. 1996. *Citizen and Subject: Contemporary Africa and the legacy of late colonialism.* Princeton, NJ: Princeton University Press.

Manuel, L. 2015. 'Não há dinheiro que compre direitos e honra dos Moçambicanos de Afungi'. *Boletim Informativo*, N° 3, 4–8, www.ctv.org.mz, accessed 23 March 2020.

Mário, T. V. n.d. 'Fábrica de gás de Palma: Plano de reassentamento vai abranger 470 famílias, http://www.civilinfo.org.mz/files/F%C3%A1brica%20de%20g%C3%A1s%20de%20Palma%20com%20area%20reduzida.pdf, accessed 23 May 2020.

Mário, T.V. and Bila, I.M. 2013. *Indústria Extractiva e Comunidades Locais: Questões Sobre Comunicação, Consultas Publicas e Impactos Sociais e Ambientais Sobre Comunidades Rurais em Tete e Cabo Delgado.* Maputo: SEKELEKANI.

Matsinhe, D. 2020. 'Mozambique: The forgotten people of Cabo Delgado'. *Daily Maverick*, https://www.dailymaverick.co.za/article/2020-05-29-mozambique-the-forgotten-people-of-cabo-delgado, accessed 29 September 2020.

Matsinhe, D. and Valoi, E. 2019. *The Genesis of Insurgency in Northern Mozambique*. Pretoria: Institute for Security Studies.

McKenzie, C. 2006. 'Forest Governance in Zambezia, Mozambique: Chinese Takeaway!' Final Report for FONGZA, http://coastalforests.tfcg.org/pubs/GovernanceZambezia-MZQ.pdf, accessed 28 July 2020.

Moyo, S. 2003. 'The land question in Africa: Research perspectives and questions'. Draft Paper presented at CODESRIA Conferences on Land Reform, the Agrarian Question and Nationalism, Gaborone, 18–19 December, and Dakar, 8–11 December.

Nabudere, W. 2001. *From Agriculture to Agricology: Toward a glocal circular economy.* Johannesburg: MISTRA.

Omar, O. 14 November 2019. 'Indústria extractiva: "Confidencialidade dos contratos limita transparência e propicia corrupção", denunciam OSC'. *Carta de Moçambique*, https://cartamz.com/index.php/sociedade/item/3633-industria-extractiva-confidencialidade-dos-contratos-limita-transparencia-e-propicia-corrupcao-denunciam-osc, accessed 23 July 2020.

Ordem dos Advogados de Mocambique (OAM). 14 October 2019a. 'Comunicado de Impresa: Reassentamento Vale', https://www.oam.org.mz/comunicado-de-impresa-reassentamento-vale, accessed 15 April 2020.

Ordem dos Advogados de Mocambique (OAM). 7 November 2019b. 'Cominicado de Imprensa: Ordem dos Advogados de Moçambique pede ao Tribunal que Condene a Mineradora Jindal', https://www.oam.org.mz/comunicado-de-imprensa-ordem-dos-advogados-de-mocambique-pede-ao-tribunal-que-condene-a-mineradora-jindal/, accessed 23 July 2020.

Pirio, G., Pittelli, R. and Adam, Y. 2018. 'The emergence of violent extremism in Northern Mozambique'. Africa Center for Strategic Studies, https://africacenter.org/spotlight/the-emergence-of-violent-extremism-in-northern-mozambique/, accessed 24 July 2020.

Richardson, B. 2010. 'Big sugar in southern Africa: Rural development and the perverted potential of sugar/ethanol exports'. *Journal of Peasant Studies,* 37 (4), 917–938.

Salimo, P. and Macuane, J.J. 2019. 'Relatório de Avaliação do Projecto Transparência e Prestação de Contas'. *Centro de Integridade Pública*, https://cipmoz.org/wp-content/uploads/2020/02/CIP-Avaliacao-do-Projecto-Accountability-Relatorio-Final-31-10-2019-Final.pdf, accessed 21 July 2020.

Sebastião, A. 4 January 2018a. 'Moçambique: População paralisa mina da Jindal'. *Deutsche Welle*, https://www.dw.com/pt-002/mo%C3%A7ambique-popula%C3%A7%C3%A3o-paralisa-mina-da-jindal/a-42012358, accessed 23 March 2020.

Sebastião, A. 10 January 2018b. 'Moçambique: Na Jindal haverá indemnizações, mas há atrasos salariais'. *Deutsche Welle*, https://www.dw.com/pt-002/mo%C3%A7ambique-na-jindal-haver%C3%A1-indemniza%C3%A7%C3%B5es-mas-h%C3%A1-atrasos-salariais/a-42095529, accessed 23 March 2020.

SEKELEKANI. 2015. *A Minha Voz: Narração de sofrimento de comunidades reassentadas em Tete*. Maputo: SEKELEKANI.

SEKELEKANI. 2016. *A Minha Voz: Narração de sofrimento ou como se incubam novos conflitos em Moçambique*. Maputo: SEKELEKANI.

SEKELEKANI. 2017. 'Impact of mining in Moatize, Mozambique', https://www.youtube.com/watch?v=xGDb05ETyHo, accessed 30 April 2020.

United Nations Conference on Trade and Development (UNCTAD). 2012. *Mozambique: Investment policy review*. New York and Geneva: UNCTAD.

Tump, T. 2019. 'Estudo sobre sinergias e concorrências entre os sectores agrícolas privado e familiar em Angola'. Unpublished Paper.

Urquhart, A.W. 1963. 'Patterns of subsistence and settlement in southwestern Angola'. National Research Council Publication 1096, National Academy of Sciences, Washington, DC.

World Bank. 2009. *Awakening Africa's Sleeping Giant: Prospects for commercial agriculture in the Guinea savannah zone and beyond.* Washington, DC: World Bank.

World Bank. 2010. *Rising Global Interest in Farmland: Can it yield sustainable and equitable benefits?* Washington DC: World Bank.

World Bank. 2017. *Mozambique Economic Update: A two-speed economy.* Washington, DC: World Bank.

Zacarias, A. 11 July 2018. 'Tete: Ordem dos Advogados critica sentença do Tribunal acerca do reassentamento'. *Deutsche Welle*, https://www.dw.com/

pt-002/tete-ordem-dos-advogados-critica-senten%C3%A7a-do-tribunal-acerca-do-reassentamento/a-44634296, accessed 23 March 2020.

Legislation

Mozambique

Regulamento Ambiental para Actividade Mineira, Decreto n° 26/2004. 20 August 2004. Maputo: Government of Mozambique, http://extwprlegs1.fao.org/docs/pdf/moz65484.pdf, accessed 9 June 2020.

Regulamento sobre o Processo de Avaliação do Impacto Ambiental, Decreto n° 45/2004. 29 September 2004. Maputo: Government of Mozambique, http://www.biofund.org.mz/wp-content/uploads/2019/01/1547551312-AIA%20reg%2045%202004-searchable_noPW.pdf, accessed 9 June 2020.

Regulamento sobre o Processo de Reassentamento Resultante das Actividades Económicas, Decreto n° 31/2012. 8 August 2012. Maputo: Government of Mozambique, https://landportal.org/library/resources/regulamento-sobre-o-processo-de-reassentamento-resultante-de-actividade-econ%C3%B3mica, accessed 9 June 2020.

Angola

Decreto sobre a Avaliação de Impacte Ambiental, Decreto nº 51/04. 2014. Luanda: Republic of Angola. http://www.gckcc.ao/attachments/article/388/Decreto%20n.%C2%BA%2051%2004,%20de%2023%20de%20Julho.pdf, accessed 9 June 2020.

Lei de Bases do Ambiente, Lei nº 5/98. 1998. Luanda: Government of Angola, http://www.saflii.org/ao/legis/num_act/ldbda149.pdf, accessed 9 June 2020.

Lei de Terras de Angola, Lei nº 9/04. 2004. Luanda: Government of Angola, http://www.gckcc.ao/attachments/article/392/Lei%20n.%C2%BA%209%2004,%20de%209%20de%20Novembro.pdf, accessed 9 June 2020.

Interviews

Fatima, F. March 2019. Interview with author, Gambos.

Fingo, D. F. March 2018. Interview with author, Lubango.

Madalena, L. March 2019. Interview with author, Gambos.

Mantemba, B. March 2019. Interview with author, Gambos.

Wakussanga, J. March 2018a. Email correspondence and telephone interview with author, Lubango.

Wakussanga, J. March 2018b. Interview with author, Lubango.

Section III

International Experiences: The state, land and political agency

NINE

Land Reform in South Africa: Lessons from Zimbabwe's radical land expropriation process

ZENZO MOYO AND TOENDEPI SHONHE

BACKGROUND: DISPOSSESSION OF LAND IN SOUTH AFRICA

South Africa's 1913 Natives Land Act configured a land ownership structure that, up to the present, has persisted despite this segregationist Act being repealed in 1991. The period between 1913 and 1991 was characterised by colonial expansion and the strengthening of segregation laws, and therefore witnessed 'millions of people being uprooted from their homes, often with untold brutality, and always without compensation' (Mothabi, 2017: 63). To reinforce this dispossession, a legal framework comprising the 1913 Act, the Natives Land and Trust Act of 1936 and the Group Areas Act of 1950 prevented Africans from acquiring land outside what had been designated as 'native reserves'. These reserves, initially covering 7 per cent of the country's landed area, increased to 13 per cent by the passing of the 1936 Act (Claassens and Matlala, 2014). These were small enclaves to which 87 per cent of the African population was forcibly confined, and these were often in areas with poor agricultural soils. As was the case in Zimbabwe (see Sadomba, 2011), this historical context of dispossession and apartheid geography, which created reserves/Bantustans and homelands (see Butler et al., 1978), played a major role in inspiring the spirit of the liberation movement (Mtisi et al., 2009). As a result, the land question featured strongly in the negotiations that led to the 1980 and 1994 moments in Zimbabwe and South Africa, respectively. Thus, the current inequitable and unsustainable land ownership structure in South Africa (and Zimbabwe before 2000) is as much a legacy of colonialism as it is of the negotiations that gave birth to majority rule (see Chapter 3 in this volume).

Contemporary analyses on socio-economic transformation in South Africa agree that land reform up to now has been slow, and as a result there has not been much transformation in terms of land ownership. At its 2017 National Conference, the ANC agreed to accelerate land reform and rural development as part of its programme of radical economic transformation. A resolution was also taken at this conference that expropriation of land without compensation would be one of the mechanisms used by government to operationalise land reform and redistribution (ANC, 2018). In their various pronouncements, the Economic Freedom Fighters (EFF) and the Black First, Land First (BLF) movement have also advocated for a radical approach to land reform (BLF, 2015; Smith, 2019). Within this context of land expropriation without compensation debate, this chapter seeks to use Zimbabwe's radical land reform approach as a lens to assess the options available for South Africa's land reform agenda. Central to the arguments is an acknowledgement that contemporary land reform bears a burden to correct historical inequities in land ownership, the subjugation of indigenous populations and the associated inequalities and poverty this has generated over the years. Considering the processes and effects of Zimbabwe's radical land repossession, the specific question is, what lessons can be derived for the benefit of land reform in South Africa? This chapter argues for a political economy approach to implementing and assessing redistributive land reform. This approach has been used by some evaluative studies in Zimbabwe's land reform. Arguments on production, accumulation and social differentiation based on these studies will be presented. Observation, a review of literature and government documents on land reform in both countries, and previous research studies conducted by the authors will be used as sources of data.

We discuss the theoretical paradigms for evaluating redistributive land reform in countries on the periphery of a capitalist world. We then consider post-independence debates and agrarian structures in Zimbabwe and South Africa, not so much as a comparison, but as a heuristic tool to capture some similarities between these two countries share. We assess some of Zimbabwe's land reform outcomes before offering some lessons – both positive and negative – that South Africa can learn from the Zimbabwean experience.

UNDERSTANDING PARADIGMS FOR EVALUATING REDISTRIBUTIVE LAND REFORM

Current debates on land reform and redistribution in South Africa are framed largely around two major narratives. One looks at the idea of efficiency and productivity in commercial farming (DLA, 2006), while the other is oriented more towards issues of transformation and social 'justice, freedom and emancipation of the formerly oppressed', and abhors privileging economistic considerations as a representation of the 'colonial present' (Kepe and Hall, 2018: 133–135). For land reform to succeed in fulfilling its intended purpose, it is key that a suitable framework or approach is adopted at its implementation. Ben Cousins and Ian Scoones (2010) discuss an array of paradigms that can be used to direct and guide the implementation or to measure the viability of land reform. Two of these paradigms are the neoclassical economics approach and the new institutional economics approach. Although slightly different, in the main these two prioritise economistic measurements, both in implementation and in assessment. 'Their central focus sees efficiency as a big factor in productivity and viability, and they therefore prefer well-functioning markets, and are proponents of market-led land reform processes' (Cousins and Scoones, 2010: 37).

Proponents of the neoclassical economics approach emphasise returns on factors of production (land, labour and capital) and are also of the view that market-led land reform is superior because it reduces market imperfections and creates security of tenure and investment, which is critical for bank credit. While it supports efficient farmers at any scale, its orientation is more towards economies of scale, which means it favours large-scale commercial farming. This differs in the new institutional economics approach, the target of which is the promotion of efficient small-scale farmers who, besides maximising on land returns, are also growth multipliers.

To the left in Cousins and Scoones' (2010) paradigms is the radical political economy approach, as well as the Marxist approach. The former prioritises rights to land and considers agrarian transformation as development. The latter examines the agrarian question, focusing on the associated transition to capitalism in agriculture. In this sense, Marxism assesses the class structure and social relations of production, property and class dynamics of capital accumulation and the connected processes of industrialisation (see Gutto, 2014). In instances where large, efficient capitalist farms are retained, the approach advocates for improved conditions of labour, or even for reforms that promote accumulation from below (see Neocosmos, 1993; Cousins, 2013).

The political economy approach – utilised in this chapter to include the use of radical political economy and Marxism – examines the extent to which land reform transforms exploitative agrarian structures and food regimes; and it promotes the development of small family farms and advocates for reform that secures rights to land and resources by peasants and farm workers (see Moyo and Yeros, 2007). According to Cousins and Scoones, viability of land reform in the context of the political economy approach 'must be assessed at a scale beyond the individual farm or land reform project and seen in the context of the new agrarian order that embodies social justice, restoration of identity, socio-economic transformation, and ecological sustainability' (Cousins and Scoones, 2010: 46).

Zimbabwe's land reform programme has been assessed in the recent past using the radical political economy and Marxists approaches (see Moyo, 2011a; 2011b; Chambati, 2013; Mkodzongi, 2013; Scoones, 2015; Shonhe, 2017; 2019; Mazwi, 2019; Muchetu, 2019), and these have concluded that there is evidence of accumulation from below.

In South Africa, scholars such as Ruth Hall and Thembela Kepe (2017) and Kepe and Hall (2018) have employed a political economy approach to assess South Africa's land reform, and these researchers have begun to draw links between radical political economy and concepts of decolonisation and decoloniality advanced by Sabelo Ndlovu-Gatsheni (2012; 2013; see also Omanga, 2020; and Chapter 2 in this volume). Similar to the political economy approach, ideas of decolonisation and decoloniality also assess redistributive land reform from the perspective of the 'colonial present' and fear some form of 'recolonisation' through stalled reforms (Kepe and Hall, 2018: 128). Following Ndlovu-Gatsheni (2012; 2013) and Chielozona Eze (2015), Kepe and Hall (2018) argue that the post-liberation project of decolonisation ought to involve the attainment of political and economic independence from the former colonisers, which must manifest itself through a total emancipation of the periphery. This, it is argued, will serve to reverse political and economic subjugation, of which land dispossession is part.

This chapter therefore argues that the way we think about redistributive land reform is a matter that requires epistemological reorientation to avoid faulty celebrations about food security premised on hollow arguments of productivity, mainly assessed through large-scale production. Kepe and Hall also argue along these lines by saying the hyper-obsession with high productivity on resettled land misses other important meanings of land, which may 'include land as a form of identity for the people concerned due to their historical roots to it', and that land itself 'could serve as a bargaining power to leverage resources or other concessions that strengthen political positions and contribute to livelihoods' (Kepe and Hall, 2018: 134).

In essence, understanding how these conceptualisations are framed, when assessing the outcomes of redistributive reforms elsewhere, could help inform policy design in South Africa as the debate on 'appropriation without compensation' gathers momentum. The following section discusses post-independence processes of land reform in South Africa and Zimbabwe to contextualise the lessons that can be shared.

POST-INDEPENDENCE LAND OWNERSHIP AND AGRARIAN STRUCTURES

Post-1994 land reform in South Africa

In an article comparing land reform processes in Zimbabwe and South Africa, Zenzo Moyo (2013) observes that, like in Zimbabwe at the commencement of its Fast-Track Land Reform Programme (FTLRP) in July 2000, landowners and landless people in South Africa agree that land redistribution is necessary. They also agree that the process has been slow and, therefore, it has not sufficiently transformed the ownership structures. However, the premises from which these two disparate groupings arrive at these similar conclusions differ substantially. While landless people want land reform to be speeded up to right the past, and to enable all citizens, especially black people, to integrate fully in the economy and enjoy full citizenship, white landowners are more driven by a desire to avoid a moment of 'rapture from the bottom', which may lead to a Zimbabwe-like chaotic land reform process (Moyo and Yeros, 2013; Moyo and Nyoni, 2013). The risk of this differentiated convergence is that while current landowners may find it necessary to release land for resettlement, they may do so without really giving away productive properties, a gesture that will fall short of landless people's expectations – which is to fully integrate into the land economy. The possibility of such an integration can be realised only through an adoption of radical, but inclusive, land reform approaches. However, for this to happen, an *a priori* question needs to be asked. What accounts for this delayed transformation in both countries?

Both Zimbabwe and South Africa went through negotiated transitions, both of which entailed compromises on the laws that would govern land reform (Hall, 2003). The negotiated settlements at independence entailed reconciling with former colonisers, which meant that the economic injustices of the past could not be tackled immediately after gaining independence. Instead, the pronouncements of reconciliation by Robert Mugabe in 1980 and Nelson Mandela in 1994 sealed compromises with capital (such as international finance institutions, and large-scale land and business owners), leading to compromised approaches that limited the possibility of an immediate remedy to inequalities associated with colonial land ownership, on account of global geopolitical considerations. This was despite the fact that the inequitable land ownership structure had featured strongly in the negotiations that led to the respective countries' independence.

For South Africa, the question that preoccupied many within the anti-apartheid movement during the transition period was whether land redistribution was to be treated as negotiable (Mafeje, 1992). Many people believed that the best approach would have been to expropriate land from those who had unduly benefited from historical dispossession. Current discussions on land reform in South Africa, epitomised by the ruling party's 2017 conference resolution of land expropriation without compensation, have sought to revisit this poignant question about the non-negotiability of radical land redistribution (ANC, 2018). It has been argued above that South Africa's land reform programme has been slow, with only 8 million hectares having been redistributed between 1994 and 2018 (Presidential Advisory Panel on Land Reform and Agriculture, 2019). From an initial target to redistribute 30 per cent of all commercial agricultural land by 2014, less than 10 per cent had been redistributed by 2018 (Presidential Advisory Panel on Land Reform and Agriculture, 2019: 12). What Arrighi writes about post-colonial states, namely that even after the attainment of democracy, the skewed and dualistic land ownership structures imposed through segregation laws still remain, applies to South Africa (Arrighi, 1967).

A cursory review of the three pillars of land reform prescribed in South Africa's 1996 Constitution – restitution, redistribution and tenure reforms – shows how this framework, developed during the transitional negotiations, has contributed to the phlegmatic transformation process. For example, section 25 of the Constitution essentially prescribes market-informed processes of compensation that should be followed in cases where land is to be expropriated. This means owners of land can deliberately stall the process by distorting market prices. It was probably with this in mind that Samir Amin (2006) had to argue that by stipulating compensation for acquired land, the post-apartheid compromise ruled out any meaningful agrarian reform.

For one, the land redistribution pillar is constrained not only by the need to compensate those whose land is to be acquired (see Hall, 2007),[1] but also the expectation that acquired land should be productive. Such approaches favour neoclassical economistic arguments that privilege property rights and security of tenure, as articulated by Hernando de Soto (2000) and Craig Richardson (2005). Over-emphasising property rights and productivity based viability, while eschewing indigenous people's right to land and cultural belonging, negates the gains of democracy. The tendency of sometimes over-privileging those with qualifications and experience in 'productive' agriculture is also not uncommon in state-led reform processes, where beneficiaries are allocated land on the basis of possessing credentials desirable for high-yield production (DLA, 2006; Scoones et al., 2010). The right to access land to attain equity, identity and belonging should also be understood as a right to gain bargaining power useful to leverage other resources and concessions that can strengthen socio-political positions for everyone and contribute to livelihoods (Kepe and Hall, 2018; Shonhe, 2020).

One of the outcomes of the early 1990s constitutional negotiations was an agreement that only land dispossession that occurred after June 1913 was to be considered for restitution (Williams, 2007). This is despite the fact that dispossessions started in the 1650s when the first settlers occupied the Cape of Good Hope. The Restitution of Land Rights Act (No. 22 of 1994) was aimed at restoring cultural land rights to the descendants of the dispossessed, without disrupting agricultural production and political stability (Hall, 2007). This pillar was intended to restore land to black people, mainly relying on the memory of the descendants of the dispossessed, and in the process hoping to restore victims' lost sense of identity. As acknowledged by the Presidential Advisory Panel on Land Reform and Agriculture (2019), despite the

1 Ntsebeza (2005) argues that the Communal Land Rights Act (No. 11 of 2004) is ineffective as evictions have continued. Hall (2007) argues the land reform has been slow and ineffective, having shifted its focus from redistribution to a mechanism for evictions. The Presidential Advisory Panel on Land Reform and Agriculture (2019) observed that the national Constitution protects the current owners of the land and gives the right to secure recourse through courts, such that without a moratorium, evictions are likely to continue.

fact that the state has allocated funds to land restitution, many claims have remained unresolved (see Chapter 7 in this volume). For those cases that have been resolved, most claimants have preferred cash payment rather than restoration or alternative land. This is usually explained by arguing that most South Africans prefer cash as they are not interested in farming, preferring urban life. The 'South African urbanisation review' by David Gardner and Nick Graham (2018) supports this thesis of urban life preference (65 per cent of South Africa's 56 million citizens reside in towns). However, this urban preference thesis should not be used to overlook the enduring rural–urban linkages and survival strategies that Doreen Atkinson writes about. She points out that 'many poor people keep their rural roots as a safety net, and many more well-off black people keep a link with their rural villages, in anticipation of retirement' (Atkinson, 2014: 43).

The levels of memory and remembrance necessary for one to prove a cultural connection to the land may be too deep a burden, even though it is required as evidence to substantiate a pre-existing right to that land. Even if a claimant succeeds in proving this linkage, many will simply not possess a cultural and identity connection with the land being claimed as to develop an appetite to resettle there. Hence the choice to opt for financial compensation, which hardly restores lost identity. Instead, this perpetuates the racially skewed land ownership patterns. Joint ventures and strategic partnerships between agribusiness, land claimants and communal property owners, seeking to maintain productivity levels, have also been pursued under the restitution pillar (see Chapter 7 in this volume). This was common in the Limpopo Province where almost 50 per cent of agricultural land was under claims. '[T]here is lack of policy detail on how these should operate and be monitored' (Kepe and Hall, 2016: 58), which has affected their performance. The imposition of the agribusiness model has also been criticised for being inappropriate for smallholder farming (Rusenga, 2020).

It cannot be missed that there are legal constraints that limit the state's ability to redistribute land quickly. For example, provisions of section 25(3) of the South African Constitution demand: 'The amount of the compensation and the time and manner of payment must be just and equitable ... having regard to all relevant circumstances, including the market value of the property' (Act No. 108 of 1996). It is clear that even though the Constitution places a lot of responsibility on the state, the corresponding powers given to the state do not match this responsibility. It seems as if what the right hand gives to the state, the left hand takes away; in other words, a negation of the right.

The preceding paragraphs have sought to show that the processes of restitution, grant-based redistribution and tenure reforms have not significantly transformed landholding structures (Hall, 2007; Gumede, 2014).[2] This is aptly revealed by statistics in the Department of Rural Development and Land Reform's 'Land audit report' (2018). The report says that out of a total of 121,924,881 hectares of land in the country, 94 per cent or 114,223,276 hectares is registered in the Deeds Office. Of the registered portion, companies (23,199,904 hectares), trusts (29,291,857 hectares) and individuals (37,800,986) own a total of 89,532,044 hectares, or 90 per cent of all registered land. Table 9.1 summarises individual land ownership by race.

Table 9.1: Individual land ownership by race in South Africa (2017)

Race	Hectares	Percentage of total
Whites	26,663,144	72
Coloureds	5,371,383	15
Indians	2,031,790	5
Africans	1,314,873	4
Other	1,271,562	3
Co-owned	425,537	1
TOTALs	**37,078,289**	**100**

Source: DLA (2018).

Faced with the figures captured in Table 9.1, the Presidential Advisory Panel on Land Reform and Agriculture (2019) is justified

2 The third pillar of land tenure reform has not been discussed here due to space limitations. However, DLA (1997), Ntsebeza (2005), Hall (2007) and the Presidential Advisory Panel on Land Reform and Agriculture (2019) discuss it in detail.

to lament that despite 25 years of democracy, 'the legacy of land dispossession has yet to be redressed, and social exclusion and economic inequality persist' as people's expectations and promises made are missed.

Post-2000 land reform in Zimbabwe

Zimbabwe's FTLRP officially started in 2000 (Scoones et al., 2010: 24). There is divergence of views on whether the ruling Zimbabwe African National Union-Patriotic Front (ZANU-PF) government triggered the radical land reform in response to defeat in the February 2000 constitutional referendum (Sachikonye, 2003), or if it was a policy initiative driven by its welfarist ideological orientation.[3] There are also suggestions that ZANU-PF may have succumbed to pressure from rural movements (Moyo, 2004; Alexander, 2006), and then co-opted an increasingly agitated war veterans movement (Sadomba, 2011) and peasants in order to mobilise against a newly formed opposition party – the Movement for Democratic Change (MDC) (Raftopoulos, 2003; Moyo, 2004). However, scholars generally agree that the FTLRP was largely chaotic and violent (Sadomba, 2011; Zamchiya, 2012). Within this context, Sam Moyo and Paris Yeros (2007) and Zvakanyorwa Sadomba (2011) posit that this violence was part and parcel of mobilisation towards a revolutionary approach within a context of an overdue reform process. Sadomba (2011) details how such a revolution was intended to secure structural changes to a neocolonial-capital alliance where elites were in positions of accumulation and the rest of the citizens faced high levels of poverty. This notion was emphasised

3 In February 2000, Zimbabwe held a referendum for citizens to accept/reject a draft constitution that had been drawn up in the preceding two years by a government-appointed, but Zanu-PF-dominated, Constitutional Commission. One of the clauses in the draft would have enabled the state to expropriate land without compensation. The newly formed MDC, together with human rights-oriented civil society organisations, campaigned rigorously for rejection of the draft. The No vote won, and the ruling party interpreted this loss as a rejection of the radical land reform clause. Either by coincidence or design, this moment marked the radicalisation of the land reform programme.

by a scholar on Zimbabwean political economy, Sam Moyo:[4]

> Zimbabwe's land reform agenda is a huge thing, much more, but the problem is that people reduce it simplistically. It is actually restructuring property relations in a broader sense. On the one hand, you are getting land, but what is actually happening is shifting the structure of the dominance of one group over other groups, not only on a racial basis, but also in terms of classes as well ... You are also shifting and restructuring class relations, of course to the extent that you minimise the elite who take many farms and big farms, which they eventually did in Zimbabwe, even though they are still less than 10 per cent of the total landholdings.

To backtrack slightly, the build-up to the FTLRP began in the late 1990s, when peasants and chiefs embarked on spasmodic but forceful land occupation activities, often with violent resistance from the state at the time (Moyo, 2001). One of the oft-cited examples is that of the Svosve people, under Chief Svosve of Marondera, who took occupation of four farms in June 1998, based on their historical claim to the land (Murisa, 2011). Occupations of this nature, of which there were many, had more to do with ancestral connections to the land than the need to have farm land, in a way speaking to issues of identity and tradition. Within the same year, some war veterans in south-eastern Zimbabwe occupied the Agricultural and Rural Development Authority's Mkwasine farm (Murisa, 2011: 113). Thus, it would not be an exaggeration to argue that rural social movements and peasants, led by war veterans and chiefs in some instances, reconceptualised the land redistribution process and challenged the state on broader structural issues. This culminated in some cooperative arrangements with the state (Sadomba, 2011). The character of these land occupations, which in part defined the nature of state-led land redistribution from 2000

4 Interview with Sam Moyo, a Zimbabwean professor of political economics, and widely considered as one of the best researchers and experts on land reform in southern Africa. The interview was conducted on 11 November 2015, a few days before he died in a car accident in India.

onwards, took the form and content of guerrilla warfare. Within this context, land reform was seen as a third Chimurenga.[5] In some areas, as alluded to earlier, there were instances where identity and citizenship issues were prioritised as rural peasants shared, within the same FTLRP agenda, their own aim of regaining ancestral land, claiming autochthonous rights that had been severed in 1930 when Zimbabwe's first Land Apportionment Act, which instituted the separation of races and the creation of native reserves, was enacted (see Floyd, 1962). In such instances, the process of land occupations was always preceded by traditional ceremonies to seek the protection of the ancestral world (Sadombe, 2011).

In practical terms, the FTLRP eschewed market-led approaches to land reform, and instead prioritised radical agrarian paradigms that sought to secure land rights for peasants and rural dwellers. But as Deborah Potts and Chris Mutambirwa (1990) and Godfrey Tawodzera et al. (2012) show, in Zimbabwe town dwellers always consider themselves to be migrants, and do not plan to permanently remain in towns. The majority, according to Potts and Mutambirwa, still preserve links with their rural villages due to 'a strong perception that the maintenance of rural links is essential as economic security for the eventualities of old age and unemployment when urban expenses could not be covered' (Potts and Mutambirwa, 1990: 677).

Thus, due to these deep rural–urban linkages, town dwellers also got absorbed into the land redistribution networks that crystallised into two modes of land allocations. Besides, the economic structural adjustment programme had radically ramped up urban poverty and induced the state to cut various welfare provisions of the past, leading to urban populations opting for the resettlement programme (Moyo, 2011b).

As a result of the nature of the third Chimurenga approach, peasants, urban dwellers and war veterans who had taken part in the land occupations of the farms got preference and were settled mainly

5 The term Chimurenga was used to refer to Zimbabwe's liberation wars. Thus, calling the FTLRP a third Chimurenga elevated the programme to the level of previous armed struggles aimed at regaining national freedom and identity.

in the A1 farms across the country.[6] This process of allocation also considered autochthon interests, and reserved plots for war veterans, women and districts that did not have commercial farms. The other model was the A2 medium- and large-scale farms that were allocated through technocratic processes by the Ministry of Lands, Agriculture and Rural Resettlement. In total, Zimbabwe's radical land reform programme transferred 13 million hectares of land from 5,400 white farmers to 219,000 smallholders and middle-scale farmers. The agrarian relations were changed from a dualistic structure, composed of large-scale commercial farming and communal area farmers, to a trimodal structure, where large-scale farmers now co-exist with the middle-scale farmers and the peasantry (Moyo, 2011b). The trimodal agrarian structure is a critical innovation in land reform for varied reasons.

First, it reflects the redistributive nature of the land reform programme as well as its land tenure reconfiguration, achieved from a process that took restitution and redistribution into account. Second, the new structure illustrates how over 13 million hectares of productive land has been redistributed, predominantly in favour of A1 smallholders[7] and communal area villagers, who now constitute 79 per cent of the farming households, up from 49 per cent in 2000 (see Table 9.2). Third, the trimodal agrarian structure shows how Zimbabwe's land redistribution preserved capitalist farming under the A2 model, where farming households increased to 13 per cent, up from 4 per cent. They hold the land under 99-year leases, even though not all of them have accessed the lease agreements to date.

6 A1 farms are made up of villagised resettled smallholder farmers who were given 6 hectares of arable land and 12 hectares sharing for grazing on a permit basis. A2 farms are the medium- to large-scale farms of 20 hectares and above that were either left with existing commercial farmers or were given to new owners post-redistribution.

7 While there are disparate definitions of small farmers, as Cousins (2013) discusses, in Zimbabwe this refers to ordinary villagised farmers and fast-track villagised resettled farmers who own an average of 6 hectares of arable land and 12 hectares of commonly held land for grazing under a permits system. The term also refers to communal farmers who own an average of 3 hectares held under customary ownership.

Table 9.2: Estimated landholdings by farmer groups: 1980, 2000 and 2010

Farm categories	Farms/households (000s)						Area held (000 ha)						Average farm size (ha)		
	1980		2000		2010		1980		2000		2010*		1980	2000	2010
	No.	%	No.	%	No.	%	Ha	%	Ha	%	Ha	%			
Family farms*	700	98	1,125	99	1,321	98	16,400	49	20,067	61	25,826	79	23	18	20
Small/middle commercial farms**	8.5	1	8.5	1	30.9	2	1,400	4	1,400	4	4,400	13	165	165	142
Large farms	5.4	1	4.956	0.4	1.371	0.1	13,000	39	8,691.6	27	1,156.9	4	2,407	1,754	844
Agro-estates	0.296	0.1	0.296	0.02	0.247	0.02	2,567	8	2,567	8	1,494.6	5	8,672	8,672	6,051
Total	**714**	100	**1,139**	100	**1,353**	100	**33,367**	100	**32,726**	100	**32,878**	100	**46.7**	**28.7**	**24.3**

Source: Moyo (2011b)

** Combines communal, old resettlement and A1 areas*
*** Combines A2 and small-scale commercial farm areas*

The greatest weakness of Zimbabwe's radical land reform programme was its politicisation, which became apparent immediately after the rejection of the constitutional referendum in 2000. Those who supported the reform programme became clustered and identified with the politics of ZANU-PF, while those who expressed opposition to the FTLRP, regardless of which aspect they disagreed with, became associated with opposition politics and, by extension, the opposition party. At that point, Zimbabwe began to witness the crystallisation of a polarisation phenomenon, which pitted redistribution and nationalism against liberal human rights (Moyo, 2018). Every socio-economic and political engagement became a simplified binary between the ruling party and the opposition party, the MDC. Thus, the politicisation of the process meant that beneficiaries of land reform in the main became those who were associated with ZANU-PF (Scoones et al., 2010; Zamchiya, 2012; 2013), while accidental beneficiaries from the opposition party could expect their offer letters to be withdrawn at any moment once that connection was exposed. Some beneficiaries had to 'act ZANU-PF' in order to be able to co-exist with the ruling party's supporters on the farms (Mkodzongi, 2013).

Another weakness is that in correcting the racial imbalance on land ownership, the Zimbabwean process neglected to emphasise the class content of the programme. By 2007, Moyo and Yeros (2007) had already noted that even though land reform in Zimbabwe was both radical and necessary, it had begun to compromise with capital, which manifested in the allocation of land to middle-scale black farmers who were to be developed into a fully-fledged capitalist class through a capital friendly tenure system. Thus, ideas of narrow nationalism, predicated on the political class, became dominant in land reform as the process sought to satisfy the needs of the politically connected. Even though land reform is meant to emphasise redistribution, transformation and decongestion of crowded spaces, many of the beneficiaries of A2 farms belonged to elites who were able to manipulate the process for their own egocentric class interests.

As a result, many high-ranking ruling party officials became owners of multiple farms, with some ministers laying claim to more than five farms each (Mambo, 2012; Moyo, 2018). Many farms were taken away from white farmers, and given to ruling party elites, peg for peg, eschewing the redistributive and decongestion thrusts. Besides this being achieved through corruption, it became a vehicle for exacerbating inequality in the country. In addition to this, and also bordering on corruption, many elites from across the political divide benefited from a farm mechanisation loan scheme, that was later scandalously converted to a grant scheme by the Reserve Bank, absolving recipients from paying back loans (Magaisa, 2020a; 2020b). These drawbacks have attracted significant attention from different land stakeholders and researchers. But it is equally important to focus on the agrarian market structure changes discussed in the following sections.

CHANGING PRODUCTION AND ACCUMULATION PATTERNS AMONG RESETTLED FARMERS

Described as violent and disruptive, Zimbabwe's land reform is portrayed as being responsible for the decline in agricultural production as well as other sectors of the economy. We discuss production patterns of the main food and cash crops over the past three decades, not so much to favour the viability-based-on-production arguments, but to show that radical land redistribution does not equate to the total destruction of livelihoods. There is a dominant view that the decline in maize and tobacco output in the early 2000s was caused by the removal of experienced and large-scale commercial farmers (LSCF), who were replaced by unskilled and inexperienced black smallholder farmers (Scoones et al., 2010). However, as Figure 9.1 demonstrates, national maize production output in communal and large-scale commercial farms started declining in the late 1990s, not post-2000, and has since begun to accelerate. The decline reached its lowest ebb in 2005, before a rise began across all farmer types. A simplistic neoclassical view would point to changes in commodity prices, for instance. However, our analysis shows that a variety of factors were at play.

Figure 9.1: Maize output in tons (1993 to 2017)

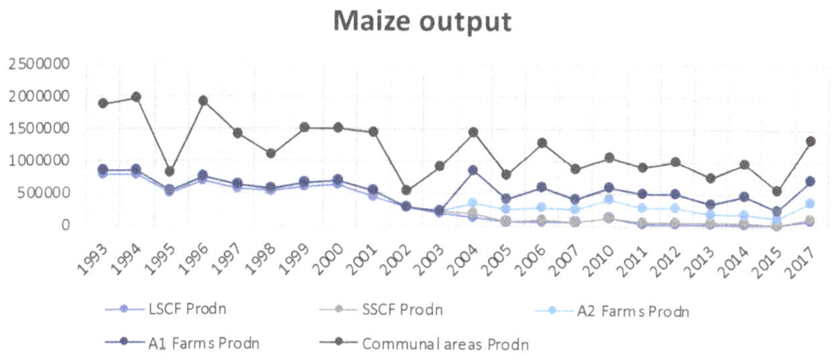

Source: Authors' compilation from the Ministry of Agriculture data.

For instance, it is widely believed that capital flight associated with economic sanctions imposed by Europe and the United States may have resulted in the decline (Scoones et al., 2010; Moyo and Nyoni, 2013), exacerbated by the hostile political environment that unnerved markets and bank credits, resulting in an overall decline in output across farming and other sectors. In the other sectors, along the commodity value chains, volume and actors in the inputs and outputs markets dropped and reconfigured significantly as the effect of capital flight consolidated. Small businesses replaced big players in the farming inputs supply and agricultural commodity markets. These changes also affected the cost of production and commodity pricing, as well as accumulation patterns in the broader economy.

Zimbabwe experienced an agricultural production revamp from 2007, seven years after the fast track began, but this positive development was stalled in 2010 to 2011 due to economy-wide challenges. Among the newly resettled farmers, production and average yield levels for A1 and A2 farmers, respectively, have been improving after the liberalisation of commodity by the Government of National Unity in 2009, as Figure 9.1 and Figure 9.2 show.

Figure 9.2: Maize yield (1990–2017)

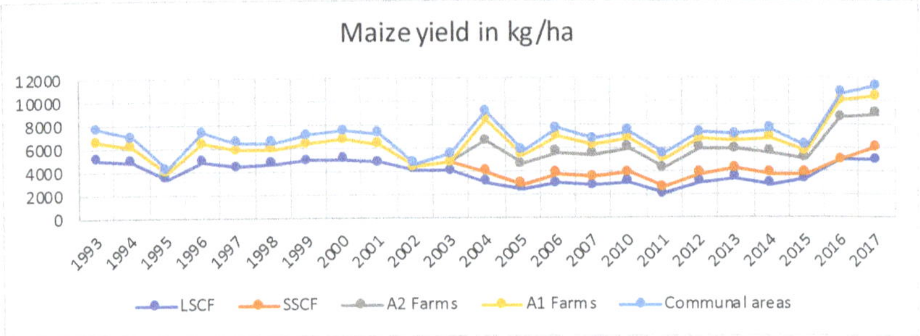

Source: Authors' compliation from the Ministry of Agriculture data.

In the same vein, the tobacco cash crop, which was produced mostly by the LSCFs prior to 2000, was on the decline since the fast-track land reform began. However, since then, tobacco production has been democratised and is now dominated by smallholders (A1 and communal areas). For example, the number of smallholders increased from a low of 6,310 in 2000, producing 7,583 million kilograms of tobacco, to an average of 123,469 smallholder growers or 87.6 per cent of tobacco producers, over the period 2013 to 2019 (see Figure 9.3). In 2018, smallholder growers produced 158.1 million kilograms, amounting to 62.8 per cent of total annual production. As a result, they earned a total of US$436.2 million, or 59.2 per cent of total income (TIMB, 2000; 2018; 2019). A similar trend was observed in other crops; for instance, smallholder growers delivered 82 per cent of the maize to the Mvurwi Grain Marketing Board depot in 2019 (Shonhe and Scoones, forthcoming).

Figure 9.3: Tobacco output (1994–2017)

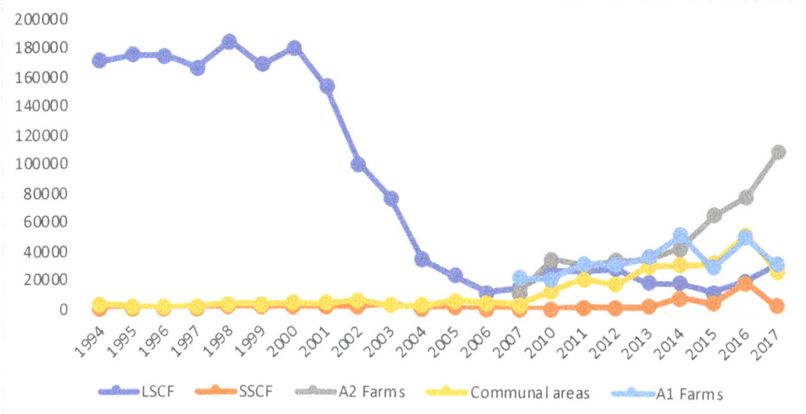

Source: Authors' compilation from the Ministry of Agriculture data.

Two decades after resettlement, how has access to land changed accumulation patterns for the farmers? The involvement of smallholder growers in commercial agriculture after land reform has resulted in increased accumulation of productive and non-productive assets by peasants (Moyo et al., 2009; Scoones et al., 2010; Shonhe, 2017; Mazwi et al., 2019). Scoones (2017) and Toendepi Shonhe (2019) have observed how farmers are now investing in urban properties, using proceeds from the sale of agricultural produce. Due to rural–urban linkages discussed earlier, urban households are increasingly dependent on food produced from their landholdings in resettled farms, which has ameliorated food shortages in towns and cities (Tawodzera et al., 2012). Besides, faced with a bank credit crunch since 2000, Shonhe (2019) observes that over 66 per cent of the farmers now rely on agricultural and off-farm income to finance agricultural production and development. These details are usually deliberately eschewed in media reports on land reform in Zimbabwe, while an 'all is not well' picture is developed.

Peasant farmers are turning the page and are producing, as well as accumulating, using the land resources that they now have.

This trend was also observed among former farm workers. These workers were mostly excluded from the land reform process as they were seen to be supportive of the opposition party – the MDC – and thus had to seek alternative livelihood options (Sachikonye, 2003; Chambati and Moyo, 2004). While Walter Chambati (2013) observes that these former farm workers secured the freedom of how to sell their labour, Shonhe et al. (forthcoming) argue that these workers have now gained access to land through rentals or illegal occupation. They are reliant on their own production for income generation. Figure 9.4 shows how workers in Mvurwi obtained their sources of livelihoods in 2018. The survey results indicate that farm workers in the LSCFs (A1 farms), and those still residing in farm compounds and unattached to specific farmers, rely on crop farming the most. Those in the A2 sector rely on artisanal and project activities, while only those working on joint venture farms rely more on farm wages.

Figure 9.4: Farm worker diversified sources of income

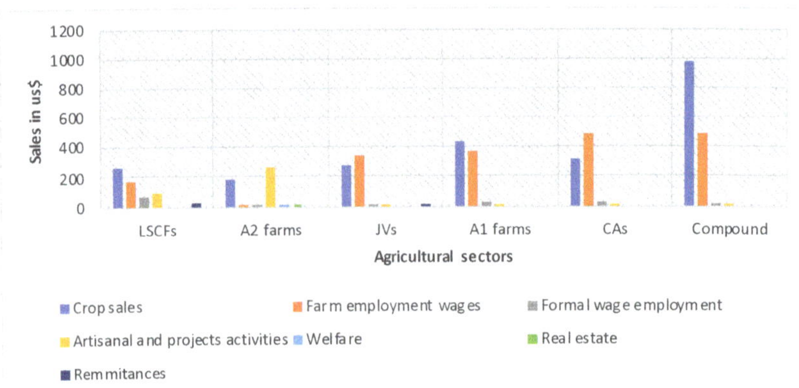

Source: Shonhe et al. (forthcoming)

Notes: JVs are joint ventures between resettled and former white farmers, Chinese or some indigenous business people.

In this sense, the FTLRP led to a shift by former farm workers from reliance on sale of labour to smallholder farming. The yesteryear farm worker has disappeared and a new one with more diversified sources of livelihoods has emerged.

LESSONS FROM THE ZIMBABWEAN EXPERIENCE

It has been established in this chapter that, just like in Zimbabwe before the FTLRP, land reform in South Africa has been very slow. The Zimbabwean case, which has altered ownership structures, has the potential to provide positive and negative lessons for South Africa.

First, the subordination of a variety of peasant questions to the agrarian modernisation project and an obsession with land reform viability-based-on-production matrices misses the bigger purpose of reform. Land redistribution is more than just taking away land from those who have it in abundance and giving to those who do not have it. Land reform offers an opportunity to restructure property relations in a very broad sense. It shifts the narrow structure of dominance by one social group over others, not only in terms of race, but also in terms of class relations. But for this to be achieved, a burden of extra vigilance should be placed on the state to ensure that land reform does not become a new site of over-accumulation, where only the elite end up with huge, multiple and idle land resources. While in theory land reform has the capacity to reverse high levels of inequality, if vigilance is not exercised to guard against over-accumulation, the opposite will happen. In Zimbabwe, many government ministers ended up with many farms due to this lack of vigilance (see Mambo, 2012). The way the farm mechanisation scheme was conducted not only points to corruption, but also the state's complicity in widening inequality by supporting those who already have at the expense of the poor.

Second, as Statistics SA (2017: 56) has shown, the percentage of persons with limited access to food stood at 21.3 in 2017, while households with limited access to food was at 24.7. The same report states that 'only 16 per cent of South African households were involved in agricultural production. Most production took place in backyard gardens' (Statistics SA, 2019: 6). Most of these household agricultural activities were concerned with food production – fruits, grains, vegetables and livestock farming. Nationally, according to the

'General household survey 2018', 'more than three-quarters (78 per cent) of households that were involved in agriculture were involved in an attempt to secure an additional source of food' (Statistics SA, 2019: 6).

These statistics show that ordinary people have not only an appetite to engage in farming, but are also conscious of the fact that self-production of food is essential in ameliorating poverty. The trimodal approach adopted in Zimbabwe during its FTLRP could be useful for South Africa to broadly decentralise food production. This reform framework allows family, small-scale, medium-scale and large-scale farms to co-exist side by side, and also ensures that minimal land is left idle. This not only helps to create jobs; it also encourages food production at a household level, which is more sustainable as a social policy intervention (see Chapter 6 in this volume).

The third lesson that the Zimbabwean experience offers is that while it is inevitable that radical redistributive land reform will upset food markets, investment opportunities and bank credit, these relationships can be re-established. How quickly the disruption is brought under control depends on how other important variables are managed. Considering how current landowners are invested in land, resistance to dispossession should be expected. However, as Figures 9.1, 9.2 and 9.3 illustrate, the period of decline in production (for both maize and tobacco) is being reversed as new landowners gain more experience, and markets begin to accept the permanency of the status quo.

In 2017, maize yield per hectare surpassed pre-land reform levels, while tobacco has since gone past the white commercial farmers' production levels across farming sectors. A major lesson is that South Africa should not expect to maintain constant production levels if radical land reform takes place, because such reform should aim for more than just issues of productivity. It is also about identity – connecting citizens to their ancestral land, democratising access to the means of production and food sovereignty. As the Zimbabwean case demonstrates, changes in land ownership have intra- and inter-party, regional and global economic and political implications, as powerful constituencies respond differently to the new settings, with patronage networks also coming into play.

A fourth lesson is derived from the far-reaching effects of reconfiguration that follows radical transformative land reform programmes. Changes in land sizes and tenure, broadening land ownership and commodity production patterns, the consequent effects on input and markets will always reconfigure value chains. For Zimbabwe, this contributed to the informalisation of the economy, which could not graduate to the formal sector due to the economy-wide challenges and diminished government capacity to intervene. The land reform ought to be seen as a complete reconfiguration of the productive forces and, therefore, post-settlement plans ought to be multisectoral. A political economy approach therefore enables an analysis of how vulnerable groups may be affected, for example, through food shortages or price hikes, and how they may respond, including, for instance, through uprisings and changes in voting patterns. For Zimbabwe, overlooking farm workers in the land reform programme was a grave error, given not only their farming experience gained over the years, but also the possibility of rendering them homeless, in addition to destroying their social networks within the farming sector (Chambati, 2017).

The fifth lesson is on the non-politicisation of the land reform process. In the Zimbabwean case, there were rapacious political entanglements that distorted the good intentions of land redistribution. The politicisation of the programme meant that one political party, ZANU-PF 'grabbed the bone and ran away with it' and, therefore, heavily tilted reform benefits towards those who belonged or sympathised with the ruling party. Most of those who got medium-scale farms (A2 model) were connected to the ruling elite, which meant that patrimonialism and corruption became a big part of the process. This led to the exclusion of many citizens, most of whom were supporters or sympathisers of opposition parties (Zamchiya, 2012). It is important that key state (not political) institutions should not be sidestepped in land reform. In fact, they should be the cog on which technical redistributive processes are centred to reduce societal polarisation.

CONCLUSION AND IMPLICATIONS FOR SOUTH AFRICA

While land and agrarian reforms are emotive and political, their socio-economic imperatives are obvious. Narratives informed by narrowly defined property rights and neoclassical economistic approaches miss important nuances that only political economy approaches can bring to the fore. While this chapter acknowledges the rapacious effects of land politics on Zimbabwe's economy, it also appreciates that the collapse of the economy was a result of multiple variables. Of course, global capital has the capacity to severely punish whoever acts singularly against its wishes. The undermining of property rights, in particular, attracts immediate retribution by global capital as it unsettles property relations. This may be inevitable for South Africa as well.

Taking into consideration the current repertoire of land reform debates in South Africa, informed by consciousness aroused by the 'radical' politics of the EFF, the adoption of the expropriation without compensation resolution of the 2017 ANC conference (ANC, 2018), and the language of civil society formations such as the BLF, it is pertinent that South Africa resolves the land question urgently. A close assessment of where Zimbabwe got it right and where it faltered as it confronted capital should be a priority for South Africa as this process unfolds. Approaching this learning process with an open mind is as crucial as it is unavoidable. Resolving the land question will inevitably disrupt ownership and production patterns. Therefore, productivity matrices should not be used exclusively to inform or to assess the success of land reform. Broader socio-economic considerations informed by a political economy analysis should be adopted. Such an approach generates new possibilities for social justice and development that is undergirded by accumulation from below. Shorn of its chaotic and violent characterisation, Zimbabwe's experience does this.

REFERENCES

African National Congress (ANC). 2018. '54th National Conference: Report and resolutions', http://joeslovo.anc.org.za/sites/default/files/docs/ANC per cent2054th_National_Conference_Report per cent20and per cent20Resolutions.pdf, accessed 12 March 2020.

Alexander, J. 2006. *The Unsettled Land: State-making and the politics of land in Zimbabwe, 1893–2003*. Oxford: James Currey.

Amin, S. 2006. *Beyond US Hegemony? Assessing the prospects for a multipolar world*. Pietermaritzburg: University of KwaZulu-Natal Press.

Arrighi, G. 1967. *The Political Economy of Rhodesia*. The Hague: Mouton.

Atkinson, D. 2014. 'Rural–urban linkages: South Africa case study'. Working Paper Series No. 125, Territorial Cohesion for Development Program, Rimisp, Santiago, Chile.

Black First, Land First (BLF). 2015. 'EFF policy discussion documents towards NPA 2014: Land and agrarian revolution', https://blf.org.za/2015/04/23/eff-policy-discussion-documents-towards-npa-2014-land-and-agrarian-revolution-2/, accessed 27 May 2020.

Butler, J., Rotberg, R. and Adams, J. 1978. *The Black Homelands of South Africa: The political and economic development of Bophuthatswana and KwaZulu*. Berkeley, CA: University of California Press.

Chambati, W. 2013. 'The political economy of agrarian labour relations in Zimbabwe after redistributive land reform'. *Agrarian South: Journal of Political Economy*, 2 (2), 189–211.

Chambati, W. 2017. 'Changing forms of wage labour in Zimbabwe's new agrarian structure'. *Agrarian South: Journal of Political Economy*, 6 (1), 79–112.

Chambati, W. and Moyo, S. 2004. 'Land reform and the political economy of agricultural labour'. African Institute for Agrarian Studies, Harare.

Claassens, A. and Matlala, B. 2014. 'Platinum, poverty and princes in post-apartheid South Africa: New laws, old repertoires', in Khadiagala, G., Naidoo, P., Pillay, D. and Southall, R. (eds.) *New South African Review 4: A fragile democracy – twenty years on*. Johannesburg: Wits University Press, 113–135.

Cousins, B. 2013. 'Smallholder irrigation schemes, agrarian reform and "accumulation from above and from below" in South Africa'. *Journal of Agrarian Change*, 13 (1), 116–139.

Cousins, B. and Scoones, I. 2010. 'Contested paradigms of 'viability' in redistributive land reform: Perspectives from southern Africa'. *Journal of Peasant Studies*, 37 (1), 31–66.

De Soto, H. 2000. *The Mystery of Capital: Why capitalism triumphs in the West and fails everywhere else*. New York: Basic Books.

Department of Land Affairs (DLA). 1997. 'White Paper on South African Land Policy', http://www.ruraldevelopment.gov.za/phocadownload/White-Papers/whitepaperlandreform.pdf, accessed 25 May 2020.

Department of Land Affairs (DLA). 2006. 'Implementation plan for the proactive land acquisition strategy', https://www.gov.za/documents/implementation-plan-proactive-land-acquisition-strategy, accessed 12 May 2020.

Department of Rural Development and Land Reform. 2018. 'Land audit report:

Phase II: Private land ownership by race, gender and nationality', https://www.gov.za/documents/land-audit-report-2017-5-feb-2018-0000, accessed 1 April 2020.

Eze, C. 2015. 'Decolonisation and its discontents: Thoughts on the postcolonial African moral self'. *South African Journal of Philosophy*, 34 (4), 408–418.

Floyd, B.N. 1962. 'Land apportionment in Southern Rhodesia'. *Geographical Review*, 52 (4), 566–582.

Gardner, D. and Graham, N. 2018. 'South African urbanisation review: Analysis of the human settlement programme and subsidy instruments', https://csp.treasury.gov.za/Resource%20_Centre/Conferences/Documents/Urbanization%20Review%20Papers/Paper%206%20-%20Analysis%20of%20HS%20Programme.pdf, accessed 25 May 2020.

Gumede, V. 2014. 'Land reform in post-apartheid South Africa: Should South Africa follow Zimbabwe's footsteps?' *International Journal of African Renaissance Studies*, 9 (1), 50–68.

Gutto, S.B.O. 2014. 'Retheorising and reconceptualising land, sovereignty, socio-economic rights and responsibility in the context of pan-Africanism and African renaissance in the 21st century'. *International Journal of African Renaissance Studies*, 9 (1), 5–15.

Hall, R. 2003. 'A comparative analysis of land reform in South Africa and Zimbabwe', in Lee, M.C. and Colvard, K. (eds.) *Unfinished Business: The land crisis in southern Africa*. Pretoria: Africa Institute of South Africa, 255–267.

Hall, R. 2007. 'Transforming rural South Africa? Taking stock of land reform', in Ntsebeza, L. and Hall, R. (eds.) *The Land Question in South Africa: The challenge of transformation and redistribution*. Cape Town: HSRC Press, 87–106.

Hall, R. and Kepe, T. 2017. 'Elite capture and state neglect: New evidence on South Africa's land reform'. *Review of African Political Economy*, 44 (151), 122–130.

Kepe, T. and Hall, R. 2016. 'Land redistribution in South Africa', https://www.parliament.gov.za/storage/app/media/Pages/2017/october/High_Level_Panel/Commissioned_Report_land/Commissioned_Report_on_Land_Redistribution_Kepe_and_Hall.pdf, accessed 20 March 2020.

Kepe, T. and Hall, R. 2018. 'Land redistribution in South Africa: Towards decolonisation or recolonisation?' *Politikon*, 45 (1), 128–137.

Mafeje, A. 1992. *In Search of an Alternative: A collection of essays on revolutionary theory and politics*. Harare: SAPES Books.

Magaisa, A.T. 17 July 2020a. 'BSR exclusive: Beneficiaries of the RBZ farm mechanisation scheme'. *Saturday Big Read*, https://www.bigsr.co.uk/single-post/2020/07/18/BSR-EXCLUSIVE-Beneficiaries-of-the-RBZ-Farm-Mechanisation-Scheme, accessed 25 July 2020.

Magaisa, A.T. 24 July 2020b. 'BSR exclusive: Beneficiaries of the RBZ

Mechanisation Scheme – 2'. *Saturday Big Read*, https://www.bigsr.co.uk/single-post/2020/07/25/BSR-EXCLUSIVE-Beneficiaries-of-the-RBZ-Farm-Mechanisation-Scheme---2, accessed 25 May 2020.

Mambo, E. 14 September 2012. 'Multiple farm-owners defy Mugabe'. *Zimbabwe Independent*, https://www.theindependent.co.zw/2012/09/14/multiple-farm-owners-defy-mugabe/, accessed 16 November 2017.

Mazwi, F. 2019. 'Changing patterns of agricultural financing following the Fast-Track Land Resettlement Programme: An interrogation of contract farming in sugar and tobacco in Zimbabwe'. PhD thesis, University of KwaZulu-Natal.

Mazwi, F., Chemura, A., Mudimu, G.T. and Chambati, W. 2019. 'Political economy of command agriculture in Zimbabwe: A state-led contract farming model'. *Agrarian South: Journal of Political Economy*, 8 (1–2), 232–257.

Mkodzongi, G. 2013. 'New people, new land and new livelihoods: A micro-study of Zimbabwe's Fast-Track Land Reform'. *Agrarian South: Journal of Political Economy*, 2 (3), 345–366.

Mothabi, T. 2017. 'A need for developmental intervention in South Africa', in Kanyenze, G., Jaunch, H., Kanengoni, A.D., Madzwamuse, M. and Muchena, D. (eds.) *Towards Democratic Developmental States in Southern Africa.* Harare: Weaver Press, 75–115.

Moyo, S. 2001. 'The land occupation movement and democratization in Zimbabwe: Contradictions of neoliberalism'. *Journal of International Studies*, 30 (2), 311–330.

Moyo, S. 2004. 'The land and agrarian question in Zimbabwe'. Working Paper presented at the Conference on the Agrarian Constraint and Poverty Reduction: Macroeconomic Lessons for Africa, Addis Ababa, 17–18 December.

Moyo, S. 2011a. 'Three decades of agrarian reform in Zimbabwe'. *Journal of Peasant Studies*, 38 (3), 493–531.

Moyo, S. 2011b. 'Changing agrarian relations after redistributive land reform in Zimbabwe'. *Journal of Peasant Studies*, 38 (5), 939–966.

Moyo, S. and Nyoni, N. 2013. 'Changing agrarian relations after redistributive land reform', in Moyo, S. and Chambati, W. (eds.) *Land and Agrarian Reform in Zimbabwe: Beyond white settler capitalism.* Dakar: CODESRIA and AIAS, 195–250.

Moyo, S. and Yeros, P. 2007. 'The radicalised state: Zimbabwe's interrupted revolution'. *Review of African Political Economy*, 34 (111), 103–121.

Moyo, S. and Yeros, P. 2013. 'The Zimbabwe model: Radicalisation, reform and resistance', in Moyo, S. and Chambati, W. (eds.) *Land and Agrarian Reform in Zimbabwe: Beyond white settler capitalism.* Dakar: CODESRIA and AIAS, 331–357.

Moyo, S., Chambati, W., Murisa, T., Siziba, D., Dangwa, C., Mujeyi, K. and Nyoni, N. 2009: 'Fast Track Land Reform baseline survey in Zimbabwe:

Trends and tendencies, 2005/06'. African Institute for Agrarian Studies, Harare.

Moyo, Z. 2013. 'Land reform in South Africa and Zimbabwe: Towards the realisation of socio-economic rights?' *Polity*, https://www.polity.org.za/article/land-reform-in-south-africa-and-zimbabwe-towards-the-realisation-of-socio-economic-rights-2013-07-16, accessed 1 April 2020.

Moyo, Z. 2018. 'Civil society, the state and democracy in Zimbabwe, 1988–2014: Hegemonies, polarities and fractures'. PhD dissertation, University of Johannesburg.

Mtisi, J., Nyakudya, M. and Barnes, T. 2009. 'Social and economic developments during the UDI period', in Raftopoulos, B. and Mlambo, A. (eds.) *Becoming Zimbabwe: A history from the pre-colonial period to 2008*. Harare: Weaver Press, 115–166.

Muchetu, R.G. 2019. 'Family farms and the markets: Examining the level of market-oriented production 15 years after the Zimbabwe Fast Track Land Reform Programme'. *Review of African Political Economy*, 46 (159), 33–54.

Murisa, T. 2011. 'Lacuna in rural agency: The case of Zimbabwe's agrarian reforms', in Helliker, K. and Murisa, T. (eds.) *Land Struggles and Civil Society in Southern Africa*. Trenton, NJ: Africa World Press, 113–154.

Ndlovu-Gatsheni, S.J. 2012. 'Coloniality of power in development studies and the impact of global imperial designs on Africa'. *Australasian Review of African Studies*, 33 (2), 48–73.

Ndlovu-Gatsheni, S.J. 2013. 'Perhaps decoloniality is the answer? Critical reflections on development from a decolonial epistemic perspective'. *Africanus*, 43 (2), 1–11.

Neocosmos, M. 1993. *The Agrarian Question in Southern Africa and "Accumulation from Below": Economics and politics in the struggle for democracy*. Uppsala: Nordic Africa Institute.

Ntsebeza, L., 2005. *Democracy Compromised: Chiefs and the politics of the land in South Africa*. Leiden: Brill.

Omanga, D. 2020. 'Decolonization, decoloniality, and the future of African studies: A conversation with Dr Sabelo Ndlovu-Gatsheni', https://items.ssrc.org/from-our-programs/decolonization-decoloniality-and-the-future-of-african-studies-a-conversation-with-dr-sabelo-ndlovu-gatsheni/, accessed 23 July 2020.

Potts, D. and Mutambirwa, C. 1990. 'Rural-urban linkages in contemporary Harare: Why migrants need their land'. *Journal of Southern African Studies*, 16 (4), 677–698.

Presidential Advisory Panel on Land Reform and Agriculture. 2019. 'Final report of the Presidential Advisory Panel on Land Reform and Agriculture', https://www.gov.za/sites/default/files/gcis_document/201907/panelreportlandreform_0.pdf, accessed 20 March 2020.

Raftopoulos, B. 2003. 'The state in crisis: Authoritarian nationalism, selective citizenship and distortions of democracy in Zimbabwe', in Hammar, A. and Raftopoulos, B. (eds.) *Zimbabwe's Unfinished Business: Rethinking land, state and nation in the context of crisis*. Harare: Weaver Press, 217–241.

Richardson, C.J. 2005. 'The loss of property rights and the collapse of Zimbabwe'. Cato Institute, https://www.cato.org/publications/economic-development-bulletin/how-loss-property-rights-caused-zimbabwes-collapse, accessed 30 May 2020.

Rusenga, C. 2020. 'Large-scale farming and land reform beneficiaries in South Africa: Lessons from a case study in Limpopo Province'. *Journal of Asian and African Studies*, https://doi.org/10.1177/0021909620937465, accessed 30 May 2020, 1–16.

Sachikonye, L.M. 2003. 'The situation of commercial farm workers after land reform in Zimbabwe'. Farm Community Trust of Zimbabwe, Harare.

Sadomba, Z.W. 2011. *War Veterans in Zimbabwe's Revolution: Challenging neo-colonialism and settler and international capital*. Weaver Press: Harare.

Scoones, I. 2015. 'Zimbabwe's land reform: New political dynamics in the countryside'. *Review of African Political Economy*, 42 (144), 190–205.

Scoones, I., Marongwe, N., Mavedzenge, B., Mahenehene, J., Murimbarimba, F. and Sukume, C. 2010. *Zimbabwe's Land Reform: Myths and realities*. Johannesburg: Jacana Media.

Shonhe, T. 2017. *Reconfigured Agrarian Relations in Zimbabwe*. Bamenda: Langaa RPCIG.

Shonhe, T. 2019. 'Land reform and new meaning of rural development in Zimbabwe'. Paper presented at the International Conference on Public Administration and Development Alternatives (IPADA), http://ulspace.ul.ac.za/bitstream/handle/10386/2682/shonhe_land_2019.pdf?sequence=1, accessed 5 August 2020.

Shonhe, T. 2020. 'The right to development and the shifting land tenure systems in Zimbabwe', in Kamga, S.D. (ed.) *The Right to Development in Africa: Issues, constraints, and prospects*. Ibadan: Pan-African University Press, 699–728.

Shonhe, T. and Scoones, I. Forthcoming. 'Private and state-led contract farming in Zimbabwe: What are the consequences for social differentiation, class formation and rural politics?' *Journal of Agrarian Change*.

Shonhe, T., Scoones, I., Murimbarimba, F. Forthcoming. 'Agricultural commercialization and changing labour regimes in Zimbabwe'. *Journal of Contemporary African Studies*.

Smith, C. 2019. 'EFF: Land question must be final by year end, with all land in state's custody'. *Fin24*, https://www.fin24.com/Economy/eff-land-question-must-be-final-by-year-end-with-all-land-in-states-custody-20190626, accessed 27 May 2020.

Statistics South Africa (Stats SA). 2017. 'General household survey 2017 statistical release', https://www.datafirst.uct.ac.za/dataportal/index.php/

catalog/723, accessed 29 May 2020.
Statistics South Africa (Stats SA). 2019. 'General household survey 2018: Measuring the progress of development in the country – May 2019', http://www.statssa.gov.za/publications/P0318/GHS2018presentation_%20FinalforSG.pdf, accessed 29 May 2020.
Tawodzera, G., Zanamwe. L. and Crush, J. 2012. 'The state of food insecurity in Harare, Zimbabwe'. Urban Food Security Series No. 13, http://www.afsun.org/wp-content/uploads/2013/09/AFSUN_13.pdf, accessed 29 May 2020.
Tobacco Industry and Marketing Board (TIMB). 2000. 'Annual Statistical Report'. Harare.
Tobacco Industry and Marketing Board (TIMB). 2018. 'Annual statistical report'. Harare, https://www.timb.co.zw/storage/app/media/Annual%20Stats%20Report/2018%20ANNUAL%20STATISTICAL%20REPORT.pdf, accessed 30 May 2020.
Tobacco Industry and Marketing Board (TIMB). 2019. 'Tobacco sales report: Weekly report 39 ending 27 September 2019'. Harare, https://www.timb.co.zw/storage/app/media/2019%20Weekly%20Report/weekly-bulletin-39-week-ending-27-september-2019.pdf, accessed 30 May 2020.
Williams, A. 2007. 'A piece of land: Black women and land in South Africa and the United States of America'. American Studies Honors Projects, Macalester College, https://digitalcommons.macalester.edu/amst_honors/2, accessed 20 April 2020.
Zamchiya, P. 2012. 'Agrarian change in Zimbabwe: Politics, production and accumulation'. PhD dissertation, University of Oxford.
Zamchiya, P. 2013. 'The role of politics and state practices in shaping rural differentiation: A study of resettled small-scale farmers in south-eastern Zimbabwe'. *Journal of Southern African Studies*, 13 (4), 937–953.

Legislation

Communal Land Rights Act (No. 11 of 2004).
Constitution of the Republic of South Africa (Act No. 108 of 1996).
Group Areas Act (No. 41 of 1950).
Natives Land Act (No. 27 of 1913).
Natives Land and Trust Act (No. 18 of 1936).
The Restitution of Land Rights Act (No. 22 of 1994).

Interview

Moyo, S. 11 November 2015. Interview with author, Zimbabwe.

TEN

Land Struggles, Democracy and Race in Brazil: Contesting the nation

Andrew Bennie

INTRODUCTION

The Movimento dos Trabalhadores Rurais Sem Terra (MST) in Brazil, or Rural Landless Workers Movement, is the largest land movement in the world and one of the most powerful social movements in Latin America, organising over one million landless families and through which over 400,000 families have accessed land. 'Land concentration in Brazil is one of the highest globally, with around one per cent of landowners occupying almost 50 per cent of rural land' (Tricontinental, 2020: 3). The movement aims to enhance democracy and development in Brazil, which it asserts are hampered by the vast social inequalities that are deeply rooted in the nation's history (Carter, 2015a). As many MST activists are at pains to point out, it is much more than simply a land access movement; it envisions and pursues a far-reaching project of democratisation and social transformation.

In this chapter I explore the construction of the MST's core political identity, 'landless', and its association with a political project of democratisation and social transformation. I situate the movement in a wider Brazilian history of colonialism, struggles over land and territory, and racial dynamics in the ongoing making of the Brazilian nation. I thus examine how the movement is part of a larger pattern of struggle over labour and land, and how it pursues the fuller achievement of citizenship through the democratisation of land access, labour and politics. While Brazil exhibits similar features of social inequality and land concentration to South Africa, the MST also emerges out of a Brazilian history and its varying relationships between colonialism, race, land and nation formation. I also attempt to examine the question of race, nation and land more specifically in Brazil through the case of *quilombo* communities, descendants of runaway slaves, fighting for land rights.

The struggles of the MST and *quilombos* are built on the material foundation of the centrality of territorial struggles in the making of the Brazilian nation as a political community. The term 'nation' is broadly understood to refer to a political community in which citizens are entitled to exercise their rights and responsibilities. In South Africa, an added dimension to this is that the form and meaning of the nation has also, to a large extent, been defined through the pursuit of freedom and democracy against colonialism and apartheid, and consequently has a strong association with who the key subjects of the nation are (Chipkin, 2007). Ivor Chipkin points out, though, that the citizen is the subject, not of the nation but of democracy (2007). Given South Africa's racial history and the centrality of racial redress in its land question, land has had strong associations with claims for citizenship and equal rights (Alexander, 2006). However, a major part of recent debates has posed the relation between land and the nation as one of authenticity – who are the authentic subjects of the nation and, in turn, to whom does the land authentically belong (Kepe and Hall, 2018)? I argue that instead of seeking to reconcile land with an authentic notion of the nation, in their struggles for deepened democracy and realisation of substantive citizenship, the MST and *quilombos* subject the standing of the nation to the depth of democracy and citizenship rights experienced by the subordinate classes.

To draw on the assertions of Robin Sheriff (2001) and Ilke Leite

(2015), they thus render the idea of the nation, and the pursuit of a more just nation, as not one of consensus around a uniform identity or static authenticity, but as a site of contestation, contradiction, inequality and, necessarily, social transformation. In further relevance to South Africa, the struggles of the MST and *quilombos* illustrate the link between historically constituted identities, and their further political construction and evolution closely tied to mobilisation from below that contests prevailing patterns of injustice relating to land, labour and the social structure of the nation. Both the political nature of the MST's struggles and the historical construction of *quilombos* point to the specificity of the relation between land and race in South Africa, and they highlight the interlinkages between race and the class dimensions of agrarian reform.

The chapter's argument and content are drawn from extensive engagement with literature on the MST, *quilombos* and Brazil, MST documents, six key informant interviews with members of the MST secretariat and militants (organisers), and 14 interviews with MST members while living in one settlement and two encampments in the state of São Paulo for a two-week period in 2016. The interviews with members of the secretariat, the national coordinating body of the MST, allowed for deeper exploration of the political history of the movement and the political subjects it works to cultivate around the land question, the successes and challenges the movement experiences, and the practicalities of building agrarian and food system alternatives. A visit to its national school, Florestan Fernandes, contributed to a deeper appreciation of the central role of education and liberatory pedagogy, practised in every aspect of the practical workings of the school as part of the MST's social transformation project. The period spent living in the settlement and encampments facilitated an exploration of the concrete experiences, histories and outlooks of MST participants, the central protagonists in fighting for the democratisation of land and labour.

This chapter starts with a brief overview of Brazilian history and land struggles, showing how, rather than the struggle against land deprivation being a key process in the making of Brazil, the struggles to *access* land as the country's social structure was being formed have also been central. This gives a historical momentum and legitimacy to struggles *for* land that is drawn on by land movements such as the MST, which feeds into the identity of its participants. Second, I explore key aspects of the rise of the MST and its approach to agrarian reform. Third, I turn to how the movement works to construct the political subject of the 'landless', drawing on histories of land struggles in the making of the Brazilian nation and the movement's own historical activities, as it interacts with the state and the structural limits to agrarian reform.

Fourth, I explicitly address the relationship between race and land in Brazil by describing the history that informs the meaning of *quilombo* as identification with a history of resistance linked to land-based forms of production and reproduction, and how this evolved as *quilombos* worked to insert this identity into the formal frameworks of the nation as a claim to rights. This draws a link between race and land, but also embeds the relationship in wider modes of production, consumption and identity. I then turn to how the struggles and identities of the MST and *quilombos* are tied to the social transformation of the nation, and the role that the national Constitution has played in legitimating modes of 'social conflict' (Carter, 2015b) in pursuit of a more democratic and materially just national order. I conclude by noting that, while land struggles have advanced contestation in the nation for deeper citizenship and democratisation, the forces confronting this in the national context are also shaped by those of neoliberal globalisation; and finally, some implications for the South African context are considered.

BRAZILIAN HISTORY AND THE RISE OF THE MST

Land concentration in Brazil is one of the highest in the world, with most land under the control of *latifundia* (essentially, unreconstructed feudal-like landowners) and national and multinational corporations that skew agricultural development policy and support to their interests, which are at odds with the needs of the peasantry (Fernandes, 2013). Its 'historical pattern of development based on deep inequality has produced a highly modernised and globalised agricultural economy that exists alongside a rural population of whom more than half live below the poverty line' (Carter, 2010: 189). This dualistic agrarian structure is similar to that in South Africa and other former settler colonies of the Global South (Jara, 2014). However, in contrast to South Africa, where the vast majority of the country's food consumption is supplied by the predominantly white, large-scale commercial farming sector that emerged from settler colonialism and mass land dispossession (Aliber and Mdoda, 2015), in Brazil 'the peasant and family farm sector, which comprises 84 per cent of all farms but occupies only 24 per cent of total agricultural land area, produces about 70 per cent of total domestic food consumption' (Graeub et al., 2016: 10).

This dualistic pattern should be viewed in light of the formation of the Brazilian peasantry out of the struggle against slavery and multiple struggles *for* land in a colonial context (Fernandes, 2013). Although 'enslavement resulted in waves of indigenous resistance, 80 per cent died from disease introduced by colonisers' (Wright and Wolford, 2003: 116), and so landowners turned to the importation of slaves from Africa. Freed and escaped slaves formed *quilombo* communities in the 1800s, where they survived on farming and natural harvesting. In the turn to the creation of a 'free' labour force at the end of the 19th century, the white elite grew increasingly anxious about being outnumbered by a 'free' black population. They were also consumed by the question of building 'a civilised nation' on the back of what they deemed were the offspring of 'African savages'. The solution was a policy of 'whitening' the nation, to build up a white labour force, and so they encouraged the immigration of mostly European peasants to Brazil (Nolen, 2015).

However, in anticipation of the end of slavery and the desire to keep land in white hands, the Brazilian Crown passed a law in 1850 that effectively handed over ownership of public lands to large landowners. This consolidated a small but powerful land-owning class with inordinate political power to exploit and oppress rural populations (Wright and Wolford, 2003; Leite, 2015). These processes also limited the ability of European immigrants to access land, thus bringing them into the land struggle as well. At the end of 19th century, while former slaves and immigrants had their labour power, neither had land; and as indigenous populations fought against further incursions into what land they had left, so the construction of the peasantry, through struggles over land, coincided with struggles for freedom as the Brazilian nation was brought into being. As Bernado Fernandes notes: 'The black Afro-Brazilian, the white European and the indigenous native converged to form the Brazilian peasantry. In constant struggle, the peasantry was being destroyed and recreated by the expansion of capitalist development, and in the process also recreating itself' (Fernandes, 2013: 275).

This dialectic between the destruction and recreation of the peasantry is underpinned by an important distinction between land and territory (Fernandes, 2013). Land relates to the physical entity of land and the formal legal delimitations that are ascribed to it, whereas territory encompasses the socio-ecological relationships on the land, through which material reproduction is secured (Sobreiro, 2015). Indeed, agricultural censuses over the last 30 years have shown how identity claims of rural groups, such as foresters, fishers, peasants and *quilombos*, are often closely connected to conceptions of territory (Leite, 2015). This diverse social base of the peasantry in the context of territorial struggles, together with their common historical and predominantly violent repression by large landowners and the state, have provided a strong class basis to the land and territorial struggles in Brazil and to the political identities mobilised around these. This has been enhanced by the increasing power of globalised agribusiness capital to shape territorial development in the second half of the 20th century. This, together with the fact that Brazil did not have state-legislated racial dispossession and segregation, means that land struggles have not hinged as uniformly on race as they have in places like South Africa, where racialised land dispossession was a defining historical pattern. However, as will be discussed in more detail later, race remains a defining feature of inequality in Brazil; the question is, therefore, how it articulates with struggles over land and territory.

RISE OF THE RURAL LANDLESS WORKERS MOVEMENT (MST)

The forms of political identification, which the MST works to build among participants, should be seen in relation to the conditions of its emergence and evolution, and the changing contexts with which it has engaged. It exists in a longer history of peasant organisations and rural workers' unions, which were widely suppressed after the dictatorship took power in 1964 (De Medeiros, 2015). In the same year, the dictatorship passed the 1964 Land Statute that stipulated that land must serve a social function, and which became codified in Brazil's democratic Constitution of 1988. However, its initial intent was not to facilitate structural agrarian reform but to dampen rural conflict, as the state sought to commercialise capitalist agriculture and large rural estates, while suppressing peasants and their demands (Fernandes, 2015). The dictatorship period thus saw the consolidation of the export-oriented agribusiness sector into the 'powerhouse' that it is today: the country is the world's largest exporter of soya, beef and sugar cane. It is thus a globally integrated sector that also exerts enormous political influence in domestic politics (Delgado, 2015).

The MST's formative period took place during a time of growing popular mobilisation in the 1980s around basic rights and democratising the country as the military's grip on power loosened. The stirrings of the movement began with the occupation of Macali Farm in the southernmost state of Rio Grande do Sul in the early hours of Brazil's National Independence Day, 7 September 1979. The MST grew out of increasing peasant land struggles across Brazil, against evictions, mega development projects such as dams, and land occupations from the late 1970s. The Pastoral Land Commission played a key role in supporting these struggles and connecting them to one another, bringing them together into national meetings, which laid the foundation for the formal establishment of the movement in 1984 (Poletto, 2015). The MST cemented its place on the national stage with its massive occupation at Encruzilhada Natalino (Natalino's Crossing) in Rio Grande do Sul in 1980.

The 'demands initially made by the MST and other peasant

organisations were feasible within a programme of "classical bourgeois agrarian reform": democratise access to land, support peasant livelihoods by integrating them into internal markets, and raise their incomes to improve their living standards' (MST, 2014: 26). The industrial bourgeoisie at the time was in favour of such a reform process as it conformed with their needs to widen the productive base of agriculture and increase the domestic market. However, the small but powerful rural oligarchy, with their grip on the state, frustrated such reforms. In addition, democratisation coincided with neoliberal reforms from the 1980s, further frustrating the agrarian reform process. Engagement with this context led the MST to evolve its demands and outlooks to wider social and political change, questioning the prevailing agrarian model. The MST thus sees its key struggle as against agribusiness and its powerful role in shaping territorial development and undermining the livelihoods of peasants. Opposition to agribusiness capital is, therefore, a key basis of class struggle, which the MST sees as uniting indigenous, *quilombo*, peasant and rural worker communities. It states (MST, 2014: 33):

> The traditional people (indigenous groups, extractivists, quilombolas), and the peasants and workers in the countryside have been key practitioners of alternatives to capitalist agriculture. They have established themselves through their resistance and their direct confrontation with capital. Thus, they can take the lead in a new model of agricultural production under the control of the workers and focused on meeting the needs and rights of all people.

Although the movement references race and has working political links with land struggles of particular Afro-descendant communities (see below), it does not explicitly locate race as a pillar of political action in relation to the land question and social change, despite the extent of racial inequality in the country. This may have something to do with the pervasiveness of the idea of Brazil as a racial democracy (Straubhaar, 2010), but it should also be viewed in relation to the history of Brazil and the contemporary array of forces, described earlier. Polls consistently find that a large majority of ordinary Brazilians are, in fact, in favour of agrarian reform (Tomaz, 2016), while the social forces that most threaten the land and human rights of indigenous, black, peasant and working-class communities are the oligarchic landowning elite, globalised agribusiness capital and supportive state policies, which help to frame a distinct class experience and character to the struggles organised by the MST.

There are three key interconnected elements to the MST's programme in pursuing this project of democratisation and development. First is what is referred to as the struggle *for* the land. The principal tactic here is the land occupation, in which a piece of land is collectively identified for occupation; landless people are mobilised and prepared for the occupation; the land is occupied and an encampment of the iconic black tarp tents are set up, in which the occupying community might wait months, or sometimes years, before the land is expropriated by the state and handed over to them. The second is mobilisation aimed at pressuring the state to implement agrarian reform in the form of production credit, services to settled communities, research, and support for agro-ecological production, education and housing.

The third is the struggle *on* the land, the elaboration of ecological and cooperative forms of production, community construction and health and education systems in the settlements established on the land that has been won (Carter and De Carvalho, 2015; Fernandes, 2015). The MST's struggle is, therefore, to advance alternative models of territorial development, what Anthony Pahnke calls 'self-governmental resistance' (2015: 1088), against the continued territorialisation of agribusiness. The movement has made important strides in this regard. One of its victories is that once settlements are established, the state is obliged to provide services like health clinics and schools. Thus, in collaboration with the state, it has established an extensive, formal education system on the settlements. A number of these schools are run fully by the MST and function according to liberatory pedagogies. Efforts to build livelihood alternatives are linked to trying to keep young people in the rural areas (see Tarlau, 2015). It has also developed peasant-centred healthcare systems on the settlements. Its experiences in developing production alternatives are nuanced. In some cases, it has established impressive production capacities, from primary production to processing of animal feed, dairy processing sold under its own brands, and the production of its own brand of *cachaca*, a popular liquor made from sugar cane (Juncal, 2014).

In addition to cooperatives on settlements through which settlers source inputs and aggregate output, there are also large cooperatives that function across settlements, such as an organic seed-producing cooperative (which sells seeds under the brand Bionatur) and a Cooperative of Technical Services, which provides technical production support to peasants across settlements. It has also established formal relationships with universities to foster research and experimentation to improve production techniques on settlements (Pahnke, 2015). However, this is not always a straightforward process: while there have been successes in the MST's programme to 'institutionalise resistance' through agro-ecology production through cooperatives, efforts here have lagged behind their achievements in education and land reform (Pahnke, 2015: 1088; Wolford, 2015). Thus, as the MST (2014; MST 4, 2016) and many analysts note, despite the movement's massive level of mobilisation, organisation and impact, the nation's agrarian structure has still not been substantially altered – as is commonly explained by those in the movement, to this day the country 'has never had agrarian reform'. This will be expanded in the following section, where I turn to the construction of political identity in the movement and the context of land and agrarian reform within which this takes place.

BUILDING THE LANDLESS IDENTITY IN PRACTICE

The core political identity of the MST is that of the 'landless worker' – *sem terra*. It mobilises a relatively wide social base around this identity – peasants, rural workers, urban workers – reflecting the fragmented nature of 'classes of labour', which national histories, coinciding with neoliberal globalisation, have produced (Bernstein, 2006). The basis of bringing these varying social actors together under the notion of landless worker is their common experience of workers on the land, working in relationships of exploitation to powerful interests (Tomaz,

2016). It thus highlights their exploitation and marginalisation under Brazil's social structure, and the historical origins of this, as well as their collective power and agency when organised as the landless. The building of this identity, however, is not arbitrary, but is rooted in the collective experience of these social groups before and within the movement's activities. This common identity is thus built through common action, one of the most important stages of which is the land occupation. As Fernandes describes: 'In these face-to-face encounters amid the land struggles, peasants have the opportunity to exchange life experiences, sharpen a sense of awareness of their status as dispossessed and exploited rural workers, and develop an identity as landless peasants' (Fernandes, 2015: 132).

The MST and the notion of landless thus also provide a space of socialisation into the moral values of the movement and its ideals of social change. Many within the MST describe it as a family and a place in which they feel valued as human beings, with agency to change their circumstances and the conditions around them. As Miguel Carter describes, 'the movement has nurtured feelings of dignity, self-confidence, and social responsibility amongst its members' (2010: 201). The power of this mode of identification is that it is also rooted in a recollection of historical peasant struggles over territory, which provides a collective memory that infuses the identity of the MST's participants (Issa, 2007; Baletti et al., 2008). As an MST organiser explains: 'In the whole history of Brazil there are people fighting for land, so this creates a culture, some kind of culture, that it's fair to fight for land. It's not something that someone will give to you as a gift, you have to fight for it. So, this is, like, in the popular consciousness' (Tomaz, 2016).

The MST also nurtures a strong sense of identification with the movement on the part of its participants. It does this through building a strong movement culture based on resistance and emancipatory ideals with a wide range of symbols (such as its iconic red flag and logo, in which the outline of Brazil frames the faces of a woman and man), songs, art, poetry, slogans and practices of *mística*, references to historic leaders of popular struggles, mass mobilisations, festivals, and MST meetings and congresses. This works to build a cultural and symbolic field of association that bolsters the peasant identity of families within the movement and is central in framing a counter-hegemonic discourse to Brazil's prevailing social relations (Carter, 2010; Fernandes, 2015).

The MST also illustrates how a form of identification around which people can be mobilised for political action does not necessarily only emerge 'from below' but can be a result of multiple institutional relationships as well, including the state. Marcelo Rosa (2012: 212) shows how the political category 'landless' emerged in the early 1960s, before the military dictatorship, in the state of Rio Grande do Sul (the same state in which the MST rose and undertook its early actions), through shifting political alliances between social movements and the state, which was responsive to the precarious conditions experienced in the rural areas. This included the mayor of a local town who formed an association for landless peasants. This led to 'the institutionalisation of the landless as a public problem' (Rosa, 2012: 212) and was further enacted when the movement undertook a series of land invasions in 1962. This 'gave social meaning to an indistinct category, the landless, that had been in government plans but did not have representatives in society', and so it was through the collective action of a movement that the category came to life and embedded the idea of the state playing a key role in addressing landlessness (Rosa, 2012: 216). The occupation at Encruzilhada Natalino in the 1980s, which laid the basis for the MST, thus drew on an existing political category to force the state to expropriate private land for resettlement.

In the context of the fight against the military dictatorship, the occupation also helped to attract public attention to the landless issue, imbuing it with further political relevance. The broad peasant mobilisations of the 1980s led the president of the transitional democratic government, José Sarney (1985–1989), to assign the National Institute for Colonisation and Agrarian Reform, which had been established in 1970, with the task of expropriating land, providing land titles and organising post-settlement support. He also instituted the Programa Nacional de Reforma Agrária (National Plan for Agrarian Reform), which promised to give land titles to 1.5 million landless peasants over four years; however, this promise went unfulfilled (Robles and Veltmeyer, 2015).

While in the 1980s the movement was oriented towards securing land and rights for rural inhabitants, by the early 1990s, it had adopted an increasingly confrontational approach towards the state in the context of repression and the closing down of political opportunities under an intolerant neoliberal president. The 1990s thus saw an increase in land occupations 'from 186 in 1995, to 450 in 1996, to 856 in 1999' (Robles and Veltmeyer, 2015: 30). A massacre of 19 peasants by police on a farm near the town of Eldorado dos Carajás in the state of Pará resulted in an upswelling of public opinion in favour of the MST, forcing the new Fernando Henrique Cardoso administration to enact more support for land settlement. Occupied by leading agribusiness representatives, the existing Ministry of Agriculture was focused largely on supporting the dominant agricultural model, and so Cardoso created the Ministry of Agrarian Development, which was tasked with enacting agrarian reform and supporting settlements. He also set new settlement goals, which led to an increase in occupations and one of the greatest rates of resettlement in the country's post-dictatorship era, with around 500,000 families resettled between 1995 and 2002 (Sauer and Mészáros, 2017: 400). However, two key limitations remained in this process. First, most of these settlements were located in economically underdeveloped regions, such as the Amazon. Second, they were undertaken within a market-based framework of land reform advised by the World Bank, which was less about agrarian transformation and more about relieving rural poverty and mitigating conflict through programmes that individualised the resettlement programme (Sauer and Mészáros, 2017).

These limitations prompted the MST to intensify its scope of vision and demands on the basis that to secure land and rights for rural inhabitants required more far-reaching political action and social change. Thus, from the mid-1990s, as it operated in a context of enhanced political opportunities and resource mobilisation, it started to develop wider working relationships with the state and other popular organisations. The combination of the two periods saw it widen its scope of political activity to a much more expansive vision of agrarian reform and societal transformation. It thus 'began to embrace a more comprehensive, holistic agenda for social change' and more solidly integrated concerns like gender equality, human rights, agro-ecology and food sovereignty into its 'class-based analysis of Brazilian reality' (Carter, 2015b: 167; MST, 2014).

During the 1980s, the Workers' Party (PT) had promoted far-reaching land reform, and so when it was elected to power in 2002, the MST's hopes were raised that these ideals and objectives could be advanced even further. However, while the movement enjoyed greater freedom as the PT ended the state's criminalisation of the movement, which had taken place under Cardoso's second term in office, the number of land occupations and settlements were lowest under the PTs administrations. From 'a high of 879 settlements established in 2005, the annual amount [*sic*] steadily decreased to only 117 in 2012' (Robles and Veltmeyer, 2015: 9). Similarly, the number of rural estates expropriated by the federal state peaked at 845 under the Cardoso administration in 1998. 'These numbers fell under the Lula government, peaking at 400 in 2005, but consistently dropped afterwards, to only 18 in 2012' (Carter, 2015b: 415). There are several reasons for these disappointing outcomes under the PT administrations. During this period, the PT actually increased support for agribusiness. Taking a 'neo-developmentalist' approach, it worked to cement Brazil as an agricultural export superpower. It took the view that this productionist model in a globalised economy would ensure growth and a positive trade balance, which would allow the state to finance its public and social investment programmes; this approach subsequently won the PT much acclaim for the drastic reductions in poverty (Saad-Filho, 2015). Furthermore, as a result of the commodities export boom, land demand and land prices increased significantly (the latter by 227 per cent in 10 years). Given that 'the state paid market value for expropriated land, this severely curtailed the extent of land reform' (Sauer and Mészáros, 2017: 402).

However, the government also expanded support and expenditure for family farming, through programmes like the National Programme for Strengthening Family Farming, which mainly provided credit for production; the passing of the Family Farming Law, which provided the framework for support to small-scale farmers; and public procurement programmes, such as the Programme for the Acquisition of Foodstuffs and the National School Nutrition Programme, which allowed for at least 30 per cent of the food destined for school nutrition programmes to be purchased from family farmers (this was subsequently slashed by the Temer government after the 2016 'coup'). These indeed benefited MST settlements (Pahnke, 2015), but, as noted by Sérgio Sauer and George Mészáros (2017), while they have played a role as rural development policies, they did not advance a land reform agenda, and budgetary support to family farming still amounted to only about 15 per cent of that given to the agribusiness sector.

However, these setbacks in land reform also reflect relative weaknesses of movements like the MST as a result of, first, increased public criminalisation of the movement, linked to increased power of agribusiness representatives inside and outside of government. This affected its ability to mobilise public pressure for land reform. Second, some have argued that the PT government's social and employment policies improved the living standards of the poorest sections of society (the core of the MST's base), thereby reducing demand for land among those groups (Fernandes, 2013). These factors have reduced what Fernandes has called the 'convening power' of agrarian social movements, referring to 'their capacity to push government into implementing more conflictual aspects of land reform, particularly expropriations and new settlements' (Sauer and Mészáros, 2017: 410). The movement has responded to this setback by intensifying its efforts to forge wider alliances among rural, indigenous and agrarian movements, and with urban and labour movements (Rosa, 2015).

It has also responded by advancing a conceptualisation of popular agrarian reform that explicitly links land reform with a new model, based on the prioritisation of production of foodstuffs (rather than export commodities) through agro-ecology and alternative social (including gender) relations (MST, 2014). The movement's contemporary situation reflects the structural and counter-agrarian reform forces that it is up against, but it has also forced the MST to re-examine its objectives and strategies in its efforts to re-energise the struggle for agrarian reform (Robles and Veltmeyer, 2015). This includes the challenges in building forms of identification around this in the movement, which will be discussed later. The meaning of race in Brazil, and its relationship with land, further illustrates the multiple material, historical and political experiences that shape forms of identification and its relationship to land.

RACE AND LAND IN BRAZIL

Central to the idea of the Brazilian nation is that it is a 'racial democracy' (Sheriff, 2001). Over 50 per cent of Brazil's population consider themselves as black or *pardo* (mixed race), descendants of the approximately 3.5 million slaves brought from today's Angola and Mozambique to work the sugar plantations in the country's north-eastern region (Araujo, 2015). After the slave trade from Africa to Brazil was abolished in 1850, and slavery within the country formally ended by 1888, Brazil came to see itself as a racial democracy, a term ascribed to it by one of its most famous liberal sociologists, Gilberto Freyre. In his 1933 book, *Casa Grande e Senzala* (*The Masters and the Slaves*), he challenged racist theories prevalent at the time. He showed that Brazilian history was a product of the blending of European, Amerindian and African cultures, and he defended the African contribution to Brazilian culture (Sheriff, 2001). The ostensibly harmonious relations that he witnessed between masters and their slaves, including sexual relations, illustrated how Brazil, he argued, was a racial democracy. This special status, he further contended, also rendered class and racial struggles redundant (Wright and Wolford, 2003).

However, in the 1970s, progressive sociologists pointed to the striking racial inequalities that persisted in the country, showing the notion of racial democracy's ideological dimensions of justifying authoritarian, oligarchic rule (Andrews, 1996). Although Brazil never experienced state-enforced racial segregation, race remains a stark marker of inequality: Afro-descendants experience much lower levels of life expectancy, education, health, income, employment and quality of life, as well as material and cultural exclusion and dispossession in urban development programmes (Keisha-Khan, 2004; Nolen, 2015). Despite these patterns and the rendering of the notion by some as a 'myth' (Araujo, 2015), it continues to exact a hold in popular belief that Brazil is a place of racial harmony, mixture and hybridity, no less among Afro-Brazilians themselves. This, writes Robin Sheriff, based on her ethnographic research with Afro-descendant residents of a favela in Rio de Janeiro, 'is one of the greatest puzzles in Brazil' (Sheriff, 2001: 4):

> ... although racism is abundantly evident in Brazil's bifurcated social structure, in the interactions that constitute everyday life for Brazilians of African descent, and in the derogatory ways that blackness is figured in speech, Brazil is renowned throughout the world as a 'racial democracy'. Neither Daniel nor his young son Tiago were deceived by this notion, but as a nationalist ideology, a cultural myth, and as a dream of how things ought to be, the force of *democracia racial* (racial democracy) is strong enough to muffle the impulse to talk – spontaneously, freely, explicitly – about the wounds of racism.

However, one of the ways in which this nationalist notion of racial democracy is increasingly being challenged is in the struggles for land and associated citizenship rights by Afro-descendant communities. The entrenchment of black poverty in urban spaces did give rise to a small 'black movement' in Brazil, emerging in the 1960s. The movement, in turn, connected with the rural land struggles of Afro-Brazilians in the form of *quilombos*, which represent an important convergence of land struggles with racial history. This relationship contributed to constituting rural slave descendant communities as political units that today play a role in contesting racial inequality in Brazil.

The meanings of *quilombo* have evolved over time as it came to be associated with Brazilian nationhood in particular ways. It is a distinctly land-based identity, originally referring to freed or escaped slaves who formed autonomous rural communities and survived on farming, fishing and gathering of natural resources, often under marginal conditions and against constant attacks from landowners and the state (Fernandes, 2013). As a historical result of the 1850 Land Law passed after the abolition of slavery, which ensured land remained concentrated in the hands of largely white landowners, those Afro-descendants who could not survive on the land moved to urban areas, feeding into the growing black urban populations that lived on the economic and political margins of urban spaces, suffering from discrimination and exclusionary development.

Over the 20th century, *quilombos* continued to defend their territories against violent attacks by big landowners and the state, and against dispossession by development projects. In the 1960s, increasing links were formed between black urban social movement struggles that were challenging racial discrimination and prejudice, such as the Unified Black Movement, whose actions gave visibility to the *quilombo* as a symbol of racial justice (Da Costa in Bowen, 2010; Leite, 2015). Resistance and social change thus came to be part of the core meanings of the term as it became associated with the mobilisation and struggle for political, economic and social liberation, and the protection of units of economic and cultural production and reproduction on the land. Hence the *quilombo* history and identity have increasingly come to represent a challenge to racial inequality. By grounding their contemporary claims to land in the history of their enslaved past, the *quilombo* can frame their demands for formalisation of their land rights as reparation for slavery (see Planas, 2017a [2014]).

At the same time, *quilombo* is not simply a racial category, but its meaning is grounded in wider histories and modes of production and reproduction. As Leite shows, 'The historical formation of these territories implodes the criteria of "skin color", valorizing much more the collective processes of organization and marginalization' (Leite, 2015: 1236). Central to *quilombo* identity, then, is struggles over land acquisition and the enjoyment of full citizenship. Given their histories, the struggle of the *quilombos* is understood as that of protecting the communities they have built, and so resistance is core to their identity. Their recognition as *quilombos,* therefore, is embedded in a particular historical relationship between Afro-descendants and the land; in particular, historical and social arrangements of territory (Leite, 2015).

This *quilombo* meaning that had been built up through relationships with land, subsequently fed into the formal frameworks of the democratic nation as they increasingly sought to stake their claim to political recognition as full rights-bearing citizens of the nation. With democratisation in the 1980s, the term came to represent a juridical device to integrate black Brazilians and racial justice into institutions of the emerging democratic order, a current referred to as *quilombismo*. As a result of the struggles and demands made by urban and rural black activists working with *quilombo* communities, three articles in the 1988 democratic Constitution afford legal protection to the collective land and cultural rights of African descendants. As such, *quilombo* also became a term claiming political recognition (Da Costa in Bowen, 2010; Leite, 2015).

Leite (2015) shows that the content of the term *quilombo* has been constructed through multiple political meanings to refer to the memories of struggles by Afro-descendants against attacks by landowners and the state on their way of being and against colonial exploitation (across the diaspora as well); as a claim to rights for compensation and restoration owed to them by the nation; and as a 'post-utopian' understanding 'rooted in the radical transformation of society' that highlights *quilombo* in terms of human rights – rights to land, as well as to life, education, health and housing, as full citizens in the framework of the nation (Leite, 2015: 1227). The democratisation of Brazil in the 1980s and the construction of the new democratic Constitution through the National Constituent Assembly, thus provided the opportunity for this *quilombo* history and identity to be formally inscribed into the national democratic order, to institutionalise it as a claim to land and social and economic rights.

SOCIAL TRANSFORMATION AND THE NATION

In her answer to the puzzle of the endurance of the racial democracy myth in Brazil, Sheriff shows that it is, in fact, much more than a myth: among poor people of colour, it is also a prescriptive claim to transformative power amid experiences of poverty and racial discrimination. Sheriff (2001: 221) notes:

> Their faith is compromised, suffused with cynicism, beset on all sides by the certain knowledge of past and future betrayals, but poor Brazilians of African descent cannot let go of *democracia racial* because it is a dream that they share with all other Brazilians. In so many ways, it is a dream that is about them, about their citizenship and their humanity, their contribution to their country, first as slaves and then as wage laborers. *Democracia racial* is, as I have noted, their moral high ground, perhaps the only one they have that is recognized, however incompletely and hypocritically, by their nation.

This desire for a 'real' racial democracy by poor Afro-Brazilians might also be seen as a metaphor for the dream of Brazil's marginalised and excluded to enjoy a transformed material and political place in the nation; to realise the full citizenship that is denied to them by the country's class inequalities and uneven distribution of political power (Carter, 2010). What both the MST and *quilombo* struggles do, then, to differing degrees, is to organise popular classes to deepen democracy and realise corresponding material improvements in their lives? The MST's and *quilombo*'s activism – by building up and mobilising around identities of full citizenship linked to the land – seeks to address inequalities by contesting the nation's existing social order, and to deepen democracy by pressuring the state to be more accountable and responsive to popular needs. The identities that they embody are thus grounded in an explicit link between social transformation and the nation. This is illustrated in how they relate to Brazil's national Constitution.

In South Africa, there was very little organic, national mobilisation around the land question in the transition to democracy (Sihlongonyane, 2005), and land had not been high on the political or policy agenda of the main liberation movement leading the constitutional negotiations, the African National Congress (ANC), which was largely urban-centred in its orientation (Levin and Solomon, 1997). In contrast, in Brazil, agrarian and *quilombo* movements actively brought their struggles and identities into the process of crafting the order of the democratic nation through the national Constitution in the 1980s. A number of the MST's demands for social change are embodied in the 1988 Constitution. As a result of the mobilisation of agrarian movements like the MST, the 1964 Land Statute, which stipulates that land must serve a social function (which includes environmental and labour standards), was incorporated into the 1988 Constitution. This statute provides the key legal justification for the MST's foremost radical tactic – land occupation. However, the occupation of land also highlights a contradiction in the Constitution between the right to property and the social right to access land. In the 1980s, the MST purposely shifted from using the prevalent term, 'invasion', to 'occupation', so as to accentuate and embody the right of land access over the right to private property (Rosa, 2012), which, in Brazil's unequal context, can serve to preserve the interests of the agrarian elite and the reproduction of injustice. This is also illustrated in the limitations of policy reform and state support for agrarian reform, discussed earlier. The occupation thus advances concrete contestation over the Constitution in the realm of society.

In the contemporary debate on expropriation of land without compensation in South Africa, some political forces portray the Constitution as an elite-crafted instrument that is an impediment to far-reaching land reform (Kepe and Hall, 2018). For the MST then, the Constitution is not an instrument reflecting national (or elite) consensus, but rather should be seen in light of the gap between the social rights guaranteed by the Constitution and the realities of inequality that deter the full development of citizenship (Carter, 2015b). The Constitution facilitates forms of social conflict in pursuit of a just national order and the material realisation of those social rights. Rather than rejecting Brazil's democratic institutions, it seeks to further democratise those institutions and ensure meaningful participation by popular classes. Through its mobilisations and forms of identification discussed earlier, it sharpens class consciousness, builds networks of trust and solidarity, and builds organising skills that enhance the capacities of its members to participate in this democratisation project. Through its activities, it has thus contributed to building a strong sense of, and capacity for, citizenship (Carter, 2010). Indeed, the movement seeks to embed social responsibility and to build transformative social actors in the image of, and to achieve, the social rights of the Constitution. As a member of the MST's National Coordination explains (Rosetti, 2016):

> Our National Constitution from 1984 established that every property, every piece of land has to have a social function. Which is very progressive … [and] which builds a comprehension of the fact that because you own land, a rural land, doesn't make you free to do whatever you want to it. It has to have a social function. So, in our land reform project, we want the peasant to exercise this principle that is in our Constitution. And that means that we have to change the way that the peasant thinks

> and relates to the land also. It's not just because he [*sic*] owns the land that he can do whatever he wants to it.

In this sense, it might be said that in its project of deepening citizenship and democratisation, the MST seeks to interpolate its members into democratic ideology by concretising the practice of formal democratic institutions (Chipkin, 2007). This is widely evident in the ways in which many MST participants explicitly link the transformation of their own material conditions to the social transformation of Brazilian society. However, the movement must also continually negotiate the meanings of the forms of political identification that it works to build in relation to the inequalities of the Brazilian nation. In attempting to build this identity of the 'peasant' corresponding to land and landless, it aims to denote a radical identity of alternative social, political and production practices.

However, at the same time, differing historical trajectories in different regions of the country make it more complex to build a uniform culture and identity based on the land, landless and peasant. For example, more extensive proletarianisation through the expansive sugar-cane plantations in the north-east of the country are linked to particular cultural expectations over the relationship between land and labour, centred on paternalistic relations, wage-earning and the vagaries of a monoculture export crop. The notion of the landless peasant was rooted in the conditions of the south, with a deeper peasant history. Building a culture around the landless peasant was more straightforward here; whereas the conditions of the much poorer, plantation-dominated and hunger-ravaged north-east have pointed to how subjective meaning-making, rooted in a particular history, can frustrate the building of the political identities described earlier across a national context (Wolford, 2015). It is therefore a question of understanding that the political identification linked to the Constitution plays a crucial role in organising resistance and mobilisation, but also that it is continually incomplete, having to grapple with contrasting contexts.

Similar to the MST, the struggles of *quilombos* against capital and undemocratic development are hinged to the elaboration of the nation through the Constitution. A *quilombo* activist explains (Da Costa in Bowen, 2010: 154):

> For the community, titled land means having their rights recognized and being empowered – such that the community has political autonomy to protect or guarantee its cultural practices and way of life. The *quilombolas* are born and raised on the land, so if they do not have the definitive title of property, they are vulnerable to expropriation.

Due to the participation of the *quilombo* movement in the 1988 Constituent Assembly, three articles of the Constitution reflect their achievement of formal political recognition for the *quilombo* identity and land struggles. Article 68 guarantees that the state will award land titles to *quilombo* communities. Article 215 declares that the state will guarantee full protection of cultural rights and expression of those, including *quilombos*, and sees protecting these rights in order to facilitate 'participating in the national civilizing process' (in Leite, 2015: 1229). In the context of Brazil's land struggles against the old predatory landed elite, continually expanding agribusiness frontiers and mega-development projects, formal land titling is crucial for *quilombo* communities to protect themselves as cultural and political groupings and their modes of reproduction. The National Coordination of Quilombo Communities has since specifically positioned its core activity as fighting for the implementation of the constitutional provision of formal land rights. Thus, as Leite argues, through the institutional incorporation of the identity of *quilombo*, resistance has been incorporated into the idea of the nation (Leite, 2015: 1232):

> The quilombo denounces a history of injustice by introducing the African diaspora into the nationalist agenda. Once 'quilombo' becomes a right, it does not lose its historical relationship to the idea of African resistance to slavery. However, it does bring this resistance within a new order, or, in other words, it brings the quilombo from the outside – from the context of Diaspora – to the inside, to the context of a nation. The sense of rebellion becomes a social pact with the Brazilian state. From the point of view of State policies, the incorporation of the quilombo into

> Brazilian society inverts the idea of resistance as conflict to the idea of resistance as a new form of social order.

In line with these constitutional provisions, various state programmes were established under the Lula administration. The Presidential Decree 4887 officially provided the process for *quilombo* communities to receive land titles and established the Palmares Cultural Foundation to undertake this process. This led to more than one million Afro-Brazilians claiming land for title on around 4.5 million acres (Planas, 2017b [2014]). In 2006, the Brasil Quilombola Program (PBQ) was established to coordinate sustainable development policies for *quilombo* territories in line with historical and cultural needs, with an emphasis on civil society involvement. Thus, in addition to land titling, the PBQ is also responsible for coordinating the provision of infrastructure and services to certified *quilombos*, economic and social development, and participation, which includes the Quilombola Social Agenda, aimed at improving access to social services (Rapaport Delegation on Afro-Brazilian Land Rights, 2008). Also, through a Presidential Decree in 2007, the National Policy for the Viable Development of the Peoples and Traditional Communities was developed to further coordinate these processes, which is made up of a forum of government and traditional communities (Leite, 2015).

However, despite these laws and programmes, slow progress has been made in land titling. Of the 5,000 or so self-identified *quilombo* communities, only about half of them have been certified and only 220 have received land titles, less than 5 per cent (Leite, 2015: 1231; Long, 2017). Part of the reason for this is that, in addition to a complicated bureaucratic system, the state remains locked in a narrow and static view of race and history when it awards land rights, with communities having to prove their connection to runaway slave societies. As discussed, *quilombo* communities have been defined as much more than their slave origins, with a more expansive grounding related to historical experience on the land and forms of economic and cultural reproduction, and alternative ways of living (Da Costa in Bowen, 2010; Planas, 2017a [2014]). The land demarcation and titling process has been further slowed down by budgetary cuts by successive government administrations (Branford and Torres, 2018). A further difficulty lies in the complexities of collective land ownership, including competing land claims (Leite, 2015).

These challenges persist, but *quilombo* struggles have contributed to the making of understandings of the nation and the history of that nation, through diverse rights linked to *quilombo* struggles being incorporated into the institutional order. The institutionalisation of their identities and demands in the articles and decrees further energised efforts by *quilombos* to formally claim land, but it also sparked renewed national discussions and debates on race, land and the need to bring Brazil's history of racial oppression and silencing, and its contemporary forms, more into the open (see Planas, 2017a [2014]). In doing this, it also brought resistance into contestation over how belonging to the nation is framed, the class interests underpinning the contestation, and the political expressions of these interests. Indeed, the future of *quilombos* came under threat after a right-wing political party, allied with rural landowners and big business lobbies, filed an application to the courts in 2004 to have Decree 4887 declared invalid. If supported by the courts, it would have made it much harder for *quilombos* to claim their land rights and would have reversed those already won, but the court rejected the legal action in 2018 (Branford and Torres, 2018). However, the case represented the forces that *quilombo* communities (and movements like the MST) are up against, pointing to an overarching factor in explaining the slow pace of *quilombo* land titling, which is the role of Brazilian and internationalised capital's grip on the uses of rural land and resources, posing a political barrier to the regulation of land for social purposes, as well as the state's support for big development projects in rural areas (Leite, 2015). The current political regime led by the neo-fascist president, Jair Bolsonaro, heightens these problems (Fogel, 2018; Phillips, 2019; Reuters, 2020). Indeed, just as the struggle for national recognition of *quilombos* is aimed at defining the nation as one in which they have full rights to equality and citizenship, so the attacks on their gains seek to undermine the identity and material base on which those claims are made. This struggle will, surely, further shape the meaning of *quilombo* as it continues its historical development along lines of class, race and citizenship struggles.

CONCLUSION

This chapter has examined how the MST and *quilombo* movements draw on and construct identities based on historical land and social struggles to contest aspects of Brazil's unjust agrarian structure. It showed how these identities evolved over changing material and political periods, grounded in histories and assertions of struggle to achieve social change. In turn, it also explored how aspects of such identities are deliberately crafted and evolved in relation to the national context, through efforts to inscribe citizenship rights and democratisation of land and labour into the nation. Indeed, this is illustrated in how the Constitution recognises, and in various ways facilitates, these struggles. It thus showed how historical struggles for land and the identities associated with these struggles can become inscribed into the nation in progressive ways, but also how their meanings evolve as they engage with changing political circumstances and with the framework of the nation, and in turn make claims to a nation that is more just and equal in material terms. This points to the role of contestation and inequality, rather than only consensus, in the idea of the nation.

The experiences of the MST and *quilombos* therefore highlight a number of possible interlinked lessons worth thinking about in the South African context. First is the role of land in building meaningful citizenship and deepened democracy – pursuing racial redress and redistribution, as part of a generalised project of democratising politics, land, labour and the economy. Second, linked to this, is an approach that therefore situates racial equality in a project of agrarian reform that does not focus narrowly on developing a black capitalist class of commercial farmers, or on simple land transfer, but is linked to a wider vision of holistic, democratic rural economies (including their urban linkages). This includes an appreciation and recognition of a diversity of land tenure systems based on differing histories, needs, uses and developmental desires, beyond just individual title (as comprehensively explored in Hornby et al., 2017). Third, this speaks to the class dimensions of agrarian reform. Given the extensive levels of unemployment, increased working-class precarity intensified by the neoliberal era and the ecological exigencies posed by the climate crisis, the significance of land in working-class reproduction and alternative strategies of development should inform agrarian reform (see Satgar, 2018; Zhan and Scully, 2018).

A further class dimension that shapes the prospects of an agrarian reform agenda, and which is illustrated strongly in the MST case, is the role that corporate power in concentrated food value chains, upstream and downstream of farming, play in circumscribing the agricultural aspects of land reform, and the implications of this for a progressive agrarian reform project (see Bernstein, 2013; Du Toit, 2018). This leads to a fourth consideration, which is that, despite the setbacks suffered by the MST and *quilombos*, the material gains they have made and the realisation of their demands in formal political frameworks is a result of extensive mobilisation from below. The lacuna of a similar movement in South Africa, capable of advocating for a progressive agrarian reform project, is indicated by the fact that only 10 per cent of commercial farmland has been transferred since 1994 and the elite capture of the land reform process (Cousins and Hall, 2017). Political organisation around land from below, therefore, is critical in forging a progressive agrarian reform project. However, the MST's and *quilombo*'s achievements and setbacks indicate how the terrain of struggle occurs in the arena of national politics and class struggles, as well as the forces of capitalist globalisation. Indeed, this calls for subordinating the precepts of globalised capital to a national development project grounded in the realisation of citizenship and socio-ecological needs.

REFERENCES

Alexander, A. 2006. 'Rights beyond the urban–rural divide: South Africa's Landless People's Movement and the creation of the landless subject'. Paper prepared for the Silencing Human Rights Conference, University of Sussex, 8–9 June.

Aliber, M. and Mdoda, L. 2015. 'The direct and indirect economic contribution of small-scale black agriculture in South Africa'. *Agrekon*, 54 (2), 18–37.

Andrews, G.R. 1996. 'Brazilian racial democracy, 1900–1990: An American counterpoint'. *Journal of Contemporary History*, 31(3), 483–507.

Araujo, A.L. 2015. 'The mythology of racial democracy in Brazil'. *Open*

Democracy, https://www.opendemocracy.net/en/beyond-trafficking-and-slavery/mythology-of-racial-democracy-in-brazil/, accessed 30 March 2020.

Baletti, B., Johnson, T.M. and Wolford, W. 2008. '"Late mobilization": Transnational peasant networks and grassroots organising in Brazil and South Africa'. *Journal of Agrarian Change*, 8 (2–3), 290–314.

Bernstein, H. 2006. 'Is there an agrarian question in the 21st century?' *Canadian Journal of Development Studies*, 27 (4), 449–460.

Bernstein, H. 2013. 'Commercial agriculture in South Africa since 1994: "Natural, simply capitalism"'. *Journal of Agrarian Change*, 13 (1), 23–46.

Bowen, M.L. 2010. 'The struggle for black land rights in Brazil: An insider's view on *quilombos* and the *quilombo* land movement'. *African and Black Diaspora: An International Journal*, 3 (2), 147–168.

Branford, S. and Torres, M. 13 February 2018. 'Brazilian Supreme Court ruling protects Quilombola land rights for now'. *Mongabay*, https://news.mongabay.com/2018/02/brazilian-supreme-court-ruling-protects-quilombola-land-rights-for-now/, accessed 30 May 2020.

Carter, M. 2010. 'The rural landless workers movement and democracy in Brazil'. *Latin American Research Review*, 45 (4), 186–217.

Carter, M. 2015a. 'Social inequality, agrarian reform, and democracy in Brazil', in Carter, M. (ed.) *Challenging Social Inequality: The Landless Rural Workers Movement and agrarian reform in Brazil*. Durham, NC: Duke University Press, 1–39.

Carter, M. 2015b. 'Origins and consolidation of the MST in Rio Grande do Sul', in Carter, M. (ed.) *Challenging Social Inequality: The Landless Rural Workers Movement and agrarian reform in Brazil*. Durham, NC: Duke University Press, 149–181.

Carter, M. and de Carvalho, M. 2015. 'Epilogue: Broken promise: The land reform debacle under the PT governments', in Carter, M. (ed.) *Challenging Social Inequality: The Landless Rural Workers Movement and agrarian reform in Brazil*. Durham, NC: Duke University Press, 413–428.

Chipkin, I. 2007. *Do South Africans Exist? Nationalism, democracy and the identity of 'the people'*. Johannesburg: Wits University Press.

Cousins, B. and Hall, R. 13 November 2017. 'South Africa is still way behind the curve on transforming land ownership'. *The Conversation*, https://theconversation.com/south-africa-is-still-way-behind-the-curve-on-transforming-land-ownership-87110, accessed 27 July 2020.

Delgado, G.C. 2015. 'The agrarian question and agribusiness in Brazil', in Carter, M. (ed.) *Challenging Social Inequality: The Landless Rural Workers Movement and agrarian reform in Brazil*. Durham, NC: Duke University Press, 43–67.

De Medeiros, L.S. 2015. 'Rural social movements, struggles for rights, and land reform in contemporary Brazilian history', in Carter, M. (ed.) *Challenging*

Social Inequality: The Landless Rural Workers Movement and agrarian reform in Brazil. Durham, NC: Duke University Press, 68–89.

Du Toit, A. 2018. 'Without the blanket of the land: Agrarian change and biopolitics in post-apartheid South Africa'. *Journal of Peasant Studies*, 45 (5–6), 1086–1107.

Fernandes, B.M. 2013. 'Re-peasantization, resistance and subordination: The struggle for land and agrarian reform in Brazil'. *Agrarian South: Journal of Political Economy*, 2 (3), 269–289.

Fernandes, B.M. 2015. 'The formation and territorialization of the MST in Brazil', in Carter, M. (ed.) *Challenging Social Inequality: The Landless Rural Workers Movement and agrarian reform in Brazil.* Durham, NC: Duke University Press, 115–148.

Fogel, B. 4 October 2018. 'Brazil flirts with a neo-fascist'. *Mail&Guardian*, https://mg.co.za/article/2018-10-04-brazil-flirts-with-a-neo-fascist/, accessed 29 March 2020.

Freyre, G. 1933. *The Masters and the Slaves: A study in the development of Brazilian civilisation.* (Translated by Putnam, S.) New York: Borzoi Books, Alfred A. Knopf.

Graeub, B.E., Chappell, M.J., Wittman, H., Ledermann, S., Kerr, R.B. et al. 2016. 'The state of family farms in the world'. *World Development*, 87, 1–15.

Hornby, D., Kingwill, R., Roysten, L. and Cousins, B. 2017. *Untitled: Securing land tenure in urban and rural South Africa.* Pietermaritzburg: University of KwaZulu-Natal Press.

Issa, D. 2007. 'Praxis of empowerment: Mística and mobilization in Brazil's Landless Rural Workers' Movement'. *Latin American Perspectives*, 34 (2), 124–138.

Jara, M. 2014. 'The solidarity economy response to the agrarian crisis in South Africa', in Satgar, V. (ed.) *The Solidarity Economy Alternative: Emerging theory and practice.* Pietermaritzburg: University of KwaZulu-Natal Press, 227–248.

Keisha-Khan, Y.P. 2004. 'The roots of black resistance: Race, gender and the struggle for urban land rights in Salvador, Bahia, Brazil'. *Social Identities*, 10 (6), 811–831.

Kepe, T. and Hall, R. 2018. 'Land redistribution in South Africa: Towards decolonisation or recolonisation?' *Politikon*, 45 (1), 128–137.

Leite, I.K. 2015. 'The Brazilian quilombo: "Race", community and land in space and time'. *Journal of Peasant Studies*, 42 (6), 1225–1240.

Levin, R. and Solomon, I. 1997. 'National liberation and village-level organization and resistance', in Levin, R. and Weiner, D. (eds.) *'No More Tears …': Struggles for land in Mpumalanga, South Africa.* Trenton, NJ: Africa World Press.

Long, C. 2017. 'For Brazil's historic slave communities, the future is uncertain'. *The Brazilian Report*, https://brazilian.report/society/2017/10/23/brazil-historic-slave-future-uncertain/, accessed 29 March 2020.

MST. 2014. 'Agrarian program of the MST: Struggle, build people's agrarian reform!' Sixth National MST Congress, http://www.mstbrazil.org/files/CRI%20-%20%20Agrarian%20Program%20of%20the%20MST%20-%20dez13.pdf, accessed 29 March 2020.

Nolen, S. 2015. 'Brazil's colour blind'. *Globe and Mail*, https://www.theglobeandmail.com/news/world/brazils-colour-bind/article25779474/, accessed 30 March 2020.

Pahnke, A. 2015. 'Institutionalizing economies of opposition: Explaining and evaluating the success of the MST's cooperatives and agroecological repeasantization'. *Journal of Peasant Studies*, 42 (6), 1087–1107.

Phillips, D. 28 November 2019. 'Indict Bolsonaro over indigenous rights, international court is urged'. *The Guardian*, https://www.theguardian.com/world/2019/nov/27/jair-bolsonaro-international-criminal-court-indigenous-rights, accessed 2 April 2020.

Planas, R. 2017a [2014]. 'Brazil's "quilombo" movement may be the world's largest slavery reparations program'. *HuffPost*, https://www.huffpost.com/entry/brazil-quilombos_n_5572236, accessed 18 March 2020.

Planas, R. 2017b [2014]. 'Afro-Brazilians demand slavery reparations because "poverty has a color"'. *HuffPost*, https://www.huffpost.com/entry/quilombos-brazil_n_5692077, accessed 18 March 2020.

Poletto, I. 2015. 'Churches, the Pastoral Land Commission, and the mobilization for agrarian reform', in Carter, M. (ed.) *Challenging Social Inequality: The Landless Rural Workers Movement and agrarian reform in Brazil*. Durham, NC: Duke University Press, 90–112.

Rapaport Delegation on Afro-Brazilian Land Rights. 2008. 'Between the law and their land: Afro-Brazilian quilombo communities' struggle for land rights'. The Bernard and Audre Rapaport Centre for Human Rights and Justice, University of Texas at Austin, https://law.utexas.edu/wp-content/uploads/sites/31/2016/02/brazil-eng.pdf, accessed 29 May 2020.

Reuters. 6 Februrary 2020. 'Brazil's Bolsonaro unveils bill to allow commercial mining on indigenous land'. *The Guardian*, https://www.theguardian.com/world/2020/feb/06/brazil-bolsonaro-commercial-mining-indigenous-land-bill, accessed 2 April 2020.

Robles, W. and Veltmeyer, H. 2015. *The Politics of Agrarian Reform in Brazil: The Landless Rural Workers Movement*. New York: Palgrave Macmillan.

Rosa, M.C. 2012. 'Landless: Meanings and transformations of a collective action category in Brazil'. *Agrarian South: Journal of Political Economy*, 1 (2), 205–231.

Rosa, M. 2015. 'Beyond the MST: The impact on Brazilian social movements', in Carter, M. (ed.) *Challenging Social Inequality: The Landless Rural Workers Movement and agrarian reform in Brazil*. Durham, NC: Duke University Press, 375–390.

Saad-Filho, A. 2015. 'Social policy for neoliberalism: The Bolsa Família Programme in Brazil'. *Development and Change*, 46 (6), 1227–1252.

Satgar, V. 2018. 'The climate crisis and systemic alternatives', in Satgar, V. (ed.) *The Climate Crisis: South African and global democratic eco-socialist alternatives*. Johannesburg: Wits University Press.

Sauer, S. and Mészáros, G. 2017. 'The political economy of land struggle in Brazil under Workers' Party governments'. *Journal of Agrarian Change*, 17 (2), 397–414.

Sheriff, R.E. 2001. *Dreaming Equality: Color, race and racism in urban Brazil*. New Brunswick, NJ: Rutgers University Press.

Sihlongonyane, M.F. 2005. 'Land occupations in South Africa', in Moyo, S. and Yeros, P. (eds.) *Reclaiming the Land: The resurgence of rural movements in Africa, Asia and Latin America*. London: Zed Books, 142–164.

Sobreiro, T. 2015. 'Can urban migration contribute to rural resistance? Indigenous mobilizations in the Middle Rio Negro, Amazonas, Brazil'. *Journal of Peasant Studies* 42 (6), 1241–1261.

Straubhaar, R. 2010. 'Trying to build a classless utopia in the land of racial democracy: The lack of racial discussion within the educational materials of the Brazilian Landless Rural Workers' Movement'. *Race, Ethnicity and Education*, 20 (2), 264–276.

Tarlau, R. 2015. 'Education of the countryside at a crossroads: Rural social movements and national policy reform in Brazil'. *Journal of Peasant Studies*, 42 (6), 1157–1177.

Tricontinental: Institute for Social Research. 2020. 'Popular agrarian reform and the struggle for land in Brazil'. Dossier No. 27, https://www.thetricontinental.org/dossier-27-land/.

Wolford, W. 2015. 'MST settlements in Pernambuco: Identity and the politics of resistance', in Carter, M. (ed.) *Challenging Social Inequality: The Landless Rural Workers Movement and agrarian reform in Brazil*. Durham, NC: Duke University Press, 310–328.

Wright, A. and Wolford, W. 2003. *To Inherit the Earth: The Landless Movement and the struggle for a new Brazil*. Oakland, CA: Food First Books.

Zhan, S. and B. Scully. 2018. 'From South Africa to China: Land, migrant labor and the semi-proletarian thesis revisited'. *Journal of Peasant Studies*, 45 (5–6), 1018–1038.

Interviews

Juncal, A. 21 October 2014. Interview with author, Eastern Cape.

MST 3. 25 June 2016. Interview with author, Mario Lago settlement, near Ribeiro Preto, Sao Paulo State. Interpretation: Christine Bugnon.

MST 4. 25 June 2016. Interview with author, Mario Lago settlement, near Ribeiro Preto, Sao Paulo State. Interpretation: Christine Bugnon.

Rosetti, N. 15 June 2016. Interview with author, member of MST National

Coordination, MST National Secretariat Office, Sao Paulo. Interpretation: Carolina Cruz.

Tomaz, F. 24 June 2016. Interview with author, MST Organiser, Ribeiro Preto, Sao Paulo State.

ELEVEN

Land, Citizenship and Nation Formation in the Occupied Palestinian Territories

QURAYSHA SOOLIMAN

'The cost of liberty is less than the price of repression.' – W. E. B. Du Bois

INTRODUCTION

Concepts such as citizenship, identity and nation formation are intricately entwined with power, domination and the historical usage of the concept of humanity. Mahmood Mamdani (2018) delineates this through his work on citizenship and colonial identity by highlighting how colonial constructions shape the native's political identity and discriminate against the native based on 'race' and 'tribe'. Israel and South Africa are settler colonies and land expropriation has negatively impacted the lives of the natives in the Occupied Palestinian Territories (OPT) and in South Africa. Land confiscation, occupation, and dispossession in the OPT have changed the individual rights of a people who were one nation but are now divided and subjugated. Palestinians struggle with a volatile citizen–subject identity constituted through the violence of the Occupation but also in the context of a Palestine that is not a state, and which has no sovereignty. The question of land expropriation in South Africa, as in Palestine, is contentious. It is also linked to the conflictual relationship between national security and civil liberties.

Palestinians collectively are described as a 'threat' and continue to be subjected to forcible displacement through the illegal confiscation of their land and natural resources. These violations are justified largely through the security and human rights argument. Black South Africans experienced similar atrocities under apartheid rule. The justifications for these actions were likewise linked to the security and human rights argument. Post-1994 South Africa has failed to successfully implement any expropriation legislation, and the apartheid-era 1975 Expropriation Act, which is not aligned with the South African Constitution, is still in force. It fails to address historical injustices and perpetuates social inequality. Several chapters in this volume cite land policy legislation as perpetuating race-based socio-economic inequality in post-apartheid South Africa (see chapters 2 and 4 in this volume).

This chapter combines the analytical frameworks of comparative settler colonialism and critical discourse analysis to examine the citizenship, identity and nation formation of the Palestinian people. It shifts the analysis of the Occupation only as an ontological category to that of the structures of Israeli settler colonialism, which can then be compared with settler colonies like South Africa. The critical discourse analysis of Palestinian activists, academics and professionals contributes to the literature on resistance, which animates the dialectical unity between oppression and resistance embodied in the settler-colonial/Israeli question on Palestinian lands. In the absence of cohesive scholarship, Zionist practices are presented as distinct yet related events that hide the structural continuities in the Zionist Israeli state, which inform policies on Palestinians inside the OPT and towards Palestinians generally. The settler-colonial framework allows for an assessment of each oppressive event, not as a singular or isolated event, but as a continuing process of subjugation. I then consider the emergence of Palestinian political identities, the quest for citizenship and the struggle to achieve national consciousness, where humanity, statehood and sovereignty is denied.

The chapter concludes with an interrogation of the political identity of Palestinians, which is linked to the idea of hope, liberation and nation-building by recounting Palestinian voices in a state that does not have sovereignty and for a people whose rightful ownership of the land is violated daily. Palestinians resist through various tactics, such as hunger strikes, peaceful protests, violence, cultural, academic and artistic contributions, in order to reclaim their land, identity and citizenship in the face of oppression by the Israeli settlers. However, it is not in the scope of this chapter to focus on the various means of resistance and its prevalence.

BACKGROUND AND CONTEXT

In his first statement as chairperson of the African Union, South African President Cyril Ramaphosa said that the 'Deal of the Century'– the so-called peace plan proposed by Donald Trump and Benjamin Netanyahu – was comparable to the South African apartheid and Bantustan or homeland systems. In referring to the unilateral US approach, Ramaphosa said that the plan and the way it was put together reminded him of how the 'apartheid regime once imposed the Bantustan system on the people of South Africa without consulting them and with all the oppressive elements which that plan had' (Tandwa, 2020). Ramaphosa was referring to the 28 January 2020 announcement in which Trump and Netanyahu engaged in unilateral decision-making about the continued belligerent Occupation of the Palestinian peoples. Since 1967, the Israeli government has endorsed policies to expand Israeli settlements on land in the OPT. This has a devastating impact, not only on Palestinians living in the OPT and East Jerusalem but also on those trapped in the caged confines of Gaza. I need to add here, that as of 1 July 2020, Netanyahu was able to submit an agreement to his cabinet (the Knesset) extending Israeli's sovereignty over the West Bank. This was in collaboration with the Trump administration and constitutes the annexation of the West Bank to Israel. This would mean, as noted by Ran Greenstein: 'A move from military rule to civilian control over the West Bank [which] would mean a radical change in the legal status of the Occupation, and transition into a full-fledged apartheid system, not just de facto (as has been the case for decades) but de jure as well' (Greenstein, 2020).

I do not deliberate on whether Israel is a racist apartheid state or if the Occupation is unlawful, as these questions have been dealt with in significant reports elsewhere (HSRC, 2009; Sooliman, 2018). This chapter is premised on Israel as an occupying, racist, apartheid state undergirded by a very specific framework of policies and procedures that can best be understood through the settler-colonial paradigm and its interrelated logics. I am thus not seeking to verify the nature of the state, but to explain why the Israeli state behaves the way it does, and what those behaviours mean with regard to Palestinian citizenship and the possibility of nation-building. This is done by incorporating the paradigm of settler colonialism and a critical discourse analysis of Palestinian responses.

Embedded in the ideology of settler colonialism are the interlinked ideologies of white supremacy and racism. Together, these ideologies constitute the discriminatory colonial instruments that threaten the territorial integrity and political independence of Palestine, hampering the potential for the development of a coherent national identity, and shifting the political identity of Palestinians towards resistance. According to Thiven Reddy (2015: 63), settler colonialism as a tool of political analysis has also been excluded in the social relations and political identities of post-1994 South Africans. This is relevant considering the legacies of racism in South Africa. It also allows for addressing the claims such as the one made about white farmers facing a 'white genocide' in South Africa (Smith, 2012). The settler-colonialism paradigm in the formation of state and subject identities contributes to an understanding of political identities, where communities considered to be racially inferior are denied historical development through policies that manipulate the land and culturally subjugate the subjects. Tshepo Madlingozi (2016: 1–2) maintains that, historically, settler-colonial states are polities of separation and apartness where:

> Settlers attempt to internally redraw the amity lines to ensure that only the settlers' way of being in the world is valorised, violently enforced and ultimately constitutionalised ... and to borrow an official designation from colonial South Africa, settlers transform the indigenes into 'foreign natives' – the disinherited, denationalised, 'invisibilised' and dispensable Others of the settler-created polity.

The settler-colonial framework analyses Zionist claims about indigeneity. This is because settlers claim in some ways to be, or having become, 'indigenous', or to be 'returning'. Bradley Burston (2014), a journalist for *Haaretz* in Israel, rhetorically asked: 'If Jews are not indigenous here [that is, in Israel-Palestine], does that mean that Jews can never be indigenous anywhere?' According to Lorenzo Veracini (2019: 575):

> The very notion of a 'Promised Land', a notion of all settlers moving towards their 'homelands' ... constitutes by definition a socio-political collective that is necessarily organised before and elsewhere, as good a definition of being exogenous as any. One cannot celebrate the movement to the land and understand oneself as having always been there ... Zionists are not indigenous to the land; they entertain a historical, that is, non-ontological relationship to it.

Theoretically, the ideologies of settler colonialism, white supremacy and racism normalise expropriation of land belonging to non-white persons and reject expropriation of land belonging to white persons. From a Palestinian context, the work of Israeli journalist and author Amira Hass (2019) supports this premise. Settler colonialism is perpetuated through the genocide and expulsion of the native peoples (Sooliman, 2014: 32). For natives, as Patrick Wolfe (2007: 333) puts it, 'the issue is that, at the hands of the settlers, they face [physical and symbolic] elimination'. Settler colonialism is defined through its claims to 'new land' and 'new identity' and is usually based on the usurpation of the native people's land (Boehmer, 2011: 257). The logic of a 'new identity' is developed mostly in the imagination and has little to do with the land or homeland that is essentially usurped (Boehmer, 2011: 257). According to Walcott (1998: 36–64), it is a case of 'no nation but the imagination'. Linguistically, it is intriguing that Elleke Boehmer argues: 'The tense of the settler colonial tends to be the future tense ... the past, the space of history, is a contested zone. This is because the one claim that the settler, by definition, is not able to make, is the claim to indigeneity, to ancestral belonging' (2011: 257).

The violence of settler colonialism is thus based on this negative indigeneity. 'In order to claim the land and affirm their identity, repression and the fencing away of the indigenous populations becomes both endemic and intractable' (Boehmer, 2011: 257–258). Significantly, 'the occupation contributes crucially to constituting the Palestinian national collective as it endeavours to erase it, which then cements the national collective where there is a sustained denial of national rights' (Veracini, 2019: 572).

In a March 2011 conference on Settler Colonial Studies held in Palestine, as noted by Omar Salamanca et al. (2012: 1–3), it was affirmed that the ideology and workings of Zionism as a political movement subjected,

> Palestine and Palestinians to structural and violent forms of dispossession, land appropriation, and erasure in the pursuit of a new Jewish state and society ... [where] the control of land is a zero-sum contest ... Consequently, transfer – a Zionist euphemism for the coordinated, at times randomly applied, plethora of legal, military, and economic tactics to expel Palestinians – has been part of Israeli policy and public discourse since the creation of the [Israeli] state ... [P]lagued by 'instability', the settler colonial structure undergirding Israeli practices takes on a painful array of manifestations: aerial and maritime bombardment, massacre and invasion, home demolitions, land theft, identity card confiscation, racist laws and loyalty tests, the wall, the siege on Gaza, cultural appropriation, dependence on willing (or unwilling) native collaboration regarding security arrangements, all with the continued support and backing of imperial powers.

It is here that the race–power nexus becomes visible as some of the colonial powers that support and endorse the Zionist state, like the United States and Australia, are themselves structurally racist, despite their democratic veneer (Sooliman, 2018). Significantly, the Western world's response to land expropriation in the OPT has been muted despite the numerous UN resolutions condemning Israeli settlement building and the confiscation of Palestinian land that 'had led to settler violence, home demolitions and denial of development' in the OPT (UN, 2016). Israel is a structurally racist state (UNESCWA, 2017) and its government has stated, according to the *Middle East Monitor* (2018), that it can

> 'legislate anywhere in the world,' that it is 'entitled to violate the sovereignty of foreign countries,' and that it 'is allowed to ignore the directives of international law in any field it desires'. A settler-colonial studies paradigm thus assists with understanding whose sovereignty underpins a specific political formation.

Finally, it should be noted that although the focus of this chapter is on Palestinians in Gaza, East Jerusalem and the OPT, I have included some discussion on Palestinian-Israeli citizens to highlight aspects of the theoretical framework and support arguments made about Israel as a structurally racist state. Sometimes, it is argued that Palestinians in Israel, the OPT and Gaza have different legal statuses that warrants a differentiated discussion. But why are they all Palestinians? The occupier state has changed their status and made them different groups with different rights. Differentiating the groups works to compartmentalise the Israeli conflict and hide the consistent harm of the Occupation. Within the settler-colonial paradigm, the structural continuities of the settler state and its racism become visible. I expand on the relationship between settler colonialism, land and white supremacy in the following section.

SETTLER COLONIALISM, WHITE SUPREMACY AND LAND EXPROPRIATION

In essence, settler colonialism constitutes a specific mode of domination that erases indigeneity by unevenly extending settler rights. The Palestinian experience is fundamentally shaped by displacement and by the Occupation. In response to this domination, Palestinians have always resisted, using different platforms and tactics. Social media have become sites of contested narratives and resistance platforms for giving Palestinians a voice. Consider the tweet of renowned Palestinian human rights lawyer and former spokesperson for the Palestine Liberation Organization, Diana Buttu (2020a): 'Netanyahu is clear: Trump is the first world leader to say it is *alright for Israel to steal land* [my emphasis].' Buttu's logic infers from the affirmation given to Netanyahu – one settler colonial to another – that the project of expropriation within the logics of settler colonialism is acceptable where the native is racialised. This perspective is supported by Trump's (and other Western leaders') rejection of a similar action (although the context is different) concerning the expropriation of the land of white farmers in South Africa.

White supremacy is constituted by particular, but distinct, interrelated logics, namely those of anti-black racism, which 'anchors capitalism', genocide, which 'anchors colonialism', and orientalism, which 'anchors war' (Smith in Sooliman, 2018). The logic of orientalism constitutes a notion of the West as a superior civilisation, where other nations or peoples are regarded as inferior and as permanent 'foreign threats to empire'; while the logic of genocide maintains that indigenous people must either disappear or keep disappearing in order to establish a 'rightful' claim of the non-indigenous people to the land (Smith in Sooliman 2018). In this way, non-indigenous people feel entitled and deem it justified to own the land, homes, resources, culture, etc. of the native people because they have disappeared. The embeddedness of the two ideologies should now be easily discernible.

Furthermore, Israel is the only country in the world to confer full citizenship based on inherited religion (Hussein, 2019). In the press conference on the 'Deal of the Century', both the United States and

Israel stated that the Palestinians (note: not Israel *and* the Palestinians) must denounce violence. This confers the status of victim onto the oppressor Israel, and the occupied Palestinians are described as the aggressors, skewing the perception, reality and narrative of the Occupation, including its inherent violence and harm to security. Since settler colonies can exist only 'through the disappearance of indigenous people', Israel is actively engaged in driving 'so many of its original inhabitants into the sand' through the 'unelaborated exercise of force', illegal settlement building and the expulsion of Bedouin populations from the villages inside Israel and in the OPT to complete its plan of 'changing the demographics' on the ground (Wolfe in Sooliman, 2018). Changing the demographics on the ground constitutes very specific actions related to land control and ownership, while changing the narrative to portray the Palestinians as the aggressors or terrorists eschews the ethical responsibility of other states to hold Israel to account.

Just like South Africa where black people were brutally exploited, dispossessed of their land and robbed of their rights to earn a livelihood through laws, such as the Glen Grey Act of 1894, the Natives Land Act of 1913, the Transvaal Asiatic Land Tenure Act of 1932, the Riotous Assemblies Act of 1930, the Asiatic Immigration Amendment Act of 1931, the Native Trust and Land Act of 1936, among others, Palestinians suffer similar aggressions. These include 'the Regularisation Law which allows Israel to retroactively expropriate private Palestinian land, the Abandoned Areas Ordinance of June 1948 and the State Property Law of 1951' (Forman and Kedar, 2003: 813–823; see also Matar, 1997; LPHR, 2017). These laws gave Israeli land officials the opportunity to normalise 'the seizure and reallocation of appropriated Arab land' (Forman and Kedar, 2003: 823).

With the reality of these usurpations, citizenship and identity formation become volatile and fluid concepts because of the struggle for meaning. Philosopher Sir Roger Scruton has stated citizenship is not enough, and it will endure only if it is associated with meanings to which the rising generation can attach its hopes and its search for identity (Hanson, 2020). Essentially, if the state does not consider its people as citizens, are citizens obliged to consider the government?

CITIZENSHIP ERASURE

The citizenship question is a hotbed in Palestine where Israel has instituted policies to strip Palestinians of their rights, identity and citizenship, a process known as 'citizenship erasure'. In this regard, consider 'the plight of East Jerusalemites, West Bankers and Gazans whose citizenship is erased due to Israeli laws and restrictions, specifically where Israel refuses to grant individuals citizenship based on family reunification as set out in the Oslo Accords' (Adamczyk, 2012: 53). In the West Bank/Gaza there are West Bankers and Gazans who entered either the West Bank or Gaza after the 1993 Oslo Accord, through the reunification process. However, Israel, the occupying power, has not approved their national identity numbers and, as a result, they cannot get effective Palestinian passports (living without citizenship and identification). After the 1967 Six-Day War, the Israeli Central Bureau of Statistics conducted a census of all its newly occupied territories, and Palestinians who were not present for any reason during this census were 'systematically excluded from the Population Registry and deprived of legal status in the OPT' (Adamczyk, 2012: 50). 'Palestinians in East Jerusalem who choose not to take Israeli citizenship are considered by the Israeli Ministry of Interior as Jordanian residents of East Jerusalem, rather than as Palestinian residents of East Jerusalem' (Maimon and Luster, 2012: 33). This 'category is applied even though they do not hold Jordanian citizenship and is about changing the demographics on the ground' (Maimon and Luster, 2012: 33).

The Palestinian Authority (PA) lacks legal authority to grant formal citizenship to Palestinians and Israel continues to administer the Population Registry (Adamczyk, 2012: 4–35). Palestinians who hold Palestinian citizenship cannot use their passport to travel outside Palestine unless the passport is approved and registered at the Israeli Ministry of Interior. During the 1967 Six-Day War, Israel occupied Gaza and the occupying power took control over the issuing of identity documents to the occupied Palestinian people. Significantly, although Israel claims that it has 'stopped occupying the Gaza Strip when it withdrew its 8,000 settlers in 2005, it continues to retain control over who receives Palestinian IDs – along with many other aspects of daily life, such as travel. Without an ID card, Palestinians cannot qualify for a passport' (El Rahman and Bailey, 2020).

Palestinian citizens of Israel are discriminated against because of their Palestinian ethnicity and have limited rights to land, housing and education. Cultural, religious and language rights are infringed upon. When Israel occupied East Jerusalem in 1967, it annexed approximately 71 square kilometres of West Bank land to Jerusalem. On 27 June 1967, the Israeli government passed the Law and Ordinance Administration (Amendment No. 11) law, which legalised the annexation of the expropriated, and now newly occupied, land from Arab East Jerusalem. As a result, more than 30 Palestinian villages and a refugee camp were brought under Israeli law and were subject to Israel's jurisdiction. As in Gaza, following the start of the Occupation, the Israeli's conducted a census of the annexed territories and issued ID cards only to those who were present. Those who were not present, despite being residents of that territory and having lived there throughout their lives, lost citizenship rights to an Israeli ID card. What is significant is that Palestinians in the annexed territory were given permanent residency, not citizenship. If one considers the legal and political implications, it becomes apparent that, because it was granted as a residency, it could be revoked. It also meant that these Palestinians were to be denied basic political rights, such as the right to vote, as they were not citizens. Subsequently, Israel has formalised laws such as the Centre of Life Policy, the Awad Decision and the Revocation of Residency based on Political Activity, which have been used to revoke the residency rights of East Jerusalem Palestinians (Buttu, 2015: 35–42).

Notably, there is a large body of literature that elaborates on the various policies instituted by Israel that affect every aspect of Palestinian life. This literature covers nation-building, cultural growth, educational development, economic advancement, and spiritual and mental prosperity. It is not in the scope of this chapter to revisit these policies; however, I will mention a few and recommend further reading. Under Israeli law, the majority of Palestinians living in Jerusalem are permanent residents rather than citizens of Israel, and their residency status is conditional on them proving that their 'centre of life' lies within the Israeli-defined municipal boundary of Jerusalem (Alsaafin, 2017). Consequently, their residency status can be revoked under any number of circumstances. Foreign citizens (except Palestinian ethnicity persons) who voluntarily choose to come and live in Israel are also granted permanent residency.

Since Israel treats Palestinians like immigrants, they live in their homes at the mercy of the authorities. They do not have rights, nor are they granted protection by the law. In this instance, the problem of citizenship is also a problem of rights and a problem of ethnicity. The Israeli authorities maintain this policy despite the fact that these Palestinians were born in Jerusalem, 'lived in the city, and have no other home ... Viewing East Jerusalem residents as foreigners who entered Israel is perplexing since it was Israel that entered East Jerusalem in 1967' (Stein, 1997: 3–7). According to *Al-Haq*, the 'Israeli residency policy not only increases humanitarian vulnerability but undermines the Palestinian presence in East Jerusalem and some parts of the West Bank (excluding Palestinians from West Bank and Gaza who are not able at all to live inside the borders of 1948 Palestine, now known as Israel)' (*Al-Haq*, 2019: 18–25).

The description above reflects the power dynamic in the bifurcated state, the emasculation of the tribal authority and the subjugation of the native through laws. Hence, even when Palestinians hold Israeli citizenship, they must renounce their Palestinian identity, especially any identity that is linked to the land (Palestine) while being forced to recognise Israel as a *Jewish* state. 'Israeli citizenship law prohibits granting of citizenship or permanent residency to Palestinians from the West Bank and Gaza Strip' (Harpaz and Herzog, 2018: 9–10). The native Palestinian can never be incorporated again into the territory usurped by the settler, despite the possibility that the usurped land/territory did in fact belong to the native Palestinian; erasing the possibility for Palestinian citizens of Israel (which is historic Palestine) to live as normal citizens. In practice, this means that Israel can confiscate Palestinian property in Jerusalem, but the Palestinian owner can never use it (Hasson, 2018). Israeli policy discriminates against Palestinian citizens of Israel in favour of Jewish citizens, sharply restricting Palestinians' access to land for housing to accommodate natural population growth (HRW, 2020). Settlements are confiscated Palestinian land on which the settlers build and live, yet Palestinians are not allowed to be close to these spaces. Then there are other apartheid practices, such as roads inside the West Bank reserved specifically for settlers but not Palestinians (HRW, 2020).

According to Rachid Khalidi (1997: 207):

> Where identity is concerned, the markers could go either way, or both ways, in such a situation: borders, security frontiers, control over antiquities, and road signs, for example, could indicate one set of things, while the educational system or the identity cards people carry could indicate something else. These different sorts of markers of course indicate clear relations of dominance and subordination …

If birth right, identification, indigeneity, belonging and residency are not recognised as criteria for citizenship, what then is the meaning of citizenship and who determines it?

THE APPROPRIATION OF A PEOPLE'S NARRATIVE

Within settler colonial ideology, the concept of native citizenship erasure works hand in hand with the distortion of the native's cultural identity and narrative. It also projects the belief of a superior versus inferior identity achieved through a process of dehumanisation. So, when Trump and Netanyahu presented what they claimed was a 'peace plan' for Palestine, despite it excluding any Palestinians from the consultation process (note Ramaphosa's comment), Palestinians all over the world reacted. The executive director of the US Campaign for Palestinian Rights, Youseff Munayyer, stated, 'Trump releases apartheid plan … This is not a peace plan; it is a war plan. A war on peace. A war on justice. A war on freedom. A war on equality' (Munayyer, 2020a). There were many condemnations of what was understood to be a belittling of Palestinians. Belittling and dehumanising the Other as a component of settler colonialism occurs through the erosion of the authentic self of the Other. This phenomenon has been discussed by

Frantz Fanon (2008) where the native wears a form of symbolic mask to shield themselves from the oppressive gaze; however, there is the risk of internalising the distorted image. W. E. B. Du Bois extrapolates on 'double-consciousness', where the identity is shredded so that one is never whole. Du Bois states: 'It is a peculiar sensation, this double-consciousness, this sense of always looking at one's self through the eyes of others, of measuring one's soul by the tape of a world that looks on in amused contempt and pity' (Du Bois, 1897).

Palestinians are revolting against contempt while developing tools for an alternative to the measurement of dignity. They are asserting their dignity in a space where racism undergirds authoritarian power. To understand the dynamics of divisions, it is necessary to focus on discourse and language. In this regard, listening to the Palestinians is paramount to seeking justice. Munayyer responded, 'Netanyahu: If only Palestinians can accept that they are worthless beings, undeserving of basic rights, Israel is prepared to make peace with them' (Munayyer, 2020b). Buttu lashed out with: 'There are 13 million Palestinians worldwide. Trump and his crew couldn't find one to sign onto his plan ... Netanyahu logic: if Palestinians agree to land theft, annexation, no refugee return, subjugation and no means of defence, Israel will negotiate with us' (Buttu, 2020b).

Palestinian-American graduate student and writer Nooran Alhamdan wrote: 'To say that Israel has "yearned for peace" since its creation is to utterly deny the state's violent legacy ... His [Netanyahu's] words explain generations of Palestinian rage, revealing that the Occupation is not just about land, but about the theft of a people's narrative' (Alhamdan, 2020). It should be noted that all Palestinians rejected Trump's plan. Palestinian President Mahmoud Abbas said, 'a thousand nos ... We will not kneel, and we will not surrender' (Daraghmeh and Akram, 2020).

Together these voices focus on issues that speak to identity, citizenship and nation-building. Significantly, an understudied perspective is that of 'the appropriation of a people's narrative'. What matters here is the way the narrative is framed. Why is the narrative in the Palestine–Israel post-conflict often presented as a 'religious conflict' or, in a historical context, why are 'rights to the land' based on biblical claims (see Elitzur, 2013; Veracini, 2019: 576)? For a nuanced perspective, consider that there are no official Israeli statements that refer to the West Bank as West Bank; they call it Judea and Samaria, based on biblical claims. Additionally, the US ambassador to Israel, David Friedman, has been seeking to adopt the Israeli name for the West Bank – Judea and Samaria – in his official remarks and statements (*Times of Israel*, 2018). Yet, historical claims are incompatible with 'indigenous place-based existence' (Veracini, 2019: 576; see also Zreik, 2016; Mamdani, 2018). Considering all of the above, why then is Israel largely portrayed as the victim and the Palestinians as the terrorists? Research has shown that Palestinian victims of Israeli aggression and the situation in Gaza are often unethically covered (Soussi, 2019). 'In almost all instances of coverage, the media deletes the human face of the Palestinian victims' (Ozohu-Suleiman, 2014: 79–88; Nikou, 2016: 45–48; 65–67).

In these nuances one must consider the dynamics of power and domination informing the historical usage of the term, humanity. Israel uses this tactic by emphasising difference. Jews versus Palestinians. Jewish superiority versus Palestinian inferiority (for a comprehensive understanding, watch the video embedded in the article in *Daily Sabah* [2019]). It is based on the nation-state Bill passed in July 2018. The Bill excludes Palestinian-Israeli citizens from the 'right to equality and collective rights' (selective humanity) because it explicitly states that Jewish rights are superior. Accordingly, the realisation of the right to national self-determination in Israel is unique to Jewish people (Lis and Landau, 2018). The Law to Amend the Cooperative Societies Ordinance (No. 8 of 2011), known as the Admissions Committees Law, allows Jewish controlled admission committees the right to reject applicants deemed 'unsuitable to the social life of the community … or the social and cultural fabric of the town' (Adalah, 2012). This process legally allows for Palestinian-Israelis to be denied the right to live in Jewish areas, legitimising the separation and exclusion of entire groups, and exposing Israel as a structurally racist state (Adalah, 2012).

THE NATIVE–SETTLER NARRATIVE

Certain Western states, especially the settler colonies and Israel, exhibit specific traits that contradict the notion of equality for all citizens, freedom and liberty. These traits include three forms of authoritarian fascism. The first is 'social apartheid which refers to the social separation of the excluded or subhuman managed through an elaborate "urban cartography"' (De Sousa Santos, 2007: 59). In apartheid South Africa, this manifested in the creation of homelands or Bantustans. In the OPT, it is about changing the realities on the ground and shifting borders and boundaries. The second description refers to contractual fascism, which means power inequalities in a civil contract where the weaker party is forced to accept despotic or unacceptable conditions imposed on them largely because they are not protected by the law. The third refers to '"territorial fascism" where social actors coerce or co-opt state institutions into exercising regulation over controlled territories' (De Sousa Santos, 2007: 59–60), such as the actions of the Jewish settlers in the OPT and Israeli settlements. With this context, comprehending Israel's arrogance and the Trump–Netanyahu pact is not difficult. Additionally, Eli Yishai, Israel's Minister of Interior Affairs stated that 'Israel belongs to the white man' (Weiler-Polak, 2020). The theoretical lens of settler colonialism gives meaning to these behaviours.

On the question of citizenship, the language used highlights how Palestinians living in Israel have what I call a volatile citizenship. Alternatively, Palestinians living in the OPT might aspire to have Palestinian citizenship, but Palestine is not formally recognised as a state by the international community. Palestine is considered as a 'non-member observer state, but not a full state' (UN, 2013). Thus, Palestinians in the OPT live in a political vacuum where citizenship and identity are developed in abstract notions of an envisaged state. In the contemporary world, citizenship includes rights and responsibilities and it acts as a source of identity for people in a society. When combined, it serves as 'an integrative function which promotes a shared identity among various social groups, and simultaneously acts as an expression of an individual's membership in a political community' (Priyadarshini, 2012).

What is the value and significance of citizenship for Palestinian-Israelis in a hostile political community and does it feature as a concept of value for Palestinians in the OPT, when freedom from Occupation is the overriding concern? Under these circumstances, is there a conflation between citizenship and national identity? For many Palestinian-Israelis, citizenship is linked to a very painful and traumatic memory of belonging. A belonging that is frustrated, but pragmatically and strategically maintained by the sense of holding on to what is rightfully theirs in the face of an apartheid state that has usurped their land, rights, identity, nation and 'homeland' (Mhajne, 2019). Such contestations over rightful ownership, identity and belonging inevitably produce the 'double-consciousness', as described by Du Bois. Palestinians are constantly confronting the violence of the apartheid, settler state and a fragmented, weakened and increasingly 'illegitimate' PA. This leads to a struggle to develop a coherent social and political identity.

But it is also here that one encounters the settler–native question, which is a 'problem of citizenship, rights, and entitlements to such resources as land and to political positions in Israel, the OPT and similarly, South Africa' (Ndlovu-Gatsheni, 2007: 31). According to Mamdani (2018: 18), 'Citizenship would be a privilege of the civilised; the uncivilised would be subject to an all-round tutelage.' Thus, the settler–native project, premised on the 'civilisational project' identified black people (and is used to derogatorily describe Palestinian Arabs till today) as barbarians. It orchestrated a system of 'indirect rule [which] divided natives into separate groups and governed each through a different set of customary law' (Mamdani, 2018: 15). This was done in order to wield power over the colonial subjects, which was a form of 'state violence'. Political leaders like General Jan Smuts stated that the African's social and political culture 'was bad, barbaric and only deserving to be stamped out root and branch' (Mamdani, 2018: 5–6).

According to Mamdani, this served as an example of the fact that the apartheid regime's plan was not only territorial segregation, but also racial segregation based on a white supremacist ideology that sought to erase African ways of life. The native–settler experience is shared by South Africans under apartheid and by Palestinians. Furthermore, the

PA is effectively shackled and controlled by Israel, which controls the PA's access to finances and even their movement. This demonstrates the infantilising and emasculating of the centres of power, where they exist among the oppressed, subjugated peoples. Israel uses this tactic as a 'form of statecraft to divide and rule' (Mamdani, 2018: 15).

According to Ronald Weitzer in Ndlovu-Gatsheni (2007: 31–32), settler societies were founded by white migrant groups who then 'assumed a super-ordinate position vis-à-vis native inhabitants and build self-sustaining states', organised around the white settlers' economic, social and political domination over the indigenous population. Weitzer argues that the solution to the native question, and in this case, what has been normalised as the Palestinian question involves 'outright elimination and forcible displacement to open the way for "quasi-European societies" to be established' (cited in Ndlovu-Gatsheni, 2007: 32). The framing of the 'problem' as a 'black problem' or 'Palestinian problem' highlights the burden and scope of prejudice, as indicated in the foregoing discussion on the responses and reactions by Western states on 'white genocide' and land expropriation in South Africa versus expropriation of Palestinian lands. This needs to be contested in the literature in the same way and with the same voracity as was done by Du Bois (1897), when he stated that 'the problem of the 20th' [and I add, the 21st] 'century is the problem of the colour line'. It should be apparent, therefore, that the questions of belonging, inclusion and rights are all neatly wrapped in the modern conceptualisation of citizenship, and are highly problematic.

PERCEPTION AND IDENTITY FORMATION IN GEOGRAPHIES OF VIOLENCE

We need to rethink the issue of land and the 'Israeli question' in Palestine from a social justice perspective. Social injustice is primarily a matter of cultural devaluation of an Othered group's culture. Correcting this grid is a matter of cultural or symbolic change. How does one change the grid when Palestinians are considered to be comparatively unworthy of respect or esteem because of institutionalised patterns of cultural value? Nancy Fraser's theory of social justice is a valuable framework in this regard. At the heart of this theory lies the 'principle of parity of participation', which highlights unequal access to resources and its impact (Armstrong and Thompson, 2009: 1). In recognising the full equality of all citizens, Fraser argues that citizens should be able to interact with each other as peers, but if one considers the fracturing of Palestine into Bantustans then it is obvious that such interaction and engagement is impossible, limiting the potential to develop a coherent identity and sense of nationhood.

The challenge to the grid has been developing since the Occupation began. The question of identity and its impact on citizenship and notions of belonging has occupied the minds of Palestinians for decades. Rashid Khalidi's book *Palestinian Identity* contributes valuable scholarship in this regard. Khalidi states that 'the narrative generated about Palestinian identity and by default, Palestinian nationalism, is distorted' (Khalidi, 1997: 176). This is something one should expect considering that the conflict and Occupation is framed positing an inverted logic so that we are told about the 'Palestinian question' and not the 'Israeli problem'. But Palestinian identity is not shaped only in relation to Israel and Zionism; it constitutes many components that Palestinians will have to resolve within themselves.

The memory, trauma, nostalgia and double-consciousness as a result of the Occupation make it difficult to reach coherence because the dimensions of Palestine are difficult to define. For Palestinians, Palestine will always be imagined through the lens of the 'internal map', that which includes places such as Jaffa and Haifa, which were cultural, economic and intellectual centres of Palestine, 'amputated' from Palestinian identity. These places belong to the Palestinian imagination and memory, unresolved as a question in the final 're-centring' of Palestinian national life (Khalidi, 1997: 204–206). In honour of this memory and in keeping with an identity that is bound to the territory, the Palestinian curriculum teaches Palestinian students from first grade that Jaffa and Haifa are Palestinian cities, visually presenting the map of Palestine, which has been the same for hundreds of years, despite the Israeli presence in the country (Abu Amer, 2020).

In contrast, the apartheid state of Israel has legislated separate development policies based on Palestinian ethnicity and in South

Africa separate development policies were legislated based on race. Much of the West Bank and Gaza, like the homelands and Bantustans in apartheid South Africa, are spatial products of a violent structure and system of settler colonialism that displaces and continues to dispossess indigenous peoples through territorial injustices. The violent design of the fragmented Palestinian and apartheid lands has been planned along what Charmaine Nelson identifies as the 'colonial cartographic imagination' (Nelson, 2017: 51–53), which destroys and distorts memory and ruptures tradition. Palestine is a land of broken treaties and agreements, which makes the cities war zones of occupied territories. Land use has become a rationalised terrain measured by racialisation and the occupier's ability to act with impunity. Structures have been designed and built, such as the separation wall, which precludes the legal landscape of the 1967 borders and severs relations between the land, people who own the land, water resources and communities. The separation of Gaza and the fragmented West Bank, designed as a colonial space of violence, erodes indigenous sovereignties. The destruction and devastation from looted landscapes have fractured families and fragmented identities.

Palestinian researcher Nader Atrash (2016) conducted a study in Gaza to determine how Israeli policies affect Gazan perceptions of Israel. Atrash found that Israeli policy from the beginning of the blockade in 2007 until the end of the 2014 war has made Gazans more negative towards Israel while showing greater support for Hamas. This signifies stronger identity formation with notions of resistance and Palestinian liberation. Furthermore, an 'overwhelming majority, 82 per cent of Gazans displayed frustration at Israeli policies towards them ... [where] the changes in Israeli policy towards Gaza have generated feelings of frustration and aggression, changing attitudes negatively' (Atrash, 2016: 12–13). In employing the frustration–aggression theory, Atrash reframes 'Gazan resistance from that of a discourse on terrorism to the realisation and acknowledging of the humanity of the Palestinian people' (Atrash, 2016: 14).

Furthermore, if, as Scruton indicates, citizenship has no meaning if the younger generation cannot attach hope and the search for identity to the notion of citizenship, then what is the value of citizenship in a context where the sovereignty of the people is compromised? The respondents in Atrash's thesis (2016: 19) explained that 'we, as graduates, have nothing to lose at this stage; there are no jobs, no security, and no hopes. However, Israel has many things to worry about and to care for, so why should we behave well with Israel' (Atrash, 2016: 19)? The question that needs to be asked is what is the benefit of citizenship for Gazans and Palestinians in the OPT – as part of a Palestinian state that has no sovereignty? Certainly, it cannot be ignored that sovereignty constitutes a fundamental component of the nation state and, thus, of nationhood and identity formation. Indeed, this brings me to a related question for South Africans living the effects of settler colonialism, apartheid, neo-apartheid and the historical plundering of resources, of which land is fundamental. What is the South African response to the reality that much of South Africa's natural mineral deposits and land resources are still not owned and are not benefiting the majority of South Africans?

CONCLUSION

Israel and erstwhile apartheid South Africa evince the same characteristics as settler colonies. Settler colonialism is defined through its claims to new land and identities. It is usually based on the usurpation of the native people's land. What occurs is a reordering of the land and the construction of geographies of violence. In the case of historical Palestine, Arab land that was and still is being appropriated and expropriated has become Israeli land. With the usurpation of the land, the natives are subject to systemic institutionalised racism through policies and laws instituted by the state, domination through different legal systems of control and the erosion of their identity, culture and dignity. The latter is maintained through an orchestrated process of dehumanisation of the native peoples, subjecting them to fear and uncertainty. This feeling is worsened by citizenship erasure and limitations on basic citizenship rights. It is also a condition of homelessness. In this instance, control of the narrative to shape perception and secure alliances with other Western states is fundamental to the existence of the settler state. These measures impact directly on nationhood, citizenship and identity formation, especially where the landscape is intentionally fractured and disjointed so that all aspects of the natives' lives are permanently trapped in spaces of violence.

In many aspects, challenging these narratives on various platforms has become a site of Palestinian resistance. In apartheid South Africa and apartheid Israel, the creation of Bantustans and homelands were designed to impoverish the native people, destroy their dignity and erode any potential for development. The above strategies also point to the impossibility of the development of a coherent and stable identity for Palestinians who are prohibited from interacting with one another normally because of restrictions on their movement. This is maintained through the extensive checkpoints and the separation wall that has usurped even more land, divided people, families, communities and even farmers from natural resources. How the land is navigated, made accessible, controlled and restricted is inherent to the realisation of Palestinian political and social identity. Control of the land is thus central to identity formation and citizenship, but also to the development of a national identity and sense of national consciousness.

Considering that Palestine is still not recognised as a state, has no sovereignty and the PA is a disempowered authority, totally dependent on Israel for its economic survival and finances, the realisation of homelessness and the perceptions of hopelessness shift to a resistance identity. Thus, conflict with the occupying authority is not only understandable but also expected. Citizenship must bring with it hope and it must be desired. Where there is no hope, the value of citizenship and an identity that is linked to a repressive state becomes precarious. The problem of Israel as an apartheid, occupying state is a moral and ethical question, just as it was in the case of apartheid South Africa. That it receives support from many Western states, despite its contraventions of international law and human rights, should demand a global, grassroots mobilisation to dismantle the apartheid state in a COVID-19 (and post-COVID-19) climate where inequalities and racism have been glaringly exposed. Fundamental to dignity, rights, citizenship, identity and nationality is a connection with and ownership of the land.

REFERENCES

Abu Amer, A. 2020. 25 June 2020. 'Israel's incitement against the Palestinian curriculum'. *Middle East Monitor*, https://www.middleeastmonitor.com/20200625-israels-incitement-against-the-palestinian-curriculum/, accessed 28 June 2020.

Adalah. 2012. 'New discriminatory laws and bills in Israel'. *Adalah*, https://www.adalah.org/uploads/oldfiles/Public/files/English/International_Advocacy/New_Discriminatory_Laws_June_2012_Update.pdf, accessed 29 January 2020.

Adamczyk, S. 2012. 'Undocumented and stateless: The Palestinian population registry and access to residency and identity documents in the Gaza Strip'. Norwegian Refugee Council, https://www.nrc.no/globalassets/pdf/reports/undocumented-and-stateless.pdf, accessed 5 March 2020.

Alhamdan, N. 29 January 2020. 'For Bibi and Trump, peace means Palestinian submission'. *972mag*, https://www.972mag.com/israel-peace-palestinian-submission/, accessed 5 February 2020.

Al-Haq. 2019. 'Joint parallel report to the United Nations Committee on the Elimination of Racial Discrimination on Israel's Seventeenth to Nineteenth Periodic Reports'. *Al-Haq*, http://www.alhaq.org/cached_uploads/download/2019/11/12/joint-parallel-report-to-cerd-on-israel-s-17th-19th-periodic-reports-10-november-2019-final-1573563352.pdf, accessed 29 January 2020.

Alsaafin, L. 18 November 2017. 'The colour-coded Israeli ID system for Palestinians'. *AlJazeera*, https://www.aljazeera.com/news/2017/11/colour-coded-israeli-id-system-palestinians-171115164848669.html, accessed 29 January 2020.

Armstrong, C. and Thompson, S. 2009. 'Parity of participation and the politics of status'. *European Journal of Political Theory*, 8 (1), 109–122.

Atrash, N. 2016. 'How do Israeli policies affect perceptions of Israel in Gaza Strip'. Master's dissertation, School of Politics and International Relations, University College, Dublin.

Boehmer, E. 2011. 'Where we belong: South Africa as a settler colony and the calibration of African and Afrikaner indigeneity', in Bateman, F. and Pilkington, L. (eds.) *Studies in Settler Colonialism*. London: Palgrave Macmillan, 257–271.

Burston, B. 29 April 2014. 'How to lie about Israel, Part two: The hard left'. *Haaretz*, https://www.haaretz.com/.premium-lying-about-israel-part-ii-the-hard-left-1.5246641, accessed 29 January 2020.

Buttu, D. 15 December 2015. 'Fractured lives: Restrictions on residency rights and family reunification in occupied Palestine'. Norwegian Refugee Council, https://www.nrc.no/resources/reports/fractured-lives-restrictions-on-residency-rights-and-family-reunification-in-occupied-

palestine/, accessed 6 March 2020.
Buttu, D. 28 January 2020a. https://twitter.com/dianabuttu/status/1222213178320277504, accessed 29 January 2020.
Buttu, D. 28 January 2020b. https://twitter.com/dianabuttu/status/1222232018877964290 and https://twitter.com/dianabuttu/status/1222215865682165760, accessed 29 January 2020.
Daily Sabah. 26 June 2019. 'Israeli students say they want to kill Arabs as teacher promotes hatred'. *Daily Sabah*, https://www.dailysabah.com/islamophobia/2018/06/26/israeli-students-say-they-want-to-kill-arabs-as-teacher-promotes-hatred, accessed 29 January 2020.
Daraghmeh, M. and Akram, F. 2020. 29 January 2020. 'Palestinians angrily reject Trump Mideast peace plan'. *AP News*, https://apnews.com/0dcb0179faf41e1870f35838058f4d18, accessed 20 June 2020.
De Sousa Santos, B. 2007. 'Beyond abyssal thinking: From global lines to ecologies of knowledges', http://www.boaventuradesousasantos.pt/media/pdfs/Beyond_Abyssal_Thinking_Review_2007.PDF, accessed 29 January 2020.
Du Bois, W.E.B. 1897. 'Strivings of the Negro people'. *The Athlantic*, https://www.theatlantic.com/magazine/archive/1897/08/strivings-of-the-negro-people/305446/, accessed 29 January 2020.
Elitzur, U. 2013. 12 April 2013. 'On three flags'. *Makorrish*, https://www.makorrishon.co.il/nrg/online/1/ART2/459/912.html, accessed 20 June 2020.
El Rahman, R.A. and Bailey, P. 12 February 2020. 'Stuck in limbo: Israel deprives thousands of Palestinians ID cards'. *The New Arab*, https://english.alaraby.co.uk/english/indepth/2020/2/12/israel-deprives-thousands-of-palestinians-id-cards, accessed 5 March 2020.
Forman, G. and Kedar, A.S. 2004. 'From Arab land to "Israel Lands": The legal dispossession of the Palestinians displaced by Israel in the wake of 1948'. *Environment and Planning D: Society and Space*, 22 (6), 809–830.
Greenstein, R. 2020. 'New Israeli government finally formed, prepares to annex West Bank Territory'. AMEC Brief No. 7, Afro-Middle East Centre (AMEC), Johannesburg.
Hanson, H.Y. 20 January 2020. 'Sir Rodger the Gadfly'. *First Things*, https://www.firstthings.com/web-exclusives/2020/01/sir-roger-the-gadfly, accessed 29 January 2020.
Harpaz, Y. and Herzog, B. 2018. 'Report on citizenship law: Israel', https://cadmus.eui.eu/bitstream/handle/1814/56024/RSCAS_GLOBALCIT_CR_2018_02.pdf?sequence=1, accessed 6 March 2020.
Hass, A. 2019. 'How the Israeli army takes Palestinian land and hands it to settlers'. *Haaretz*, https://www.haaretz.com/israel-news/.premium-how-palestinian-land-goes-from-the-army-to-the-settlers-1.7004514, accessed 29 January 2020.

Hasson, N. 2018. 16 April 2015. 'Supreme Court rules: Israel can confiscate Palestinian property in Jerusalem'. *Haaretz*, https://www.haaretz.com/supreme-court-israel-can-confiscate-palestinian-property-in-jerusalem-1.5352107, accessed 20 June 2020.

Human Rights Watch (HRW). 2020. 'Israel: Discriminatory land policies hem in Palestinians'. *HRW*, https://www.hrw.org/news/2020/05/12/israel-discriminatory-land-policies-hem-palestinians, accessed 20 June 2020.

Human Sciences Research Council (HSRC). 2009. 'Occupation, colonialism, apartheid? A re-assessment of Israel's practices in the occupied Palestinian territories under international law'. Research Report, http://www.hsrc.ac.za/en/research-data/view/4634, accessed 20 June 2020.

Hussein, M. 5 December 2019. 'First global conference on Israeli apartheid'. *Middle East Monitor*, https://www.middleeastmonitor.com/20191205-first-global-conference-on-israeli-apartheid-2/, accessed 29 January 2020.

Khalidi, R. 1997. *Palestinian Identity: The construction of modern national consciousness*. New York: Columbia University Press.

Lawyers for Palestinian Human Rights (LPHR). 3 March 2017. 'Sanctioning land expropriation in the occupied Palestinian territory: Israel's new "Land Regularisation Law"', https://lphr.org.uk/blog/sanctioning-land-expropriation-occupied-palestinian-territory-israels-new-land-regularisation-law/, accessed 5 February 2020.

Lis, J. and Landau, A. 19 July 2018. 'Israel passes controversial Jewish nation-state Bill after stormy debate'. *Haaretz*, https://www.haaretz.com/israel-news/israel-passes-controversial-nation-state-bill-1.6291048, accessed 29 January 2020.

Madlingozi, T. 2016. 'On settler colonialism and post-conquest "constitutionness": The decolonising constitutional vision of African nationalists of Azania/South Africa'. Draft chapter, https://www.academia.edu/33747352/On_Settler_Colonialism_and_Post-Conquest_Constitutionness_The_Decolonising_Constitutional_Vision_of_African_Nationalists_of_Azania_South_Africa?email_work_card=abstract-read-more, accessed 9 May 2020.

Maimon, O. and Luster, T. 2012. 'Permanent residency: A temporary status set in stone'. *Ir Amim*, http://www.ir-amim.org.il/sites/default/files/permanent%20residency.pdf, accessed 6 March 2020.

Mamdani, M. 2018. *Citizen and Subject: Contemporary Africa and the legacy of late colonialism*. Princeton, NJ: Princeton University Press.

Matar, I. 1997. 'The quiet war: Land expropriation in the occupied territories'. *Palestine–Israel Journal of Politics, Economics and Culture*, http://www.pij.org/details.php?id=476, accessed 20 February 2020.

Mhajne, A. 29 January 2019. 'Surveillance, political threats, daily discrimination: What it's like to be a Palestinian citizen in Israel'. *Haaretz*, https://www.haaretz.com/israel-news/.premium-what-it-s-like-to-be-a-palestinian-

citizen-in-israel-1.6878243, accessed 19 February 2020.
Middle East Monitor (MEMO). 21 September 2018. 'Israel declares it is above the law'. *Middle East Monitor*, https://www.middleeastmonitor.com/20180921-israel-declares-it-is-above-the-law/, accessed 29 January 2020.
Munayyer, Y. 2020a. https://twitter.com/YousefMunayyer/status/1222215394703880196, accessed 29 January 2020.
Munayyer, Y. 28 January 2020b. https://twitter.com/YousefMunayyer/status/1222216427941376001, accessed 29 January 2020.
Ndlovu-Gatsheni, S. 2007. 'Tracking the historical roots of post-apartheid citizenship problems: The Native Club, restless natives, panicking settlers and the politics of nativism in South Africa'. ASC Working Paper No. 72, African Studies Centre, Leiden, https://www.academia.edu/663140/Tracking_the_historical_roots_of_post-apartheid_citizenship_problems_the_Native_Club_restless_natives_panicking_settlers_and_the_politics_of_nativism_in_South_?auto=download, accessed 19 February 2020.
Nelson, C. 2017. 'Interrogating the colonial cartographic imagination'. *American Art*, 31 (2), 51–53.
Nikou, A. 2016. 'Framing the Gaza conflict: U.S. media portrayals of Palestinian Arabs', https://www.researchgate.net/publication/264604468_Framing_the_Gaza_conflict_US_media_portrayals_of_Palestinian_Arabs, accessed 29 January 2020.
Ozohu-Suleiman, Y. 2014. 'War journalism on Israel/Palestine: Does contra-flow really make a difference?' *Media, War & Conflict*, 7 (1), 85–103.
Priyadarshini, S. 2011. 'Citizenship and national identity', in Acharya, A. (ed.) *Citizenship in a Globalizing World*. New Delhi: Pearson Education.
Reddy, T. 2015. *South Africa, Settler Colonialism and the Failures of Liberal Democracy*. London: Zed Books.
Salamanca, O.J., Qato, M., Rabie, K. and Samour, S. 2012. 'Past is present: Settler colonialism in Palestine'. *Settler Colonial Studies*, 2 (1), 1–8.
Smith, A. 2012. 'Indigeneity, settler colonialism, white supremacy', in HoSang, D.M., LaBennett, O. and Pulido, L. (eds.) *Racial Formation in the Twenty-First Century*. Berkeley, CA: University of California Press, 65–90.
Sooliman, Q. I. 2014. 'South African foreign policy and human rights: South Africa's foreign policy on Israel (2008–2014) in relation to the Palestinian question'. Master's thesis, Faculty of Law, University of Pretoria.
Sooliman, Q. I. 2018. 'Is Israel an apartheid state?' *E-International Relations*, https://www.e-ir.info/2018/08/28/is-israel-an-apartheid-state/, accessed 5 February 2020.
Soussi, A. 17 March 2019. 'Why the media fails to cover Palestine with accuracy and empathy'. *Al Jazeera*, https://www.aljazeera.com/indepth/features/media-fails-cover-palestine-accuracy-empathy-190316225136995.html, accessed 29 January 2020.

Stein, Y. 1997. 'The quiet deportation: Revocation of residency of East Jerusalem Palestinians'. HaMoked: Centre for the Defence of the Individual, http://www.hamoked.org/items/10200_eng.pdf, accessed 19 January 2020.

Tandwa, L. 9 February 2020. 'Ramaphosa compares US, Israel plans for Jerusalem to that of apartheid regime'. *News24*, https://www.news24.com/SouthAfrica/News/ramaphosa-compares-us-israel-plans-for-jerusalem-to-that-of-apartheid-regime-20200209, accessed 10 February 2020.

Times of Israel. 25 April 2018. 'Friedman said seeking to call West Bank "Judea and Samaria" in statements'. *Times of Israel*, https://www.timesofisrael.com/friedman-seeking-to-call-west-bank-judea-and-samaria-in-official-statements/, accessed 20 June 2020.

United Nations (UN). 2013. 'Status of Palestine in the UN: Non-member observer state status: SecGen report', https://www.un.org/unispal/document/auto-insert-182149/, accessed 19 February 2020.

United Nations (UN). 2016. 'Israel's settlements have no legal validity, constitute flagrant violation of international law, Security Council reaffirms', https://www.un.org/press/en/2016/sc12657.doc.htm, accessed 5 February 2020.

United Nations Economic and Social Commission for Western Asia (UNESCWA). 15 March 2017. 'ESCWA launches report on Israeli practices towards the Palestinian people and the question of apartheid'. UNESCWA, https://www.unescwa.org/news/escwa-launches-report-israeli-practices-towards-palestinian-people-and-question-apartheid, accessed 15 February 2020.

Veracini, L. 2019. 'Israel–Palestine through a settler-colonial studies lens'. *Interventions*, 21 (4), 568–581.

Walcott, D. 1998. 'The muse of history', in *What the Twilight Said*. London: Faber, 36–64.

Weiler-Polak, D. 8 May 2020. 'Israel enacts law allowing authorities to detain illegal migrants for up to 3 years'. *Haaretz*, https://www.haaretz.com/israel-s-new-infiltrators-law-comes-into-effect-1.5167886, accessed 29 January 2020.

Wolfe, P. 2006. 'Settler colonialism and the elimination of the native'. *Journal of Genocide Research*, 8 (4), 387–409.

Wolfe, P. 2007. 'Palestine, Project Europe and the (un-)making of the new Jew: In memory of Edward W. Said', in Curthoys, N. and Ganguly, D. (eds.) *Edward Said: The legacy of a public intellectual*. Carlton: Melbourne University Press, 313–337.

Zreik, R. 2016. 'When does a settler become a native? (with apologies to Mamdani)'. *Constellations*, 23 (3), 351–364.

Legislation

South Africa

Asiatic Immigration Amendment Act (No 15 of 1931).
Glen Grey Act (No. 25 of 1894).
Natives Land Act (No. 27 of 1913).
Native Trust and Land Act (No. 18 of 1936).
Riotous Assemblies Act (No. 19 of 1930).
Transvaal Asiatic Land Tenure Act (No 35 of 1932).

Israel

Abandoned Areas Ordinance of June 1948.
Law and Ordinance Administration (Amendment No. 11).
Law to Amend the Cooperative Societies Ordinance (No. 8 of 2011), known as the Admissions Committees Law.
State Property Law of 1951.

CONCLUSION

Nation Formation, Citizenship and Rethinking Land Reform

KHWEZI MABASA AND BULELWA MABASA

INTRODUCTION

This book focuses on three central questions: what are the contested meanings of land in South Africa? How should South Africans incorporate the contested meanings of land into governance and policy formulation in pursuit of a socially cohesive nation? What is the best way to recognise these varied meanings of land as conducive for social cohesion and nation formation? This conclusion discusses the main recommendations for addressing these questions and citizens' discontent regarding post-apartheid land policy failures. We provide some insights into how to approach the land question in South Africa differently using the core findings. The main purpose is to posit proposals that are suitable for resolving policy gaps and political challenges that have emerged in implementing the post-apartheid government's land reform programme (Hall and Ntsebeza, 2007; Cousins and Walker, 2015). All the policy implementation failures highlight the shortcomings of a technocratic approach that reproduces land-based inequalities and overlooks how citizens relate to land beyond the formal markets.

Constitutional expropriation debates and productivist agricultural paradigms have dominated deliberations on South Africa's unresolved land question (Kirsten, 2006; Sihlobo and Kirsten, 2018). This book adds a different dimension to ongoing land debates by placing identity and nation formation at the centre of the discourse on land reform in post-apartheid South Africa. It primarily argues that land power relations and policy debates are constitutive components of nation-building. Land shapes essential pillars in nation formation, such as citizenship, political identity, heritage, a sense of belonging and social disparities. These pillars cannot be fully understood within a land-based productivity analysis paradigm. Thus, it is important to go beyond the productivist land paradigm and explore the contested meanings of land in society. This book reveals a diverse set of economic (livelihood), cultural, political and sociological factors underpinning South Africans' views on land reform. These varied meanings challenge traditional land reform perspectives articulated by government and private sector policy-makers over the past 26 years. They encourage South Africans to adopt different approaches to formulating and implementing land policy frameworks for tenure, redistribution and restitution.

This volume presents some recommendations on how to integrate the contested meanings of land into land legislation and regulatory governance. The proposals do not cover every single aspect of land legislation, but they direct land stakeholders towards some essential starting points. Contested meanings of land shape different aspects of human development and rights. These cannot be reduced to a single piece of legislation or policy. Land reform policy, therefore, cannot be applied as a separate policy outside other policies governing, in particular, cultural development, heritage resources and religious practices.

Land-based active citizenry, political agency and local organising feature prominently. These themes emanate from fieldwork by some of the authors with different civil society groups and communities. The evolution of land-based citizenship in South Africa and other countries was examined, with the aim of identifying lessons for transforming land politics. This volume does not focus on land struggle and usage in South Africa's urban areas, although it does allude to some of the legislative debates around land tenure in urban townships and informal settlements.

We argue that local citizen and civil society participation in land regulatory governance is pivotal. It forms a basis for resisting ongoing land dispossession, corruption and lack of consultation in land development decision-making. Furthermore, organising around land-based rights advances the aims of accountability and transparency in land policy implementation. The state failures cannot be resolved solely through legislative changes. Success in pursuing comprehensive land reform requires political agency that deepens democracy in land governance systems in different social contexts across rural and urban areas. It is impossible to analyse state failures in land reform outside relations with traditional leaders and private sector companies, for instance, as the evidence connects state failures with elite private sector and traditional authority interests.

The arguments on the contested meanings of land and citizenship explain the gaps between policy objectives and successful implementation. This is clearly expressed in the debates on land development, tenure and restitution. Existing land policy frameworks do not complement black South Africans' historical relations to land and the values attached to it. This challenge is exacerbated by the post-apartheid state's failure to fully remove the underlying colonial principles shaping land legislation. By connecting the land and national questions through discussions on the diverse meanings of land in our society, one gains insights into how to interpret citizens' discontent regarding land policy failures and what steps are required to ameliorate these concerns. The calls for land access and redress persist, even in the context of increased urbanisation and marginalisation of agrarian livelihoods. Land in South Africa has deeper political and cultural value; it is as the heart of reconstructing and remaking the South African nation.

Recommendations are organised around two cross-cutting themes: (1) nation-building, social cohesion and land reform; and (2) agrarian livelihoods, land and citizenship. The recommendations outlined in Section I focus on the relationship between nation-building and the diverse meanings of land. These proposals explain how the multiple meanings of land can be integrated into legislation and governance frameworks regulating land redress and tenure. The recommendations explained in the Section II focus on land development, agrarian transformation and citizenship. These proposals analyse the measures required to address unequal power relations between the state, private companies, traditional leaders and communities in land development decision-making processes. Overall, the core recommendations present both legislative policy-oriented and political proposals that could potentially strengthen land reform in South Africa. It is important to highlight the two-tiered policy and political governance recommendations approach in laying out some solutions for South Africa's unresolved land question.

NATION-BUILDING, SOCIAL COHESION AND LAND REFORM

According to MISTRA (2014: 95), 'The erosion of national identity emerges when disparate identities such as race, class, ethnic group and gender assume prominence at the risk of undermining national consciousness and identity.' Further, MISTRA states that 'apart from the economic and political realms, nation formation should generally take place in the cultural spaces' (2014: 96). This book takes the nation formation debate further by illustrating that land reform is at the heart of nation-building and rethinking nation formation. This finding comes out strongly in the contributions by Yacoob Abba Omar (Chapter 1), Andrew Bennie (Chapter 10) and Quaraysha Sooliman (Chapter 11). These chapters place land justice at the centre of nation-building in South Africa, Brazil and Palestine, respectively. It is important to conceptualise land justice and policy developments outside of parochial nationalist views, which emerge from settler colonialism and contemporary strands of exclusive nationalism.

This book recommends connecting land policy-making with inclusive nation-building and social cohesion principles developed in struggles to overcome authoritarian settler colonialism and apartheid. These principles are expressed in historically significant documents such as the Freedom Charter and the country's Constitution.

Land reform is a constitutive element of nation formation rather than a separate policy area, which is limited to productivist market considerations or technocratic legislative discussions. Land ownership and power relations inform core building blocks of nation-building, such as political identity, social cohesion, citizenship and belonging. The aim of approaching land as a constitutive part of rebuilding the South African nation through deepening social cohesion requires three core recommendations, which are highlighted in the following sections.

Contested meanings in land redress and tenure policy

Land has varied meanings, permeating both the material and non-material areas of human development. These meanings include, religious, spiritual, cultural, heritage and identity formation. The varied meanings of land are elevated in the chapters focusing on social conflict or policy failures related to land development and restitution. In Chapter 7, Sithandiwe Yeni's examines former labour tenants' claims and concludes that land is not necessarily required for its commercial agricultural or farming purposes. The labour tenants' primary concern is using land claims for redress purposes, given the violent and inhumane manner in which their families were dispossessed historically. Their notion of land compensation is associated with deeper meanings related to reclaiming ancestral lands, maintaining livelihoods, preserving cultural heritage and securing a place of belonging for future generations. David Coplan and Kearabetswe Moopelo's illuminate the point on contested land meanings further in Chapter 5. Their findings explain community and broader civil society resistance to a mining development project in Limpopo. The advocacy for protecting the land emanates from spiritual, medicinal, religious and heritage values associated with the land.

The first recommendation of this book stems from these chapters and proposes legislative reforms to accommodate these varied meanings of land in policy implementation. One of the proposals focuses on the Restitution of Land Rights Act (No. 22 of 1994). This legislation states that land claimants whose claims have been investigated, settled and finalised are legally entitled to restitution 'of a right in land'. Section

1 of this Act defines a 'right in land' as either 'the restoration of a right in land' or 'equitable redress'. Equitable redress is subsequently interpreted as either/or a combination of a 'right in alternative land' and 'the payment of compensation' (Restitution of Land Rights Act). The government needs to consider the different meanings of land when it formulates instruments for compensation. This is crucial for determining what constitutes fair, just and adequate land redress. South Africa cannot continue to use limited market-oriented compensation models, which have led to social conflict and the further marginalisation of affected communities.

This proposal should be streamlined into other pieces of legislation that affect land development and restitution. We specifically cite the example of mining-related land development regulation policy because it features prominently throughout this book. Section 54 (3) of the Mineral and Petroleum Resources Development Act (MPRDA, No. 28 of 2002) deals with determining compensation that is payable to an owner or occupier of land that has been destroyed through mining and prospecting. The state has not adequately considered the varied meanings or values of land in regulating the determination of compensation. It has relied largely on market-based compensation frameworks in mining-related land development cases. This approach is limited and causes disputes about compensation, settlement agreements and relocations. The ultimate result is the deepening of social disparities and unequal land power relations in South Africa, which erode national identity and nation-building.

Several laws have been enacted to protect the rights of people whose land tenure is insecure in urban and rural settings. However, statistics demonstrate that post-1994 evictions exceed those implemented in the last decade of the apartheid era. It is estimated that more than 2.3 million people were forcibly removed from their homes on farms by 2004 (Presidential Advisory Panel on Land Reform and Agriculture, 2019: 48). There are no definitive data on eviction trends since 2004, but evidence from civil society and farm-worker advocacy groups suggests that evictions have not stopped. The recent Bulelani Qolani eviction incident in the City of Cape Town demonstrates the post-apartheid state's failure to secure land tenure for working-class citizens in South Africa. Despite the suspension of landowners' abilities to execute eviction orders during COVID-19, the City of Cape Town, nevertheless, continued to evict and demolish informal structures without a court order (Kiewit, 2020). The incident subsequently led to the Human Rights Commission and the Housing Assembly instituting legal action against the conduct of the City of Cape Town. A significant point to note here is that the COVID-19 pandemic compelled the government to act decisively and prohibit all evictions. The state has largely failed to halt evictions over the past 26 years, especially in rural areas where land tenure is most precarious (Wagerif et al., 2005; High-Level Panel, 2017). Bulelwa Mabasa (Chapter 2), Peter Delius and William Beinart (Chapter 3) and Fani Ncapayi (Chapter 4) present alternative ways of approaching land tenure. They emphasise removing colonial and apartheid influences in property law and tenure legislation, which reduces customary tenure to communal ownership. These chapters further challenge the existing policy frameworks governing traditional leaders' roles in customary land tenure.

The main findings from these chapters are synthesised into this book's second recommendation, which discusses elements of an alternative tenure system, suitable for building socially cohesive land power relations in South Africa. This recommendation proposes several options for resolving the long-standing land tenure insecurity experienced by working-class citizens in rural and urban areas. The primary one is eradicating the dual tenure system, which excludes most of South Africa's black majority population. This dualism supports the underlying principles embedded in apartheid separate development strategies. It equally undermines the land tenure rights of poor South Africans in rural and urban settings. The transition towards a variegated but single tenure system requires fundamental changes in the formulation of property and customary land laws.

This book calls for a new tenure system that recognises a diverse set of precolonial landholdings within black African communities. These include individual, family and homestead landholdings. It proposes infusing this alternative approach with the lived realities and meanings of how indigenous communities govern landholding, devoid of colonial distortions. An additional significant tenure proposal emphasises building state capacity to restructure the country's Deeds Registry Act (No. 34 of 1937, as amended in 2019) and land titling systems (see chapters 2 and 3 in this volume). These two elements are essential for transitioning to an inclusive tenure structure. The current registration and titling systems are based on market principles of land exchange and formal land rights, enshrined in Roman-Dutch and English common law (Beinart et al., 2017). This volume proposes amending both systems, so that they accommodate the diverse off-register land rights. It encourages government to improve land record-keeping and administrative capacity within the context of facilitating registrations in the transition to a single system.

The last tenure proposal focuses on the role of intermediaries and traditional authorities in customary land governance, prescribed in legislation. These pieces of legislation include the Traditional Leadership and Governance Act (No. 41 of 2003), the Communal Land Rights Act (No. 11 of 2004), the Traditional Courts Bill (2008) and the Traditional and Khoisan Leadership Act (No. 3 of 2019). This volume proposes that these Acts be overhauled, as they curtail the land rights and tenure of citizens, especially in rural areas. This trend is caused by two factors: colonial distortions in customary land tenure and collusion between traditional authorities and private companies. The political and social agency of citizens is surrendered into the hands of traditional leaders or hierarchical traditional councils. Although the system of traditional leaders is sanctioned in the Constitution, the state is cautioned against regulating this system in a manner that subverts citizens' land tenure and democratic rights in the former bantustans.

The third recommendation calls for strengthening political agency and citizen oversight of land tenure and development. This is essential for shaping land policies around the experiences of landless citizens and communities with the least secure tenure. Social disparities and land inequalities in South Africa will persist in the absence of an engaged citizenry at the local level. The political agency emphasis builds on what Deborah James (2013: 29) describes as 'land-based citizenship'. This book's proposition calls for deepening democracy and accountability in the land governance policy area. It supports reclaiming citizenship through challenging the notion that traditional leaders own land falling within customary land tenure (see Chapter 4 in this volume). Additionally, land-based citizenship encourages direct decision-making in communities when private sector actors propose land development projects.

AGRARIAN LIVELIHOODS, LAND AND CITIZENSHIP

This section focuses on the book's recommendations aimed at developing inclusive land policy frameworks, which create conditions for a socially cohesive and united nation. It analyses the measures required to address unequal power relations between the state, private companies, traditional leaders and communities decision-making processes on land development. The emphasis is placed on recommendations that fall within the areas of legislative policy reforms and land governance politics. This section examines the following three themes: (1) land-based citizenship; (2) the state, land and agrarian reforms; and (3) gender and the agrarian question.

Land-based citizenship

Fani Ncapayi (Chapter 4), David Matsinhe (Chapter 8) and Andrew Bennie (Chapter 11) encourage citizens to push governments towards refining and fully implementing policy regulations governing commercial land development. The findings from South Africa and international case studies illustrate that dispossession persists. This contemporary dispossession undermines citizens' land rights, agrarian livelihood strategies, civil liberties, heritage resources and cultural freedoms. The MPRDA and the National Environmental Management Act (NEMA, No. 107 of 1998) are designed to ensure adequate local community consultation prior to mining-related land development decisions. But the evidence presented confirms that both state authorities and companies fail to consult adequately with communities.

Private companies, especially mines, continue to initiate commercial projects without inclusive and legitimate community consent, and they circumvent legislation regulating the ecological aspects of land use. In some cases, violence, intimidation and assassinations are used to curtail community resistance to commercial land development projects (Global Initiative, 2020). This publication, therefore, recommends that the extent and meaningfulness of adequate consultation with communities by private enterprises is explained thoroughly and clarified in legislation. There is contention over what constitutes credible engagement with a community, especially in the South African context where land laws recognise intermediaries such as traditional leaders, community property associations and community trusts as custodians of community interests. This is complicated further by the communalism approach running through government's legislated customary land tenure framework (see chapters 2 and 3 in this volume). The recent Gauteng Local Division judgment in the Xolobeni case, paves the way for adequate consultation by granting communities legal access to mining licence application documents. Citizens deliberating on commercial land development in their areas have struggled to get full access to these documents in the past. This inadequate access to information made it difficult for civil society groups to hold state authorities and private companies accountable in land development processes. The recent judgment legally compels state authorities to make this information available to the public (Ellis, 2020). Local communities are in a better position to make informed decisions about the impact of mining in their communities.

In addition, the National Heritage Resources Act (NHRA, No. 25 of 1999) should be amended to strengthen and deepen the protection of intangible heritage resources. These resources include, but are not limited to, sacred sites like rivers, mountains and caves, which are considered to be significant for black African communities' spirituality, religion and sense of belonging. The sacred sites must be protected and not automatically viewed as secondary to short-term, commercial land development gains (see Chapter 5 in this volume). These two recommendations on clarifying consent and protecting heritage amplify the necessity of democratising land governance through citizen engagement and accommodating deeper meanings of land within communities.

Previous studies on non-state actors' roles in land policy formulation focus on political parties, business sector associations, research-based non-governmental organisations, traditional leaders and contributions from academics. The accounts on grassroots, land civil society groups are minimal and they mostly examine national organisations such as the Landless People's Movement and the National Land Committee (Greenberg, 2004; Hall and Ntsebeza, 2007; Sidwell, 2015). This book emphasises the role of local community or civil society groups in land and agrarian policy advocacy. These groups represent former labour tenants, women organising around agrarian livelihoods, citizens residing on communally owned land, and civil society groups pursuing cultural and religious campaigns. The international case studies elevate the voices of peasant communities and land social movements.

These civil society experiences present important lessons for strengthening land governance politics in South Africa. The first lesson is the necessity to connect local land-based community struggles with national campaigns on land justice. Second, participation in the local community or civil society groups assists individuals to reclaim their citizenship and political identities, which have been subverted by historical and modern land dispossession. Third, state responses to land justice demands, which impact on nation-building and formation, are shaped primarily by the strengths or weaknesses of land-driven social movements in a country.

The state, land and agrarian reforms

Khwezi Mabasa (Chapter 6) and Zenzo Moyo and Toendepi Shonhe (Chapter 9) illustrate that class and gender inequalities are reproduced when state intervention favours large-scale commercial agriculture. David Matsinhe (Chapter 8) and Andrew Bennie (Chapter 10) explain how governments facilitate the dispossession of peasant lands in Angola, Mozambique and Brazil. This state capture by elite interests is carried out in order to establish large extractive corporate economic activities, such as mining, energy and large-scale agriculture. In all these cases, the dispossessions violated different forms of human rights and destroyed land-based livelihoods.

State authorities are encouraged to transcend the policy biases towards productivist agrarian structures, which overlook the diversity of land-based agrarian livelihoods in communities. Government policy orientation needs to purposefully support the restructuring of South Africa's agrarian structure. Emphasis should be placed on strengthening existing agrarian and land-based livelihood activities in communities by providing subsidies, securing land tenure, and facilitating improved access to global commons such as land, water and other natural resources. This form of state intervention will decrease the race, class and gender inequalities that persist in the post-apartheid agrarian structure. More importantly, pursuing transformative agrarian restructuring strengthens nation-building because the agrarian question in South Africa is connected with social cohesion and nation formation. It is multi-layered and brings to the fore different aspects of social transformation that go beyond agrarian production debates. This relationship between agrarian transformation, land redress and nation formation in the Global South is examined in other researched analyses. Land and agrarian reforms are discussed as a catalyst for challenging colonial and neocolonial power relations in society (Moyo et al., 2013).

The complicity of local and national state authorities in some cases of contemporary land dispossession warrants urgent attention. It erodes the legitimacy of public institutions and compromises social compacting. Government cannot fulfil its role in nation-building if officials undermine social cohesion through circumventing legislative prescripts or perpetuating market-oriented biases while carrying out land regulatory duties. The underlying problems include narrow class interests, patronage networks and corruption. South Africa's current ranking in the Corruption Perceptions Index measured by Transparency International is 44 out of 100 points (Trading Economics, 2020). It reflects the extent of corruption in society, which erodes state institutions and regulatory capacity in land policy implementation. The strengthening of several pieces of legislation, such as the MPRDA and the NEMA, will hold state authorities accountable in land regulatory processes. The provisions dealing with consultation and public participation of communities and interested and affected parties, also needs to be strengthened in legislation to deter the tendency to leave this issue to interpretation by the courts. In addition, local police stations and courts need to protect the constitutional rights of land civil society organisations. This includes carrying out proper criminal investigations in violence and murder cases of local land activists. But it is important to highlight that legislative changes are not sufficient or the ultimate panacea; these must be supported by land rights-based local community citizen agency, which connects with broader, national civil groups organising around land transformation.

Gender and the agrarian question

The emphasis on gendering agrarian transformation contributes to the critique of productivist land development in several ways. It illuminates how the productivist policy orientation overlooks the importance of unpaid labour and social reproduction in communities. These sociological factors have shaped land and agrarian livelihoods in black African communities throughout the evolution of South African capitalism (see chapters 6 and 7 in this volume). An additional value of the gendered paradigm lies in its emphasis on women organising around land rights and agrarian transformation. This shows that agrarian livelihood activity in working-class communities should not be reduced to food production concerns. Women's participation in localised agrarian-based social reproduction activities serves an additional purpose of asserting citizenship. The gendered analysis reveals how the socio-economic costs of unequal land access and continued dispossession are externalised onto households. Women deal with the negative economic, social and ecological trends produced by unequal land and agrarian structures.

Legislation governing land and agrarian development should consider the structural inequalities experienced by black African women in low-income communities. This gendered approach must not limit social reproduction in society to commercial market participation. South African women continue to shape agrarian development in the country in different ways. A clear example is the women-led subsistence agriculture undertaken in the informal sector, which sustains families and facilitates black African women's citizenship (see Chapter 6 in this volume). But the sector receives minimal state support because of policy biases, which direct land development towards large-scale, market-oriented agriculture. Policy interventions should support small-scale women producers in the subsistence economy. These include resolving the gender disparities in accessing land and providing supporting infrastructure to preserve the land. Additionally, government is advised to support women producers through procurement measures that build local food system linkages. The restructuring of state procurement must be complemented by introducing changes in retail market structures, which marginalise small-scale producers. All these support interventions complement the aim of decreasing gendered social disparities in the transition towards a socially inclusive agrarian structure. A society's ability to curtail different types of inequality determines the failure or success of its nation-building process.

The recommendations above support the book's main arguments in several ways. First, they emphasise legislative and political proposals that solidify citizen consultation and oversight in land development negotiations. These proposals affect essential pieces of legislation, such as the MPRDA, the NHRA and the NEMA. They equally support elevating citizen participation to protect land rights that cut across socio-economic, cultural, religious and spiritual freedoms. This last point supports this volume's broader contention on understanding and integrating contested meanings of land in land policy governance. Second, the recommendations cover state policy orientation and capacity in land governance. There are several proposals for reorientating the state's policy paradigm and regulatory oversight in land policy implementation. The recommendations cannot be implemented without the common thread of strengthening and supporting land-based citizen agency. The emphasis on the state's role in land governance and agrarian transformation is equally important for social cohesion and nation-building. Land-based social divisions and disparities increase when government officials or institutions are captured by narrow commercial interests. This state capture overlooks broader community socio-economic interests, reproduces inequalities and undermines citizens' rights. All these factors detract from inclusive socio-economic development.

Third, the recommendations illustrate that agrarian reforms in the context of social cohesion and nation-building need to reduce class and gender inequalities. A gendered approach to agrarian reforms should be embedded in policy development. This gendered approach necessitates examining forms of agrarian livelihoods and social reproduction activities that fall outside traditional market structures. The suggested measures for gender redress cannot be separated from class inequalities in South Africa's agrarian structure. The policy biases towards large-scale commercial agriculture highlight the intersection between class and gender inequalities.

CONCLUSION

This publication contributes to land reform narratives and policy debates by advancing a holistic approach, which is centred on analysing the varied multiple meanings of land in South Africa. It primarily argues that these contested meanings of land have been overlooked in policy-making. Recommendations on how to accommodate these contested meanings of land into existing land governance policy frameworks have been offered. These proposals cover essential policy areas such as land redress, tenure and development. The book's approach to land elevates a deep understanding of citizenship, which is intrinsically connected with contested meanings of land and governance politics in land reform. Land is conceptualised as a pivotal component of citizenship because it determines identity, human rights, a sense of belonging and nation-building. This understanding of citizenship also accommodates the need for more national and local organising around land politics. Active citizenship (especially in rural areas) is presented as a measure to address state capture in land governance. This book's recommendations connect land reform, citizenship and agrarian transformation to highlight that the land and national questions are inseparable in post-apartheid South Africa. The answers to these questions lie in a nuanced, calibrated approach that continually tests policies with the lived realities in communities. It must affirm and integrate the contested meanings of land that exist in different parts of South Africa. These multiple meanings of land are not only necessary but crucial in the context of introducing land reforms aimed at purposefully strengthening social cohesion and nation-building.

Future policy considerations and research

The recommendations contained in this book do not address all land policy questions or challenges in detail. There are several themes that require further research and investigation, which fall outside the research scope of this publication. The first theme is the need to discuss the relationship between different forms of land use and an alternative political economy model. State, community and private capital relations are discussed extensively in this publication, but the authors did not specifically present evidence on different land use and alternative ways of restructuring the entire South African political economy. Second, the publication proposes factoring in contested meanings of land into land redress and development policy frameworks regulating compensation. This proposal needs to be taken further and discussed in formal policy processes with the relevant stakeholders. However, the fundamental contention stands that it is not sustainable to interpret non-market and intangible values of land as secondary considerations in land redress measures.

Third, some concerns have been raised regarding the constitutional timelines that determine how the Restitution of Land Rights Act is applied. It only recognises land claims brought by families or communities that were dispossessed of land as a result of discriminatory laws or practices that took place on or after 19 June 1913. The Restitution Act emanates from section 25 (7) of the Constitution. The timeline imposition limits access to land redress as some communities were dispossessed of land long before the cut-off date. This constitutional conundrum has significant impacts on land redress.

REFERENCES

Beinart, W., Delius, P. and Hay, M. 2017. *Rights to Land: A guide to tenure upgrading and restitution in South Africa*. Johannesburg: Jacana Media.

Cousins, B. and Walker, C. 2015. *Land Divided: Land reform in South Africa for the 21st century*. Johannesburg: Jacana Media.

Ellis, E. 14 September 2020. 'Game-changing Xolobeni judgment orders applications for mining licences to be made public'. *Daily Maverick*, https://www.dailymaverick.co.za/article/2020-09-14-game-changing-xolobeni-judgment-orders-applications-for-mining-licences-to-be-mad, accessed 19 September 2020.

Global Initiative against Transnational Organised Crime. 14 September 2020. 'eMpembeni mirrors the scourge of mining-related assassinations in KZN'. *Daily Maverick*, https://www.dailymaverick.co.za/article/2020-09-14-empembeni-mirrors-the-scourge-of-mining-related-assassinations-in-kzn/, accessed 22 August 2020.

Greenberg, S. 2004. 'The Landless People's Movement and the failure of post-apartheid land reform'. Centre for Civil Society, http://ccs.ukzn.ac.za/files/Greenberg%20LPM%20RR.pdf, accessed 10 June 2020.

Hall, R. and Ntsebeza, L. 2007. 'Introduction', in Ntsebeza, L. and Hall, R. (eds.) *The Land Question in South Africa: The challenge of transformation and redistribution*. Cape Town: HSRC Press, 1–28.

High-Level Panel on the Assessment of Key Legislation and the Acceleration of Fundamental Change. 2017. 'Report of the High-Level Panel on the assessment of key legislation and the acceleration of fundamental change', https://bit.ly/3ivfXeH, accessed 1 December 2019.

James, D. 2013. 'Citizenship and land in South Africa: From rights to responsibilities'. *Critique of Anthropology*, 33 (1), 26–46.

Kiewit, L. 25 August 2020. 'High court declares the City of Cape Town's lockdown evictions illegal'. *Mail&Guardian*, https://www.google.com/amp/s/mg.co.za/news/2020-08-25-high-court-declares-the-city-of-cape-towns-lockdown-evictions-illegal/%3Famp, accessed 11 September 2020.

Kirsten, J. 2006. 'Socio-economic dynamics of the South African agricultural sector'. Trade Policy Brief No. 10, South African Institute for International Affairs.

MISTRA. 2014. *Nation Formation and Social Cohesion: An enquiry into the hopes and aspirations of South Africans*. Johannesburg: MISTRA.

Moyo, S., Jha, P. and Yeros, P. 2013. 'The classical agrarian question: Myth, reality and relevance today'. *Journal of Political Economy*, 2 (1), 93–119.

Presidential Advisory Panel on Land Reform and Agriculture. 2019. 'Final report of the Presidential Advisory Panel on Land Reform and Agriculture', https://www.gov.za/sites/default/files/gcis_document/201907/panelreportlandreform_0.pdf, accessed 1 August 2020.

Sidwell, L. 2015. 'Social movements, mobilisation and political parties: A case study of the Landless People's Movement, South Africa', in Bénit-Gbaffou, C. (ed.) *Popular Politics in South African Cities: Unpacking community participation*. Cape Town: HSRC Press, 70–92.

Sihlobo, W. and Kirsten, J. 2018. 'A compendium of essays on land reform in South Africa', https://agbiz.co.za/uploads/AgbizNews18/181207_Land%20Reform%20Essays%20Final.pdf, accessed 27 May 2020.

Trading Economics. 2020. 'South Africa corruption index', https://tradingeconomics.com/south-africa/corruption-index#stats, accessed 11 September 2020.

Wagerif, M., Russell, B. and Grundling, I. 2005. *Still Searching for Security:*

The reality of farm dweller evictions in South Africa. Polokwane: Nkuzi Development Association.

Legislation

Communal Land Rights Act (No. 11 of 2004).
Deeds Registry Act (No. 34 of 1937, as amended in 2019).
Mineral and Petroleum Resources Development Act (MPRDA, No. 28 of 2002).
National Environmental Management Act (NEMA, No. 107 of 1998).
National Heritage Resources Act (NHRA, No. 25 of 1999).
Restitution of Land Rights Act (No. 22 of 1994).
Traditional and Khoisan Leadership Act (No. 3 of 2019).
Traditional Courts Bill (2008).
Traditional Leadership and Governance Act (No. 41 of 2003).

Court cases

South African Human Rights Commission and Others v The City of Cape Town (8631/2020).
Baleni and Others v Minister of Mineral Resources and Others 2019 (2) SA 453 (GP)

INDEX

www.ingramcontent.com/pod-product-compliance
Lightning Source LLC
LaVergne TN
LVHW052022200926
848481LV00005B/1560

Laura Wright is a barrister at 4 Pump Court. Specialising in technology and IP disputes, Laura is ranked as a "Leading Junior" in Legal 500 in the field of IT and Telecoms. Laura is regularly instructed in a wide range of technology-related disputes involving computer systems, internet services and software across a variety of industry sectors.

Laura's academic background encompasses both law and technology. In 2022 Laura completed an MSc in Computing Science at Imperial College London.

Laura is a committee member of the Society for Computers and Law Junior Lawyers' Group. She frequently writes on the topic of technology law, and in recent years co-authored the "AI and Professional Liability" chapter of The Law of Artificial Intelligence (Sweet & Maxwell), as well as the IP section of the AI chapter of the Encyclopaedia of IT Law (Thomson Reuters).

Rebecca Keating is a barrister at 4 Pump Court with a particular focus on technology disputes. She is called to the Bar of England and Wales and the Bar of Ireland.

Rebecca is ranked as a "Rising Star" in Legal 500 in the field of IT and Telecoms and as a "Leading Junior" in Crypto and Blockchain Assets. She has been instructed on a wide range of technology-related disputes from project failures, the use of artificial intelligence, cyber-attacks, cryptoassets to quantum computers.

Rebecca is Co-Chair of the Society for Computers and Law Women in Technology group, an editorial member of the Tech Disputes Network and committee member of TECBAR. She has published several articles on the topic of technology and the law in both national and international publications and is a contributing author to the Law of Artificial Intelligence (Sweet & Maxwell) and the AI chapter for the Encyclopaedia of IT Law (Thomson Reuters).